WOMEN WRITERS IN THE ROMANTIC AGE

Women Writers in the Romantic Age

John Claiborne Isbell

https://www.openbookpublishers.com
Translations and notes ©2025 John Claiborne Isbell

This work is licensed under a Creative Commons Attribution-NonCommercial 4.0 International license (CC BY-NC 4.0). This license allows you to share, copy, distribute and transmit the work for non-commercial purposes, providing attribution is made to the author (but not in any way that suggests that he endorses you or your use of the work). Attribution should include the following information:

John Claiborne Isbell, *Women Writers in the Romantic Age*. Cambridge, UK: Open Book Publishers, 2025, https://doi.org/10.11647/OBP.0458

Further details about CC BY-NC licenses are available at https://creativecommons.org/licenses/by-nc/4.0/.

All external links were active at the time of publication unless otherwise stated and have been archived via the Internet Archive Wayback Machine at https://archive.org/web.

Digital material and resources associated with this volume are available at https://doi.org/10.11647/OBP.0458#resources.

Information about any revised edition of this work will be provided at https://doi.org/10.11647/OBP.0458

ISBN Paperback: 978-1-80511-551-9
ISBN Hardback: 978-1-80511-552-6
ISBN Digital (PDF): 978-1-80511-553-3
ISBN Digital ebook (EPUB): 978-1-80511-554-0
ISBN HTML: 978-1-80511-555-7
DOI: 10.11647/OBP.0458

Cover image: the Brontë sisters (Anne, Emily and Charlotte) by Patrick Branwell Brontë, oil on canvas, ca. 1834. ©National Portrait Gallery, London

Cover design: Jeevanjot Kaur Nagpal

Contents

Introduction	1
Acknowledgements	11
1. Writers from British North America	13
Canada	13
The United States: The Eighteenth Century	17
The United States: The Nineteenth Century	27
2. Writers from France	83
France	83
3. Writers from German Lands	101
Germany	101
4. Writers from Habsburg Territories	115
Austria	115
Croatia	117
Czechia	120
Hungary	122
Slovenia	124
5. Writers from Latin America and the Caribbean	125
Argentina	129
Bolivia	129
Brazil	130
Chile	132
Colombia	133
Cuba	133
Ecuador	136

Peru	137
Uruguay	139
Costa Rica	140
El Salvador	140
Guatemala	140
Haiti	140
Honduras	140
Mexico	140
Nicaragua	141
Paraguay	141
Venezuela	141
6. Writers from Ottoman Europe	**143**
Greece	143
Romania	146
Serbia	146
Albania	147
Bulgaria	147
7. Writers from Romanov Territories	**149**
Latvia	150
Lithuania	150
Poland	151
Russia	156
Ukraine	164
Estonia	167
8. Writers from Scandinavia	**169**
Denmark	169
Finland	175
Iceland	180
Norway	180
Sweden	184

9. Writers from Spain and Portugal	193
Portugal	193
Spain	195
10. Writers from the British Isles	203
Great Britain: The Eighteenth Century	203
Great Britain: The Nineteenth Century	226
Ireland	262
11. Writers from the Italian Peninsula	285
Italy	285
12. Writers from the Low Countries	293
Belgium	293
The Netherlands	295
13. Writers from the Swiss Confederation	301
Switzerland	301
Conclusion: La Condition féminine	303
Selected Bibliography	307
Index	335

Introduction

This book reviews 650 women writers in 51 national traditions, broadly covering all Europe and both Americas. Its time frame is 1776–1848, a period bracketed by two revolutions, first in the Thirteen Colonies and then later across Europe. "We the people," runs the preamble to the United States Constitution, and the 1776 and 1848 revolutions are marked by two texts with radically different ideas of what "the people" means: Jefferson's *Declaration of Independence* and Marx's *Communist Manifesto*. 1848 is also, tellingly, the date of the *Declaration of Sentiments* at the First Women's Rights Convention in Seneca Falls, NY, which reprises Jefferson's famous text adding the words "and women" to his androcentric articles. We have argued at length elsewhere for a view of Romantic art, throughout this vast region, as a reflection of the age's revolutionary upheavals: in politics, where the maps of Europe and the Americas are redrawn; in industry, where steam power transforms human capacity and opens the great rivers of the world to Western gunboats; and in the culture of the book, where stereotype printing and wood paper make possible massive print runs to meet a new and expanded reading public, one with new expectations for art.[1] Somewhat ironically, the complex emergence of nationalism which these events precipitate has tended to silo scholarship into essentially national traditions, in which an overview of the whole field—Europe and the European diaspora, for lack of a better phrase—is occluded if not lost entirely. This book aims to address that blind spot, arguing that there is no other way to view the entire global phenomenon of 'Romanticism' as such.

The book is a sequel to our previous, preponderantly male-author study, *An Outline of Romanticism in the West*.[2] That study of Europe and

---

[1] John Claiborne Isbell, *The People's Voice: A Romantic Civilization, 1776–1848* (Bloomington, IN: Lilly Library, 1996).

[2] John Claiborne Isbell, *An Outline of Romanticism in the West* (Cambridge, UK: Open Book Publishers, 2022), https://doi.org/10.11647/OBP.0302

the two Americas argued that the dearth of women writers in national Romantic historiographies, outside the English-speaking world, could reflect a relative lack of research in the field. In further pursuing that research, it has become clear that the field has indeed been explored unevenly. Tracing women writers across fifty-one national traditions, a remarkable disproportion emerges. Our initial English-language search yielded zero women writers in thirteen traditions, with thirty-eight nations noting anywhere from one woman writer to hundreds in the Anglo-American world. This glaring disproportion may offer a spur to future research. It seems obvious that Mexican women, for instance, did not lay aside their pens for seventy years as their country achieved independence; and indeed, our subsequent research identified a study on women writers in convents in colonial Mexico, where understandably a writing tradition was maintained. Moreover, as noted, the initial research for this volume was conducted primarily in English; the bibliography though lists a half-dozen Spanish and Portuguese works on Latin American women writers which offer avenues for further work. Universally, this volume's author lists should expand as research continues, that is our hope. The volume is in that sense nothing more, as Staël once put it, than a stone brought to the collective pyramid of knowledge.

Our goal has been to name every woman writer in a European language that our initial search revealed, from St Petersburg to Lima and between 1776 and 1848. This means reviewing the 650 women writers that we have recuperated—a refreshingly large number. For each author, dates, full name, and a brief description are given, providing an ongoing, somewhat encyclopedic resource and a ground plan for future research. Democratically, each author entry is limited to a ten-line maximum; and democratically, we set out to list every woman writer we have thus far found in this vast region who saw print, either during her lifetime or subsequently. We have no wish to sequester professional from 'unprofessional' women writers, or to prioritize the one over the other: indeed, to our mind, doing so fundamentally misrepresents the female writing experience during this period, when publication was both harder to come by and frowned upon by the patriarchal establishment. It is no coincidence that the volume contains memoirs written solely for family members years after the fact, or manuscript diaries and autobiographies later unearthed in family archives. They form an integral part of the rich pageant of women's writing at the time, and they deserve their moment in the sun if we are to understand the fundamental ways in which men and women picked up a pen during this age in very different manners and with very different expectations. Let these voices be heard in their diversity. Finally, to make our project more welcoming to the eye, American and British women writers are here divided by century. So many women writers have been recuperated in these two traditions that offering them *en bloc* would, we believe, fatigue the reader.

Our method is twofold; or put another way, this book operates in a double continuum. First, it offers 650 brief author entries under fifty-one national headings, reviewing the several hundred known women writers Europe and the two Americas produced during the period. This provides a brief, encyclopedic overview. Second, the book offers twenty-one author extracts, with translation, in seventeen European languages. The national traditions selected are intended to provide a representative introduction to this corpus, stretching from Russia west to Ireland and from the United States to Peru. The English and Spanish languages feature more than once, given their diasporas; Swedish features twice, given that the Finnish women writers we have thus far identified in the period wrote exclusively in Swedish or German. These various extracts may perhaps prevent the study from becoming a bare aggregate of biographical author entries, breathing life and context into one overriding question: namely, can a pattern of Romantic creation be detected in the corpus of women's writing produced in European languages during the Romantic age? The question seems worth asking, and perhaps the beginning of an answer can also be elaborated. That start to an answer will be found in the contextual commentary that accompanies our extracts, discussing to what extent these writers are impacted both by the age's multiple revolutionary events and by its patriarchal structures.

A note on names. Each brief entry provides the writer's full name and dates as known. Many of these 650 women writers at some point published anonymously or pseudonymously; pseudonyms are listed in square brackets, and a brief "known as" accompanies especially long and confusing names, say of Claire de Duras. Each extract also lists each known marriage with date and the partner's full name.

How then are the twenty-one extracts selected? If the book is comprehensive, the representative extracts are necessarily selective, and representation, as the French discovered in the 1790s, is a tricky business. To begin with, these have depended on European and American library holdings, which in some measure reflect authorial success. Thus, the Dutch novelist Anna Louisa Geertruida Bosboom-Toussaint sold across Europe at the time, and the American poet Phillis Wheatley has largely remained in print since publication. Many national traditions here reviewed leave little room for choice: we have, for instance, identified just one Greek woman writer in the period, Elisavet Moutzan-Martinengou, and though her works are often absent in the libraries of America and Western Europe, she is here in extract. A certain mix of bestsellers and the unknown thus emerges, reflecting contemporary realities. We have also endeavored to feature both verse and prose in our extracts, though prose predominates, much as it appears to predominate throughout our extensive corpus, in part because of the multiplicity of prose genres, from philosophy to memoir. Our previous volume on thirty French women writers taught us that drama lends itself less well to presentation in short extracts, and we have selected accordingly.[3] In prose fiction, we have chosen to extract opening passages, since we find incipits revelatory and the comparison between them illuminating. And finally, we have sought out literary and historical interest throughout.

National traditions, which often fail to reflect either contemporary geopolitical realities or the movement of persons, are indicated by simple use of the national descriptor for our fifty-one section headings: we say Finland, for instance, though these Finnish writers mostly wrote in Swedish, or Latvia, starring Julie de Krüdener who wrote in French. Irish, British, and United States writers are thus given separate headings representing their different modern national traditions, though the many Scottish authors here identified appear within the British tradition Scotland joined in 1707. The risk of anachronism in such an enterprise is both significant and worth avoiding; that is why those modern national traditions that pay homage to these writers are grouped under thirteen more contemporary chapter headings, from "Writers from Ottoman Europe" to "Writers from Latin America and the Caribbean," with a

---

[3] John Claiborne Isbell, *Destins de Femmes: French Women Writers, 1750–1850* (Cambridge, UK: Open Book Publishers, 2023), https://doi.org/10.11647/OBP.0346

brief geopolitical context provided to open each chapter, an outline of the broader historical framework in which these different women lived and wrote, and the institutional structures that their region's various nascent national movements inhabited.

Our task as we see it is to lay the groundwork for future research. To that end, a review of the current state of the field seems in order. Let us begin with studies on Romanticism. Without duplicating the review we conducted in 2022 to open *An Outline of Romanticism in the West*, it seems apparent that a wealth of national studies exists, and a smaller number of global ones, focused mostly on Europe to the exclusion of the New World, Latin America in particular. Notably, there is the five-volume series of essays on Romanticism in the *Comparative History of Literatures in European Languages* (Amsterdam: John Benjamins, 1988–2008), which covers the Americas intermittently. Two other comparative studies cover Europe with the Americas absent: *European Romanticism: A Reader*, edited by Stephen Prickett (2010), offers sixteen short essays on a range of national Romanticisms, followed by about nine hundred pages of bilingual extracts; while *The Oxford Handbook of European Romanticism*, edited by Paul Hamilton (2016), covers a range of European literatures with some gaps, such as the Southern Slavs and the Low Countries. The present volume, like our previous *Outline*, thus offers something new to scholarship in its ecumenical reach.

Reviews of women writers in the Romantic age are a different matter. Again, a wealth of national studies exists, notably in the Anglo-American tradition, though Germany and France are well represented. These studies figure in our bibliography. Many good studies review women throughout history, and they too figure in our bibliography, for instance Anne Commire and Deborah Klezmer, *Women in World History: A Biographical Encyclopedia*, 17 vols (Waterford, CT: Yorkin Publications, 1999–2002), Katharina M. Wilson, *An Encyclopedia of Continental Women Writers*, 2 vols (New York and London: Garland Publishing, 1991), and Katharina M. Wilson, Paul Schlueter, and June Schlueter, *Women Writers of Great Britain and Europe: An Encyclopedia* (London: Garland, 1997). Let us leave these aside for now, since our goal is to address the Romantic age specifically. Similarly, comparatist work on the Enlightenment is tangential to our task: Elizabeth Cook, *Epistolary Bodies: Gender and Genre in the Eighteenth-Century Republic of*

Letters (Stanford, CA: Stanford University Press, 1996), say, or Rebecca Cypess, *Women and Musical Salons in the Enlightenment* (Chicago, IL: University of Chicago Press, 2022). The same goes for Victorian studies, such as Linda H. Peterson, *The Cambridge Companion to Victorian Women's Writing* (Cambridge: Cambridge University Press, 2015). In short, global studies of Romantic women writers are infrequent. The Gothic genre marks an exception here: Emma Clery, *The Rise of Supernatural Fiction, 1762–1800* (Cambridge: Cambridge University Press, 1995); Eugenia C. DeLamotte, *Perils of the Night: A Feminist Study of Nineteenth-Century Gothic* (Oxford: Oxford University Press, 1990); William Hughes, David Punter, and Andrew Smith, *The Encyclopedia of the Gothic*, 2 vols (Chichester: Wiley-Blackwell, 2013); even Montague Summers, *A Gothic Bibliography* (London: The Fortune Press, 1941). Beyond the Gothic, pickings seem thin: Katherine Sobba Green, *The Courtship Novel, 1740–1820: A Feminized Genre* (Lexington, KY: University Press of Kentucky, 1991); Susanne Kord, *Women Peasant Poets in Eighteenth-Century England, Scotland, and Germany: Milkmaids on Parnassus* (London: Camden House, 2003); Jacqueline Letzter and Robert Adelson, *Women Writing Opera: Creativity and Controversy in the Age of the French Revolution* (Berkeley, CA: University of California Press, 2001); or Patrick H. Vincent, The *Romantic Poetess: European Culture, Politics, and Gender, 1820–1840* (Durham, NH: University of New Hampshire Press, 2004). In short, global overviews of women writers in the Romantic era seem relatively few in number, and those that exist tend to be thematic. The present volume is designed to fill that gap, addressing the question of whether a feminine Romantic age manifests across Europe and the European diaspora, one shaped and created by women writers.

What, then, does one encounter in the pages of this book? Death in childbirth, distressingly often. Tuberculosis. Bad marriages with little prospect of divorce. Debtors' prison. Time as amanuensis for a male writer, fathers in particular. Career choices: governess, teacher, director of a girls' school; dressmaker, mill worker, weaver, spy. Tailor, in the case of Maria Engelbrecht Stokkenbech, who spent years disguised as a man, smoking, drinking, and playing cards with her male coworkers, urinating through a horn, before being found out, tried, and forbidden by the government from wearing men's clothes. Writer as a last resort, to avoid penury, to feed one's children. Displeasure at being "obligated to any man breathing," in the case of Jane Elizabeth Moore. Scientists and Quakers; lesbians, spinsters, mothers of twelve. Pseudonymous and anonymous writers, facing misattribution at the time and a sudden drop in positive reviews when one's gender identity is revealed. The unpublished, by choice or by the luck of the draw: Phillis Wheatley for instance could not, it turned out, publish again after freedom. Polyglots in large number. Autodidacts. Travelers, voluntary and otherwise, across empire and diaspora: America, China, India, South Africa, Southeast Asia, Australia, the Antilles. The bourgeois, the noble, the daughters of silk throwsters and linen drapers, those who appealed to the Royal Literary Fund. Fighters for causes, again in large number, including those who joined action to words: abolitionists, early suffragists, hymn writers, temperance crusaders. The guillotined. Speakers for the enslaved and the outcast, for every minority: Romany, Jewish, Native American, the colonized, the poor; for women, for prisoners, for those imprisoned for debt; for those Frantz Fanon calls the wretched of the Earth. This sympathy for the minority, the voiceless, and the oppressed, I have argued, is a quintessentially Romantic impulse, and in it, one may perhaps find the legacy of the Romantic period that frames this corpus of lives and works. It lies at the origins of nationalism—giving a voice, *vox populi*, to the voiceless masses—and it recurs throughout these pages, crossing barriers of language and regime and appearing with some frequency among the different women we encounter, with their different reasons for writing. As much as any pattern, it distinguishes this text.

"The Romantic Age" is a necessarily fluid concept. What then lies beyond this book's perimeter? In space, we have restricted our project to Europe and the European diaspora, the argument being that a "Romantic Age" *per se* does not exist in the period chosen, 1776–1848, outside of that ambit. Our earlier *Outline of Romanticism in the West* looks briefly in its epilogue at three different 'Romantic movements' outside the Eurosphere—in Japan, India, and the Ottoman Empire—and finds that the works concerned are all written after 1850. One may note that the borders of the Eurosphere were themselves fluid at the time, extending beyond the Americas into Australia, Africa, and Asia. Those various colonial presences, from Macau to South Africa, duly feature in this book. In time, one must delimit a chronological span somewhere, and we have done so. Thus, like the Assing sisters, Emily Dickinson is absent—she was just leaving school in 1848 and did not begin to organize her poetry for another decade. 1776 and 1848 are seismic enough, we believe, to support the weight here accorded them. But it is quite true that Romanticism colors outside the lines. The *Declaration of Independence* is itself a somewhat arbitrary benchmark in the American revolutionary process, and that is particularly true of Boston, where the enslaved Phillis Wheatley published her poems in 1773. Opening this volume with her work—and she wrote thereafter, though she could not publish—seems a suitable means of underlining that truth.

As we trace out the boundaries of this collection, it becomes apparent that these exist in more than space and time alone; the very business of identifying someone as an author is tricky. As Virginia Woolf noted in *A Room of One's Own*, "I would venture to guess that Anon, who wrote so many poems without signing them, was often a woman."[4] Many women in our period indeed wrote and published pseudonymously or anonymously; many women also surely collaborated uncredited on work by men they knew. An interesting new monograph, *Breaking Conventions*, thus reviews the extent to which the woman's part in its five couples' publications was compromised or elided.[5] It seems fair to say in these circumstances that identifying and reclaiming all women writers in the Romantic Age is a task that can be begun but not completed. And that is quite appropriate. Let other scholars then continue and correct the work here begun.

Our overriding hope in this work is exactly that: to provide tools for future research, to inspire readers to delve into the data accumulated in these pages. Perhaps an extract in one of our various languages will light a fire in a reader; perhaps a footnote will name a monograph that seems worthy of a look. The footnotes, like the bibliography, are designed, first to indicate where further information on a given author may be found, and second, to guide research. There is some duplication: the bibliography largely contains items mentioned in the

---

4   Virginia Woolf, *A Room of One's Own* (New York: Harcourt, Brace and Company, [1937]), p. 85.
5   Patricia Auspos, *Breaking Conventions: Five Couples in Search of Marriage-Career Balance at the Turn of the Nineteenth Century* (Cambridge, UK: Open Book Publishers, 2023), https://www.openbookpublishers.com/books/10.11647/obp.0318. This text also has valuable information on women as amanuenses.

footnotes, assembling a small library of sources for work on women writers in the Romantic age from Russia to Peru. Author monographs, of which a good number are listed here, appear only in the footnotes; and similarly, local studies—say, on Texas or Kentucky, in the United States section—do not feature in the bibliography, which is already long. The lion's share of footnotes cites author monographs and reference works such as encyclopedias, meaning that individual page numbers seem otiose; readers are invited to consult encyclopedia entries entire or to look through author monographs at leisure. The bibliography in turn, like the index, offers a handy overview of publications in the field of Romantic women's studies, and is partitioned like the book itself into national and regional headings. As for the translations, they reproduce published versions whenever possible—for French, Polish, or Spanish, for instance. When not, they are my own responsibility, begun with Google Translate and subsequently reviewed both by me and by a qualified native speaker of that language, as the acknowledgements document.

Acknowledgements

This book has taken some time to complete, as is perhaps only proper. Bibliographical research took me to libraries in Europe, Asia, and North America: in Paris, the Bibliothèque nationale de France and the Mediathèque du Musée du quai Branly—Jacques Chirac; in London, The British Library; in Cambridge, Massachusetts, Harvard's Widener Library; in Almaty, The National Library of Kazakhstan; in Oslo, The National Library of Norway; in Palo Alto, Stanford University Library; in San Francisco, The University of California at Berkeley Library; and in Vienna, the Universitätsbibliothek Wien, in all of which library staff were unfailingly helpful. The internet, that two-edged sword, provided many initial leads, notably Wikipedia. I was sponsored in this research by two university programs whose help made the final book possible: at the Université Paris Est-Créteil, the LIS Laboratory—*Lettres, Idées, Savoirs*—and its co-director, Anne Raffarin; at the University of Vienna, the Department of Slavonic Studies and its head, Stefan Newerkla. To these two programs and their directors go my heartfelt thanks.

A variety of individuals also helped immeasurably over the long months of assembling this volume, most particularly with my numerous extracts and translations: Vladislav Beronja, Luiza Duarte Caetano, Márta Csire, William Gilbreath, Rosemary Lloyd, Thomas Mikula, Roger Paulin, Naděžda Salmhoferová, Nataliya Shpylova-Saeed, Todd Sjoblom, and Harry van der Linden. Special thanks go to Roger Paulin, Schroeder Professor of German emeritus at The University of Cambridge and my former German professor, who reviewed the German sections in their entirety and offered unfailing support for the project from inception to completion. My wife Margarita Madanova Isbell did many things, as always, over the years this project took, among them reviewing my translation from the Russian, in which, as always, any errors are my own. I would also like to thank the team at Open Book

Publishers who oversaw the production of the book. This study has indeed been some time in the making, and so I extend my thanks back to my former students and colleagues at The University of Cambridge, Durham University, Indiana University Bloomington, the Université de Paris-XIII, and The University of Texas Rio Grande Valley, indeed back to Klosterschule Gaesdonck and the Lycée international in Saint-Germain-en-Laye, my first posts. My journey has been a shared one and these have been my companions. A special thanks goes to the Lilly Library at Indiana University Bloomington, where in 1996, I produced an exhibition and catalogue, *The People's Voice: A Romantic Civilization, 1776–1848*, that did much to encourage my thinking on Romanticism along more ecumenical or global lines. Sometimes as we arrive, only the dust or salt of the journey remains to indicate how far we have come; Ithaka is further than one imagines. I dedicate this book to those students and colleagues and to my wife Margarita, who has seen the book move from the unreal to the real, as the *Upanishads* put it. May it encounter sympathetic eyes.

1. Writers from British North America

The region of British North America, consolidated after the French loss of Quebec and Louisiana in 1763—or what after 1776 and American independence became the separate Canadian and United States national traditions—has done considerable work reclaiming women writers from the period 1776–1848. My English-language research identifies fourteen Canadian women writers in this period and for the United States, thirty-three in the eighteenth century and 159 in the nineteenth, outpacing any other national reclamation project but the British. The sheer volume of American women writers recovered, as in the case of British writers, has caused us to divide these two traditions by century.

Canada (14 writers)

Emily Elizabeth Shaw Beavan (1818–6 August 1897), born in Belfast, emigrated to New Brunswick with her family in 1836. Here, she married Frederick Williams Cadwalleder Beavan in 1838. In 1843, they emigrated to England, where she published *Sketches and Tales Illustrative of Life in the Backwoods of New Brunswick, North America* before emigrating to Australia in 1852. She also wrote poems and short stories. She died in Sydney.[1]

Julia Catherine Beckwith (10 March 1796–28 November 1867), born in New Brunswick to a francophone mother and an anglophone father, grew up there, in Novia Scotia, and in Quebec. Her (and arguably Canada's) first novel, *St. Ursula's Convent*, written at age seventeen,

---

1 George Williams Brown, *Dictionary of Canadian Biography*, 15 vols (Toronto: University of Toronto/Université Laval, 1966–2005 https://www.biographi.ca/en/).

appeared in 1824 in 165 copies. She married George Henry Hart in 1822, moving with him to the United States where she published her second novel, *Tonnawanda*. Beckwith returned to New Brunswick in 1831 with her husband and six children, and there wrote a third novel, *Edith*, which remained in manuscript.[2]

Deborah How Cottnam (c. 1725/1728–31 December 1806), a colonial poet and schoolmistress baptized in Massachusetts, was raised in Nova Scotia but returned to Boston a prisoner in 1744 during King George's War. By 1774, she ran a school in Salem for the Loyalist gentry, which she moved to Novia Scotia in 1777 with the outbreak of the Revolutionary War, then later to New Brunswick. She was married to Samuel Cottnam from 1742 until his death in 1780. Her selected poems saw publication in 1845.[3]

Eliza Lanesford Cushing (19 October 1794–4 May 1886), born in Massachusetts, published two anonymous novels in Boston, *Saratoga* and *Yorktown*, before marrying Frederick Cushing in 1828 and then moving to Montreal with her sister in 1833. Widowed in 1845–1846, the two sisters founded a monthly girls' magazine, *The Snow-Drop*. Cushing later edited *The Literary Garland*, where the two published poetry and prose, from 1850–1851; Cushing also published short stories and plays in both Canada and the United States. Her sister Harriet Vaughan Cheney appears here under United States nineteenth-century women writers.[4]

Sarah Herbert (October 1824–22 December 1846), born in Ireland, emigrated to Canada with her family in 1826. Their ship sank off the coast of Nova Scotia, her mother dying soon after. Herbert submitted poetry and stories to journals such as *The Olive Branch, The Novascotian*, and *The British North American Wesleyan Methodist Magazine*. In 1843, her serial novel *Agnes Maitland* won a contest sponsored by *The Olive Branch*, of which she became editor and proprietor in 1844, publishing Harriet Beecher Stowe among others. She died of consumption in 1846.[5]

---

2 *Dictionary of Canadian Biography*; Eugene Benson and William Toye, eds. *Oxford Companion to Canadian Literature*, 2nd edition (Oxford: Oxford University Press, 1997).

3 *The Canadian Encyclopedia* (https://www.thecanadianencyclopedia.ca/en); *The Oxford Dictionary of National Biography* [DNB] (https://www.oxforddnb.com/); *Dictionary of Canadian Biography*.

4 William New, ed. *Encyclopedia of Literature in Canada* (Toronto: University of Toronto Press, 2002).

5 *Dictionary of Canadian Biography*; Linda H. Peterson, ed. *The Cambridge Companion to Victorian Women's Writing* (Cambridge: Cambridge University Press, 2015).

Anne Langton (24 June 1804–10 May 1893), an English portrait and landscape painter, emigrated to Canada with her parents in 1837 to join her brother after her family had fallen on hard times. Here, she published her early memoirs as *A Gentlewoman in Upper Canada*.[6]

Maria Morris Miller (12 February 1813–29 October 1875), a botanical painter, was born and died in Halifax, Nova Scotia, where in 1840 she married Garret Trafalgar Nelson Miller. She presented her works to Queen Victoria and received royal patronage. Besides three catalogs of Nova Scotian wildflowers, 1840–1866, Miller published a volume of poetry with her sister in 1856, *Metrical Musings*.[7]

Maria Monk (27 June 1816-summer of 1849) published the *Awful Disclosures of Maria Monk* in 1836, purporting to be memoirs of seven years in a Montreal convent, a tale of sexual slavery to priests and infanticide. It sold 26,000 copies amid a mood of anti-Catholic hysteria. Monk moved to Philadelphia with her partner, Graham Monk, where the birth of a child out of wedlock in 1838 alienated most of her followers. Several inconsistencies, and the news that she had spent seven years in the Magdalen Asylum for Wayward Girls, suggest that the book was a hoax.[8]

Susanna Moodie, née **Strickland** (6 December 1803–8 April 1885), born in England, published her first children's book, *Spartacus*, in 1822. She married John Moodie in 1831, emigrating with him to Upper Canada in 1832. Her memoir *Roughing it in the Bush* appeared in 1852, with a sequel in 1853. She also published poetry and novels. Margaret Atwood devoted a volume of poetry to her.[9]

Ellen Kyle Noel [or **Mrs. J.V. Noel**] (22 December 1815–20 June 1873) emigrated to Kingston, Ontario where she married John le Vavasour Noel in 1833. She ran a seminary for women in Savannah, Georgia from about 1836–1847, then returning to Kingston. Noel wrote stories and serialized novels for Montreal and Toronto periodicals: the *Canadian Illustrated News*, the *Saturday Reader*. Her works include *The Abbey of Rathmore, and Other Tales*; *The Cross of Pride*; *Hilda*; and *Passion and Principle*.[10]

---

6   *Dictionary of Canadian Biography*; www.archives.gov.on.ca.
7   *Dictionary of Canadian Biography*; thecanadianencyclopedia.ca.
8   *Dictionary of Canadian Biography*; Gordon Stein. *Encyclopedia of Hoaxes* (Detroit, MI: Gale Research, 1993).
9   *Dictionary of Canadian Biography; Dictionary of National Biography* [DNB], 'Strickland, Agnes (1796–1874).'
10 Lorraine McMullen and Sandra Campbell, eds. *Pioneering Women: Short Stories by Canadian Women. Beginnings to 1880* (Ottawa: University of Ottawa Press, 1993).

Louise-Amélie Panet [or **Berczy**] (27 January 1789–24 March 1862), a poetess and painter born in the city of Quebec, married William Bent Berczy in 1819 and died in Quebec.[11]

Hannah Maynard Pickard [or **A Lady**] (25 November 1812–11 March 1844), born in Vermont, moved to Concord, Massachusetts with her family aged three, then to Wilbraham and Boston from 1826–1828. Here, Pickard taught at two sabbath schools and wrote for the *Sabbath School Messenger*, *Guide to Holiness*, and other periodicals. She wrote poems, sketches, and prose and published two novels which saw several editions: *Procrastination, or, Maria Louisa Winslow*, 1840, and *The Widow's Jewels: In Two Stories*, 1844. In 1838, Pickard began teaching at the Wilbraham Academy. She married Humphrey Pickard in 1841, relocating to Saint John, New Brunswick in Canada, where he preached. Pickard died of heart failure aged thirty-two. The posthumous *Memoir and Writings of Mrs. Hannah Maynard Pickard*, 1845, included her history, diary, correspondence, and some other writings.[12]

Dame Elizabeth Posthuma Simcoe (22 September 1762–17 January 1850), an English heiress, artist, and diarist, lost both father and mother before baptism, when her aunt adopted her. In 1782, she married John Graves Simcoe, later the first Lieutenant Governor of Upper Canada, with whom she had eleven children. Besides her 595 watercolors of what became Toronto, her diary was published in 1911.[13]

Grizelda Elizabeth Cottnam Tonge [or **Portia**] (1803–19 May 1825), born in Nova Scotia, sailed to join her father in Guyana in 1825, where she died of a tropical disease. Her poems were written under the pen name 'Portia.'[14]

---

11 *Canadian Women Artists History Initiative* (https://www.concordia.ca/finearts/art-history/research/cwahi.html).
12 *Dictionary of Canadian Biography*; George Maclean Rose. *A Cyclopædia of Canadian Biography* [...] (Toronto: Rose Publishing Company, 1886); *Canada's Early Women Writers* (https://cwrc.ca/project/canadas-early-women-writers).
13 *Dictionary of Canadian Biography*.
14 Ibid.

The United States: The Eighteenth Century
(33 writers)

Phillis Wheatley,
Poems on Various Subjects, Religious and Moral (1773)

> On Being Brought from Africa to America
> 'Twas mercy brought me from my *Pagan* land,
> Taught my benighted soul to understand
> That there's a God, that there's a *Saviour* too:
> Once I redemption neither sought nor knew.
> Some view our sable race with scornful eye,
> "Their colour is a diabolic die."
> Remember, *Christians*, *Negroes*, black as *Cain*,
> May be refin'd, and join th' angelic train.[15]

As the slaveowner John Wheatley remarks in his prefatory letter to this collection, "Phillis was brought from *Africa* to *America*, in the Year 1761, between Seven and Eight Years of Age." She was thus around twenty when she published this poem, having overcome the barriers of language, culture, and continued enslavement to do so. What seem to be her own prefatory remarks on the poems, after the customary demurrals, add with startling confidence, "we presume they have too much Merit to be cast aside with Contempt." (p. iv). Her master's letter, she concludes, sufficiently indicates the disadvantages regarding learning she has faced, and that is certainly the case.

It bears saying that this is a good poem. The rhyme is undemanding, but the Augustan heroic couplets are well-managed: end-stopped as the eighteenth century preferred, with one routine syntactical contortion in line 4 and just two poeticisms, the word "sable" and the phrase "th'angelic train." The language seems in fact unusually limpid for this period against which Wordsworth revolted a generation later in his quest for ordinary speech. The argument, in turn, covers considerable ground in eight lines, from the old slavers' pretention that enslavement saved souls, through outright

---
15 In *The Poems of Phillis Wheatley*, ed. Julian D. Mason, Jr. (Chapel Hill, NC: University of North Carolina Press, 1966), p. 7.

racism—the essentialist claim that black skin is *per se* diabolic—to the redemptive argument that any human soul may be saved and thus worthy of Heaven. The entire poem, in short, is couched in the discourse of the oppressor. One may speculate that Wheatley, in her twelve years of enslavement, had had time for other thoughts than these European tropes; other poems in this collection are without exception longer productions. But the tropes are handled with skill, and the concluding antithesis to answer the overtly racist opening has a certain barbed weight.

One may note some resemblance between this short poem's redemptive narrative and that of the famous hymn "Amazing Grace," written in December 1772, i.e. almost simultaneously, and published in 1779. Wheatley opens "'Twas mercy brought me," while John Newton opens verse two, "'Twas grace that taught my heart to fear." The juxtaposition is curious, given that the abolitionist Newton was a reformed slave trader and Wheatley, a victim of that trade. And in fact, the whole story of her volume's publication is thought-provoking. The volume appeared in Boston and London (where Newton then preached), with three prefatory texts: from Wheatley herself, from her slaveowner, John Wheatley, and from an assembly of Boston notables, including the colony's governor and the revolutionary John Hancock, which examined Wheatley to determine whether she had been able to write the poems herself. Thomas Jefferson for his part, who unlike George Washington did not free his slaves in his will, refused to see any value in Wheatley's poetic production.[16] Black, female, and carried into slavery, the confidence Wheatley displays in her volume's opening text is all the more inspiring when one considers the range of obstacles she faced. Finally, let us note that the word *freedom* does not feature in this short text, very much in the air though it was in colonial Boston in 1773, where Wheatley wrote.

Abigail Adams (22 November 1744–28 October 1818), born in Massachusetts to a Congregationalist minister and slaveholder, was the wife and mother of United States presidents. She married John Adams in 1764 and they had six children. In 1784–1788, the couple were in Paris

---

16 Thomas Jefferson, *Notes on the State of Virginia: With Related Documents*, ed. David Waldstreicher (New York: Palgrave, 2002), p. 178.

and London, where John was posted. John became president in 1797–1800, dying in 1826. The adult Adams, a Unitarian, opposed slavery and advocated for women's rights, though marked by conservatism. She and her husband exchanged 1,200 letters.[17]

Hannah Adams (2 October 1755–15 December 1831), born in Massachusetts, was perhaps the first professional woman writer in the United States. Self-taught, Adams later taught Latin and Greek, publishing three major works: the ecumenical *A View of Religions*, 1784; *A Summary History of New-England*, 1799; and *History of the Jews*, 1812. A self-proclaimed Unitarian, her acquaintances included John Adams, a distant cousin, and the abbé Grégoire. She wrote a short autobiography before her death.[18]

Katharine Greene Amory (22 November 1731–22 April 1777), born in Boston, married John Amory in 1756. They had ten children. She kept a Loyalist diary during the Revolutionary War, leaving Boston for London in 1775, where she died. The diary was published in 1923.[19]

Abigail Abbot Bailey (2 February 1746–11 February 1815), born in New Hampshire, married Major Asa Bailey in 1767. He was physically abusive and adulterous. They had seventeen children before Bailey learned that Asa had raped their daughter. Asa attempted to resettle the family in New York, which had stricter divorce laws; Bailey finally obtained a divorce in 1792. Struggling to support her children, Bailey found families in New Hampshire with whom they could live; her memoirs, written for her church, were published in 1815, the year she died.[20]

---

17   *Encyclopædia Britannica* (https://www.britannica.com/); Phyllis Lee Levin, *Abigail Adams: A Biography* (New York: St. Martin's Press, 1987).
18   *Who Was Who in America: Historical Volume, 1607–1896* (Chicago, IL: Marquis Who's Who, 1967); Dumas Malone, ed. *Dictionary of American Biography*, 22 vols (New York: Charles Scribner's Sons, 1928–1958); Anne Commire and Deborah Klezmer, eds. *Women in World History: A Biographical Encyclopedia*, 17 vols (Waterford, CT: Yorkin Publications, 1999–2002).
19   James Henry Stark, *The Loyalists of Massachusetts and the Other Side of the American Revolution* (Boston: W.B. Clarke Co., 1909).
20   Anne Commire et al., eds. *Women in World History* (1999–2002); Eugenia C. DeLamotte, Natania Meeker, and Jean F. O'Barr, eds. *Women Imagine Change: A Global Anthology of Women's Resistance from 600 B.C.E. to Present* (London: Routledge, 1997); Margo Culley, ed. *A Day at a Time: The Diary Literature of American Women from 1764 to the Present* (New York: Feminist Press at CUNY, 1985).

Lucy Barnes (6 March 1780–29 August 1809), born in New Hampshire to a Unitarian Universalist minister, proselytized for universal salvation before her early death. Her letters, dissertations, and poems were published posthumously in a 71-page pamphlet as *The Female Christian*.[21]

Ann Eliza Bleecker (October 1752–23 November 1783), born in New York to American Dutch gentry, married John James Bleecker in 1769. Bleecker's mother and infant daughter died while the family fled to Albany during the Revolutionary War, her sister during the return journey. Bleecker's pastoral poems and short stories, first appearing in her letters, were published posthumously by her daughter in 1793; her Indian Captivity novel *The History of Maria Kittle* was republished in 1797.[22]

Jemima Condict (24 August 1754–14 November 1779) was born and died in New Jersey. She kept a diary in partial numerical code with several mentions of the Revolutionary War. It was published in 1930.[23]

Rebecca Dickinson (25 July 1738–31 December 1815), born in Massachusetts, was apprenticed as a gownmaker around the age of twelve. She began keeping a diary in her thirties, describing Revolutionary events and her struggles with her Calvinist faith, which was published posthumously. Dickinson declined marriage at least three times; her success as a gownmaker enabled her to live independently as she desired.[24]

Elizabeth Sandwith Drinker (27 February 1735–24 November 1807), who lived and died in Philadelphia, married Henry Drinker in 1761. She kept a 2,100-page diary which was published in 1889. Federalist and Quaker, Drinker's diary sheds light on Quakerism and life in Philadelphia before and after the Revolutionary War. Henry, who was neutral and pacifist, was arrested for treason in 1777; Drinker appealed to George Washington and secured Henry's release in 1778.[25]

---

21 E.R. Hanson, *Our Woman Workers: Biographical Sketches of Women Eminent in the Universalist Church for Literary, Philanthropic and Christian Work* (Chicago, IL: Star and Covenant Office, 1884).

22 Jared Gardner, *Master Plots: Race and the Founding of an American Literature, 1787–1845* (Baltimore, MD: Johns Hopkins University Press, 2000); Sharon M. Harris, *Executing Race: Early American Women's Narratives of Race* (Columbus, OH: The Ohio State University Press, 2005).

23 Elizabeth Evans, *Weathering the Storm; Women of the American Revolution* (New York: Charles Scribner's Sons, 1975).

24 Marla Miller, *Rebecca Dickinson: Independence for a New England Woman* (Boulder, CO: Westview Press, 2014).

25 Elaine Forman Crane, ed. *The Diary of Elizabeth Drinker: The Life Cycle of an Eighteenth-Century Woman* (Philadelphia: University of Pennsylvania Press, 2010).

Margaretta Faugères (11 October 1771 – 9 January 1801), born in New York City, was the daughter of Ann Eliza Bleecker, whose manuscripts she published after 1790 in *The New York Magazine* alongside her own poems and prose. She married Peter Faugères in 1792. In 1791, she published *Fine Feelings Exemplified in the Conduct of a Negro Slave*, an abolitionist riposte to Thomas Jefferson, and in 1797, the pamphlet *The Ghost of John Young* in opposition to capital punishment. In 1795, she wrote the play *Belisarius: A Tragedy*, on human rights as exemplified by the French Revolution.[26]

Jenny Fenno (1765?-?) may have been the Jennet Fenno who was born in 1765. Her volume *Original Compositions in Prose and Verse* of 1791 contains around seventy poems, mostly in heroic couplets, and fifteen prose works. Fenno begins by justifying herself as a woman writer; several elegies for Boston's Second Baptist Church suggest she may have been a member.[27]

Elizabeth Graeme Fergusson [or **Betsy Graeme**] (3 February 1737–23 February 1801), born in Pennsylvania, met Laurence Sterne and George III while visiting London in 1764. She secretly married Hugh Henry Fergusson in 1772; her father died the next month and under colonial law, she became a *feme covert*—all her inherited property belonged to her husband. Henry left for London in 1778, Fergusson remaining in Pennsylvania. Her property was confiscated in 1779 as belonging to her Loyalist husband, and it took her two years to regain it, as chronicled in her letters and poems.[28]

---

26 Sharon M. Harris, *Women's Early American Historical Narratives* (London: Penguin Classics, 2003); Sharon M. Harris, *Executing Race* (2005).

27 Claire Buck, ed. *Bloomsbury Guide to Women's Literature* (London: Bloomsbury, 1992); James A. Levernier and Douglas R. Wilmes, eds. *American Writers before 1800: A Biographical and Critical Dictionary* (Westport, CT: Greenwood Press, 1983); Carla Mulford, Amy E. Winans, and Angela Vietto, eds. *American Women Prose Writers to 1820* (Detroit, MI: Gale Research, 1999); Janet M. Todd, ed. *A Dictionary of British and American Women Writers, 1660–1800* (Totowa, NJ: Rowman & Allanheld, 1985); Lina Mainiero et al., eds. *American women Writers: A Critical Reference Guide from Colonial Times to the Present*, 5 vols (New York: Frederick Ungar, 1979–1994), https://archive.org/details/americanwomenwri0000unse; Cathy N. Davidson et al., eds. *The Oxford Companion to Women's Writing in the United States* (Oxford: Oxford University Press, 1995).

28 Cathy N. Davidson et al., eds. *The Oxford Companion to Women's Writing in the United States* (1995); Edward T. James, Janet Wilson James, and Paul Samuel Boyer, eds. *Notable American Women, 1607–1950: A Biographical Dictionary*, 3 vols (Cambridge, MA: Harvard University Press, 1971).

Sarah Logan Fisher (1751–1796), born in Pennsylvania, married Thomas Fisher in 1772. She kept a diary after 1777—the year George Washington lodged at their family estate—in which she records her Quaker and Loyalist views. Thomas was imprisoned for eight months that year with other Quakers as a suspected Tory. The couple refused to use the continental money, and that prohibited them from engaging in trade. Fisher's diary was published in 1958.[29]

Hannah Webster Foster (10 September 1758/59–17 April 1840), born in Massachusetts, was the mother of writers Harriet Vaughan Cheney and Eliza Lanesford Cushing, both listed here. Foster began writing on politics in the Boston press in the 1770s. In 1785, she married Rev. John Foster. She published her epistolary novel *The Coquette; or, The History of Eliza Wharton* anonymously in 1797. Based on a true story of seduction, it sold well, but her name first appeared in it after 1866. In 1798, Foster published *The Boarding School; or, Lessons of a Preceptress to Her Pupils*, which sold less well. She then returned to journalism, moving to Montreal to be with her daughters at her husband's death in 1829.[30]

Winifred Marshall Gales (10 July 1761–26 June 1839), born in England, married Joseph Gales Sr. in 1784. Gales published a novel, *The History of Lady Emma Melcombe and Her Family*, in 1787, and *The Sheffield Independent* with Joseph until 1794 when he fled to continental Europe. Gales joined him in Germany and the couple emigrated to Philadelphia in 1795, then to North Carolina where in 1804, Gales published *Matilda Berkely; or, Family Anecdotes*, the first known novel by a resident of that state. Firm Unitarians and Jeffersonian Republicans, the couple left Raleigh for Washington, D.C. in 1833.[31]

Grace Growden Galloway (1727–1782), born in Pennsylvania, married Joseph Galloway in 1753. Joseph, Speaker of the Pennsylvania House from 1766, was removed in 1775 as a Loyalist. He fled to the British with their daughter and Galloway became a social pariah, as recorded in her diary, which she began the day after Joseph fled. When

---

29   www.encyclopedia.com
30   *Encyclopædia Britannica*; Carol Kort, *A to Z of American Women Writers* (New York: Facts on File, 2000); Paul Lauter, ed. *The Heath Anthology of American Literature*, 5th edition, 5 vols (New York: Houghton Mifflin Company, 2005).
31   William S. Powell, *Dictionary of North Carolina Biography*, 6 vols (Chapel Hill, NC: University of North Carolina Press, 2016); Enid C. Gilberthorpe, *Book Printing at Sheffield in the Eighteenth Century* (Sheffield, UK: Sheffield City Libraries, 1967).

she refused to evacuate her property—confiscated in her husband's name—the state put new locks on her doors. Her testament willing the property to her daughter was honored after the Treaty of Paris in 1783.[32]

Hannah Griffitts (1727–1817), born in Pennsylvania, lived in Philadelphia until her death. A Quaker, she wrote elegies and sharp political satires celebrating colonial opposition to the British, which she circulated among her female acquaintanceship, though a few appeared in print. Some sixty of her poems feature in her cousin Milcah Martha Moore's commonplace book, published in 1997.[33]

Mary Jane 'Mercy' Harbison (18 March 1770–9 December 1837), born in New Jersey, married John Harbison in 1787. In western Pennsylvania in 1792, Harbison was captured with her three small children by Native Americans, who killed two of the children. After several days, she escaped with the third, giving a deposition of her captivity to the magistrates in Pittsburgh.[34]

Susannah Willard Johnson (20 February 1729/30–27 November 1810), born in Massachusetts, married Captain James Johnson in 1757, having fourteen children in all. She was captured with her family during an Abenaki raid in 1754, at the outbreak of the French and Indian War. They were marched to Quebec, then held for ransom until sold into slavery to the French. She returned to New Jersey in 1757. Johnson dictated her captivity memoir in 1796, using her surviving letters, notes, and diary, and edited subsequent editions.[35]

Rebecca Hammond Lard (**Laird**) (7 March 1772–28 September 1855), born in Massachusetts, married Samuel Laird in 1801, moving

---

32 Linda K. Kerber, *Women of the Republic: Intellect and Ideology in Revolutionary America* (Chapel Hill, NC: University of North Carolina Press, 1980); Carol Berkin, *First Generations: Women in Colonial America* (New York: Hill and Wang, 1996); Carol Berkin, *Revolutionary Mothers: Women in the Struggle for America's Independence* (New York: Knopf, 2005); Paul Engle, *Women in the American Revolution* (Chicago, IL: Follett, 1976).

33 *American National Biography*; Susan M. Stabile, *Memory's Daughters: The Material Culture of Remembrance in Eighteenth-Century America* (Ithaca, NY: Cornell University Press, 2004).

34 Horace Kephart, ed. *The Account of Mary Rowlandson and Other Indian Captivity Narratives* (Mineola, NY: Dover Publications, 2005).

35 Emma Lewis Coleman, *New England Captives Carried to Canada Between 1677 and 1760 during the French and Indian Wars*, 2 vols (Portland, ME: Southworth Press, 1925).

to Indiana after 1819. In 1820, she published the volume *Miscellaneous Poems on Moral and Religious Subjects* in Vermont, followed by a twelve-page booklet, *On the Banks of the Ohio*, in 1823—the first known poem to be published by an Indiana resident.[36]

Milcah Martha Moore (1740–1829) was born on the island of Madeira, moving to Pennsylvania in 1761. In 1767, Moore married her cousin Charles Moore and was expelled from the Society of Friends, rejoining it at his death in 1801. Between the 1760s and 1778, Moore kept a commonplace book (first published in 1997) featuring poems by over a dozen female acquaintances. Some of these, and some of her own poems, appeared in the 1787 textbook she edited for young readers entitled *Miscellanies, Moral and Instructive, in Prose and Verse*.[37]

Sarah Wentworth Apthorp Morton (August 1759–14 May 1846), born in Boston, married Perez Morton in 1781, later Speaker of the Massachusetts House. In about 1787, Perez began an affair with Morton's younger sister, who committed suicide. In 1792, Morton published her anti-slavery poem *The African Chief*, though her father had been a slave trader. Morton published three more volumes of poetry, 1790–1799, and an autobiographical sketch in 1823.[38]

Judith Sargent Stevens Murray (1 May 1751–9 June 1820), born in Massachusetts, married John Stevens in 1769. In 1786, John fled the United States to avoid debtors' prison, dying soon after; in 1788, Murray married the Universalist Rev. John Murray. Murray recorded her over 2,500 letters in letter books, discovered in 1984; between 1782 and 1816, she also published books, essays, poems, and plays, notably her essay *On the Equality of the Sexes*, written in 1779 and published in 1790, two years before Mary Wollstonecraft.[39]

Elizabeth Porter Phelps (24 November 1747–1 January 1817), born in Massachusetts, married Charles Phelps, Jr. in 1770. Phelps kept a

---

36 Fred D. Cavinder, *The Indiana Book of Records, Firsts, and Fascinating Facts* (Bloomington, IN: Indiana University Press, 1985).
37 Susan M. Stabile, *Memory's Daughters* (2004); Catherine La Courreye Blecki and A. Wulf, eds. *Milcah Martha Moore's Book: A Commonplace Book from Revolutionary America* (University Park, PA: Pennsylvania State University Press, 1997).
38 *Encyclopædia Britannica*.
39 Linda K. Kerber, *Women of the Republic* (1980); Sheila L. Skemp . *First Lady of Letters: Judith Sargent Murray and the Struggle for Female Independence* (Philadelphia, PA: University of Pennsylvania Press, 2011).

manuscript diary for 54 years, an important source on farm and domestic life at the turn of the nineteenth century.[40]

Martha Laurens Ramsay (3 November 1759–10 June 1811), born in South Carolina, married David Ramsay in 1787. They had eleven children. Ramsay's mother died in 1770 and she was raised by her uncle, who moved to England, then France after 1775. Her father, a wealthy plantation owner and slave trader, became President of the Second Continental Congress in 1777. Captured by the British, he joined Ramsay in France from 1782–1784, when she returned to Charleston. Her diary and letters were published posthumously by her husband.[41]

Susanna Rowson, née **Haswell** (1762–2 March 1824), born in England, moved to Massachusetts in 1767. During the Revolutionary War in 1778, the family's property was confiscated, and they were returned to England. She married William Rowson in 1786, publishing her novel *Charlotte Temple* in 1791. It has had over 200 editions. In 1793, the couple returned to Philadelphia as actors, where Rowson wrote a novel, an opera, a musical farce, and an address to American troops. Rowson left the stage in 1797, running a school and publishing more novels, plays, a spelling dictionary, and two books on geography.[42]

Anna Young Smith (5 November 1756–3 April 1780), born in Philadelphia, married Dr. William Smith in 1775. She shared her poems within Philadelphia's literary circles from 1773 until her marriage. Most were published posthumously, though Smith's revolutionary *Elegy to the Memory of the American Volunteers* appeared in *The Pennsylvania Magazine* in 1775.[43]

Annis Boudinot Stockton (1 July 1736–6 February 1801), born in Pennsylvania, married Richard Stockton around 1757. Richard signed the *Declaration of Independence*; George Washington, with whom she corresponded, visited their Princeton home. It was plundered by

---

40   Marla R. Miller, *The Needle's Eye: Women and Work in the Age of Revolution* (Amherst, MA: University of Massachusetts Press, 2006).
41   Margaret Simons Middleton , *David and Martha Laurens Ramsay* (New York: Carlton Press, 1971).
42   *Encyclopædia Britannica*; Emily Stipes Watts, *The Poetry of American Women from 1632 to 1945* (Austin, TX: University of Texas Press, 1977).
43   Janet M. Todd, ed. *British and American Women Writers* (1985); Lorna Sage, Germaine Greer, and Elaine Showalter, eds. *The Cambridge Guide to Women's Writing in English* (Cambridge: Cambridge University Press, 1999); Taryn Benbow-Pfalzgraf, ed. *American Women Writers*, 2nd edition (Detroit: St. James Press, 2000).

Cornwallis during the Revolutionary War, while Richard, imprisoned by the British, died in 1781. Stockton's brother served as President of the Continental Congress in 1782–1783. Stockton published odes, pastorals, elegies, sonnets, epitaphs, and hymns, and was read in Europe. Her unpublished poems later tripled her complete works in length.[44]

Mercy Otis Warren (25 September 1728–19 October 1814), born in Massachusetts, married James Warren in 1754; he later became Speaker of the Massachusetts House. Warren, who corresponded with the revolutionary figures John Adams, Patrick Henry, John Hancock, and Thomas Jefferson, also published observations on the United States Constitution in 1788, advocating for a Bill of Rights; a collection of poems and plays in 1790; and in 1805, a three-volume history of the American Revolution.[45]

Helena Wells, later **Whitford** (1761?–1824), born in South Carolina, moved to London with her family in 1777. The State of South Carolina later seized their colonial property. Wells ran a school in London with her sister from 1789–1799; she married Edward Whitford in 1801. Wells published two novels and two treatises on education between 1798 and 1809.[46]

Phillis Wheatley Peters, also spelled **Phyllis** and **Wheatly** (c. 1753–55 December 1784), born in Africa, was abducted and sold into slavery in Massachusetts in 1761. Wheatley, whose first given name was that of the slave ship that transported her, was reading Greek and Latin by the age of twelve and wrote her first surviving poem at fourteen. Wheatley published her first book of poems in London in 1773; she was manumitted in 1774, her former owners dying in 1774–1778. She married John Peters in 1778; her 1779 proposal for a second volume of poems failed for lack of patrons. Peters was imprisoned for debt in 1784; Wheatley died that year aged thirty-one, her infant daughter dying the same day.[47]

---

44 Carla Mulford, ed. *Only for the Eye of a Friend: The Poems of Annis Boudinot Stockton* (Charlottesville, VA: University of Virginia Press, 1995).

45 *Oxford Dictionary of National Biography* [DNB] (Oxford: Oxford University Press, https://www.oxforddnb.com/); Katharine Anthony, *First Lady of the Revolution: The Life of Mercy Otis Warren* (New York: Doubleday & Co., 1958).

46 *Dictionary of National Biography* [DNB].

47 David Waldstreicher. *The Odyssey of Phillis Wheatley: A Poet's Journeys Through American Slavery and Independence* (New York: Farrar, Straus and Giroux, 2023).

Eliza Yonge Wilkinson (7 February 1757–1806?), born in South Carolina to a slave-owning family, married Joseph Wilkinson in 1774. He died the following year, and she married Peter Porcher in 1786. Twelve of Wilkinson's letters from 1779–1781 were published, heavily edited, in 1839.[48]

The United States: The Nineteenth Century (159 writers)

Lois Bryan Adams (14 October 1817–28 June 1870), born in New York, moved to Michigan with her family in 1823. In 1841, she married James Randall Adams, a newspaper editor who died in 1848. Adams published in the Michigan and the New York press, contributing to and editing *The Michigan Farmer* during the 1850s.[49]

Lucy Bakewell Audubon (18 January 1787–18 June 1874), born in England, emigrated with her family to Connecticut in 1798. In 1808, she married John James Audubon, whose ornithological work she made financially possible, working as a teacher and governess. They settled in Kentucky. Audubon also arranged the publication of John's *Birds of America*, 1827–1838, and edited *The Life of John James Audubon*.[50]

Delia Salter Bacon (2 February 1811–2 September 1859), born in a log cabin in Tallmadge, Ohio, relocated to New England soon after. In 1831, she published *Tales of the Puritans* anonymously; in 1832, she beat Edgar Allan Poe in a short story contest. Bacon moved to New York in 1836, publishing a play there in 1839. After 1845, Bacon worked on her theory that a group led by (the unrelated) Francis Bacon had authored Shakespeare's plays. Nathaniel Hawthorne, Ralph Waldo Emerson, and Walt Whitman admired her. Bacon's trip to England in 1846, with a minister, caused controversy. She spent her last years in lunatic asylums in England and the United States.[51]

---

48 Janet M. Todd, ed. *British and American Women Writers* (1985); Carla Mulford et al., eds. *American Women Prose Writers to 1820* (1999).

49 William Turner Coggeshall, *The Poets and Poetry Of The West: With Biographical and Critical Notices* (Columbus, OH: Follett, Foster & Co., 1860).

50 Carolyn E. DeLatte, *Lucy Audubon: A Biography* (Baton Rouge, LA: Louisiana State University Press, 1982).

51 Viviane Constance Hopkins, *Prodigal Puritan: A Life of Delia Bacon* (Cambridge, MA: Harvard University Press, 1959).

Margaret Jewett Smith Bailey (1812?–17 May 1882), born in Massachusetts, converted to Methodism aged seventeen and journeyed to the Oregon Country as a missionary in 1837. In 1839, she married William J. Bailey, whom she divorced in 1854 because of his drinking and abuse. She contributed prose and poetry to *The Oregon Spectator* after 1846, the first local poet to be published west of the Rocky Mountains. Falsely accused of fornication at the mission, and a divorcee, Bailey published *The Grains* in 1854 to clear her name. It is the first known novel to be published in Oregon. Only three copies were extant before republication in 1986.[52]

Margaret L. Bailey, née **Shands** (12 December 1812–1888), born in Virginia, moved with her family to the Cincinnati area aged about six. She married Dr. Gamaliel Bailey in 1833; they had twelve children, of whom six survived infancy. From 1844–1852, Bailey edited *The Youth's Monthly Visitor*. The couple moved to Washington, D.C. in 1846, where she hosted an abolitionist salon. Bailey edited *The National Era* in 1859–1860; her poems appeared in her periodicals and her husband's and were uncollected at her death.[53]

Harriette Newell Woods Baker (19 August 1815–26 April 1893), born in Massachusetts, published her first short story aged eleven. In 1835, aged twenty, she married Rev. Abijah Richardson Baker. After the marriage, Baker continued to publish, also assisting her husband after 1850 in editing two monthly periodicals. Several of Baker's 200-odd moral and religious tales were republished in England and translated into French and German; her 1861 tale *Tim: The Scissors Grinder* sold half a million copies.[54]

---

52 Jean M. Ward and Elaine A. Maveety, eds. *Pacific Northwest Women, 1815–1925: Lives, Memories, and Writings* (Corvallis, OR: Oregon State University Press, 1995).

53 Rufus Wilmot Griswold, *The Female Poets of America* (Philadelphia, PA: Carey and Hart, 1849); William Turner Coggeshall, *The Poets and Poetry of the West* (1860); Graham Russell Hodges, *Encyclopedia of African American History, 1619–1895: From the Colonial Period to the Age of Frederick Douglass*, 3 vols (Oxford: Oxford University Press, 2006).

54 George Derby and James Terry White, eds. *The National Cyclopædia of American Biography* […], 63 vols (New York: J. T. White, 1891–1984); Frances Elizabeth Willard and Mary Ashton Livermore, *A Woman of the Century: Fourteen Hundred-seventy Biographical Sketches Accompanied by Portraits of Leading American Women in All Walks of Life* (Buffalo, NY: Moulton, 1893).

Martha Violet Ball (17 May 1811–22 December 1894), born in Boston, was a teacher for thirty years, operating a Boston school for young African American girls with her sister in 1833–1839. She helped edit *The Home Guardian*, a periodical for intemperate women and girls, for 27 years from 1837. Ball was an active abolitionist and missionary organizer throughout her life, facing a pro-slavery mob in Philadelphia in 1838. She also published several small volumes with some success.[55]

Charlotte Mary Sanford Barnes (1818–14 April 1863), born in Massachusetts to an acting family, made her stage debut at the age of three. Her New York stage debut in 1834 earned mixed reviews. Barnes had more success as a playwright, following two successful adaptations with her original blank verse drama in 1837, *Octavia Bragaldi, or, The Confession*, which she performed in New York and then in England in 1841. Barnes continued writing and performing until her death; her original works were collected in 1848, but her adaptations and translations do not survive.[56]

Sidney Frances Bateman, née **Cowell** (29 March 1823–13 January 1881) was born to an acting family in America and married Hezekiah Linthicum Bateman aged sixteen. In the 1850s, the couple moved to St Louis, then New York, then London where Hezekiah managed the Lyceum Theater. Bateman managed the Lyceum for three years after her husband's death in 1875, then managed the Sadler's Wells Theater until her death. Bateman also published several plays, notably *Self*, 1857, which had some success.[57]

Elise Justine Bayard Cutting (16 August 1823–1853), born in New York, married Fulton Cutting in 1849. Cutting published poems frequently in the New York City periodicals *The Knickerbocker* and *The Literary World*, most signed "E.J.B.' or 'E.B.C.,' her initials, and thus sometimes difficult to identify.[58]

---

55 Frances Elizabeth Willard et al. *A Woman of the Century* (1893); Patricia Okker, *Our Sister Editors: Sarah J. Hale and the Tradition of Nineteenth-Century American Women Editors* (Athens, GA: University of Georgia Press, 1995); Jean Fagan Yellin and John C. Van Horne, *The Abolitionist Sisterhood: Women's Political Culture in Antebellum America* (Ithaca, NY: Cornell University Press, 1994).

56 Lina Mainiero et al., eds. *American Women Writers* (1979–1994); Miriam López Rodríguez and María Dolores Narbona Carrión, eds. *Women's Contribution to Nineteenth-Century American Theatre* (Valencia: Universitat de València, 2004).

57 Hugh Chisholm, ed. *Encyclopædia Britannica*, 11th edition, 29 vols (Cambridge: Cambridge University Press, 1910–1911), "Bateman, Hezekiah Linthicum." Also this: https://archive.org/details/playsprosepoetry00barn/page/n5/mode/2up

58 Lina Mainiero et al., eds. *American Women Writers* (1979–1994); George Derby et al, eds. *The National Cyclopædia of American Biography* (1891–1963); Rufus W. Griswold. *The Female Poets of America* (1849).

Mary C. Billings, née **Ward** [after first marriage, **Granniss**; after second marriage, **Webster**; after third marriage, **Billings**] (12 July 1824– 2 March 1904), born in Connecticut, was married three times, in 1845, 1869, and 1885, and widowed three times. Her first published poem was written at the age of twelve. Billings, a universalist minister later doing missionary work in Texas, continued to publish frequently in northern periodicals, her works sometimes being compiled in book form. Her first book, *Emma Clermont*, appeared in 1849.[59]

Sarah Tittle Bolton, née **Barrett** (18 December 1814–4 August 1893), born in Kentucky, moved with her family to Indiana around the age of three. At the age of thirteen, Bolton's first published poem appeared. She married Nathaniel Bolton in 1831, publishing poetry and helping with her husband's career editing a newspaper and in state politics. The couple were in Europe from 1855–1858. Nathaniel died soon after their return; Bolton remarried in 1863 but left for Europe for several years then returned to Indiana, continuing to publish poetry and to advocate for women's property rights.[60]

Anne Charlotte Lynch Botta (11 November 1815–23 March 1891), born in Vermont, was the daughter of a United Irishman banished from Ireland after 1798. He died in 1819 and the family moved to Connecticut, then Rhode Island in 1838, where Botta taught and hosted a salon. Botta moved to Manhattan in 1845, there hosting the city's leading literary salon, where she presented Edgar Allan Poe. Besides frequent periodical publications, her volume *Poems* appeared in 1848. She married Vincenzo Botta in Europe in 1855; he published a posthumous memorial of her in 1893.[61]

Maria Gowen [or **Gowan**] **Brooks** (1794–11 November 1845), born in Massachusetts, married John Brooks at around the age of nineteen, a man some thirty years older and her guardian after her father's death. Brooks also changed her name from Abigail to Maria. She published her first volume of poetry in 1820: *Judith, Esther, and other Poems*. John died in

---

59 Susan Hill Lindley and Eleanor J. Stebner, *The Westminster Handbook to Women in American Religious History* (Louisville, KY: Westminster John Knox Press, 2008); E.R. Hanson, *Our Woman Workers* (1884).
60 Edward T. James et al., eds. *Notable American Women, 1607–1950* (1971); Dumas Malone, ed. *Dictionary of American Biography* (1928–1958).
61 D.C. Gilman, H. T. Peck, and F. M. Colby, eds. *New International Encyclopedia*, 17 vols (New York: Dodd, Mead, 1902–1904).

1823 and Brooks left for her brother's coffee plantation in Cuba. In 1825, Brooks began publishing her epic poem *Zophiël*, which earned praise from Robert Southey and Edgar Allan Poe. In Europe in 1829–1831, she met Southey and the Marquis de Lafayette. Other poems and prose followed, in print and manuscript.[62]

Phoebe Hinsdale Brown, née **Hinsdale** (1 May 1783–10 October 1861), born in New York, lost her parents in infancy and her grandparents at age ten, when she was taken in by her sister for eight years as a sort of servant. Brown then could not write her name. In 1805, she married Timothy H. Brown, a housepainter. Between 1824–1857, she published two Sunday school books, some poems in the periodical press, and various hymns, often anonymously, including "I Love to Steal Awhile Away," 1824. Her autobiography remained unpublished.[63]

Charity Bryant (22 May 1777–6 October 1851), born in Massachusetts, was the aunt of the poet William Cullen Bryant. In 1797, Bryant began working as a teacher. In 1807, she met Sylvia Drake, who remained her lifelong companion. They ran a tailoring business together and were accepted as a couple by their community. Bryant wrote many poems but instructed them all to be burned. The few that remain are mostly acrostic and addressed to Drake. The two are buried in Vermont under a shared headstone.[64]

Juliet Hamersley Lewis Campbell [or **Judith Canute**] (5 August 1823–26 December 1898), born in Pennsylvania, attended the Moravian Young Ladies' Seminary after 1835. In 1842, she married James Hepburn Campbell. Campbell's poems appeared in some prominent anthologies: *The American Female Poets* and *Read's Female Poets of America* in 1848, *The Female Poets of America* in 1849. In 1862, Campbell published the long poem *Legend of Infancy of Our Savior: A Christmas Carol*. Campbell also published one known novel, *Eros and Antieros; or, The Bachelor's Ward*, in 1857, as 'Judith Canute.' It was republished the following year under her own name but with a new title. The novel narrates the heroine Viola's good education; Campbell's father was Chief Justice of the Pennsylvania Supreme Court.[65]

---

62   Lina Mainiero et al., eds. *American Women Writers* (1979–1994).
63   Joyce Appleby, Eileen Cheng, and Joanne Goodwin, *Encyclopedia of Women in American History*, 3 vols (Armonk, NY: Sharpe Reference, 2002).
64   Rachel Hope Cleves. *Charity and Sylvia: a Same-Sex Marriage in Early America* (Oxford: Oxford University Press, 2014).
65   Lina Mainiero et al., eds. *American Women Writers* (1979–1994); Rufus Wilmot

Francesca Anna Canfield, née **Pascalis** [or **Salonina**] (August 1803–23 May 1833), born in Pennsylvania, moved to New York City as a child with her family. At school, she learned French, Italian, Spanish, and Portuguese, translating Verri's *Le notti romane* and a volume of Lavater. Her prose and verse appeared in various periodicals, including the *Mirror* and the *Minerva*, often signed 'Salonina.' She married Palmer Canfield, in whose *Canfield's Lottery Argus* she also published. Canfield contracted tuberculosis at nineteen and died of it ten years later. Her husband died the same year, preventing his edition of her works.[66]

Julia Abigail Fletcher Carney [or **Julia**, **Minnie May**, **Frank Fisher**, **Sadie Sensible**, **Minister's Wife**, **Rev. Peter Benson's Daughter**] (6 April 1823–1 November 1908), born in Massachusetts, married Rev. Thomas J. Carney in 1849. Told by her mother "Never let me see any more of your poetry," Carney hid her work until she began publishing in the Lancaster and Concord local papers at age fourteen. She taught from 1840–1849, publishing Sunday school instruction books and poems and sketches in reformist journals. From 1849, Carney wrote under various monikers for periodicals including the *Christian Freeman*, the *Rose of Sharon*, the *Lily of the Valley*, the *Phrenological Journal*, *Midland Monthly*, the *New Covenant*, the *New York National Agriculturist*, the *Universalist Miscellany*, the *Ladies' Repository*, and the *Boston Olive Branch*. She published two volumes of poetry, *Gifts from Julia* and *Poetry of the Seasons*.[67]

Anna Ella Carroll [or **Hancock**] (29 August 1815–19 February 1894), born in Maryland to the 1830–1831 governor, was raised by her father as his aide. In the 1850s, he joined the anti-immigrant but also pro-labor and anti-slavery Know Nothing party. In 1856, Carroll campaigned for Millard Fillmore, who carried Maryland; she published two books, *The Star of the West* and the anti-Catholic *The Great American Battle*, along with several pamphlets. With Lincoln's election in 1860, Carroll freed her slaves, working to keep Maryland in the Union and after Fort Sumter, publishing a series of pamphlets laying out the constitutional grounds for Lincoln's war powers. She also submitted a successful memorandum

---

Griswold. *The Female Poets of America* (1849).

66 Rufus Wilmot Griswold, *The Female Poets of America* (1849); James Grant Wilson and John Fiske, *Appletons' Cyclopædia of American Biography*, 6 vols (New York: D. Appleton & Co., 1887–1889).

67 E.R. Hanson, *Our Woman Workers* (1884).

arguing for attack via the Tennessee and Cumberland rivers, not the Mississippi, and advised Lincoln that permanent emancipation would require a constitutional amendment. Her war work went unpaid.[68]

Alice Cary (26 April 1820–12 February 1871), born in Ohio, was raised Universalist, the older sister of Phoebe Cary. The two began publishing poetry in the press in 1837, over their stepmother's objections. Alice's "The Child of Sorrow" appeared in 1838 and was praised by Edgar Allan Poe, Horace Greeley, and Rufus Griswold, who included the sisters in *The Female Poets of America* and wrote the preface for their 1849 *Poems of Alice and Phoebe Cary*. The sisters moved to New York City in 1850, where their salon drew John Greenleaf Whittier, P.T. Barnum, Elizabeth Cady Stanton, Horace Greeley, and others. Alice Cary wrote verse and prose for the *Atlantic Monthly*, *Harper's*, *Putnam's Magazine*, the *New York Ledger*, the *Independent*, and other periodicals. Besides her collected articles, she wrote novels and poems including *The Clovernook Children* and *Snow Berries, a Book for Young Folks*.[69]

Phoebe Cary (4 September 1824–31 July 1871), born in Ohio, was the younger sister of Alice Cary. The two were largely self-educated. Phoebe Cary for a short time edited *Revolution*, a periodical published by Susan B. Anthony. The sisters appeared in Rufus Griswold's *The Female Poets of America*, who prefaced their 1849 *Poems of Alice and Phoebe Cary*. They moved to New York City in 1850, where Phoebe Cary published two volumes of verse: *Poems and Parodies* in 1854 and *Poems of Faith, Hope and Love* in 1867. Several of her poems were set as hymns, including "Nearer Home;" her *Hymns for all Christians* appeared in 1869. In their joint housekeeping, Phoebe took the lead, Alice being an invalid. Alice died of tuberculosis; Phoebe of hepatitis five months later. They are buried together.[70]

Virginia Randolph Cary (30 January 1786–2 May 1852), born most likely at her parents' Tuckahoe plantation in Virginia, had twelve

---

68 Janet L. Coryell, *Neither Heroine nor Fool: Anna Ella Carroll of Maryland* (Kent, OH: Kent State University Press, 1990).

69 Eugene Ehrlich and Gorton Carruth, *The Oxford Illustrated Literary Guide to the United States* (Oxford: Oxford University Press, 1982); James Grant Wilson et al. *Appletons' Cyclopædia* (1887–1889).

70 Greeley, Horace, *Eminent Women of the Age; Being Narratives of the Lives and Deeds of the Most Prominent Women of the Present Generation* (Hartford, CT: S.M. Betts & Company, 1868); Eugene Ehrlich et al., *The Oxford [...] Guide to the United States* (1982).

siblings including Thomas Mann Randolph, Jr., later Governor of Virginia. After her mother's death in 1789, Cary moved to Monticello, Virginia, with Thomas, who was the son-in-law of Thomas Jefferson. Her sister Ann married Gouverneur Morris. In 1805, Cary married her cousin Wilson Jefferson Cary. After his death in 1823, she published four books: *Letters on Female Character, Addressed to a Young Lady, on the Death of Her Mother* and *Mutius: An Historical Sketch of the Fourth Century*, both in 1828; *Christian Parent's Assistant*, 1829; and *Ruth Churchill; or, The True Protestant: A Tale for the Times*, 1851.[71]

Luella Juliette Bartlett Case, née **Bartlett** (30 December 1807–1857), born in New Hampshire, was the granddaughter on the Governor of New Hampshire, whose life she was writing when she died. In 1828, she married Eliphalet Case and moved to Lowell, Massachusetts, where Eliphalet edited various newspapers. About 1845, the couple moved west. Eliphalet became editor of the *Cincinnati Enquirer*, to which Case contributed prose and poetry. She also contributed to *The Rose of Sharon, The Ladies' Repository, The Star of Bethlehem*, and *The Universalist Review*, and wrote hymns. In 1848, Case left her husband and returned to New Hampshire. She died either in September 1857 or on 10 October 1857. Her poems include "Joan of Arc in Prison."[72]

Eliza Jane Cate (1812–1884), born in New Hampshire, worked in the cotton mills in New Hampshire and Massachusetts. In Lowell, Cate wrote for the *Lowell Offering*, in which she published fiction under several pen names including 'D,' 'Jennie,' 'Jane,' 'E. J. D,' and 'Frankin, NH.' Cate continued publishing with the journal's successor, the *New England Offering*, including "Rights and Duties of Mill Girls." Her fictional series, *Lights and Shadows of Factory Life in New England* first appeared in *The New World* in 1843, describing the lives of female mill workers and allegedly selling 20,000 copies. Cate also published in the *Olive Branch, Godey's Lady's Book*, and *Peterson's Magazine*. She wrote eight books, including *A Year with the Franklins: Or, To Suffer and Be Strong*, 1846, *Rural Scenes in New England*, 1848, and *Jenny Ambrose; or, Life in the Eastern States*, 1866.[73]

---

71 Janice E. McKenney, *Women of the Constitution: Wives of the Signers* (Lanham, MD: Scarecrow Press, 2012).

72 E.R. Hanson, *Our Woman Workers* (1884); William Turner Coggeshall. *The Poets and Poetry of the West* (1860); Bela Chapin. *The Poets of New Hampshire, Being Specimen Poems of Three Hundred Poets of the Granite State, with Biographical Notes* (Claremont, NH: Charles H. Adams, 1883).

73 Judith A. Ranta, *Women and Children of the Mills: An Annotated Guide to Nineteenth-*

Frances Manwaring Caulkins (26 April 1795–1869), born in Connecticut, lost her father before her birth. Caulkins was largely self-taught, marrying Philemon Haven in 1807 and limited in schooling thereafter, though she read French and Latin and later studied German and Italian. Philemon died in 1819. Caulkins was first published in the *Connecticut Gazette* in 1816. She ran a small school for young ladies from 1820–1829, then a ladies' academy in New London in 1829–1832, then again teaching in Norwich from 1832–1834. In New York, 1836–1842, Caulkins published two tracts with the American Tract Society in print runs approaching a million copies, followed in verse and prose by *Children of the Bible* and *Child's Hymn-Book*, then the *Tract Primer* in 1847, *Bible Studies* in 1854–1859, and *Eve and her Daughters* in 1861. In 1852, Caulkins published *The History of New-London*. Her extensive manuscripts subsist.[74]

Betsey Guppy Chamberlain (29 December 1797–1886), born in New Hampshire, lost her mother aged four, through whom she may have had Abenaki heritage. Her father was involved in twenty-nine Superior Court cases, 1799–1828. Betsey married Josiah Chamberlain in 1820, who died in 1823. In 1828, Chamberlain sued her father to recover her dowry; despite success, she was forced to sell her small farm and travel to work in the mills. In 1834, she married Thomas Wright in Lowell. From 1840–1843, Chamberlain published thirty-three prose pieces in the *Lowell Offering* and from 1848–1850, five more in the *New England Offering*, under various pseudonyms—'Betsey,' 'B.C.,' 'Jemima,' 'Tabitha.' Her 1842 pieces *The Indian Pledge* and *A Fire-Side Scene* are satirical early protests against the treatment of Native Americans. In 1843, Chamberlain married Charles Boutwell in Illinois, having four husbands in total.[75]

Elizabeth Margaret Chandler (24 December 1807–2 November 1834), born to a Quaker family in Delaware, lost both her parents by the age of nine; she moved then to Philadelphia to live with a grandmother. Chandler drew national attention at eighteen with her 1825 poem "The

---

Century American Textile Factory Literature (Westport, CT: Greenwood Publishing Group, 1999).

74 Jennifer Scanlon and Shaaron Cosner, *American Women Historians, 1700s-1990s: A Biographical Dictionary* (Westport, CT: Greenwood Publishing Group, 1996).

75 Judith A. Ranta, *The Life and Writings of Betsey Chamberlain: Native American Mill Worker* (Boston, MA: Northeastern University Press, 2003).

Slave-Ship." Benjamin Lundy invited her to contribute to his journal, *The Genius of Universal Emancipation*, where she called for immediate emancipation and for the better treatment of Native Americans. Many of her articles reappeared elsewhere, and her design "Am I not a Woman and a Sister?" became the masthead for *The Liberator*'s ladies' section. The Chandlers moved to a farm in the Michigan Territory in 1830. Still writing and editing, Chandler also founded the Logan Female Anti-Slavery Society, which created a main link on the Underground Railroad. She died aged twenty-six; posthumous volumes of essays and poems followed.[76]

Essie Blythe Cheesborough [or **Motte Hall**, **Elma South**, **Ide Delmar**, and **E. B. C.**] (1826–29 December 1905), born in South Carolina, was educated by private tutors in Philadelphia and Charleston. She contributed to the *Southern Literary Gazette, Russell's Magazine*, and various other Southern literary journals, including *Land We Love*. After the Civil War, she contributed to the *Watchman* in New York City and to *Family Journal, Wood's Household Magazine*, and *Demorest's*. Cheesborough never published a book, although she left voluminous manuscripts on a variety of subjects.[77]

Harriet Vaughan Cheney (9 September 1796–14 May 1889) was born in Massachusetts into a Unitarian family where her mother, Hannah Webster Foster, and her sister, Eliza Lanesford Cushing, also wrote. Both are listed here. In 1820, she and her sister published *The Sunday-School, or Village Sketches*. The anonymous romance *A Peep at the Pilgrims in Sixteen Thirty-Six: A Tale of Olden Times* and *The Rivals of Acadia: an Old Story of the New World* followed in 1824 and 1827. Cheney married Edward Cheney in 1830 and moved to Montreal, as did her sister. The two contributed fiction and essays to the *Literary Garland*, Canada's leading literary magazine, though Cheney still published longer works in Boston: for instance, *Sketches from the Life of Christ* in 1844. The two founded and edited *The Snow-Drop*, a girls' magazine, between 1846–1852, after the deaths of their husbands.[78]

---

76 Marcia J. Heringa Mason, ed. *Remember the Distance That Divides Us: The Family Letters of Philadelphia Quaker Abolitionist and Michigan Pioneer Elizabeth Margaret Chandler, 1830–1842* (East Lansing, MI: Michigan State University Press, 2004).
77 Daniel E. Sutherland, *The Confederate Carpetbaggers* (Baton Rouge, LA: LSU Press, 1988).
78 Lorraine McMullen et al., *Pioneering Women* (1993).

Caroline Chesebro' (30 March 1825–16 February 1873), born in New York, was educated at a seminary there before taking a position at the Packer Collegiate Institute in Brooklyn. In 1848, Chesebro' was engaged as a contributor to *Graham's American Monthly Magazine*. Between 1848 and 1851, her stories also appeared in *Holden's Dollar Magazine, The Knickerbocker, Sartain's, Peterson's Magazine*, and *Godey's Lady's Book*, collected in *Dream-Land by Daylight, A Panorama of Romance*, 1851. In 1852 came the novel *Isa, a Pilgrimage*, which occasioned a controversy with her dedicatee Alice Cary. *Victoria, or the World Overcome* followed in 1856, and more prose and verse in *Harper's Magazine, The Atlantic Monthly*, and *Appletons' Journal*, along with other works. After 1865, Chesebro' returned to teaching at Packer Collegiate Institute. She was the founder of *The Packard Quarterly*.[79]

Lydia Maria Child (11 February 1802–20 October 1880), born in Massachusetts, published the novel *Hobomok* anonymously in 1824, set in 1620s New England. In 1826, she founded *The Juvenile Miscellany*, closing in 1834 as her abolitionism affected sales. In 1828, she married David Lee Child and moved to Boston, publishing novels, poetry, and manuals: *The Mothers Book, The Frugal Housewife*. It saw thirty-three printings in twenty-five years. In 1833, Child published *An Appeal in Favor of That Class of Americans Called Africans*, the first American anti-slavery work in book form, followed by shorter tracts. She campaigned for equal female membership in the American Anti-Slavery Society, whose journal she edited after 1840. She also sheltered runaway slaves and wrote anti-slavery fiction, as well as poetry, notably "Over the River and through the Wood." During the 1860s, Child also wrote pamphlets on Native American rights.[80]

Emily Chubbuck, later **Emily Judson** [or **Fanny Forester**] (23 August 1817–1 June 1854), born in New York, became a teacher in 1834. In 1840, she entered the Utica female seminary; she published her first novel, *Charles Lynne*, in 1841. After 1844, Chubbuck corresponded with Nathaniel Parker Willis, who published her in his *New York Mirror* and helped her publish in *The Columbian* and *Graham's Magazine*. Chubbuck met Adoniram Judson in

---

79   Nina Baym, *Woman's Fiction: A Guide to Novels by and about Women in America, 1820–70* (Champaign, IL: University of Illinois Press, 1993).
80   Lydia Moland, *Lydia Maria Child: A Radical American Life* (Chicago, IL: University of Chicago Press, 2022).

1845 and they were married in 1846, sailing to Burma where Adoniram was a missionary. He died at sea in 1850 and Chubbuck returned consumptive to the United States. Chubbuck published *The Great Secret*, 1842; *Allan Lucas*, 1843; *Alderbrook*, 1846; *Trippings in Author Land*, 1846; *An Olio of Domestic Verses*, 1852; *Kathayan Slave*, 1853; and *My Two Sisters* (1854), to some acclaim, along with a memoir of her husband's second wife in 1850.[81]

Eunice Hale Cobb, née **Waite** (27 January 1803–2 May 1880), born in Maine, lost her father aged five and was raised by her Calvinist grandparents. Her mother remarried when she was ten. In 1821, she published "The First Article" in the Boston *Universalist Magazine*, filling one quarter of the issue. That year, she began a diary, which she kept until she died. She married Rev. Sylvanus Cobb in 1822 and assisted in his ministry, also writing hymns and poems, settling eventually in Boston. Cobb contributed often to Universalist periodicals, both prose and verse; she also contributed to public welfare, via Sunday schools and temperance work for instance, and she attended the first Women's Rights Convention in Worcester, Massachusetts. Cobb cofounded the Ladies' Physiological Institute of Boston and was its first elected president. Her papers are at Radcliffe College.[82]

Margaret Coxe (1805–14 September 1855), born in New Jersey, educated herself at home in a good library. Coxe wrote several books, including *The Young Lady's Companion*, *Wonders of the Deep*, and *Botany of the Scriptures*. Her book *Claims of the Country on American Females* was published in 1842, followed by *Floral Emblems; or, Moral Sketches from Flowers* in 1845. In 1843, Coxe founded the Cincinnati Female Seminary. In 1850, John Zachos became co-owner and principal of the seminary; in 1851, the two became co-owners and principals of the Cooper Female Institute in Dayton, Ohio.[83]

Hannah Mather Crocker (27 June 1752–11 July 1829), born in Massachusetts to the Mather family, was the niece of Thomas Hutchinson, last Governor of the Massachusetts Bay colony. In 1779, she married Joseph Crocker. The couple had

---

81 George H. Tooze, ed. *The Life and Letters of Emily Chubbuck Judson (Fanny Forester)*, 7 volumes (Macon, GA: Mercer University Press, 2010-).

82 George Bancroft Griffith, *The Poets of Maine: A Collection of Specimen Poems from Over Four Hundred Verse-Makers of the Pine-Tree State* (Portland, ME: Elwell, Pickard & Co, 1888); E.R. Hanson, *Our Woman Workers* (1884).

83 Henry Gardiner Adams, ed. *A Cyclopædia of Female Biography: Consisting of Sketches of All Women Who Have Been Distinguished by Great Talents, Strength of Character, Piety, Benevolence, or Moral Virtue of Any Kind* (London: Groombridge & Sons, 1857).

ten children. Crocker founded St Anne's Lodge, a fraternal lodge for women, for which she may have written the unpublished *North Square Creed* in 1787. She founded the School of Industry in 1812 to educate the female children of the Boston poor. In 1818, she published *Observations on the Real Rights of Women, with Their Appropriate Duties, Agreeable to Scripture, Reason and Common Sense*, the first book on the rights of women by an American; her *Reminiscences and Traditions of Boston*, describing the Revolutionary War, appeared in 2011. Her other works include *A Series of Letters on Free Masonry* and *The School of Reform*.[84]

Susan (Akin) Crowen [or **Mrs T.J. Crowen**] (1 September 1821–7 October 1870), born in New York, moved with her family to New York City as an infant. In 1839, she married Thomas J. Crowen. The couple had nine children. Crowen's works include *The Management of the Sick Room, with Rules for Diet Cookery*, 1844; *The American Lady's System for Cookery*, 1847; and *Every Lady's Book: an Instructor in the Art of Making Every Variety of Plain and Fancy Cakes, Pastry, Confectionary, Blanc Mange, Jellies, Ice Creams, also for the Cooking of Meats, Vegetables, &c. &c.*, 1848. Her cookbooks were reprinted throughout the 1850s and 1860s, and there are modern reprints.[85]

Eunice Powers Cutter (16 October 1819–10 May 1893), born in Massachusetts, lost her mother early. In 1843, she became precept of the Quaboag Seminary in Warren, marrying Calvin Cutter, a physician. Calvin published a university textbook, *Anatomy and Physiology*, in 1846, much reprinted before revision in 1848 and 1852 with Cutter's help. Cutter published her own *Human and Comparative Physiology*, aimed at schoolchildren, in the early 1850s. Between 1848 and 1857, Cutter traveled with her husband and lectured to women's groups throughout New England about health. The couple moved to Kansas in 1857 as friends of John Brown and campaigners for Kansas entering the Union as a free state. Cutter's 1856 article "The Missouri River Pirates" was reprinted in *The National Anti-Slavery Standard*. In 1861, the Cutters returned to Massachusetts to work for the war effort and then to update their popular works.[86]

---

[84] Taryn Benbow-Pfalzgraf, ed. *American Women Writers* (2000); *American National Biography*; John R. Shook, ed. *The Dictionary of Early American Philosophers*, 2 vols (New York: Continuum, 2012).

[85] Mrs. Thomas J. Crowen, *Every Lady's Book: an Instructor in the Art of Making Every Variety of Plain and Fancy Cakes, Pastry, Confectionary, Blanc Mange, Jellies, Ice Creams, also for the Cooking of Meats, Vegetables, &c. &c.*, (New York: T.J. Crowen, 1848).

[86] Elizabeth Wagner Reed. *American Women in Science Before the Civil War* (Minneapolis, MN: University of Minnesota, 1992).

Lucretia Maria Davidson (27 September 1808–27 August 1825), born in New York, died of tuberculosis aged sixteen but left 278 poems of various lengths. Her work was praised by Edgar Allan Poe, Robert Southey, and Marceline Desbordes-Valmore, who wrote an ode to her. Southey wrote a study comparing her to Thomas Chatterton which helped her reputation, while Poe found her actual work less impressive than Southey's mythmaking. Catherine Sedgwick wrote a biographical sketch which appeared in Davidson's *Poetical Remains*. Davidson's sister Margaret also wrote and also died young of consumption: the two were published together in 1850.[87]

Margaret Miller Davidson (26 March 1823–25 November 1838), born in New York, was Lucretia Davidson's younger sister. Her work was edited by Washington Irving after her death from tuberculosis at age fifteen. Irving wrote *Biography and Poetical Remains of the Late Margaret Miller Davidson* in 1841; by 1864, the book had seen twenty editions. Poe preferred her work to her sister's, admiring the long poem *Lenore* in particular.[88]

Mary Elizabeth Moragne Davis, née **Moragne** [or **A Lady of South Carolina**; **M. E. Moragne**] (1815–1903), born in South Carolina to a Huguenot planter family, began keeping a diary in 1834. In 1838, she published the prizewinning "The British Partizan" in the *Augusta Mirror*. The "Rencontre" followed in 1841, and "Joseph, a Scripture Sketch, in Three Parts," a long piece of blank verse. That year, she withdrew a piece from the *Mirror*: "The Walsingham Family, or, A Mother's Ambition." In 1842, she married Rev. William Hervey Davis. In 1888, Davis published *Lays from the Sunny Lands*. In 1951, *The Neglected Thread a Journal from the Calhoun Community, 1836–1842* appeared posthumously.[89]

Anna Peyre Dinnies, née **Shackleford** [or **Moina**] (7 February 1805– 8 August 1886), born in South Carolina, was educated in a Charleston seminary. In 1830, she married John C. Dinnies and moved to St Louis, where John published the monthly *St. Louis Medical and Surgical Journal*. In 1845 or 1849, the couple moved to New Orleans. In 1847, Dinnies

---

87 Henry Gardiner Adams, ed. *A Cyclopædia of Female Biography* (1857); James Grant Wilson et al. *Appletons' Cyclopædia* (1887–1889).
88 Edward T. James et al., eds. *Notable American Women, 1607–1950* (1971).
89 Barbara A. White, *American Women's Fiction, 1790–1870: A Reference Guide* (London: Routledge, 2013).

published *The Floral Year, Embellished with Bouquets of Flowers, Drawn and Colored from Nature. Each Flower illustrated with a Poem*. Dinnies also published several poems in the press, both before and after marriage, among them "Chrysanthemum," "The Wife," "Wedded Love," and "Love's Messenger." "The Conquered Banner" however was by another author using the pen name 'Moina.'[90]

Mary Ann H. Dodd, later **Shutts** (5 March 1813–18 January 1878), born in Connecticut, was educated in Hartford at Mrs. Kinnear's Seminary. Her first published articles appeared in 1834 in the *Hermenethean*, a Hartford college magazine. After 1835, she began contributing to *The Ladies' Repository* in Boston and to the annual *Rose of Sharon*. A Universalist, Dodd often published in denominational journals. Her *Poems* appeared in 1843 or 1844, and *Frederick Lee, or, The Christmas Present* in 1847. In 1855, she married Henry Shutts.[91]

Sarah Mapps Douglass (9 September 1806–8 September 1882), born in Pennsylvania, attended college in the early 1820s and taught briefly in New York City. In 1825, she began teaching in Philadelphia; in 1833, after teaching briefly at the Free African School for Girls, she founded her own school for African American girls. In 1838, the Philadelphia Female Anti-Slavery Society took over the school, retaining her as headmistress. In 1831, Douglass collected money for *The Liberator*, to which she also contributed; that year, she also helped found the Female Literary Association for African American women. As 'Zillah' and possibly 'Sophonisba,' Douglass also published in *The Colored American* and the *Anglo-African Magazine*. In 1833, Douglass co-founded the Philadelphia Female Anti-Slavery Society, marrying William Douglass in 1855. Douglass was buried in an unmarked grave.[92]

Julia Louisa Dumont, née **Corey** (October 1794–2 January 1857), born in Ohio, lost her father as an infant. Her mother remarried and moved to New York. In 1811–1812, Dumont taught in schools in New York state. In 1812, she married John Dumont, later a candidate for

---

[90] Henry Gardiner Adams, ed. *A Cyclopædia of Female Biography* (1857); George Derby et al., eds. *The National Cyclopædia of American Biography* (1891–1984).

[91] James Grant Wilson et al., *Appletons' Cyclopædia* (1887–1889); Rufus Wilmot Griswold. *The Female Poets of America* (1849).

[92] Margaret Hope Bacon, *Sarah Mapps Douglass, Faithful Attender of Quaker Meeting: View from the Back Bench* (Philadelphia, PA: Quaker Press of Friends General Conference, 2003).

Governor of Indiana. The couple moved to Indiana in 1814, where Dumont opened a school and contributed poetry to the Cincinnati *Literary Gazette*, including "Poverty," "The Pauper to the Rich Man," and "The Orphan Emigrant." In 1834–1836, she wrote stories for the *Cincinnati Mirror*, winning two prizes. These and stories first appearing in the *Western Literary Journal* and *The Ladies' Repository* appear in her 1856 volume *Life Sketches from Common Paths: A Series of American Tales*, published in New York City. Dumont lost five children early. She died of consumption in 1857.[93]

Elizabeth Jessup Eames, née **Elizabeth Jessup** [or **Stella** and **Mrs. E. J. Eames**] (26 June 1813-November 1856), born in New York, began publishing in 1831 as "Stella." In 1834, the family moved to Illinois. Eames contributed regularly to the *New Yorker*, whose editor Horace Greeley was attached to her, and to the *New-York Tribune*, where Margaret Fuller was a friend. She also published in *Graham's Magazine* and the *Southern Literary Messenger*; Edgar Allan Poe admired her work. In 1837, she married the Illinois farmer Walter S. Eames and the couple moved to New York. Walter drowned in 1851, and Eames died of consumption in 1856. A volume of her poems appeared before her death; she also appears in Rufus Griswold's *Female Poets of America*. Her *The Lost Shell Ballad* appeared in 1858.[94]

Amanda Maria Corey Edmond [or **A.M.E.**] (24 October 1824–30 May 1862), born in Massachusetts, married James Edmond in 1844. Edmond wrote much of her work from age fourteen to twenty; in 1844, she published *The Broken Vow and Other Poems*, reviewed by Edgar Allan Poe for the *Broadway Journal*. That year also saw *Willie Grant; or, The Little Pharisee; The Vase of Flowers: A Gift for the Young* followed in 1846, *Ralph Mobrey: or, The Child of Many Prayers* in 1847 and *Early Days: Pieces in Prose and Verse for the Young* in 1848. Edmond went on to publish *Forget Me Not: A Gift for Sabbath School Children* in 1854, *Religious and Other Poems* in 1872, and a *Memoir of Mrs. Sarah D. Comstock* also in 1854.[95]

---

93 William Turner Coggeshall, *The Poets and Poetry of the West* (1860); Meredith Nicholson, *The Hoosiers* (New York: Macmillan, 1916).

94 Caroline May, *The American Female Poets: With Biographical and Critical Notices* (Philadelphia, PA: Lindsay & Blakiston, 1848); Rufus Wilmot Griswold, *The Female Poets of America* (1849).

95 www.eapoe.org; www.brooklinehistoricalsociety.org; www.librarycompany.org

Elleanor Eldridge (26 March 1784/1785?-c. 1845), born in Rhode Island with Narragansett and African American ancestry, purchased a lot of land in Providence and there built a house, then a second property adjacent to it, worth about $4,000, on a $240 loan. Her creditor then died, whereupon his brother attached the property, sold it by the sheriff, and himself purchased it for the exact amount of the mortgage. Eldridge however was not a woman to submit quietly to such behavior. Assisted by the state Attorney General and some of the leading citizens of Providence, Eldridge campaigned to recover her property and lived there to old age. To finance her case, she wrote *Memoirs of Elleanor Eldridge* in 1838, which sold several editions. A companion volume, *Elleanor's Second Book*, was published in 1847.[96]

Elizabeth Fries Ellet, née **Lummis** (18 October 1818–3 June 1877), born in New York, studied modern languages at Aurora Female Seminary in Aurora, her first publication, aged sixteen, being a translation of Silvio Pellico. In 1835, she published *Poems, Translated and Original*, containing her tragedy *Teresa Contarini*, performed in New York City; she also married William Henry Ellet and the couple moved to South Carolina. In 1839, Ellet published *The Characters of Schiller. Scenes in the Life of Joanna of Sicily* and *Rambles about the Country* followed. Ellet published in the *American Monthly*, the *North American Review*, the *Southern Literary Messenger*, and elsewhere. In 1845, she returned to New York City and published *The Women of the American Revolution*. Ellet was involved in a scandal with Edgar Allan Poe and Frances Sargent Osgood, Ellet later implying that Poe was insane. Other books followed.[97]

Jane Evans Elliot, née **Jane Smith Evans** (7 April 1820–5 December 1886), born in North Carolina, married Alexander Elliot in 1847 and moved to Ellerslie Plantation. Elliot kept a diary from 1837–1882, describing her life from Antebellum to Reconstruction, including her views on slavery. The plantation was raided during Sherman's march to Fayetteville, and Elliot lost a nephew at the Battle of Cold Harbor. Her diaries were published in 1908.[98]

---

96 Joyce Appleby et al.. *Encyclopedia of Women in American History* (2002).
97 Drake, Francis Samuel, *Dictionary of American Biography, Including Men of the Time* [...] (Boston, MA: James R. Osgood & Co., 1872).
98 Jennie E. McNeill, ed. *Diary of Mrs. Jane Evans Elliot, 1837–1882* (Raleigh, NC: Edwards & Broughton Printing Company, 1908).

Emma Catherine Embury, née **Manley** [or **Ianthe**] (25 February 1806–10 February 1863), born in New York City, was contributing verse and prose to the *New York Mirror* by the age of twenty. In 1828, she married Daniel Embury, a banker, and published her first volume of poetry: *Guido, a Tale: Sketches from History and Other Poems*, followed by her prose *Pictures of Early Life* in 1830. She was briefly lady co-editor for *Graham's Magazine* in Philadelphia and was a salon regular alongside Anne Lynch Botta and Frances Sargent Osgood. Embury also published *Constance Latimer: or, The Blind Girl*, 1838; *American Wild Flowers*, 1845; and *Glimpses of Home Life* and *The Waldorf Family*, both in 1848. In later life, Embury was an invalid and withdrew from society. *Poems of Emma C. Embury* and *Prose Writings of Emma C. Embury* appeared posthumously in 1869 and 1893.[99]

Eliza Farnham (17 November 1815–15 December 1864), born in New York, moved to Illinois in 1835 and there married Thomas J. Farnham in 1836. The couple returned to New York in 1841. In 1843, Farnham wrote a series for *Brother Jonathan* refuting the call for women's suffrage. In 1844, thanks to Horace Greeley and others, she was appointed matron of the women's ward at Sing Sing Prison, though she resigned amid controversy in 1848. Moving to Boston, she there helped manage the Institution for the Blind. From 1849–1856, Farnham was in California, thereafter spending time on both coasts assisting destitute emigrants. She published *Life in the Prairie Land*, 1846; *California, In-Doors and Out*, 1856; *My Early Days*, 1859; *Woman and Her Era*, 1864; and *The Ideal Attained: Being the Story of Two Steadfast Souls*, 1865. She was an atheist.[100]

Eliza Ware Farrar, née **Rotch** (12 July 1791–22 April 1870), born in Dunkirk, France, left for England as a child due to the French Revolution. The family lost everything and sent her to her grandparents in Massachusetts. Here, she joined the Friends Meeting but was later disowned for her liberal views. In 1828, she married John Farrar, a Harvard professor. Farrar published actively in Boston from 1830–1837: *The Children's Robinson Crusoe*, 1830; *The Story of the Life of Lafayette*, 1831; *John Howard*, 1833; *Youth's Letter-Writer*, 1834; *The Adventures of Congo in*

---

99 Denise D. Knight, ed. *Writers of the American Renaissance: An A-to-Z Guide* (Westport, CT: Greenwood Press, 2003).
100 Edward C. Atwater, *Women Medical Doctors in the United States before the Civil War: A Biographical Dictionary* (Rochester, NY: University of Rochester Press, 2016).

Search of his Master, 1835; and *The Young Lady's Friend*, 1836. *Recollections of Seventy Years* followed in 1866. Farrar also wrote the manuscript *Memorials of the Life of Elizabeth Rotch, Being the Recollections of a Mother, by her Daughter, Eliza Farrar*, now in the New Bedford Whaling Museum. Her correspondence also survives.[101]

Susan Augusta Fenimore Cooper (17 April 1813–31 December 1894), born in New York, studied in Europe while traveling with her family. Daughter of the writer James Fenimore Cooper, she later served as his amanuensis. Cooper published various works: *Elinor Wyllys—A Tale*, 1845; *Rural Hours*, 1850; *The Lumley Autograph*, 1851, a satirical essay; *Mt. Vernon: A Letter to the Children of America*, 1859; *Female Suffrage: A Letter to the Christian Women of America*, 1870; and *Rhyme and Reason of Country Life*, 1885. Cooper also edited John Leonard Knapp's *Country Rambles in England; or, Journal of a Naturalist*, 1853. Cooper was a gifted artist and perhaps did the plates for *Rural Hours*, a book which influenced Darwin and Thoreau. She was active in charity work, 1868–1886, founding a Cooperstown orphanage in 1873.[102]

Eliza Lee Cabot Follen (15 August 1787–26 January 1860), born in Massachusetts to the Cabot family, lost her mother in 1809 and her father in 1819, after which she headed the household. She married Charles Follen in 1828; he died in 1840. Follen founded a Sunday school and edited two Sunday school periodicals, the *Christian Teacher's Manual*, 1828–1830, and the *Child's Friend*, 1843–1850. She published *The Well-Spent Hour*, 1827, *Selections from Fénelon*, 1829, *The Sceptic*, 1835, *Sketches of Married Life*, 1838, *Poems*, 1839, *The works of Charles Follen, with a Memoir of his Life*, 5 vols, 1846, *The Lark and the Linnet*, 1854, *To Mothers in the Free States* and *Anti-Slavery Hymns and Songs*, 1855, *Little Songs*, 1856, *Twilight Stories*, 1858, and *Home Dramas*, 1859. Follen was a zealous abolitionist. She wrote several Universalist hymns and translated from French and German, including fairy tales.[103]

---

101 James Grant Wilson et al. *Appletons' Cyclopædia* (1887–1889).
102 Rochelle L. Johnson and Daniel Patterson, eds. *Susan Fenimore Cooper: New Essays on* Rural Hours *and Other Works* (Athens: University of Georgia Press, 2001); Daniel Patterson, Roger Thompson, and J. Scott Bryson, eds. *Early American Nature Writers: A Biographical Encyclopedia* (Westport, CT: Greenwood Press, 2008).
103 Caryn Hannan, *Massachusetts Biographical Dictionary* (Boston, MA: State History Publications, 2008); James Grant Wilson et al., *Appletons' Cyclopædia* (1887–1889).

Sarah Margaret Fuller (23 May 1810–19 July 1850), born in Massachusetts, became known in her thirties as the best-read person in New England. Her first journal article was in 1834. Her father died in 1835 and Fuller took work teaching in Boston, then Providence, holding her first Conversation in 1839. That year, Ralph Waldo Emerson asked her to edit *The Dial*, which she did from 1840–1842. She published *Summer on the Lakes* in 1844 and *Woman in the Nineteenth Century* in 1845, considered the first major feminist work in the United States. In 1844, Fuller moved to New York as a critic, then editor, for Horace Greeley's *New-York Tribune*, publishing over 250 columns. In 1846, Fuller was sent to Italy as a war correspondent, meeting Giuseppe Mazzini and Giovanni Angelo Ossoli, with whom she had a son. The family drowned in 1850 with Fuller's manuscript history of the Roman Republic. Posthumous works followed.[104]

Anna Rosina Kliest Gambold (1 May 1762–1821), born in Pennsylvania, was head teacher in Bethlehem's Seminary for Young Ladies from 1788–1805. In 1805, she married John Gambold and moved to Georgia to evangelize among the Cherokee people, establishing a school. In 1819, Gambold published an article in the *American Journal of Science and Arts* on the use of flowers in Cherokee medicine. Their Moravian mission was shuttered by the United States government when removing the Cherokee from their ancestral lands. Gambold kept a mission diary, published in 2007. She died and was buried at the mission cemetery.[105]

Sarah Ann Haynsworth Gayle, née **Haynsworth** or **Haynesworth** (18 January 1804–30 July 1835), born in South Carolina, moved to Claiborne, Alabama as a child with her family. In 1819, she married John Gayle, who later became Governor of Alabama. She died of lockjaw following a dental operation, leaving a journal for the years 1827–1835 which the *Encyclopedia of Alabama* calls "unique as the only surviving account of early Alabama life written by a woman."[106]

Caroline Howard Gilman [or **Mrs. Clarissa Packard**] (8 October 1794–15 September 1888), born in Massachusetts, lost her parents young

---

104 Matteson, John, *The Lives of Margaret Fuller: A Biography* (New York: W.W. Norton, 2012).
105 Susan Hill Lindley et al., *Women in American Religious History* (2008).
106 Thomas McAdory Owen, *History of Alabama and Dictionary of Alabama Biography*, 4 vols (Chicago, IL: S.J. Clarke publishing Company, 1921).

and grew up with older siblings. Her first published poem, "Jephtha's Rash Vow," was at age sixteen; another appeared in 1817 in the *North American Review*. In 1819, she married Rev. Samuel Gilman, who later wrote Harvard's alma mater. The couple moved to Charleston, South Carolina, where he served as Unitarian pastor from 1819–1858. In 1832, Gilman launched *The Rosebud*, a juvenile weekly paper, then *The Southern Rose*, containing instructions for young slaveholders and critical reviews of abolitionist literature. *Recollections of a New England Housekeeper* appeared here in 1835, then *Recollections of a Southern Matron* in 1836. Other works include *Poetry of Traveling in the United States*, 1838; *Tales and Ballads*, 1839; and *Ruth Raymond*, 1840, to some success.[107]

Abba Goddard [or **A. A. G.**, **A. A. Goddard**, and **A. G. A.**] (20 July 1819–26 November 1873), born in Connecticut, moved to Lowell, Massachusetts with her family in 1834, where her father worked at the Lowell Machine Shop. An 1845 list of authors in the *Lowell Offering* credits her; it was widely read by the Lowell Mill Girls. In 1846, The *Trojan Sketchbook* of Troy, New York, featured Goddard as editor and contributor of the essay "Legend of the Poestenkill," a love story between a Mohawk man and a Dutch settler. During the Civil War, Goddard served as a nurse for wounded soldiers in Portland, Maine and wrote about the war in the Portland newspaper, traveling 600 miles to help the wounded and raising donations on their behalf.[108]

Eliza Anderson Godefroy [or **Beatrice Ironside**] (?–2 October 1839), born in Maryland, married Henry Anderson in 1799. He had abandoned Anderson and their daughter by 1801. In 1805, she traveled to Europe, vainly attempting to convince Napoleon to recognize a marriage between her friend Elizabeth Patterson Bonaparte and his youngest brother Jérôme-Napoléon. Returning to Baltimore, Anderson joined the *Companion and Weekly Miscellany*, becoming editor in 1806. Her contributions are hidden by pseudonyms. In 1806, she launched a new magazine, *The Observer*, first anonymously, then using the pen name 'Beatrice Ironside' and addressing the novelty of a female editor

---

107 Denise D. Knight, ed. *Writers of the American Renaissance* (2003); D.C. Gilman et al., eds. *New International Encyclopedia* (1902–1904).
108 Harriet H. Robinson. *Massachusetts in the Woman Suffrage Movement. A General, Political, Legal and Legislative History from 1774, to 1881* (Boston, MA: Roberts Brothers, 1883).

directly. Histories have overlooked her role. In 1807, her translation of Sophie Cottin's *Claire d'Albe* brought renewed attacks, and she decided to close the journal. In 1808, she married Maximilian Godefroy, moving to France in 1819.[109]

Hannah Flagg Gould (3 September 1789–5 September 1865), born in Massachusetts, kept house early for her father, a Revolutionary War veteran perhaps referenced in some of her poems: "The Scar of Lexington," "The Veteran and the Child," and so forth. Her poems appeared in various periodicals and in subsequent collections: *Poems*, 1832; *Esther: A Scriptural Narrative*, 1835; *Poems*, 3 vols, 1836; *The Golden Vase, a Gift for the Young*, 1843; *Gathered Leaves and Miscellaneous Papers*, 1846; *New Poems*, 1850; *The Diosma: a Perennial*, 1851; *The Youth's Coronal*, 1851; *The Mother's Dream, and other Poems*, 1853; *Hymns and Other Poems for Children*, 1854; and *Poems for Little Ones*, 1863. Gould was much recited by schoolchildren. A standout poem is "A Name in the Sand."[110]

Rebecca Gratz (4 March 1781–27 August 1869), born in Pennsylvania, was an active member of Philadelphia's first synagogue. Her father descended from a long line of Silesian rabbis. In 1801, Gratz helped establish the Female Association for the Relief of Women and Children in Reduced Circumstances, for families of war veterans. In 1815, she helped found the Philadelphia Orphan Asylum, remaining its secretary for forty years. She founded a Hebrew Sunday school in 1838 and presided until 1864. In 1819, Gratz co-founded the Female Hebrew Benevolent Society of Philadelphia, acting as secretary for almost four decades. In 1850, in *The Occident*, she proposed a Jewish foster home, which was founded in 1855. She may be the model for Walter Scott's Rebecca in *Ivanhoe*, thanks to their mutual friend Washington Irving.[111]

Jane Lewers Gray (1796–18 November 1871), born in Northern Ireland, was educated at a Moravian Seminary before marrying the Presbyterian Rev. John Gray and sailing with him to Bermuda in 1820. After eighteen months in New Brunswick, the couple moved to New

---

109 Patricia Okker, *Our Sister Editors* (1995).
110 Rufus Wilmot Griswold, *The Female Poets of America* (1849); Joyce Appleby et al., *Encyclopedia of Women in American History* (2002); Gabriele Kass-Simon, Patricia Farnes, and Deborah Nash, *Women of Science: Righting the Record* (Bloomington, IN: Indiana University Press, 1993).
111 Isidore Singer et al., eds. *The Jewish Encyclopedia* [...], 12 vols (New York: Funk and Wagnalls, 1901–1906).

York City, then Easton, Pennsylvania, where he ministered for 45 years. Gray's hymn, "Hark to the Solemn Bell," appeared in the *Presbyterian Collection of Psalms and Hymns* of 1843; other hymns and poems appeared at home or abroad, "Sabbath Reminiscences" appearing in England. A posthumous volume of *Selections from the Poetical Writings of Jane Lewers Gray* was printed for private distribution in New York in 1872.[112]

Mary Griffith, née **Corré** (1772–1846), was born in France, her father emigrating to the United States in 1776 and doing well in business in New York City. Corré married John Griffith, who died in 1815. She began publishing short stories in the New York press. In 1820, Griffith purchased an estate in New Jersey and became interested in the natural sciences, publishing her results in scientific and literary journals. Her works included *Our Neighborhood, or Letters on Horticulture and Natural Phenomena*, 1831; *Camperdown, or News from Our Neighborhood* and *Discoveries in Light and Vision*, both 1836; *The Two Defaulters*, 1842; and *Three Hundred Years Hence*, published in 1950 but originally in *Camperdown* and the first known utopian novel by an American woman.[113]

Sarah Moore Grimké (26 November 1792–23 December 1873), born in South Carolina, is often regarded as the mother of the women's suffrage movement. From age twelve, Grimké taught Sunday school to the plantation slaves but was prevented from teaching them to read, a law she defied. Grimké became a Quaker after moving to Philadelphia in 1821, campaigning for abolition and the female vote. In 1827, Grimké went to Charleston to "save" her sister; Angelina converted and moved to Philadelphia in 1829, both reaching thousands on the abolitionist and suffragist circuit. Finding that her brother had three mixed-race sons, Grimké adopted them and sent them to Harvard and Princeton. Grimké also published *An Epistle to the Clergy of the Southern States*, 1836, and *Letters on the Equality of the Sexes and the Condition of Women*, 1838. She then ceased public speaking until 1861, when she campaigned for President Lincoln.[114]

---

112 Rufus Wilmot Griswold, *The Female Poets of America* (1849); Edwin Francis Hatfield, *The Poets of the Church. A Series of Biographical Sketches of Hymn-Writers with Notes on their Hymns* (New York: A.D.F. Randolph, 1884).
113 Robt S. Cox, "A Spontaneous Flow: The Geological Contributions of Mary Griffith, 1772–1846." *Earth Sciences History* 1993, 12 (2): 187–195.
114 Larry Ceplair, ed. *The Public Years of Sarah and Angelina Grimké: Selected Writings 1835–1839* (New York: Columbia University Press, 1989); Pamela R. Durso. *The Power of Woman: The Life and Writings of Sarah Moore Grimké* (Macon, GA: Mercer University Press, 2003).

Angelina Emily Grimké Weld (20 February 1805–26 October 1879), born in South Carolina, was the younger sister of Sarah Moore Grimké, the two living together as adults until Angelina married the abolitionist Theodore Dwight Weld in 1838. In Charleston in 1829, Angelina called on her Presbyterian church to condemn slavery and was expelled. That year, she left for the North, never seeing Charleston or her mother again. In 1835, William Lloyd Garrison published Weld's letter to him in *The Liberator*, amid Quaker controversy. In 1836, Weld's *An Appeal to the Christian Women of the South* was publicly burned in South Carolina. In 1837, the sisters joined the first Anti-Slavery Convention of American Women. Weld published *Letters to Catharine Beecher* in 1838, then *Letters on the Province of Woman*, facing an arsonist pro-slavery mob that year in Philadelphia. The sisters' *American Slavery as It Is* appeared in 1839.[115]

Harriet Ward Sanborn Grosvenor (22 January 1823–7 September 1863), born in New Hampshire, married Edwin Prescott Grosvenor in 1843 and moved to Newburyport, Massachusetts. Grosvenor published fifteen books: *My Sister Emily*, 1847; *A Sabbath in My Early Home*, 1850; *Unfading Flowers*, 1851; *The Little Word No: Or, Indecision of Character*, 1853; *Agnes Thornton: Or, School Duties* and *Helen Spencer: Or, Home Duties*, both 1854; *Right and Wrong*, 1855; *Ellen Dacre*, 1858; *Capt. Russel's Watchword* and *Life's Lessons*, 1859; *The Old Red House, The Drunkard's Daughter*, and *Blind Ethan, A Story for Boys*, all 1860; *Why the Mill Was Stopped*, 1861; *Climbing the Mountain*, 1862; and *Noonday: A Life Sketch*, 1863. After her husband's death in 1856, Grosvenor supported her family by writing. She also wrote hymns and broadsides.[116]

Mary Whitwell Hale [or **Y.L.E.**] (29 January 1810–17 November 1862), born in Massachusetts, contributed prose sketches early to the *Boston Evening Gazette*. Hale taught intermittently until 1833, when she became preceptress at the Bristol Academy in Taunton, Massachusetts before opening a private school in that town. Several of her hymns appeared in *The Christian Register* under the initials 'Y.L.E.,' the concluding letters of her name. In 1840, a volume of her *Poems* appeared in Boston. Hale left Taunton in 1842 for Keene, founding a new school where she taught for many years. At the outbreak of the Civil War, Hale became secretary of the Cheshire County Soldiers' Aid Society, still writing hymns and odes. She died in Keene.[117]

---

115 Larry Ceplair, ed. *The Public Years of Sarah and Angelina Grimké* (1989); Ellen H. Todras, *Angelina Grimké, Voice of Abolition* (North Haven, CT: Linnet Books, 1999).
116 "The Library of Congress Name Authority File." Library of Congress.
117 Emma Raymond Pitman, *Lady Hymn Writers* (London: T. Nelson and sons, 1892).

Sarah Josepha Buell Hale (24 October 1788–30 April 1879), born in New Hampshire, married David Hale in 1813. He died in 1822 and Hale wore black for the rest of her life. In 1823, Hale published a volume of poems called *The Genius of Oblivion*, followed in 1827 by her first novel, *Northwood: Life North and South*, in which Hale proposed relocating the nation's slaves to freedom in Liberia, an early engagement with slavery in fiction. Hale then moved to Boston to edit the *Ladies' Magazine*, 1828–1836. Her *Poems for Our Children*, with "Mary Had a Little Lamb," appeared in 1830. In 1837, Hale began work as editor of *Godey's Lady's Book*, where she published the great names of the day to over 150,000 subscribers, retiring in 1877. Hale also published nearly fifty volumes in her life, novels and poems. Hale published *Woman's Record*, helped to found Vassar College and worked to make Thanksgiving a national holiday.[118]

Louisa Jane Hall, née **Park** (7 February 1802–8 September 1892), born in Massachusetts, first published anonymously at twenty in the *Literary Gazette* and elsewhere. Her father had edited the Federalist *New-England Repository* after 1804, then opened the Boston Lyceum for Young Ladies in 1811, where Hall studied. In 1831, Hall followed her father to Worcester, Massachusetts; Hall was partially blind for some years, during which he read to her. Hall published the poem *Miriam, a Dramatic Sketch* in 1837, though it was begun in 1826, and *Joanna of Naples, an Historical Tale* in 1838. *Hannah, the Mother of Samuel the Prophet*, another verse play, followed in 1839. She married the Unitarian Rev. Edward B. Hall in 1840, moving with him to Providence, Rhode Island. She also published a volume of *Verse and Prose* in 1850. Edward died in 1866, and Hall returned to Boston in 1872.[119]

Sarah Ewing Hall (30 October 1761–8 April 1830), born in Pennsylvania, married John Hall in 1782. The couple had eleven children. After eight years on a Maryland farm, the family returned to Philadelphia in 1790. In 1805, they moved to New Jersey, eventually returning to Philadelphia in 1811. Hall contributed essays to the Philadelphia Federalist magazine *Port Folio*; in 1818, she published *Conversations on the Bible*. Her letters and essays appeared posthumously in 1833 as *Mrs. Sarah Hall, Author of Conversations on the Bible*.[120]

---

118 Muriel L. Dubois, *To My Countrywomen: The Life of Sarah Josepha Hale* (Bedford, NH: Apprentice Shop Books, 2006); Patricia Okker, *Our Sister Editors* (1995).
119 Rufus Wilmot Griswold, *The Female Poets of America* (1849); Caroline May, *The American Female Poets* (1848).
120 Dumas Malone, ed. *Dictionary of American Biography* (1928–1958); *American National Biography*.

Mary Elizabeth Hewitt, later **Mary Elizabeth Stebbins** [or **Ione** and **Jane**] (23 December 1807/1818?–9 October 1894), born in Massachusetts, lived in Boston with her widowed mother until she married James Lang Hewitt around 1827, moving then to New York City. Hewitt's early poems appeared in *The Knickerbocker*, the *Southern Literary Messenger*, and elsewhere, under her pseudonyms. In 1845, she published *The Songs of Our Land, and Other Poems*, then *Poems, Sacred, Passionate, and Legendary* in 1854; she also edited *The Gem of the Western World*, 1850; *The Memorial: Written by Friends of the Late Mrs. Osgood*, 1851; *Heroines of History*, 1852; and *Lives of Illustrious Women of All Ages*, 1860. In 1854, she married Russell Stebbins. The proposed birthdate of 1818 seems improbable given Hewitt's first marriage.[121]

Harriett Low Hillard (18 May 1809–1877), born in Massachusetts, followed her uncle to China from 1829–1833 as a companion for her aunt in Portuguese Macau. As the only unmarried young woman visitor in the colony, she was much invited. Canton, in China proper, being closed to women, she and her aunt dressed as boys to visit and caused an international incident when discovered. In 1836, after their return, Low married John Hillard and settled in London. In 1848, John's bank failed, and the family moved to Brooklyn. John died in 1859. Hillard's Macau diary fills nine volumes or 947 pages. An abridged version appeared in 1900; a complete edition began in 2002. The journal is in the Library of Congress.[122]

Ellen Sturgis Hooper (17 February 1812–3 November 1848), born in Massachusetts, married physician Robert William Hooper in 1837. Regularly published in Ralph Waldo Emerson's *The Dial*, Hooper's poems also appeared in Elizabeth Peabody's *Aesthetic Papers*, 1849, and the final stanzas of her *The Wood-Fire* appear in Henry David Thoreau's *Walden*, 1854. Hooper died of tuberculosis at age 36. Her friends included Nathaniel Hawthorne and Margaret Fuller.[123]

Lucy Hooper (4 February 1816–1 August 1841), born in Massachusetts, moved with her family to Brooklyn at age fourteen, where she soon became an anonymous contributor to the *Long Island*

---

121 Rufus Wilmot Griswold, *The Female Poets of America* (1849); Sarah Josepha Hale. *Woman's Record, or Sketches of All Distinguished Women from the Creation to A.D. 1854* […], 2nd edition (New York: Harper & Bros, 1855).
122 John Rogers Haddad, *The Romance of China: Excursions to China in U.S. Culture, 1776–1876* (New York: Columbia University Press, 2008).
123 Denise D. Knight, ed. *Writers of the American Renaissance* (2003).

Star. Her prose articles were collected and published as *Scenes from Real Life* in 1840. Hooper died of tuberculosis aged twenty-five in 1841. Her *Poetical Remains* appeared in 1842, followed by the *Complete Poetical Works* in 1848. The bulk of Hooper's prose writings remains uncollected. She is remembered for her flower book, *The Lady's Book of Flowers and Poetry to which are added a Botanical Introduction, a Complete Floral Dictionary, and a Chapter on Plants in Rooms*, 1842.[124]

Esther Allen Howland (13 July 1801–14 April 1860), born in Massachusetts, married Southworth Allen Howland in 1823, moving with him to Worcester, Massachusetts. In 1844, Howland published *The New England Economical Housekeeper, and Family Receipt Book*, which sold 1500 copies in its first fifteen weeks and continued printing yearly, with a modified title after 1849, into the 1870s. Recipes included chowder, salt cod, Johnny-Cake and a fruited Boston pudding, alongside medical and housekeeping advice such as a method of CPR or this saying attributed to Thomas Jefferson: "Never buy what you do not want because it is cheap."[125]

Rebekah Hyneman, née **Gumpert** (8 September 1812–10 September 1875), born to a mixed Jewish-gentile household in Pennsylvania, mastered French, German, and Hebrew through self-study. She married Benjamin Hyneman in 1835, the couple having two children before Benjamin disappeared on a business trip to Texas in 1839, presumed murdered. Hyneman and her sons formally converted to Judaism in 1845. She soon regularly contributed stories, essays, poems, and translations of foreign authors to *The Occident and American Jewish Advocate* and *The Masonic Mirror and Keystone*. Her work was often on Jewish themes. Between 1846–1850, she published the verse "Female Scriptural Characters" in *The Occident*. *The Leper and Other Poems*, with over eighty poems, appeared in 1853. Her two sons died during the Civil War, one while interned at the infamous Andersonville Confederate prison camp.[126]

---

124 Charles Dexter Cleveland, *A Compendium of American Literature, Chronologically Arranged, with Biographical Sketches of the Authors* [...] (Philadelphia, PA: Biddle, 1858).

125 Esther Allen Howland, *The Practical Cook Book and Economical Housekeeper's Guide* (Boston, MA: Roberts Brothers, 1865).

126 Isidore Singer et al., eds. *The Jewish Encyclopedia* (1901–1906).

Rebecca Cox Jackson (15 February 1795–1871), born in Pennsylvania to a free Black family, married Samuel S. Jackson and worked as a seamstress before her religious awakening in 1830. She divorced when her husband failed to teach her to read and write. Jackson joined a Shaker community in New York, whose practice of celibacy she admired, but left after experiencing racial discrimination there, moving with her lifelong companion Rebecca Perot to Philadelphia. There, in 1859, Jackson established a Shaker community ministering primarily to Black women, still active in 1908. Jackson continued as Eldress until her death in 1871. Her autobiography, written in 1830–1864, was published in 1981: *Gifts of Power: The Writings of Rebecca Cox Jackson, Black Visionary, Shaker Eldress*. Shakers preach a dual Mother-Father godhead, and Jackson's feminism or 'womanism' was rooted in her egalitarian religiosity.[127]

Maria James (11 October 1793–11 September 1868), born in Wales, emigrated aged about seven with her family to Dutchess County, New York, where her father worked in the slate quarries. At the age of ten, James's parents placed her with the family of Rev. Freeborn Garrettson, where she lived until 1810. Besides household tasks, James read Hannah More, *The Pilgrim's Progress*, the common hymnbook, and the New Testament. She left to learn dressmaking but returned to household work, mainly in the nursery, composing poetry in her free time. In 1833, the wife of Bishop Alonzo Potter showed her husband James's *Ode on the Fourth of July 1833*. Bishop Potter arranged for her poems to be published with a preface by him: *Wales and other Poems*, 1839.[128]

Charlotte A. Jerauld, née **Fillebrown** [or **Charlotte**] (16 April 1820–2 August 1845), born in Massachusetts, lost her father aged nine. In early childhood, the family moved from Cambridge to Boston, where her school was visited by Daniel Webster and Henry Clay, who read some of her work and told her: "I wish you were a boy; I would make a statesman of you." At age fifteen, she went to work at a bookbindery which bound *The Ladies' Repository*. After publishing some poetry, Jerauld published her first prose there in 1841: "Emma Beaumont." Several prose contributions to the *Repository* followed.

---

127 Henry Louis Gates, Jr. *The Signifying Monkey: A Theory of African-American Literary Criticism*. New York: Oxford University Press, 1989).
128 Rufus Wilmot Griswold, *The Female Poets of America* (1849); James Grant Wilson et al. *Appletons' Cyclopædia* (1887–1889).

A zealous Universalist, Jerrauld also published in the *Rose of Sharon*, the *Universalist Quarterly*, the *Miscellany*, the *Union*, and the *Star of Bethlehem*. In 1843, she married J.W. Jerrauld. She died in childbirth and was buried with her infant. Her *Poetry and Prose*, with a memoir of the author, was published in 1860.[129]

Margaret Johnson Erwin Dudley (4 March 1821–28 August 1863), born in Mississippi, was the niece of Richard Mentor Johnson, ninth Vice President of the United States. She spoke fluent French. In 1843, Dudley married James Erwin of Tennessee, who died in 1851. She remarried in 1855 to Dr. Charles William Dudley, living at Mount Holly, a plantation she had acquired in 1854. It housed 100 enslaved people, making Dudley one of the largest slaveholders in Mississippi. Dudley freed her slaves in 1858; she described the South as "stagnant," and believed men and women to be equal. A staunch supporter of Abraham Lincoln, Dudley criticized *Uncle Tom's Cabin* as "jejune, sentimental, and piffling." In 1981, her descendant John Seymour Erwin edited a collection of her letters, 1821–1863. Their location is now unknown, and the book contains many factual errors.[130]

Elizabeth Lichtenstein Johnston (28 May 1764–1848), daughter of a Russian immigrant, married William Martin Johnston in 1779; the couple had ten children. She and her family were loyal to England during the Revolutionary War. Johnston wrote about her experiences in her book, *Recollections of a Georgia Loyalist*, in 1836. Her son James William Johnston was twice Premier of the Colony of Canada.[131]

Eliza Grew Jones (30 March 1803–28 March 1838), born in Rhode Island, married Rev. Dr. John Taylor Jones in 1830. Two weeks later, the couple was assigned to work in Burma. After two years, they were transferred to Siam. Jones's major work was a Siamese-English dictionary completed in 1833 and thought lost until its manuscript was identified in the British Museum Library in 2007. Later, Jones also created a

---

129 Virginia Blain, Patricia Clements, and Isobel Grundy, *The Feminist Companion to Literature in English—Women Writers from the Middle Ages to the Present* (London: B.T. Batsford Limited, 1990); E.R. Hanson. *Our Woman Workers* (1884).

130 Harry S. Laver, *Citizens More Than Soldiers: The Kentucky Militia and Society in the Early Republic* (Lincoln, NE: University of Nebraska Press, 2007); Elizabeth Fox-Genovese and Eugene D. Genovese, *The Mind of the Master Class: History and Faith in the Southern Slaveholders' Worldview* (Cambridge, UK: Cambridge University Press, 2005).

131 *Dictionary of Canadian Biography*.

Romanized script for writing the Siamese language and wrote portions of biblical history in Siamese. Jones died in Bangkok of cholera in 1838, aged thirty-four. She is buried in the Bangkok Protestant Cemetery.[132]

Juliette Augusta Magill Kinzie (11 September 1806–15 September 1870), born in Connecticut, married John H. Kinzie in 1830, moving with him to Detroit and then Fort Winnebago, where John was an Indian sub-agent to the Ho-Chunk nation (Winnebago people). After the Winnebago were forced to move west to the Mississippi River in 1832, the Kinzies left Wisconsin territory in 1833 to move to Chicago. There, the Kinzies helped found St. James Church, now the seat of the Episcopalian Diocese of Chicago; St. Luke's Hospital; and the Chicago Historical Society. In 1844, Kinzie anonymously published *Narrative of the Massacre at Chicago, August 15, 1812, and of Some Preceding Events*. Her *Wau-Bun: The "Early Day" in the North West*, 1856, recounted Kinzie's experiences at Fort Winnebago and her family's experiences during the Black Hawk War. A novel, *Walter Ogilby*, followed in 1869.[133]

Caroline Mathilda Stansbury Kirkland (11 January 1801–6 April 1864), born in New York City, married William Kirkland in 1828, settling in Geneva, New York until 1835, when they moved to Detroit, Michigan. In 1837, they founded the village of Pinckney on land William had purchased. Here, Kirkland published *A New Home—Who'll Follow?* under the pseudonym Mary Clavers, followed by *Forest Life*. In 1843, the family left Michigan for New York City, where Kirkland published *Western Clearings* in 1845 and William became editor of the *New York Evening Mirror* and the *Christian Inquirer*. He died in an accident in 1846. From 1847–1849, Kirkland edited the *Union Magazine*. She also opened a school for girls and a salon, welcoming Edgar Allan Poe, William Cullen Bryant, and others. Abroad in 1848 and 1850, she met Charles Dickens and the Brownings. Harriet Martineau was a close friend.[134]

Eliza (Buckminster) Lee (1792–1864), born in New Hampshire, married Thomas Lee of Boston. She wrote *Sketches of New England Life*, 1837; *Naomi, or Boston Two Hundred Years Ago*, 1848; and memoirs of her father and brother, 1849. Lee also translated from the German and wrote a life of the German novelist Jean Paul in 1842. In 1858, she published a historical novel, *Parthenia, the Last Days of Paganism*.[135]

---

132 Dana Lee Robert, *American Women in Mission: a Social History of Their Thought and Practice* (Macon, GA: Mercer University Press, 1997).
133 *American National Biography*.
134 Paul Lauter, ed. *The Heath Anthology of American Literature* (2005).
135 D.C. Gilman et al., eds. *New International Encyclopedia* (1902–1904).

Hannah Farnham Sawyer Lee (5 November 1780–27 December 1865), born in Massachusetts, married George Gardiner Lee in 1807. George died in 1816, leaving Lee with three daughters. Lee then lived with her brother until his death in 1858. Lee's first novel, *Grace Seymour*, appeared in 1830; then, *The Backslider*, 1835; *Three Experiments of Living, Elinor Fulton, The Contrast, or Modes of Education, The Harcourts*, and *Rich Enough: A Tale of the Times*, all in 1837; *Historical Sketches of the Old Painters*, 1838; *The Life and Times of Martin Luther*, 1839; *Rosanna, or Scenes in Boston*, 1839; *The Life and Times of Thomas Cranmer*, 1841; *Tales*, 1842; *The Huguenots in France and America*, 1843; *The World Before You, or the Log Cabin*, 1847; *Stories from Life*, 1849; and so forth. *Three Experiments* sold 20,000 copies in its first two months and saw over thirty U.S. editions, though Lee's writing was not acclaimed.[136]

Jarena Lee (11 February 1783–3 February 1864), born into a free Black family in New Jersey, worked from age seven as a live-in servant with a white family. In 1804, Lee was introduced to Christianity, moving to Philadelphia where she continued in domestic service. Lee struggled with suicidal thoughts until her calling in 1807, but Bishop Allen told her the Methodist Church had no women preachers. She married Joseph Lee in 1811; he too did not want her to preach. Joseph died six years later. Bishop Allen at last endorsed her as a "traveling exhorter" in 1819; Lee preached even in the South, where she risked enslavement, facing continued hostility. In 1836, Lee published an autobiography, the first Black woman to do so. In 1852, the African Methodist Episcopal Church forbade women preachers. Lee then vanished from the record, though she spoke at the American Anti-Slavery Society convention in 1853.[137]

Mary Elizabeth Lee [or **M.E.L.** and **A Friend**] (23 March 1813–23 September 1849), born in South Carolina, entered school in Charleston aged ten. In 1833, she began contributing pseudonymously to *The Rose Bud, The Southern Rose, Graham's Magazine, Godey's Lady's Book*, and the *Southern Literary Messenger*. Her first book *Social Evenings, or Historical Tales for Youth* appeared in Massachusetts in 1840, Lee writing for northern and southern periodicals alike. She also produced various translations from the French, German, and Italian. Always in poor

---

136 James Grant Wilson et al., *Appletons' Cyclopædia* (1887–1889).
137 Carla L. Peterson, *Doers of the Word: African American Women Speakers and Writers in the North (1830–1880)* (New York: Oxford University Press, 1995).

health, Lee died aged thirty-six in 1849. *The Poetical Remains of the late Mary Elizabeth Lee, with a Biographical Memoir* appeared in 1851.[138]

Eliza Leslie (15 November 1787–1 January 1858), born in Pennsylvania, moved with her family to England for six years when she was five years old. After her father's death in 1803, her mother ran a series of boarding houses. Leslie's first book was based on class notes, though she called the recipes original: *Seventy-Five Receipts for Pastry, Cakes, and Sweetmeats*, 1828, went through eleven editions by 1839. Leslie's *Directions for Cookery, in its Various Branches*, 1837, sold at least 150,000 copies and remained in print into the 1890s, making it the century's most popular cookbook. She published nine cookbooks in all, including a French cookbook and an entire book of cornmeal recipes; she also wrote fiction and nonfiction for children and adults, publishing extensively in the press. From 1836–1845, Leslie edited *The Gift*, an annual gift book featuring Edgar Allan Poe, Henry Wadsworth Longfellow, and Ralph Waldo Emerson.[139]

Octavia Walton Le Vert, née **Octavia Celestia Valentine Walton** (11 August 1810–12 March 1877), born in Georgia, spoke French, Spanish, and Italian. Her father was appointed Florida's first territorial secretary in 1821; in Pensacola, Le Vert translated French and Spanish documents for him. She met Edgar Allan Poe and Washington Irving in the 1820s-1830s, corresponding with them thereafter. In Washington, D.C., she met Daniel Webster, John C. Calhoun, and Henry Clay, with whom she became close. Le Vert moved with her parents to Mobile, Alabama in 1835, where she married Dr. Henry Strachey Le Vert in 1836. Abroad in 1853 and 1855, Le Vert met Queen Victoria, Napoleon III, and Pope Pius IX, as told in her *Souvenirs of Travel*, 1857. Henry died in 1864 and afterward, Le Vert left Mobile for Georgia. Her *Souvenirs of Distinguished People* and *Souvenirs of the War* were both left unpublished.[140]

Estelle Anna Lewis, née **Sarah Anna Robinson** [or **Stella**] (April 1824–24 November 1880), born in Maryland, by age twenty had

---

[138] Barbara A. White, *American Women's Fiction* (2013); Sidney Ernest Bradshaw. *On Southern Poetry Prior to 1860...* (Richmond, VA: B.F. Johnson publishing Company, 1900).

[139] John Seely Hart, *The Female Prose Writers of America. With Portraits, Biographical Notices, and Specimens of Their Writings* (Philadelphia, PA: E.H. Butler & Co., 1852).

[140] Frances Gibson Satterfield, *Madame Le Vert: A Biography of Octavia Walton Le Vert* (Edisto Island, SC: Edisto Press, 1987).

translated the *Aeneid* into English verse, published stories in the *Family Magazine*, and published *Records of the Heart*, 1844. In 1841, she married Sidney D. Lewis and moved to Brooklyn with him, where they hosted a salon. They divorced in 1858, and Lewis thereafter resided mostly in England. She published *The Child of the Sea and Other Poems*, 1848, *The Myths of the Minstrel*, 1852, and an essay series in *Graham's Magazine*, "Art and Artists in America;" then three tragedies, *Helemah; or, The Fall of Montezuma*, 1864, *Sappho of Lesbos*, 1868, which was played in Greek in Athens, and *The King's Stratagem; or, The Pearl of Poland*, 1873. Her *Poetical Works*, 1858, appeared in French. Alphonse de Lamartine compared her to Petrarch, Edgar Allan Poe to Sappho. She was then forgotten.[141]

Deborah Norris Logan (19 October 1761–2 February 1839), born to a Quaker family in Pennsylvania, lost her father aged five and was largely self-educated. In Philadelphia, she heard the first-ever public reading of the *Declaration of Independence* before a small crowd. It failed to impress. In 1781, she married George Logan, who entered politics. Logan meanwhile found a correspondence between William Penn and George's grandfather, editing it in eleven manuscript volumes first published entire in 1870–1872. From 1815, she kept a diary in seventeen volumes now held by the Historical Society of Pennsylvania. She also kept an extensive correspondence and published a small amount of poetry. After her husband's death, she wrote a *Memoir of Dr. George Logan of Stenton*, published in 1899.[142]

Judith Lomax (25 September 1774–19 January 1828), born in Virginia, lived on her father's plantation until his death in 1816. A financial reverse in 1815 estranged her from many of her relatives, and she thereafter supported herself in Port Royal, Virginia. Ecumenical in her beliefs, Lomax remained Anglican. She kept a notebook after 1819 of her efforts to rebuild the Episcopal Church in Virginia after the Revolutionary War; it was published in 1999 as *The Sabbath Journal of Judith Lomax*. Her *Notes of an American Lyre* appeared in 1813 with a dedication to Thomas Jefferson, whom she had met at Monticello. It is the first self-standing volume of poetry published by a woman in Virginia.[143]

---

141 James Lawrence Onderdonk, *History of American Verse (1610–1897)* (Chicago, IL: A.C. McClurg, 1901); James Grant Wilson et al., *Appletons' Cyclopædia* (1887–1889).
142 Heidi Brayman Hackel and Catherine E. Kelly, *Reading Women: Literacy, Authorship, and Culture in the Atlantic World, 1500–1800* (Philadelphia, PA: University of Pennsylvania Press, 2009).
143 David S. Shields, ed. *American Poetry: The Seventeenth and Eighteenth Centuries* (New

Marguerite St. Leon Loud, née **Barstow** (17 April 1812–4 November 1889), born in Pennsylvania, was educated at home. In 1834, she married the piano maker John Loud and soon began contributing verse and prose to periodicals such as the *United States Gazette* and the *Saturday Courier*. Loud wrote the story "The Hermit of Wysauking;" her volume of poetry, *Wayside Flowers*, appeared in 1851. Edgar Allan Poe praised her work.[144]

Maria White Lowell (8 July 1821–27 October 1853), born in Massachusetts, was raised in an Ursuline convent burned by a mob in 1834. Involved in temperance and women's rights, she attended Margaret Fuller's first Conversation in 1839. An 1843 visit to Quakers in Philadelphia strengthened her abolitionism. She married James Russell Lowell in 1844, the couple moving to Philadelphia in 1845, where James published in abolitionist journals. Plagued by ill-health, Lowell died aged thirty-two in 1853. Her poems were privately printed by her husband after her death in 1855. Emily Dickinson knew her work and Henry Wadsworth Longfellow published a poem of hers, "The Grave of Keats," in an 1874 anthology. Amy Lowell found Lowell's work better than her husband James's, saying that he had said the same.[145]

Mary Tyler Peabody Mann, née **Peabody** (16 November 1806–11 February 1887), born in Massachusetts, learned ten languages at home. Mann taught in Maine for a year in 1824, relocating to Boston to teach with her sister Elizabeth in 1825. From 1833–1835, Mann went with her sister Sophia to Cuba as a governess. Back in Salem, she taught until 1840, marrying Horace Mann in 1843 and setting out that day for Europe. The couple returned in 1853. Horace had been appointed secretary to the Massachusetts Board of Education in 1837, and Mann devoted much time to assisting him. After his death in 1859, Mann and her sister Elizabeth opened the country's first public kindergarten, publishing the *Moral Culture of Infancy and Kindergarten Guide* in 1863. Mann also wrote *The Flower People*, 1838; *Life and Works of Horace Mann*, 1865; and *Juanita, a Romance of Real Life in Cuba*, 1887, among other texts.[146]

York: Library of America, 2007); Susan Hill Lindley et al., *Women in American Religious History* (2008).

144 Rufus Wilmot Griswold, *The Female Poets of America* (1849); Caroline May. *The American Female Poets* (1848).

145 Hope Jillson Vernon, *The Poems of Maria Lowell, With Unpublished Letters and a Biography* (Providence, RI: Brown University Press, 1936).

146 Monika M. Elbert, Julie E. Hall, and Katharine Rodier, eds. *Reinventing the Peabody Sisters* (Iowa City, IA: University of Iowa Press, 2006).

Elizabeth Louisa Mather, née **Foster** (7 January 1815–5 February 1882), born in Connecticut, married Eleazer Watrous Mather in 1837. Mather wrote prose and verse for the *Ladies' Repository* from 1847–1874, and for the *Universalist Union*, the *Trumpet, Ambassador, Golden Hide, Odd Fellows' Offering*, and the *Lily of the Valley*. She wrote on religion, capital punishment, and women's suffrage. *From Hadlyme Hills, Poems and Prose by E. Louisa Mather*, 1956, is a compilation work by her descendants.[147]

Caroline May [or **Caromaia**] (c. 1820–5 March 1895), born in Croydon, England, came to New York City with her family in 1834. May began to publish poetry under her pseudonym 'Caromaia;' in 1848, she edited *American Female Poets, With Biographical and Critical Notices*. A literary feud ensued between May and Rufus Griswold, editor of *Female Poets of America*. May later edited several other anthologies and at least three volumes of her own poetry: *Poems*, 1864; *Hymns on the Collects for Every Sunday in the Year*, 1872; and *Lays of Memory and Affection*, 1888. Her father died in Philadelphia in 1857, May living and teaching thereafter at a girls' school in Pelham, New York.[148]

Sarah Carter Edgarton Mayo (17 March 1819–9 July 1848), born in Massachusetts, taught herself French and Latin and began contributing to journals aged sixteen. Mayo edited *The Rose of Sharon* from 1840–1848 and was associate editor of the Boston *Universalist and Ladies' Repository* from 1839–1842. Between 1836 and 1844, she published *The Palfreys, Ellen Clifford*, and *Memoirs of Mrs. Julia W. Scott*, and compiled *The Poetry of Women, The Flower Vase, Spring Flowers, The Floral Fortune Teller, Language and Poetry of Flowers* and *Fables of Flora*. Her earnings allowed her to support her family and put her younger brother through Harvard. He died after graduation in 1847. Mayo married Amory Dwight Mayo in 1846 and the couple moved to Gloucester, Massachusetts. They had a daughter in September 1847; Mayo's health then deteriorated, and she died some months later aged twenty-nine.[149]

Louisa Susannah Cheves McCord (3 December 1810–23 November 1879), born in South Carolina, was the daughter of Langdon Cheves, Speaker of the United States House of Representatives in 1814–1816.

---

147 E.R. Hanson, *Our Woman Workers* (1884).
148 James Grant Wilson et al., *Appletons' Cyclopædia* (1887–1889).
149 Dumas Malone, ed. *Dictionary of American Biography* (1928–1958); *American National Biography*; James Grant Wilson et al., *Appletons' Cyclopædia* (1887–1889).

As a young woman, she became owner of Lang Syne Plantation; she married David James McCord in 1840. He died in 1855. In 1848, McCord published the lyric collection *My Dreams*; the tragedy *Caius Gracchus* followed in 1851. From 1849, after her 1848 *Sophisms of the Protective Policy. A Translation from the French of Bastiat*, she contributed secessionist pro-slavery prose to *The Southern Quarterly Review*, *The Southern Literary Messenger*, and perhaps *De Bow's Review*, also opposing women's suffrage. From 1861, she worked for the Confederate Soldiers' Relief Association and local military hospital. She helped erect the Confederate monument in Columbia, South Carolina in 1879 before her death.[150]

Frances Harriet Whipple Green McDougall (1805–1878), born in Rhode Island, founded the periodical *The Original* in 1829, which folded after two issues. She published poems in the press after 1830. In 1838, she anonymously published the *Memoirs of Eleanor Eldridge, a Colored Woman*, which sold 30,000 copies. *The Mechanic* followed in 1841, then *Might and Right* in 1844. For a period in 1842, she edited *The Wampanoag*, and thereafter contributed to *The Nineteenth Century* and *The Univercoelum and Spiritual Philosopher*. In 1848, she became editor of *The Young People's Journal of Science, Literature, and Art*. Around 1842, McDougall married Charles Green, moving with him to Connecticut; they divorced in 1847 and she moved to New York City, where she taught botany. In 1861, she moved to San Francisco, writing and lecturing against slavery and for women's rights. She married William McDougall in 1862.[151]

Maria Jane McIntosh [or **Aunt Kitty**] (1803–25 February 1878), born in Georgia, lost both her parents in 1835 and joined her brother in New York City. McIntosh then lost her fortune in the Panic of 1837 and wrote to earn a living. Her story "Blind Alice" in 1841 was an immediate success; *Conquest and Self-Conquest* followed in 1844, then *Praise and Principle*, 1845; *Two Lives, to Seem and to Be*, 1846; *Aunt Kitty's Tales*, 1847; *Charms and Counter Charms*, 1848; *Woman in America: Her Work and Reward*, 1850; *The Lofty and the Lowly* and *Evenings at Donaldson Manor*, 1852; *Emily Herbert*, 1855; *Violet, or the Cross and Crown*, 1856; *Meta Gray*, 1858; and *Two Pictures*, 1863. Much of her work was reprinted in London.[152]

---

150 Leigh Fought, *Southern Womanhood and Slavery: A Biography of Louisa S. McCord, 1810–1879* (Columbia, MO: University of Missouri Press, 2003).
151 Sarah C. O'Dowd, *A Rhode Island Original: Frances Harriet Whipple Green McDougall* (Lebanon, NH: University Press of New England, 2004).
152 John Seely Hart, *The Female Prose Writers of America* (1852); Amy E. Hudock and Katharine Rodier, *American Women Prose Writers, 1820–1870* (Detroit, MI: Gale

Louisa Medina (c.1813–1838) [or **Louisa Honore de Medina, Louisa Medina Hamblin**, or **Louisine**], born in Europe, allegedly spoke Greek, Latin, French, Spanish, and English in her teens and began writing for London annuals at the age of twelve. At nineteen, Medina came to the United States, reaching Philadelphia in 1831 and moving to New York City, where she tutored in French and Spanish. Medina became governess to Bowery Theatre manager Thomas S. Hamblin's children, then his chief playwright after 1833 and among the day's leading dramatists. She published poetry, short stories, and about thirty-four melodramas of which eleven survive, many presumed lost in Bowery Theatre fires, plays both wildly successful and much admired. Medina adapted Edward Bulwer-Lytton, Robert Montgomery Bird, and others, the *Last Days of Pompeii* with its erupting volcano onstage being credited with saving the Bowery.[153]

Penina Moïse (23 April 1797–13 September 1880), born in South Carolina to a French Jewish family from Sint Eustatius, went to work aged twelve to support the family at her father's death. Moïse began publishing hymns and poetry after 1830 in the *Home Journal*, the Washington *Union*, and other publications; she also published the book of poems *Fancy's Sketch-Book*, 1833, and *Hymns Written for the Use of Hebrew Congregations*, 1856, for use in her Charleston synagogue, Beth Elohim.[154]

Abby Jane Morrell, née **Wood** (17 February 1809–?), born in New York, lost her father aged two. In 1824, she married Captain Benjamin Morrell. From 1829–1831, the couple sailed on her husband's fourth voyage, stretching from New Zealand to Liberia. It is chronicled in her *Narrative of a Voyage to the Ethiopic and South Atlantic Ocean, Indian Ocean, Chinese Sea, North and South Pacific Oceans, in the Years 1829, 1830, 1831*, ghost-written by Samuel Knapp and published in 1833. Morrell is the first woman to describe the Antarctic in print. She approves of colonization but advocates for reform. More recent scholarship has favored her husband's account, finding cliché in her writing for which

---

Research, 2001).
153 Miriam López Rodríguez and María Dolores Narbona Carrión, eds. *Women's Contribution to Nineteenth-Century American Theatre* (Valencia: Universitat de València, 2004).
154 James Grant Wilson et al., *Appletons' Cyclopædia* (1887–1889); Dumas Malone, ed. *Dictionary of American Biography* (1928–1958).

Knapp may in part be responsible. Benjamin died in 1839 and Morrell is little recorded thereafter. Her death date is uncertain.[155]

Lucretia Mott, née **Coffin** (3 January 1793–11 November 1880), born in Massachusetts, was sent aged thirteen to a Quaker school in New York, where James Mott taught her before she became a teacher there at fifteen. The family moved to Philadelphia in 1809, Mott and James marrying in 1811. In 1821, Mott was recognized by her Friends Meeting as a minister, traveling throughout the United States. In 1835, she co-founded the American Anti-Slavery Society, attending each Anti-Slavery Convention of American Women, 1837–1839. In 1840, she attended the General Anti-Slavery Convention in London but was segregated as a woman. She published her *Sermon to the Medical Students* on race in 1849; after 1850, Mott's home became a stop on the Underground Railroad. Mott also campaigned for legal equality in marriage, organizing the Seneca Falls Convention in 1848 and publishing *Discourse on Woman* in 1850.[156]

Anna Cora Mowatt Ritchie, née **Ogden**, later **Mowatt**, later, **Ritchie** [or **Isabel, Henry C. Browning**, and **Helen Berkley**] (5 March 1819–21 July 1870), born in France, came to the United States aged six. In 1834, she eloped with James Mowatt. Her first book, *Pelayo, or The Cavern of Covadonga*, appeared in 1836, then *Reviewers Reviewed* in 1837. Mowatt published in *Graham's Magazine, Godey's Lady's Book*, and elsewhere. Her play *Gulzara* appeared in *The New World*. She wrote a biography of Goethe and two novels, *The Fortune Hunter* and *Evelyn*. In 1841, her public readings were witnessed by Edgar Allan Poe. Her play *Fashion* appeared in 1845, earning rave reviews; and she began acting, touring the United States and Europe. James died in 1851; Mowatt's *Autobiography of an Actress* appeared in 1853. President Franklin Pierce attended her wedding with William Foushee Ritchie in 1854. She wrote several more books.[157]

Harriet Newell, née **Atwood** (10 October 1793–30 November 1812), born in Massachusetts, joined the First Congregationalist Church in

---

155 Abby Jane Morrell, *Narrative of a Voyage to the Ethiopic and South Atlantic Ocean, Indian Ocean, Chinese Sea, North and South Pacific Oceans in the Years 1829, 1830, 1831* (Cambridge, UK: Cambridge University Press, 2012).
156 Otelia Cromwell, *Lucretia Mott* (Cambridge, MA: Harvard University Press, 1958).
157 Eric Wollencott Barnes, *The Lady of Fashion: The Life and the Theatre of Anna Cora Mowatt* (New York: Scribner, 1954).

Roxbury in 1809. In 1812, she married Rev. Samuel Newell, a missionary to the Burman empire, sailing the same month to Calcutta where the British East India Company denied them residence. Taking ship to Mauritius, Newell gave birth to a child who died after five days. Newell died in Mauritius some weeks later, aged nineteen. Her letters and journal were published posthumously and saw several editions. She was the first American to die in foreign mission service.[158]

Rebecca S. Nichols, née **Reed** [or **Ellen** and **Kate Cleaveland**] (28 October 1819–21 June 1903), born in New Jersey, moved as a child to Kentucky with her family, where she married the printer Willard Nichols in Louisville in 1838. The couple moved to St Louis, Missouri in 1840, where Willard edited a newspaper, then to Cincinnati from 1841–1851. Nichols published her first poems in the *Louisville News-Letter* and *Louisville Journal* as 'Ellen.' In 1844, she published *Berenice, or the Curse of Minna, and other Poems*. Nichols edited the Cincinnati periodical *The Guest* after 1846, to which she contributed, as to *Graham's Magazine*, *The Knickerbocker*, and other periodicals, including to the *Cincinnati Herald* as 'Kate Cleaveland.' In 1851, Nichols published a longer volume, *Songs of the Heart and of the Hearth-Stone*, in Philadelphia. The *Cincinnati Commercial* afterward paid her for a poem a week.[159]

Asenath Hatch Nicholson (24 February 1792–15 May 1855), born in Vermont, became a teacher before marrying Norman Nicholson and moving to New York. They ran a boarding-house. Norman died in 1844 and Nicholson traveled to Ireland, walking through virtually every county, then Scotland, publishing *Ireland's Welcome to the Stranger, or, An Excursion through Ireland in 1844 & 1845, for the Purpose of Personally Investigating the Condition of the Poor* in 1847. Returning to Ireland after 1846, Nicholson wrote *Annals of the Famine in Ireland, 1847, 1848 and 1849*. She also contacted the *New-York Tribune* and *The Emancipator* and organized aid. She again walked the country distributing bibles, food, and clothing. In 1835, Nicholson authored the first American vegetarian cookbook, *Nature's Own Book*. She also published *Kitchen Philosophy for Vegetarians*, and *Loose Papers*, 1853, about her eight years in Europe.[160]

---

158 Anne Commire et al., eds. *Women in World History* (1999–2002).
159 William Turner Coggeshall, *The Poets and Poetry of The West* (1860); Thomas Buchanan Read, *The Female Poets of America: With Portraits, Biographical Notices, and Specimens of Their Writings* (Philadelphia, PA: E.H. Butler & Company, 1849).
160 Maureen O'Rourke Murphy, *Compassionate Stranger: Asenath Nicholson and the Great Irish Famine* (Syracuse, NY: Syracuse University Press, 2015).

Frances Sargent Osgood, née **Locke** (18 June 1811–12 May 1850), born in Massachusetts, was first published at fourteen in the *Juvenile Miscellany*. In 1835, she married Samuel Stillman Osgood and the couple moved to England, where Osgood published two lyric volumes, *A Wreath of Flowers from New England* and *The Casket of Fate*, returning to Boston, then New York City in 1839. Osgood published in literary magazines, sometimes as 'Kate Carol' or 'Violet Vane.' In 1841, she published *The Poetry of Flowers and the Flowers of Poetry*; then *The Snowdrop, a New Year Gift for Children*; *Rose, Sketches in Verse*; and *Puss in Boots*, 1842; *The Marquis of Carabas*, 1844; and *Cries in New York*, 1846. After 1845, Elizabeth Ellet suggested that Osgood's and Edgar Allan Poe's friendship was not platonic, retracting under threat and blaming Poe; the Osgoods moved to Philadelphia. Her work was much admired.[161]

Susan Paul (1809–1841), born in Massachusetts, began her abolitionist career in the New England Anti-Slavery Society. In 1833, a delegation led by William Lloyd Garrison visited her classroom and invited her students, aged three to ten, to form the Juvenile Choir of Boston, exposing white audiences to a Black choir. Paul also became one of the first Black members of the Boston Female Anti-Slavery Society and co-founded a temperance society in the 1830s. She published one book: *Memoir of James Jackson*, 1835, the first biography of an African American published in the United States. Jackson was a student of Paul's who died at age six. Though advertised in *The Liberator*, the Orthodox Congregational Sabbath School Society and the Baptist Sabbath School Society would not accept her work. Paul died of tuberculosis in 1841.[162]

Elizabeth Palmer Peabody (16 May 1804–3 January 1894), born in Massachusetts, taught in Boston after 1822. In 1834–1835, she taught at Amos Bronson Alcott's experimental Temple School, publishing her *Record of a School* after its 1835 closing. Peabody then opened a bookstore at her home, 1840–1852, where Margaret Fuller's Conversations were held from 1839. Her library offered several hundred titles in several European languages and published Nathaniel Hawthorne. Peabody was for a time business manager of the Transcendentalist *The Dial*, which published her translation from the French of a chapter of the *Lotus Sutra*

---

161 Emily Stipes Watts, *The Poetry of American Women* (1977).
162 Shirley J. Yee, *Black Women Abolitionists: A Study in Activism, 1828–1860* (Knoxville, TN: University of Tennessee Press, 1992).

in 1844, the first known Buddhist scripture published in English. She opened a kindergarten in 1860, writing books on the topic after a visit to Germany, editing the *Kindergarten Messenger* in 1873–1877 and helping establish the institution in America. She also fought for Native American and African American rights.[163]

Lydia Jane Wheeler Peirson [or **Pierson**] (1802–1862), born in Connecticut, moved with her parents to New York at age sixteen and married Oliver Peirson two years later. The couple moved to Liberty Township, Pennsylvania, in the Allegheny Mountains, in 1821, where Peirson wrote extensively for magazines and newspapers, more prose than poetry. She published two volumes of poems in 1846–1847: *Forest Leaves* and *The Forest Minstrel*. In 1849, Peirson edited the *Lancaster Literary Gazette*; she also contributed often to the *Ladies' Garland*, the *Southern Literary Magazine* and *The New Real*. Peirson moved to Adrian, Michigan in 1853, dying there in 1862. Her writings are uncollected.[164]

Adaliza Cutter Phelps (1823–3 June 1852), born in New Hampshire, lived and died in Jaffrey. Much of her writing is religious in theme, though she first joined the Congregational Church late in life. A volume of her collected poetry, *The Life of Christ and Other Poems*, appeared posthumously in Boston in 1852, with an introduction by her husband.[165]

Elizabeth Wooster Stuart Phelps [or **H. Trusta**] (13 August 1815–29 November 1852), born in Massachusetts, was the daughter of the theologian Moses Stuart. In 1832, Phelps studied in Boston's Mount Vernon School, first publishing in headmaster Jacob Abbott's *The Religious Magazine*. She returned to Andover in 1834 suffering from partial blindness and temporary paralysis. In 1842, she married Austin Phelps in Boston, the couple returning to Andover in 1848. In 1849, Phelps began publishing: *Little Kitty Brown and Her Bible Verses*, 1851; *Kitty Brown and Her City Cousins*, 1852; *Kitty Brown and Her Little School*, 1852; *Kitty Brown Beginning to Think*, 1853. Other works followed: *The Sunny Side; or, The Country Minister's Wife*, 1851; *A Peep at Number Five; or, A Chapter in the Life of a City Pastor*; 1852; and

---

163 Megan Marshall, *The Peabody Sisters: Three Women Who Ignited American Romanticism* (Boston, MA: Houghton Mifflin Company, 2005).

164 Sarah Josepha Hale, *Woman's Record* (1855); James Grant Wilson et al. *Appletons' Cyclopædia* (1887–1889).

165 Bela Chapin, *The Poets of New Hampshire* (1883).

so forth. *The Sunny Side* sold more than 500,000 copies and earned international recognition.[166]

Rachel Parker Plummer (22 March 1819–19 March 1839), born in Illinois, married Luther M. Plummer aged fourteen, moving with forty-nine other families to Arkansas in 1830 en route to Texas. In 1834, the group built Fort Parker on the Navasota River in the Comancheria. In 1836, a Comanche party attacked, taking five prisoners. Plummer describes rape, torture, murder, a scalp dance, and an attempt to burn her alive. She was sold back by the Comanche in 1837, dying two months after her third childbirth, the infant two days later. Her father, accused of murdering another woman and child, had fled with the Plummers in freezing rain, and Plummer was already in poor health. Her book, *Rachael Plummer's Narrative of Twenty One Months' Servitude as a Prisoner Among the Commanchee Indians*, became a sensation on publication in Texas in 1838. Her father republished it in 1844. One questions its impartiality.[167]

Margaret Prior, née **Barrett**, later **Allen**; then, **Prior** (1773–7 April 1842), born in Virginia, lost her mother as a child. In 1789, she married William Allen of Baltimore, lost at sea in 1808. Prior moved to New York City, where she married the Quaker William Prior in 1814. He died in 1829. In 1819, Prior became a Methodist; soon after, she joined the board of the New York Asylum for Orphans, also visiting the penal House of Refuge which opened in 1825 and opening a school for the poor in the Bowery. In 1834, Prior joined the New York Female Moral Reform Society as an urban missionary. The reports of her visits were published posthumously in *Walks of Usefulness, or, Reminiscences of Mrs. Margaret Prior*, in 1851. Prior also established a soup kitchen. She gave up snuff when she became a temperance activist.[168]

Sarah Louisa Forten Purvis [or **Ada, Magawisca**] (1814–1884), born to the free Black Forten family in Pennsylvania, in 1833 founded the Philadelphia Female Anti-Slavery Society with her mother and her two sisters. Some attribution questions remain for Purvis's poetry; a

---

166 Lina Mainiero et al., eds. *American Women Writers* (1979–1994); Nina Baym, *Woman's Fiction* (1993).
167 Frank X. Tolbert, *An Informal History of Texas: the Story of Texas from Cabeza de Vaca to Temple Houston* (New York: Harper and Brothers, 1961).
168 Joyce Appleby et al., *Encyclopedia of Women in American History* (2002); Susan Hill Lindley et al., *Women in American Religious History* (2008).

Quaker abolitionist, Eliza Earle Hacker, may have authored some 'Ada' poems attributed to Purvis. Purvis published her poem "An Appeal to Women" in 1837. Her dozen published poems in *The Liberator*, 1831–1835, include "The Grave of the Slave," 1831, and "A Slave Girl's Farewell," 1835. Purvis's 15 April 1837 letter to Angelina Grimké discusses the intersection of abolitionist and feminist goals. In 1838, Purvis married Joseph Purvis, with whom she had eight children. She died either in 1857 or 1884. Purvis's pen name Magawisca is taken from Catherine Sedgwick's 1827 novel *Hope Leslie*.[169]

Mary Traill Spence Lowell Putnam (3 December 1810–1 June 1898), born in Massachusetts, was the sister of James Russell Lowell. Putnam became fluent in French, Italian, German, Polish, Swedish, and Hungarian. She married Samuel R. Putnam in 1832 and the couple traveled abroad for some years. Putnam wrote for magazines until 1844, when she translated from the Swedish Fredrika Bremer's *The Handmaid*. From 1848–1850, Putnam contributed articles to the *North American Review* on Polish and Hungarian literature, and from 1850–1851, to the *Christian Examiner* on the history of Hungary. In 1850, Putnam published a *History of the Constitution of Hungary*. She became known for her controversy with Francis Bowen, editor of the *North American Review*, during the 1848 revolutions in Hungary. Putnam published memoirs of her son and father, a novel, two abolitionist dramas, and *Fifteen Days* between 1861–1885.[170]

Mary Randolph (9 August 1762–23 January 1828), born in Virginia, was the sister of Thomas Mann Randolph Jr., Governor of Virginia. She grew up at Tuckahoe Plantation. In 1780, Randolph married her first cousin once removed, David Meade Randolph, moving to the family plantation Presquile. Around 1795, George Washington appointed David the U.S. Marshal of Virginia and the couple moved to Richmond. David was a Federalist and open critic of Thomas Jefferson, who removed him from office after his own election. In 1807, Mary Randolph opened a boarding house in Richmond; in 1810, her household included nine slaves. Randolph

---

169 Jessie Carney Smith and Linda T. Wynn, *Freedom Facts and Firsts: 400 Years of the African American Civil Rights Experience* (Canton, MI: Visible Ink Press, 2009); Anne Commire et al., eds. *Women in World History* (1999–2002).

170 George Derby et al., eds. *The National Cyclopædia of American Biography* (1891–1984); D.C. Gilman et al., eds. *New International Encyclopedia* (1902–1904).

may have invented the refrigerator. By 1819, she had moved to Washington, D.C., where in 1824 she published *The Virginia House-Wife*. With over 500 recipes, including for tomatoes, it was republished at least nineteen times before the Civil War. She is buried at Arlington National Cemetery.[171]

Martha Meredith Read (1773-March 1816), born in Pennsylvania, married John Read in 1796. Read published two novels both set in part in Philadelphia and in part in Santo Domingo, *Monima, or the Beggar Girl*, 1802, and *Margaretta; or, the Intricacies of the Heart*, 1807, along with the essay *A Second Vindication of the Rights of Women*, echoing Mary Wollstonecraft, in 1801. Read's first novel, part of the second, and her essay were all serialized in Isaac Ralston's newspaper *The Ladies' Monitor*.[172]

Therese Albertine Luise von Jakob Robinson [or **Ernst Berthold, ein Frauenzimmer, Talvj**] (26 January 1797–13 April 1870), born in Halle, Germany, followed her father in 1806 or 1807 to the University of Charkow, Russia (now Kharkiv, Ukraine) for three to five years, where she began to study Slavic languages. They moved to St Petersburg in 1810 or 1811, then back to Halle in 1816. Robinson translated Walter Scott, then published *Volkslieder der Serben*, 1826, praised by Johann Wolfgang von Goethe. In 1828, she married Edward Robinson, moving to Andover, Massachusetts in 1830, then Boston in 1833. In 1834, Robinson translated John Pickering's "Indian Languages of North America" and published her *Historical View of the Slavic Languages*. Her *Popular Poetry of the Teutonic Nations* followed in 1836, then a treatise on Ossian in 1840. She later published history and novels, returning to Germany in 1863.[173]

Rebecca Rush (1 January 1779–1850), born in Pennsylvania, published *Kelroy*, her only known publication, in 1812. The War of 1812 overshadowed it.[174]

Elizabeth Elkins Sanders (12 August 1762–19 February 1851), born in Massachusetts, lost her father aged one. In 1782, she married Thomas Sanders. She published her first pamphlet at the age of sixty-six: *Conversations, Principally on the Aborigines of North America*, 1828. In it, Sanders decries the forced removal of Creeks and Cherokees from their

---

171 Edward T. James et al., *Notable American Women* (1971).
172 Joseph Fichtelberg, "Heart-felt Verities: The Feminism of Martha Meredith Read." *Legacy* (1998) 15.2: 125–138.
173 Irma Elizabeth Voigt, *The Life and Works of Therese Robinson (Talvj)* (PhD thesis) (Champaign, IL: University of Illinois, 1913).
174 James Grant Wilson et al., *Appletons' Cyclopædia* (1887–1889): "Rush, Jacob."

ancestral lands and the atrocities committed against Native Americans by the US military, calling Andrew Jackson "a second Robespierre." A sequel followed in 1829: *The First Settlers of New England*. At age eighty-two, Sanders began a new series of pamphlets on missionary work: *Tract on Missions*, 1844; *Second Part of a Tract on Missions*, 1845; and *Remarks on the "Tour Around Hawaii," by the Missionaries, Messrs. Ellis, Thurston, and Goodrich*, 1848. Sanders feared for the native cultures of Pacific Islanders and had harsh words for Calvinism, perhaps influencing Herman Melville.[175]

Leonora Sansay, née **Honora Davern** (11 December 1773–1821), born in Pennsylvania, lost her father at sea a few weeks later. Aaron Burr became her patron in the late 1790s, perhaps persuading her to marry Louis Sansay, a planter from Saint-Domingue (later Haiti). In 1803, the Sansays sailed for Haiti, as described in her 1808 *Secret History; or, The Horrors of St. Domingo*, based on her letters to Burr. The Sansays left Haiti for Cuba, where Louis's jealousy caused Sansay to flee for Jamaica, then Philadelphia. In 1806–1807, Sansay played a part in Burr's alleged conspiracy. In 1809, she published the novel *Laura*, then possibly, after departing for London, *Zelica: The Creole*, 1820; *The Scarlet Handkerchief*, 1823; and *The Stranger in Mexico* (not extant).[176]

Esther "Hetty" Saunders (1793–15 December 1862), born into slavery in Delaware around 1793, escaped with her father and brother in 1800 by crossing the Delaware River. Saunders was taken in and educated by a New Jersey Quaker family, Joseph and Ann Brick Hall. Saunders's collected poems were published in 2001: *I Love to Live Alone: The Poems of Esther "Hetty" Saunders*. She also wrote *The Hill of Age* to honor Judy Wyring, a 109-year-old Black woman. She is buried at Salem Friends Burial Ground, New Jersey.[177]

Jane Johnston Schoolcraft [or **Bamewawagezhikaquay**] (31 January 1800–22 May 1842), born in the Northwest Territory (later Michigan), was the granddaughter of an Ojibwe war chief and daughter of a Belfast fur trader. In 1823, she married Henry Rowe Schoolcraft, a US Indian agent

---

175 Edward T. James et al., *Notable American Women* (1971); Lina Mainiero et al., eds. *American Women Writers* (1979–1994).
176 Carla Mulford et al., eds. *American Women Prose Writers to 1820* (1999).
177 Sibyl E. Moses, *African American Women Writers in New Jersey, 1836–2000. A Biographical Dictionary and Bibliographic Guide* (New Brunswick, NJ: Rutgers University Press, 2006).

and later a seminal figure of American cultural anthropology. Schoolcraft wrote poems and Ojibwe stories in English and Ojibwe; Henry published extracts in 1826–1827 in his *The Literary Voyager*, a founding text in Native American publishing history. He then compiled Ojibwe information from his wife in the six-volume *Indian Tribes of the United States*, 1846, commissioned by the United States Congress. These Ojibwe materials were the main source for Henry Wadsworth Longfellow's 1855 *Song of Hiawatha*. The couple moved to New York City in 1841, where Schoolcraft died. Her complete writings appeared in 2007.[178]

Julia H. Scott, née **Kinney** (4 November 1809–5 March 1842), born in Pennsylvania, taught in Towanda, where she conducted the first Sunday school in 1830. There, she met Dr. David L. Scott; they married in 1835, settling in Towanda. Before marriage, Scott published a good deal of prose and verse in Universalist periodicals and in the literary press. She also published *The Sacrifice: A Clergyman's Story* in 1834. Scott died of consumption aged thirty-three; after her death, a volume of her *Poems* appeared with a memoir by Sarah Carter Edgarton Mayo.[179]

Catharine Maria Sedgwick (28 December 1789–31 July 1867), born in Massachusetts, was the daughter of the Speaker of the United States House of Representatives. She was cared for as a child by Elizabeth Freeman, a former slave whose freedom her father had won in court. Sedgwick published the novels *The New England Tale*, 1822; *Redwood*, 1824; *Hope Leslie*, 1827, with its heroine Magawisca; *Clarence*, 1830; *The Linwoods*, 1835, set during the Revolution; *Home*, 1835; *The Poor Rich Man, and the Rich Poor Man*, 1836; *Live and Let Live*, 1837; and *The Irish Girl, and Other Tales*, 1850. She also published for children: *The Travellers*, 1825; *The Deformed Boy*, 1826; *Stories for Young Persons*, 1840; and *The Boy of Mount Rhigi*, 1848. Visiting Europe in 1839, Sedgwick published *Letters from Abroad*, 1841. Among her many other published works is *Slavery in New England*, 1853. She is buried near Freeman.[180]

Lydia Huntley Sigourney, née **Lydia Howard Huntley** (1 September 1791–10 June 1865), born in Connecticut, published fifty-two books and in nearly 300 periodicals in her lifetime. Sigourney opened a girls' school in

---

178 Robert Dale Parker, ed. *The Sound the Stars Make Rushing Through the Sky: The Writings of Jane Johnston Schoolcraft* (Philadelphia, PA: University of Pennsylvania Press, 2007).
179 Caroline Mehetabel Fisher Sawyer, *Memoir of Mrs. Julia H. Scott: with her Poems and Selections from her Prose* (Boston, MA: A. Tompkins, 1860).
180 Lucinda L. Damon-Bach and Victoria Clements, *Catharine Maria Sedgwick: Critical Perspectives* (Lebanon, NH: University Press of New England, 2003).

Norwich, Connecticut in 1811, then another in Hartford from 1814–1819, when she married Charles Sigourney. Her works include *Moral Pieces in Prose and Verse*, 1815; the long poem *Traits of the Aborigines of America*, 1822; *A Sketch of Connecticut Forty Years Since*, 1824; *Poems*, 1827; and *Evening Readings In History*, 1833. *Letters to Young Ladies*, 1833, after which she gave up anonymity, was printed more than twenty-five times. *Sketches* and *Poems* followed, both in 1834; *Pocahontas, and Other Poems*, 1841; and so forth. Sigourney was perhaps the best-known authoress in America after 1833. During the lyceum movement, till the 1870s, Sigournean Societies were founded from Georgia to Kansas in her honor.[181]

Elizabeth Oakes Smith, née **Prince** [or **E**] (12 August 1806–16 November 1893), born in Maine, lost her father at sea in 1809. In 1823, she married Seba Smith. Smith may have written for Seba's journals; she wrote for *The Yankee* in 1828–1829; in 1833, she briefly edited Seba's *Courier*, and by the late 1830s, she contributed often to his and other periodicals. The family moved to New York City in 1838. Smith contributed to *Godey's Ladies' Book*, *Snowden's Ladies' Companion*, and other journals, and published the novel *Riches Without Wings*. *The Sinless Child and Other Poems*, 1842, preceded the novels *The Western Captive*, 1842, and *The Salamander*, 1848. She wrote "Woman and Her Needs" for Horace Greeley's *New-York Tribune*, 1850–1851, and began lecturing on women's rights. Other novels and articles followed, until her son was arrested for transporting slaves from Africa in 1861. Smith published less thereafter.[182]

Margaret Bayard Smith (20 February 1778–7 June 1844), born in Pennsylvania, lost her mother in 1780 and was sent to a Moravian boarding school in Bethlehem. In 1800, she married Samuel Harrison Smith, a friend of Thomas Jefferson, and the couple moved to Washington, D.C., where they were frequent White House guests. Samuel founded the city's first newspaper, the *Daily Intelligencer*, Smith writing often for this and other publications, signed or anonymously. She published a novel in 1824, *A Winter in Washington, or Memoirs of the Seymour Family*; also, *What is Gentility?* in 1825. Smith wrote several biographical profiles, including one of her close friend Dolley Madison,

---

181 Gary Kelly, ed. *Lydia Sigourney: Selected Poetry and Prose* (Peterborough: Broadview Press, 2008).

182 Timothy H. Scherman, ed. *Elizabeth Oakes Smith: Selected Writings*, 2 vols (Macon, GA: Mercer University Press, 2023–2024).

published in 1836. Her reputation is based primarily on a collection of her letters and notebooks, 1800–1841, published in 1906 as *The First Forty Years of Washington Society*.[183]

Elizabeth Cady Stanton, née **Cady** (12 November 1815–26 October 1902), born in New York, studied mathematics, languages (Greek), philosophy, and law. Her father was a justice on the state supreme court; her mother an abolitionist, though the family owned at least one slave before 1827. In 1840, Stanton married Henry Brewster Stanton. On honeymoon, the couple attended London's World Anti-Slavery Convention, whose male members voted that women could attend in silence on a balcony. Stanton like Lucretia Mott was appalled; the two women became close friends. In 1848, Mott came to the Stantons' home in Seneca Falls, NY, and the two organized the Seneca Falls Convention, attended by Frederick Douglass and 300 others, where Stanton read her *Declaration of Sentiments*, starting a long battle for suffrage and equal rights. Stanton met Susan B. Anthony in 1851, writing and organizing until her death in 1902.[184]

Ann Sophia Stephens [or **Jonathan Slick**] (30 March 1810–20 August 1886), born in Connecticut, lost her mother early. In 1831, she married Edward Stephens and the couple moved to Portland, Maine. Here, they co-founded the *Portland Magazine*, in which Stephens's early work appeared before its sale in 1837. The couple then moved to New York City, she taking the job of editor to *The Ladies' Companion*. Over the next few years, Stephens wrote over twenty-five serial novels, plus verse and prose for periodicals including *Godey's Lady's Book* and *Graham's Magazine*. Stephens started her own magazine, *Mrs Stephens' Illustrated New Monthly*, in 1856; it later merged with *Peterson's Magazine*. She is credited as the progenitor of the dime novel genre, starting with her *Malaeska, the Indian Wife of the White Hunter*, published in 1860.[185]

Lavinia Stoddard, née **Stone** (29 June 1787–8 November 1820), born in Connecticut, moved with her family to New Jersey as an infant. In 1811, she married Dr. William Stoddard. The couple moved to Troy, New York, and there established an academy. Stoddard often published

---

183 Edward T. James et al., *Notable American Women* (1971).
184 Elisabeth Griffith, *In Her Own Right: The Life of Elizabeth Cady Stanton* (Oxford: Oxford University Press, 1985).
185 Sherry Lee Linkon, *In Her Own Voice: Nineteenth-century American Women Essayists* (New York: Taylor & Francis, 1997); Edward T. James et al., *Notable American Women* (1971).

poems in periodicals, notably "The Soul's Defiance," much reprinted in nineteenth-century American anthologies of verse. She died aged thirty-three. [186]

Harriet Elisabeth Beecher Stowe (14 June 1811–1 July 1896), born in Connecticut, lost her mother aged five. In 1832, Stowe moved to Cincinnati, Ohio, to join her father. She married Rev. Calvin Ellis Stowe in 1836, the couple moving to Brunswick, Maine, where they housed several fugitive slaves. Stowe published *Uncle Tom's Cabin* in 1851–1852, just after congress's passage of the Fugitive Slave Act of 1850, in the newspaper *The National Era*. Within a year, the book had sold 300,000 copies. Stowe later stirred controversy with a seeming defense of the Highland Clearances on behalf of Elizabeth Campbell, Duchess of Argyll. She first published in 1834: *A New England Sketchbook*, and continued publishing extensively thereafter into the late 1870s, both prose and verse, both fiction and non-fiction.[187]

Mary Amelia Swift (17 September 1812–1 November 1875), born in Connecticut, became principal of the Litchfield Female Academy in 1833. Here, she published *First Lessons in Natural Philosophy–Part First* in 1833, then *First Lessons on Natural Philosophy for Children–Part Second* in 1836, the year she left the academy and also published *Poor but Happy, or, the Villagers of Ban de la Roche and the Children of Icolumbkill*. Between 1833–1884, there were thirty-four editions or revisions of the *First Lessons*, which were translated into Burmese and Japanese. In 1845, Swift married Henry Augustus Swift, settling in Brooklyn. She is among the first women authors of a scientific textbook.[188]

Cynthia Taggart (1801/1804–1849), born in Rhode Island, lived in constant pain from infancy. Her education was neglected, and she first thought of writing when illness closed all other activities to her, in about 1822. Taggart lived with her widowed sister, near the coast; she wrote at night when unable to sleep. Friends collected and published her poetry in 1834, with an autobiography, to avert poverty. The book saw three editions, the last in 1848.[189]

---

186 Rufus Wilmot Griswold, *The Female Poets of America* (1849).
187 Joan D. Hedrick, *Harriet Beecher Stowe: A Life* (Oxford: Oxford University Press, 1994).
188 Elizabeth Wagner Reed, *American Women in Science* (1992).
189 Rufus Wilmot Griswold, *The Female Poets of America* (1849); Sarah Josepha Hale, *Woman's Record* (1855).

Jane Agnew Taylor, née **Jane Ellen Agnew** (c. 1817/1820–3 May 1904–1907), born in New Jersey, married J. Orville Taylor in 1835 or 1836. Taylor wrote *The Girls School Book No. 1* as early as 1837 and it was in its fourth edition by 1839. That year, she published *Physiology for Children*, which was widely distributed and substantially revised in 1848. Taylor's 1858 *Wouldst Know Thyself!, or, The Outlines of Human Physiology* was a condensed version of her earlier works, with a second edition in 1860.[190]

Tabitha Gilman Tenney (7 April 1762–2 May 1837), born in New Hampshire, married Samuel Tenney in 1788. Samuel was elected to Congress that year. In 1801, Tenney published *Female Quixotism, Exhibited in the Romantic Opinions and Extravagant Adventures of Dorcasina Sheldon*. It has been called the most popular novel written in America prior to *Uncle Tom's Cabin* in 1852. It went through at least five editions and was still in print in the 1850s.[191]

Caroline Matilda Warren Thayer (c. 1785–1844), born in Massachusetts, married James Thayer in 1809. In 1818, she opened a school on Canandaigua Lake; in 1819, she became a superintendent at Wesleyan Seminary in New York City, though dismissed in 1821 for her association with the New Jerusalem Church. Thayer moved to Joseph Hoxie's Academy in New York City for several years, then to teach in Kentucky in 1824, then in Mississippi by 1831. She wrote poetry, novels, and children's literature with a religious bent: *The Gamesters; Religion Recommended to Youth, in a Series of Letters; Elegy; Reflections; Stanzas; Ode to Cause of the Greeks; The Miracle Spring; First Lessons in the History of the United States;* and *The Widow's Son*.[192]

Eliza Townsend (June 1788–12 January 1854), born in Massachusetts, contributed anonymous poems to the *Monthly Anthology*, the *Unitarian Miscellany*, the *General Repository and Review*, and *The Port Folio*, among other magazines, for instance an "Occasional Ode" condemning Napoleon in 1809. Later, Townsend published more religious poetry, among these "The Incomprehensibility of God."[193]

---

190 Elizabeth Wagner Reed, *American Women in Science* (1992).
191 Samuel Austin Allibone, *A Critical Dictionary of English Literature, and British and American Authors, Living and Deceased, from the Earliest Accounts to the Middle of the Nineteenth Century* [...], 3 vols (Philadelphia, PA: J.B. Lippincott & Co., 1859–1871).
192 Peter Rawlings, *Americans on Fiction, 1776–1900*, 3 vols (London: Pickering & Chatto, 2002).
193 Rufus Wilmot Griswold, *The Female Poets of America* (1849).

Mary Townsend (14 May 1814–8 July 1851) was born in Pennsylvania to a Quaker family which joined the Hicksites at the Hicksite Separation. Townsend may have had tumors in her uterus; she eventually lost her sight and taught herself a sort of braille. She anonymously published *Life in the Insect World* in 1844, reflecting her use of microscopes. With her sister Hannah, she also published *The Anti-Slavery Alphabet* in 1846, sold at anti-slavery fairs to raise funds for abolition. After 1847, Townsend worked on a rhyming history of England for children, though her sister's part is perhaps larger than her own. Her achievements were mostly forgotten until Elizabeth Wagner Reed's *American Women in Science before the Civil War* in 1992. A descendant is now editing Townsend's works—for instance, *Hannah, Mary, and Elizabeth: Poems and Letters circa 1840–1851*, 2018.[194]

Louisa Caroline Tuthill, née **Huggins** [various pen names] (6 July 1799–1 June 1879), born in Connecticut, married Cornelius Tuthill in 1817, settling in New Haven. Tuthill wrote regularly for *The Microscope* during its existence. Cornelius died in 1825, leaving Tuthill with four children. She began publishing regular anonymous contributions to periodicals and some small anonymous volumes. After 1839, her *Young Ladies' Reader* went through several editions. *The Young Lady's Home* followed that year, then a series of small volumes for children: *I Will Be a Gentleman*, 1844, twenty editions; *I Will Be a Lady*, 1844, twenty editions; and so forth. In 1848, Tuthill published a *History of Architecture from the Earliest Times*, the first in the United States. The *Success in Life* series followed in 1849–1850: *The Merchant*; *The Lawyer*; *The Mechanic*; *The Artist*; *The Farmer*; and *The Physician*. Tuthill was often republished in England.[195]

Mary Elizabeth Van Lennep, née **Hawes** (16 April 1821–27 September 1844), born in Connecticut, did charity work as a child and taught Sunday school. Van Lennep kept a diary, 1841–1843, which survived. She also wrote letters and poetry. In 1843, she married Rev. Henry John Van Lennep; that year, the couple sailed for Smyrna (now Izmir), in the Ottoman Empire, with her piano. In 1844, they transferred to Constantinople (now Istanbul), where Van Lennep was to run an Armenian girls' school. She contracted dysentery and typhus and died that year aged twenty-three. Van Lennep's mother published a *Memoir*

---

194 Elizabeth Wagner Reed, *American Women in Science* (1992).
195 Joyce Appleby et al., *Encyclopedia of Women in American History* (2002); John Seely Hart, *The Female Prose Writers of America* (1852).

of Mrs. Mary E. Van Lennep: Only Daughter of the Rev. Joel Hawes, D.D. and Wife of the Rev. Henry J. Van Lennep, Missionary in Turkey in 1847.[196]

Julia Rush Cutler Ward (5 January 1796–9 November 1824), born in Massachusetts, married Samuel Ward in 1812 aged seventeen, settling in New York City. Heading the banking house of Prime, Ward & King, Samuel was perhaps the most influential financier in America. The Wards had seven children, Ward dying aged twenty-eight a week after giving birth to her last. Ward wrote occasional poems, one added to Rufus Griswold's *Female Poets of America* in 1878.[197]

Katharine Augusta Ware (1797–1843), born in Massachusetts, wrote a poem aged fifteen on the death of Robert Treat Paine, later published in his collected works. In 1819, she married Charles A. Ware, earning recognition for her occasional odes on public events appearing in literary journals: one on Lafayette was presented to him in Boston, another on the governor of New York, DeWitt Clinton, was recited at the opening of the Erie Canal. In 1828, Ware launched a literary periodical, *The Bower of Taste*, which continued for some years. She moved to Europe in 1839, publishing *The Power of the Passions and Other Poems* in London in 1842 and dying in Paris the following year.[198]

Catharine Harbison Waterman, née **Waterman**, later **Esling** (12 April 1812–6 April 1897), born in Pennsylvania, published under her maiden name in the *New York Mirror*, the *Annuals*, *Graham's Magazine*, and *Godey's Lady's Book*. She wrote hymns such as "Come Unto Me," published in 1839 in *The Christian Keepsake*. She married Captain George J. Esling of the Merchant Marine in 1840, settling in Rio de Janeiro until 1844, when the couple returned to Philadelphia. Waterman edited *Friendship's Offering for 1842* in 1841. In 1850, her poems were collected and published as *The Broken Bracelet and Other Poems*. Waterman also wrote *The Book of Parlour Games* in 1853 and *Flora's Lexicon* in 1857. In her later years, she gave up writing.[199]

---

196 Dana Lee Robert, *American Women in Mission* (1997); James Grant Wilson et al., *Appletons' Cyclopædia* (1887–1889).
197 Rufus Wilmot Griswold, *The Female Poets of America* (1849).
198 Rufus Wilmot Griswold, *The Female Poets of America* (1849); Samuel Austin Allibone, *A Critical Dictionary of English Literature* (1859–1871).
199 Rufus Wilmot Griswold, *The Female Poets of America* (1849); Caroline May, *The American Female Poets* (1848); Thomas Buchanan Read, *The Female Poets of America* (1849).

Amelia Ball Coppuck Welby, née **Coppuck** [or **Amelia** or **'Minstrelgirl'**] (3 February 1819–3 May 1852), born in Maryland, moved to Louisville, Kentucky with her family in 1834 or 1835, marrying George B. Welby in 1838. She wrote poetry as 'Amelia' for the Louisville *Journal* from 1837–1847. Rufus Wilmot Griswold and Edgar Allan Poe admired her work; a volume of her poems appeared in 1844 and went through fifteen editions in the next fifteen years. Welby was among the most popular poets in the Antebellum South. She died in Louisville two months after giving birth to her only child, a son.[200]

Anna Maria Wells, née **Foster** (1795–19 December 1868), born in Massachusetts, was baptized on September 20, 1795, her father dying that Fall. Foster was the half-sister of Frances Sargent Osgood. In 1821, she married Thomas Wells, publishing *Poems and Juvenile Sketches* in 1830. Thomas left his wife and four children in 1834 to go to sea, returning before 1840, Wells living in South Carolina for a time, where she published her "Auto-biography of Amelia Sophia Smink" in the *Southern Literary Journal* in 1838. Wells published *The Flowerlet. A Gift of Love* in Boston in 1842. By 1850, Wells was in New York City, though back in Boston by 1855. Here, she published *Patty Williams's Voyage. A Story Almost Wholly True* in 1866, contributing children's verse to *The Nursery* and *Our Young Folks*, among other venues.[201]

Jane Kilby Welsh [or **Welch**] (25 January? 1783–12 September 1853), whose life is little known, published *A Botanical Catechism: Containing Introductory Lessons for Students in Botany. By a Lady* in Northampton, Massachusetts in 1819 and *Familiar Lessons in Mineralogy and Geology: Designed for the Use of Young Persons and Lyceums: in Two Volumes* in Boston in 1832–1833. Welsh was one of twenty-two women described by Elizabeth Wagner Reed in *American Women in Science before the Civil War* in 1992. She is also one of just six women who were primary authors of works among the 1465 authors noted by Curtis P. Schuh in his *Mineralogy & Crystallography: An Annotated Biobibliography of Books Published 1469 Through 1919*.[202]

---

200 Wade Hall, *The Kentucky Anthology: Two Hundred Years of Writing in the Bluegrass State* (Lexington, KY: University Press of Kentucky, 2005); Frances Elizabeth Willard et al., *A Woman of the Century* (1893).

201 Rufus Wilmot Griswold, *The Female Poets of America* (1849); Kenneth M. Price and Susan Belasco Smith, *Periodical Literature in Nineteenth-century America* (Charlottesville, VA: University of Virginia Press, 1996).

202 Elizabeth Wagner Reed, *American Women in Science* (1992); Kristine Larsen, *The Women Who Popularized Geology in the 19th Century* (New York: Springer, 2017).

Sarah Helen Power Whitman (19 January 1803–27 June 1878), born in Rhode Island, married John Winslow Whitman in 1828. John had been co-editor of the *Boston Spectator and Ladies' Album*, where Whitman published poetry using the name 'Helen.' He died in 1833 and the couple never had children; Whitman also had a heart condition that she treated with ether she breathed in through her handkerchief. Whitman crossed paths with Edgar Allan Poe in 1845, he declining to be introduced. In 1848, they resumed contact via poems. Poe visited Whitman in 1848, regretting her friendships with Margaret Fuller and Elizabeth F. Ellet. The two discussed marriage; Rufus Wilmot Griswold makes much of this. Whitman's *Hours of Life, and Other Poems* appeared in 1853; in 1860, she published *Edgar Allan Poe and His Critics*, aimed especially at Griswold. Whitman's will left money for charity and for a volume of her poems.[203]

Catharine R. Williams (31 December 1787–11 October 1872), born in Rhode Island, lost her mother as a child; her father being at sea, she was raised by aunts. In 1824, she married Horatio N. Williams, settling in New York State. It was an unhappy marriage and Williams returned to Providence two years later. Here, she opened a school, then published her *Original Poems* in 1828, which did well. A prose story, "Religion at Home," came out in 1829; then *Tales, National and Revolutionary* in 1830; a satirical novel, *Aristocracy*, in 1832; the *History of Fall River*, 1833; then a second series of *Tales* in 1835. Williams then published *The Biography of Revolutionary Heroes*, 1839, and traveled in Canada prior to publishing *Neutral French: The Exiles of Nova Scotia* in 1841. Her *Annals of the Aristocracy of Rhode Island* came out in 1843–1845. Williams was a suffragist connected to the Dorr Rebellion. She left a manuscript novel.[204]

Elizabeth Washington Gamble Wirt (30 January 1784–24 January 1857), born in Virginia, married William Wirt in 1802, a future Attorney-General of the United States. The Wirts lived in Virginia and Washington, D.C.; after William's death in 1834, Wirt moved to Florida. To entertain her ten children, Wirt wrote *Flora's Dictionary*, an alphabetical list of over 200 flowers with their scientific name, symbolic meaning, and verse featuring the flower in question, with texts explaining plant morphology and Linnaean

---

203 Kenneth Silverman, *Edgar A. Poe: Mournful and Never-ending Remembrance* (New York: Harper Perennial, 1991).
204 Sidney Smith Rider, *Bibliographical Memoirs of Three Rhode Island Authors, J.K. Angell, Frances H. (Whipple) McDougall, Catharine R. Williams* (Providence, Rhode Island: S.S. Rider, 1880).

nomenclature. Published anonymously in 1829, the book went through several reprintings before Wirt was credited in 1835. A wide variety of similar books began appearing in the 1840s, often by writers less interested in science than Wirt was. The Wirts' voluminous correspondence subsists.[205]

Sarah "Sally" Sayward Barrell Keating Wood (1 October 1759–6 January 1855), born in Maine, married Richard Keating in 1778; Richard died five years later, and Wood married General Abiel Wood in 1804. Abiel died in 1811. Wood wrote Gothic novels: *Julia and the Illuminated Baron*, 1800; *Dorval; or, the Speculator*, 1801; *Amelia; or, the Influence of Virtue, an Old Man's Story*, 1802; *Ferdinand and Elmira: A Russian Story*, 1804; and *Tales of the Night*, 1827. Wood published anonymously as 'A Lady from Massachusetts' until Maine became a state in 1820, when she became 'A Lady from Maine' on her last title page. She is known as Maine's first novelist. Her manuscript work, *War, the Parent of Domestic Calamity: A Tale of the Revolution*, is at the Library of the Maine Historical Society in Portland.[206]

Jane Taylor Worthington, née **Lomax** (2 February 1821–26 May 1847), born in Virginia, published prose and verse almost exclusively in the *Southern Literary Messenger*. In 1843, she married Dr. Francis Asbury Worthington, son of the Governor of Ohio; the couple settled in Ohio, where Worthington died in Cincinnati. Her works include hymns: "It Visiteth the Desolate;" stories: "Life and Love" and "Ravenel Hall. A Tale in Two Parts;" and poems: "Lines to One Who Will Understand Them," "Moonlight on the Grave," "Sleep," "The Common Bramble," "The Child's Grave," "The Withered Leaves," "The Poor," "To the Peaks of Otter," and "To Twilight." There is no collection of her works.[207]

---

205 Jack Kramer, *Women of Flowers: A Tribute to Victorian Women Illustrators* (New York: Stewart, Tabori & Chang, 1996).
206 Karen A. Weyler. "Sally Sayward Barrell Keating Wood." *Legacy* (1998). 15.2: 204–212.
207 Rufus Wilmot Griswold, *The Female Poets of America* (1849); Samuel Austin Allibone, *A Critical Dictionary of English Literature* (1859–1871).

2. Writers from France

France in the period 1776–1848 experienced three revolutions, three monarchies (Old Regime, Restoration, and July Monarchy), a first and second republic, and a first empire. Not only was the region constitutionally in flux, its borders in 1810 briefly extended from Rome, the Empire's second city, to Lübeck on the Baltic. Napoleon's troops were on their way to Moscow. Our focus however is the emergent national tradition, and I have identified forty-six French women writers for the period, more than for any tradition outside the English-speaking world.

France (46 writers)

George Sand, *Indiana* (1832)

PREMIÈRE PARTIE.

I.

Par une soirée d'automne pluvieuse et fraîche, trois personnes rêveuses étaient gravement occupées, au fond d'un petit castel de la Brie, à regarder brûler les tisons du foyer et cheminer lentement l'aiguille de la pendule. Deux de ces hôtes silencieux semblaient s'abandonner en toute soumission au vague ennui qui pesait sur eux ; mais le troisième donnait des marques de rébellion ouverte ; il s'agitait sur son siège, étouffait à demi haut quelques bâillements mélancoliques, et frappait la pincette sur les bûches pétillantes, avec l'intention marquée de lutter contre l'ennemi commun.

Ce personnage, beaucoup plus âgé que les deux autres, était le maître de la maison, le colonel Delmare, vieille bravoure en demi-solde, homme jadis beau, maintenant épais, au front chauve, à la moustache grise, à l'œil terrible ; excellent maître devant qui tout tremblait, femme, serviteurs, chevaux et chiens.

Il quitta enfin sa chaise, évidemment impatienté de ne savoir comment rompre le silence, et se prit à marcher pesamment dans toute la longueur du salon, sans perdre un instant la roideur convenable à tous les mouvements d'un ancien militaire, s'appuyant sur les reins et se tournant tout d'une pièce, avec ce contentement perpétuel de soi-même qui caractérise l'homme de parade et l'officier-modèle.[1]

PART 1

I.

On a chilly wet autumn evening, in a little manor house in Brie, three people, lost in thought, were solemnly watching the embers burn in the fireplace and the hands make their way slowly round the clock. Two of these silent individuals seemed submissively resigned to the vague boredom that oppressed them. But the third showed signs of open rebellion: he moved about restlessly in his chair, half stifled a few melancholy yawns, and struck the crackling logs with the tongs, obviously trying to fight against the common enemy.

This person, who was much older than the other two, was the master of the house, Colonel Delmare, a retired army officer, who had once been handsome but now was heavy and bald with a grey moustache and a fierce look; he was an excellent master who made everyone tremble, wife, servants, horses, and dogs.

At last he left his chair, having obviously lost his patience at not knowing how to break the silence, and began to tramp up and down the room. But he did not for a moment relax the stiff movements of an old soldier, keeping his back straight, turning in one movement with the permanent smugness typical of the parade officer on duty.[2]

After Sand's author's prefaces of 1832, 1842, and 1852, readers come to this scene of domestic life. The scene would likely have been impossible a half-century earlier. At least four relatively fashionable Romantic tropes appear: Rousseau's reverie, Chateaubriand's the vague, Senancour's ennui, and Staël's melancholy. But there is more to it than that. This is a leisurely opening, and that leisure depends on nothing happening: three protagonists in a salon do nothing much for the opening half a page. Just as epic poets were for centuries taught to begin *in medias res*, in the middle of things, so novels prior to the Romantic period, both epistolary and narrative, tend to move quickly into plot: one thinks of Voltaire or Fielding, or indeed of Victor Hugo's 1831 *Notre Dame de Paris*, which opens with the bells of Paris ringing. Even Laurence Sterne, that

---

1   In George Sand, *Oeuvres complètes*, ed. Béatrice Didier, 1832 (Paris: Champion, 2008), *Indiana*, ed. Brigitte Diaz, pp. 87–88.
2   George Sand, *Indiana*, tr. Sylvia Raphaël (Oxford: Oxford University Press, 1994), p. 15.

trailblazer for digression, opens *Tristram Shandy* in 1759 with his hero's conception. Sand here ignores that novelistic imperative.

Sand instead does two things: she gives us setting, rather as Honoré de Balzac gives us the Pension Vauquer to open 1835's *Le Père Goriot*—she creates a mood; and she gives us character. Mood is in a sense the opposite of plot: the one is static, the other dynamic. As the Impressionists in the 1860s found beauty and meaning in the commonplace and the everyday, so Sand finds it in an autumn evening with a fire in the grate; as Claude Monet saw that Rouen cathedral at dawn was unlike Rouen cathedral in the afternoon, so Sand saw that the mood of a rainy autumn evening is unique and particular and worthy of expression. As for character, Sand further saw that properly defined, character is plot's creation: her retired colonel is who he is because of his past military service, which in the France of 1832 at once suggests France's Revolutionary and Napoleonic Wars. Just as Balzac's Colonel Chabert of 1832 is out of place in Restoration France, so Sand's Colonel Delmare by the fire gives marks of "rébellion ouverte," a term charged with meaning after 1789 and another commonplace Romantic trope. It is no coincidence that Sand opened her novel thus as the dust of 1830's July Revolution settled—France's second revolution in forty years.

Indiana, it turns out, is the wife of the older Colonel Delmare, trapped in a loveless marriage. As the plot progresses, her search for love leads her to their neighbor Raymon, who has already seduced her servant, Noun. Pregnant and now abandoned, Noun drowns herself. The novel travels between France and Réunion, then the Île Bourbon, returning to witness the Revolution of 1830, then departing again for Réunion, where Indiana and her cousin Ralph—the third person in the opening scene—plan a *Liebestod*. The conclusion shows them instead living on that island in the manner of Jacques-Henri Bernardin de Saint-Pierre's best-selling *Paul et Virginie*, 1783.

Marie Catherine Sophie de Flavigny, Comtesse d'Agoult [or **Daniel Stern**] (31 December 1805–5 March 1876), born in Frankfurt-am-Main to a French émigré father and a German Jewish convert mother, was bilingual, meeting Goethe as a child. In 1827, d'Agoult married Charles Louis Constant, Comte d'Agoult. Her salon drew writers and musicians from Vigny to Chopin to Heine. In 1833, d'Agoult began her liaison with Franz Liszt; her novel *Nélida*, 1846, is an anagram of their third child's name, Daniel. Their daughter Cosima married Richard Wagner. D'Agoult's 1850 *Histoire de la Révolution de 1848* remains a reference point.[3]

Hortense Thérèse Sigismonde Sophie Alexandrine Allart de Méritens [or **Prudence de Saman L'Esbatx**], known as **Hortense Allart** (7 September 1801–28 February 1879), born in Milan, lost her father at sixteen, her mother at twenty. Allart was the niece of Sophie Gay and cousin of Delphine de Girardin. She found work as a governess but was there impregnated and abandoned by the Comte de Sampayo. In 1824, she published letters on Staël. *Gertrude* followed in 1828, then books on history, politics, and philosophy. Allart had liaisons with Sand, Chateaubriand, Sainte-Beuve, and others; in 1843, she married Napoléon Louis Frédéric Corneille de Méritens de Malvézie.[4]

Virginie Ancelot, née **Marguerite Louise Virginie Chardon** (15 March 1792–20 March 1875), born in Dijon, debuted as a painter in the Salon of 1814. Around 1819, she married Jacques-François Ancelot. He lost his post in 1830, and Ancelot collaborated in his vaudevilles and memoirs between 1832–1835. Ancelot's own plays, mostly in prose, were staged in Paris from 1835–1848 and collected in 1848; she also published several novels from 1839–1866, and salon memoirs. From 1824, Ancelot hosted Lacretelle, Hugo, Sophie Gay, Delphine de Girardin, Rachel, Juliette Récamier, Guizot, Saint-Simon, Musset, Stendhal, Chateaubriand, Vigny, Lamartine, Mérimée, and Delacroix in one of Paris's last great literary salons.[5]

Sophie d'Arbouville, née **Sophie Lecat de Bazancourt** (28 October 1810–22 March 1850), born in Paris, was the granddaughter of Sophie d'Houdetot. Aged twenty-two, she married François d'Arbouville, a general she accompanied on campaigns. She published her poems anonymously; her short stories in *La Revue des deux mondes* appeared without her permission. Sainte-Beuve frequented her Paris salon, alongside Mérimée and Chateaubriand. Her *Poésies et nouvelles* appeared posthumously in 1855.[6]

---

3   Charles Dupêchez, *Marie d'Agoult, 1805–1876* (Paris: Plon, 1994).
4   Helynne Hollstein Hansen, *Hortense Allart: The Woman and the Novelist* (Lanham, MD: University Press of America, 1998).
5   Sophie Marchal, *Virginie Ancelot, femme de lettres au xixe siècle* (Lille: ANRT, Université de Lille III, 1998).
6   Léon Séché, *Muses romantiques: Madame d'Arbouville d'après ses lettres à Sainte-Beuve:*

Angélique Arnaud [or **Marie Angélique Bassin**] (23 December 1797–9 April 1884), born in Gannat, married Louis Arnaud in 1820. Arnaud began publishing republican articles in periodicals after 1833—*L'Avenir des femmes, Droit des femmes, La Femme, La Solidarité*. Feminist, socialist, and Saint-Simonian, her novels met with some success and with an admirer in George Sand.[7]

Félicie Marie Émilie d'Ayzac (1801–26 March 1881), born in Paris, became a teacher at sixteen and taught for thirty-five years. She translated Horace in 1822, winning a prize in 1823 from the Académie des jeux floraux; in 1833, she published *Soupirs poétiques*, whose second edition was crowned by the Académie française in 1842. D'Ayzac also studied medieval statuary, winning more prizes with her work on Chartres in 1849 and Saint-Denis in 1860–1867.[8]

Marguerite Victoire Babois (6 October 1760–18 March 1839), born in Versailles, lost her mother at fifteen and was placed in a convent, leaving in 1780 to marry Jacques-Nicolas Gosset. She obtained a divorce in 1793. In 1806, Babois met the painter Jean-Jacques Karpff [or Casimir de Colmar], living with him until his death in 1829. Her uncle Ducis encouraged her to publish; her *Élégie sur la mort de sa fille âgée de cinq ans* had nine editions between 1804–1815. Babois also published a volume of *Élégies nationales* and some volumes in other poetic genres; she influenced Desbordes-Valmore, Hugo, and Lamartine.[9]

Sophie, Baronne de Bawr, née **Alexandrine-Sophie Goury de Champgrand** (8 October 1773–31 December 1860), illegitimate daughter of a marquis and an opera singer, studied music with Grétry and Boieldieu. During the Terror, Bawr married Jules de Rohan-Rochefort; he was guillotined soon after. In 1801, she married Claude-Henri de Saint-Simon, and after a divorce, the Baron de Bawr, though again widowed. She supported herself by writing songs, novels, plays, and

---

1846–1850: documents inédits, portraits, vues et autographe (Paris: Mercure de France, 1909).

7   Alexandra K. Wettlaufer, *Portraits of the Artist as a Young Woman: Painting and the Novel in France and Britain 1800–1860* (Columbus, OH: Ohio State University Press, 2011).

8   Axel Duboul, *Les Deux Siècles de l'Académie des Jeux floraux*, 2 vols (Toulouse: Édouard Privat, 1901).

9   Domenico Gabrielli, *Dictionnaire historique du Père-Lachaise: xviiie et xixe siècles* (Paris: Amateur, 2002).

musical theater; her *Suite d'un bal masqué* had 246 performances between 1813 and 1869. Bawr published her *Souvenirs* in 1853.[10]

Fanny de Beauharnais, née **Marie-Anne-Françoise Mouchard** (4 October 1737–2 July 1813), married Count Claude de Beauharnais in 1753 and later became godmother to their great-niece Joséphine. After separating from her husband, Beauharnais hosted a salon and devoted herself to literature. Her works—poetry, long poems, novels, from her *Mélanges de poésies fugitives et de prose sans conséquence* in 1772 to her *Le Voyage de Zizi et d'Azor* in 1811—were sometimes attributed to Dorat and other male friends.[11]

Louise Swanton Belloc, née **Anne-Louise Chassériau Swanton** (1 October 1796–6 November 1881), born in La Rochelle, published her first translation in 1818 and began writing for the *Revue encyclopédique*. She married Jean-Hilaire Belloc in 1821; the poet Hilaire Belloc was her grandson. Belloc knew Hugo, Stendhal, and Lamartine, but also Dickens, Harriet Beecher Stowe, and Maria Edgeworth; sadly, her correspondence was later destroyed. She translated Dickens, Gaskell, Scott, Moore, Goldsmith, Byron, Edgeworth, and Stowe's *Uncle Tom's Cabin*, herself authoring over forty books including a life of Byron. Belloc often collaborated with her close friend Adélaïde de Montgolfier, alongside whom she is buried.[12]

Louise-Angélique Bertin (15 January 1805–26 April 1877) was born in Roches, daughter of Louis François Bertin, owner of the *Journal des Débats*. She studied counterpoint with the teacher of Berlioz and Liszt. Her works included an opéra-comique in 1827, *Le Loup-garou*, and the opera *Fausto* in 1831. In 1836, the Paris Opéra staged her *La Esmeralda*, with libretto by Victor Hugo, performed for only six nights due to rowdy audiences. Critics were condescending to this polio survivor, but Berlioz dedicated to her the first version of his *Les Nuits d'été*. Bertin also left twelve cantatas, some instrumental work, five chamber symphonies, and two volumes of poetry, the first of them being awarded a prize by

---

10 Jacqueline Letzter and Robert Adelson, *Women Writing Opera: Creativity and Controversy in the Age of the French Revolution* (Berkeley, CA: University of California Press, 2001).
11 Erick Noël, *Les Beauharnais, une fortune antillaise, 1756–1796* (Genève: Droz, 2003).
12 Gustave Vapereau, *Dictionnaire universel des contemporains* […], 2nd edition (Paris: Hachette et Cie, 1861).

the Académie française.¹³

Adélaïde Charlotte Louise Éléonore, Comtesse de Boigne, known as **Adélaïde de Boigne** (19 February 1781–10 May 1866), born in Versailles, was the playmate of the first *dauphin*. In England in 1798, she married Benoît, Comte de Boigne, separating in 1802. She returned to France in 1804, with ties to Staël and Juliette Récamier. After 1814, her salon united the old nobility with the worlds of politics, diplomacy, and literature. The July Monarchy saw her salon grow more political; Rémusat, visiting in 1832, noted Broglie, Guizot, and Thiers alongside Mérimée. It took ten years for her memoirs to come out unexpurgated, with several aristocratic families attempting to censor them. Boigne was the author of two novels, which appeared posthumously.¹⁴

Amélie-Julie [or **Émilie**] **Candeille** (30/31 July 1767–4 February 1834), born in Paris, performed before the king at the age of seven. She joined a Masonic lodge in 1781, meeting Olympe de Gouges, and debuted at the Académie royale de musique in 1782 as Iphigénie in Gluck's opera. In 1785, she debuted at the Comédie-Française; Talma became a friend. After 1789, Candeille frequented the salons of Mme de Lameth, Helvétius, and Condorcet. She married Jean Simons in 1798 but grew close to the painter Girodet from 1800 until his death in 1824, managing his career. She also published historical novels and contributed to the *Annales de la Littérature et des arts*. She married the painter Antoine-Hilaire-Henri Périé in 1823.¹⁵

Suzanne Rosette [or **Rosine**] **de Chabaud-Latour** (15 September 1794- 28 May 1860), born in Nîmes, was the governess of François Guizot's children. She published an English language manual and translated several works of John Newton, abolitionist author of the hymn "Amazing Grace." After 1830, she became active in the evangelical chapel on rue Taitbout in Paris, frequented by Protestant society including Staël's daughter Albertine, whose husband the Duc de Broglie worked for abolition under the July Monarchy.¹⁶

Louise-Marie-Victoire "Victorine" de Chastenay (11 April 1771–9 May 1855), born in Paris, studied the sciences and Latin, German,

---

13 *Grove Music Online*.
14 Françoise Wagener, *La Comtesse de Boigne 1781–1866* (Paris: Flammarion, 1998).
15 *Grove Music Online*; Jacqueline Letzter et al., *Women Writing Opera* (2001).
16 Daniel Robert, *Textes et documents relatifs à l'histoire des Eglises réformées en France Période 1800–1830* (Geneva: Librairie Droz, 1962).

English, Spanish, Italian, and music as a child. She became abbess of Épinal in 1785, though she took no vows; the abbey was dissolved in 1789. As the Revolution became violent, the family fled Paris to Burgundy, where Chastenay's father was denounced in 1794, though acquitted at trial. Chastenay began translating in 1797—Goldsmith's *Deserted Village*, Radcliffe's *Mysteries of Udolpho*—publishing her own works from 1802–1816: *Le Calendrier de Flore; Du Génie des peuples anciens; Les Chevaliers normands en Italie et en Sicile. De l'Asie ou considérations religieuses, philosophiques et littéraires sur l'Asie* followed in 1832, and lastly her memoirs for 1771–1815 in 1896. These had seen twenty-four editions by 1987. Unmarried, Chastenay lived in relative isolation after 1816.[17]

Louise Colet, née **Revoil de Servannes** (15 August 1810–9 March 1876), born in Aix-en-Provence, married Mouriès Hippolyte Raymond Colet, a professor at the Paris Conservatoire de musique, in 1834. In 1835, Colet published her first book of poems, winning a prize from the Académie française and going on to win three further prizes from that institution. Her salon was frequented by Hugo, Musset, Vigny, Baudelaire, and other painters and politicians. In 1846, she met Gustave Flaubert, a young unknown, in the sculptor James Pradier's studio. The liaison did not last, though Colet left her husband in 1847. She also wrote prose. Flaubert later attacked her work, unlike Hugo who admired it.[18]

Marie Louise Sophie de Grouchy [or **de Condorcet**] (8 April 1764–8 September 1822), born in Meulan, married Marie Jean Antoine Nicolas de Caritat, Marquis de Condorcet in 1786. Condorcet started a salon attended by Turgot, Beaumarchais, Gouges, and Staël alongside visitors such as Jefferson, Beccaria, and perhaps Adam Smith. The Cercle Social, committed to equal rights for women, met at her house. When her husband went into hiding, Condorcet encouraged him to write and edited his *Esquisse d'un tableau historique des progrès de l'esprit humain*, 1795. Condorcet's most important publication is her *Lettres sur la sympathie*, added in 1798 to her translation of Smith's *Theory of Moral Sentiments* and then neglected. She later edited her husband's complete

---

17 Olivier Grandjean, *Quelques femmes célèbres de Bourgogne. Victorine de Chastenay, érudite et mémorialiste sous la Révolution et l'Empire* (Vievy: Editions de l'escargot savant, 2010).

18 Francine du Plessix Gray, *Rage and Fire: Life of Louise Colet - Pioneer Feminist, Literary Star, Flaubert›s Muse* (New York: Simon & Schuster, 1994).

works.[19]

Marie Sophie Risteau Cottin (22 March 1770–25 August 1807), born in Paris, married Jean Paul Marie Cottin in 1789. Denounced as an aristocrat in 1793, he was found lifeless in his bed; his widow paid a large part of their fortune to Fouquier-Tinville in a vain attempt to save two family members. Cottin wrote *Claire d'Albe*, 1799, in two weeks, published anonymously, and gave a friend the proceeds; the success of *Malvina*, 1800, and *Amélie Mansfield*, 1802, revealed her identity. Cottin declined to publish her poetry; her poem *La Prise de Jéricho* with its Jewish heroine was published posthumously. Other novels preceded her early death.[20]

Marie de Vichy-Chamrond, Marquise du Deffand (25 September 1696–23 August 1780), born in the family château in Burgundy, married the Marquis du Deffand at twenty-two. In Regency Paris, she frequented libertine circles and met Voltaire. In 1742 she began her correspondence with the great names of the age: Voltaire, Walpole, d'Alembert, Lespinasse, the Duchesse de Luynes. She opened her salon in 1749 to Voltaire, d'Alembert, Fontenelle, Marivaux, Helvétius, to painters, sculptors, and architects. Losing her sight at fifty-six, du Deffand took her niece Julie de Lespinasse as a reader, separating from her vehemently after discovering that Lespinasse was meeting salon guests independently.[21]

Jeanne Deroin (31 December 1805–2 April 1894), born in Paris, married Antoine Ulysse Desroches in 1832 but refused to take his name. In 1848, she and Désirée Gay co-founded *La Politique des Femmes* (later *L'Opinion des femmes*), a journal for women by a society of workers. In 1849, Deroin became the first woman to campaign in a French legislative election. Proudhon thought her eccentric, and even Sand and d'Agoult found her initiative misplaced. That year, Deroin was elected to the central committee of an organization linking over a hundred workers' associations. A police raid in 1850 put Deroin in prison until 1851. She left for England after the 1851 *coup d'État*, dying in poverty despite a

---

19 Thierry Boissel. *Sophie de Condorcet, femme des Lumières, 1764–1822* (Paris: Presses de la Renaissance, 1988).
20 Silvia Lorusso, *Le Charme sans la beauté, vie de Sophie Cottin* (Paris: Classiques Garnier, 2018).
21 Inès Murat, *Madame du Deffand, 1696–1780: la lettre et l'esprit* (Paris: Perrin, 2003).

government pension after 1871.[22]

Marceline Félicité Josèphe Desbordes-Valmore (20 June 1786–23 July 1859), born in Douai, set out for Guadeloupe in 1801 with her mother, who died in 1803. Desbordes returned to Douai, becoming an actress at the age of sixteen. She met Talma, Marie Dorval, and Mademoiselle Mars. From 1808–1812, Desbordes was engaged, but the fiancé's family refused a marriage to a former actress. Desbordes resumed acting. In 1817, she married Prosper Lanchantin, known as Valmore. In 1819 Desbordes-Valmore published *Élégies et Romances*. Several more volumes of poetry followed. Her works earned her a royal pension and several academic distinctions. Her admirers include Sainte-Beuve, Balzac, Baudelaire, Verlaine, and Aragon.[23]

Julienne Joséphine Gauvin [or **Juliette Drouet**] (10 April 1806–11 May 1883), born in Fougères, lost her mother at birth, her father in 1807, and was placed with a wet-nurse, then in a convent, before being raised by an uncle. Around 1825, she became the mistress of the sculptor James Pradier. He encouraged her to act, and she began in 1828, taking her uncle's name. Though booed in *Marie Tudor*, 1833, Drouet was extremely beautiful; Victor Hugo fell in love. She abandoned acting and devoted herself to him. In 1852, having organized his flight from the Second Empire, Drouet accompanied Hugo to exile. He rented a house for her within eyesight, though later cheating on her with her chambermaid. She wrote him over 22,000 letters during the fifty years of their liaison. He did not attend her funeral.[24]

Claire Louisa Rose Bonne, Duchesse de Duras, née **de Coëtnempren de Kersaint**, known as **Claire de Duras** (27 February 1777–16 January 1828), born in Brest, left France for Martinique at her father's death in 1793, then the United States, Switzerland, and London where she married Amédée Bretagne Malo de Durfort, Duc de Duras in 1797, returning to Paris in 1800. During the Restoration, she furthered Chateaubriand's political career, while her salon became a center for Parisian literary and social life. At Chateaubriand's insistence, Duras published *Ourika* anonymously in 1823, about an African heroine, one of the three novels

---

22 Didier, Béatrice, Antoinette Fouque, and Mireille Calle-Gruber, eds. *Dictionnaire universel des créatrices*, 3 vols (Paris: Éditions des femmes, 2013).
23 Aimée Boutin, *Maternal Echoes: The Poetry of Marceline Desbordes-Valmore and Alphonse de Lamartine* (Newark, DE: University of Delaware Press, 2001).
24 Henri Troyat, *Juliette Drouet: La prisonnière sur parole* (Paris: Flammarion, 1997).

she wrote, along with *Édouard*, 1825, and the unpublished *Olivier ou le Secret*, written in 1822.²⁵

Alexandrine des Écherolles, née **Alexandrine Giraud des Écherolles** (26 September 1779–11 April 1850), born in Moulins, became lady in waiting to the Wurtemberg children from 1807 until her death. She published her memoirs of the Terror, *Quelques années de ma vie*, in 1843.²⁶

Louise Florence Pétronille Tardieu d'Esclavelles d'Épinay, known as **Louise d'Épinay** (11 March 1726–17 April 1783) was the daughter of the Baron d'Esclavelles. Épinay was put in a convent awaiting marriage, then married off at nineteen to the Marquis d'Épinay; his prodigality and adultery led to a separation of property in 1749. Around 1747, she met Rousseau, for whom she prepared the little house known as *l'Hermitage*. The prickly Rousseau moved out in 1757, but the two had a marked influence on each other. Soon after, d'Épinay retired from public life, remaining at home for a select company: Grimm, Diderot, d'Alembert, Marivaux, Marmontel, Saint-Lambert, Suard, Raynal, d'Holbach, Galiani. Voltaire was another friend. She took over Grimm's *Correspondance littéraire* during his absence.²⁷

Jeanne-Justine Fouqueau de Pussy (27 September 1786–1863), founder of the girls' magazine *Journal des Demoiselles*, edited the magazine from 1833–1852. She also wrote children's literature.²⁸

Sophie Gay, née **Marie Françoise Sophie Nichault de la Valette** (1 July 1776–5 March 1852), born in Paris, was presented aged two to Voltaire. In 1793, she married Gaspard Liottier, divorcing in 1799 to marry Jean Sigismond Gay, Baron de Lupigny. Her revolutionary salon drew Benjamin Constant, Chateaubriand, Talma, Juliette Récamier, and the Marquise de Custine. In 1802, Gay published her novel *Laure d'Estell* anonymously, also composing songs and verse romances. In 1813, she published *Léonie de Montbreuse*, then novels, five-act comedies, dramas, and opera librettos. Her restoration salon featured Hugo, Soumet, Lamartine, Vigny, Soulié, Sue,

---

25   Chantal Bertrand-Jennings, *D'un siècle l'autre: romans de Claire de Duras* (Jaignes: Chasse au Snark, 2001).

26   Germain Sicard, *Justice et politique: la Terreur dans la Révolution française* (Toulouse: Presses de l'Université Toulouse 1 Capitole, 1997).

27   Élisabeth Badinter, *Mme du Châtelet, Mme d'Épinay: ou l'ambition féminine au xviiie siècle* (Paris: Flammarion, 2006).

28   Wendelin Guentner, *Women Art Critics in Nineteenth-Century France: Vanishing Acts* (Newark, DE: University of Delaware Press, 2013).

Balzac, Janin, and Dumas; also, the painters Gérard, Girodet-Trioson, Isabey, and Horace Vernet. After 1830, she published several historical novels.[29]

Anne-Hyacinthe Geille de Saint-Léger [or **Anne-Hyacinthe de Colleville**] (26 March 1761–18 September 1824), born in Paris, published her first novel in 1781. She knew the dramatist La Harpe through her father, a fellow freemason. Colleville also published poems in periodicals and wrote two one-act comedies in prose, 1783–1788, for the boulevard theaters. She published three more novels between 1802–1806.[30]

Stéphanie Félicité, Marquise de Sillery, Comtesse de Genlis, known as **Félicité de Genlis** (21 January 1746–31 December 1830) married Charles Alexis Brûlart, Marquis de Sillery, Comte de Genlis, in 1763. Genlis joined the Orléans household as a companion to the Duchesse de Chartres, with whose husband she seems to have begun an affair almost at once. She also educated the future King Louis Philippe. Genlis met Rousseau and Voltaire and was the friend of Buffon, Marmontel, Bernardin de Saint-Pierre, Talleyrand, and Juliette Récamier; she hosted a salon in 1788–1791. During the Terror, her husband and lover were both guillotined; emigration made writing her primary source of income. Genlis returned to France in 1801, spying for Bonaparte. Her works extend to 140 volumes.[31]

Delphine Gay de Girardin [or **Vicomte de Launay**] (24 January 1804–29 June 1855), daughter of Sophie Gay, born in Aix-la-Chapelle (Aachen), met Nodier, Vigny, Latouche, Soumet, and Deschamps by the age of sixteen, publishing volumes of poetry in 1824 and 1825. She married Émile Delamothe, known as Émile de Girardin, in 1831, abandoning poetry for her dazzling chronicles in the newspaper *La Presse*, 1836–1848. Girardin wrote works of fiction including *La Canne de Monsieur de Balzac*, 1836, prose and verse dramas, and one-act comedies like *La joie fait peur*, 1854. Her salon was frequented by Gautier, Balzac, Musset, Hugo, Desbordes-Valmore, Lamartine, Liszt, Dumas père, and George Sand.[32]

---

29   Henri Malo, *Une muse et sa mère: Delphine Gay de Girardin* (Paris: Émile-Paul Frères, 1924).
30   Claire Buck, ed. *Bloomsbury Guide to Women's Literature* (1992).
31   Bonnie Arden Robb, *Félicité de Genlis: Motherhood in the Margins* (Newark, DE: University of Delaware Press, 1995).
32   Madeleine Lassere, *Delphine de Girardin: journaliste et femme de lettres au temps du*

Marie Olympe Gouze [or **Olympe de Gouges**] (7 May 1748–3 November 1793), born in Montauban, married a man thirty years her elder in 1765, Louis Yves Aubry. He died in 1766. Gouges reached Paris in the early 1770s and took the name 'Olympe de Gouges.' Here, she founded a small troupe of actors, sold in 1787. Her 1784 play *Zamore et Mirza* was staged in 1789 under the title *L'Esclavage des Noirs*. A second abolitionist play and treatise followed. In 1788–1789, Gouges declared herself a monarchist, becoming a republican after 1792. Almost all her writings, notably her 1791 *Déclaration des droits de la femme et de la citoyenne*, call for women to participate in public debate. Gouges also called for the right to divorce and for freedom from religious vows. She was guillotined in 1793.[33]

Anne-Marie Lacroix, née **Anne-Marie Allotte de Chancelay** (1732–1802), who was possibly born in 1736, married Théodore Lacroix in 1757. In 1802 she published the anonymous novel *Constantine, ou le danger des préventions maternelles*.[34]

Henriette Lucy Dillon, Marquise de La Tour-du-Pin Gouvernet (25 February 1770–2 April 1853), born in Paris, married Frédéric Séraphin, Comte de Gouvernet, later Marquis de La Tour-du-Pin, in 1787. Gouvernet was lady-in-waiting to Marie-Antoinette from 1787–1789, witnessing the Estates General, the Women's March on Versailles, and the *Grande Peur*. During the Terror, she emigrated to New York. She was close to Talleyrand during his exile, returning with her husband in 1796. Bonaparte's Brumaire coup allowed her husband to resume his diplomatic career, until their son was involved in the Duchesse de Berry's anti-Orléanist plot of 1831. Following her husband's death in 1837, Gouvernet moved to Italy. Her memoir was written at fifty and not published until 1906.[35]

Julie Jeanne Éléonore de Lespinasse (9 November 1732–23 May 1776), born in Lyon, was the natural child of the Comtesse d'Albon and possibly the Comte de Vichy-Chamron. Her alleged father then married the comtesse's daughter, and Julie was raised as governess

---

romantisme (Paris: Perrin, 2003).

33 Annie K. Smart, *Citoyennes: Women and the Ideal of Citizenship in Eighteenth-Century France* (Newark, DE: University of Delaware, 2011).
34 Neil Jeffares, *Dictionary of Pastellists Before 1800* (London: Unicorn Press, 2006).
35 Caroline Moorehead, *Dancing to the Precipice: The Life of Lucie de la Tour du Pin, Eyewitness to an Era* (New York: HarperCollins, 2009).

to her nephews and nieces, who may also have been her half-siblings. Her aunt, du Deffand, appointed her as reader in her salon when her sight began to fail, an arrangement lasting from 1754–1763, when du Deffand discovered that Lespinasse was receiving salon guests early. Lespinasse opened her own salon in 1764, receiving her aunt's regular guests alongside Condillac, Condorcet, Diderot, Turgot, and others. She inspired lifelong passion in d'Alembert.[36]

Constance Marie Pipelet or Constance, Princesse de Salm (7 September 1767–13 April 1845), born in Nantes, married Jean-Baptiste Pipelet de Leury in 1789 and settled in Paris, publishing poetry in periodicals. In 1794, her *Sapho, tragédie mêlée de chants* was staged in Paris. In 1795, Pipelet was the first woman admitted to the Lycée des arts, participating in the 1797 *Querelle des femmes auteurs*. She divorced in 1799. Pipelet published epistles, cantatas, and ballads. In 1803, she married Joseph, Count zu Salm-Reifferscheidt-Dyck, who took the title of prince in 1816; she published thereafter as the Princesse de Salm. The couple lived in Germany and in Paris, where Salm held a salon featuring Dumas, Stendhal, and others.[37]

Marie-Françoise Raoul [or **Fanny Raoul**] (19 December 1771– 9 December 1833), born in Saint-Pol-de-Léon, lost her mother in childbirth. Moving to Paris as a young woman, she frequented the salons of Thérésa Tallien, Juliette Récamier, and Germaine de Staël. With the support of Constance de Salm, she published *Opinion d'une femme sur les femmes* in 1801. In 1813, Raoul published the novel *Flaminie ou les erreurs d'une femme sensible* and her *Fragments philosophiques et littéraires*. Three brochures followed, including one on the *Charte constitutionnelle* in 1814. In 1814–1815, Raoul edited and published a liberal periodical, *Le Véridique*, which she may have largely written herself.[38]

Claire Élisabeth Jeanne de Vergennes, Comtesse de Rémusat, known as **Claire de Rémusat** (5 January 1780–16 December 1821), daughter of a director of taxes, lost father and grandfather to the guillotine on the same day. In 1796, she married Auguste Laurent de Rémusat, a family friend and widower. In 1802, aged twenty-two, she was chosen by Madame

---

36 Pierre E. Richard, *Lettres et papiers de famille: Madame du Deffand, Julie de Lespinasse* (Paris: Classiques Garnier, 2022).
37 Béatrice Didier et al., eds. *Dictionnaire universel des créatrices* (2013).
38 Geneviève Fraisse, *Muse de la raison: la démocratie exclusive et la différence des sexes* (Aix-en-Provence: Alinéa, 1989).

Bonaparte, wife of the First Consul, as lady of honor at the Tuileries. Her husband was named a prefect of the palace. Both rose at court over the years, and the couple hosted a successful salon. Talleyrand penned her portrait in 1811. Rémusat left memoirs and an important correspondence, notably with her husband and with her son Charles.[39]

Marie-Jeanne Riccoboni, née **Laboras de Mézières** (25 October 1713–7 December 1792) was born in Paris. Her father abandoned them. Housed in a convent and destined to stay there, Marie-Jeanne persuaded her mother to take her back at fourteen. In 1734, she married Antoine François Riccoboni, son of the director of the Comédie italienne. They separated in 1761. Riccoboni first performed in the Comédie italienne in 1734. She frequented the salon of d'Holbach and possibly of Helvétius, befriending Marivaux, Adam Smith, and David Hume, but later withdrew from salon life. After 1757, Riccoboni wrote ten novels. She translated five English plays and wrote one herself. She died in poverty in 1792.[40]

Antoinette Henriette Clémence Robert (6 December 1797–1 December 1872), born in Mâcon, published her first poem, on the birth of the Duc de Bordeaux, in 1820. Robert moved to Paris at her father's death in 1830. Here, from 1844–1864, she published popular historical novels influenced by Eugène Sue on republican and socialist themes; in 1860, she also co-edited the memoirs of Giuseppe Garibaldi.[41]

Marie Jeanne 'Manon' Roland de la Platière, née **Phlipon** (17 March 1754–8 November 1793), born in Paris, was placed with a wet nurse until the age of two. At eleven, she was put in a convent. She met the economist Jean Marie Roland de La Platière in 1776, and they married in 1780. Roland joined the Club des Jacobins in 1791; her salon welcomed Brissot, Pétion, Robespierre, and others. Jean Marie became Minister of the Interior in 1792, and Roland played a major role in his ministry. Attacks from the Montagne led her husband to resign. At the arrest of the Girondins, Roland was arrested and imprisoned; she appeared before the Tribunal six days after Gouges. Her husband learned of her

---

39 Paul de Rémusat, ed. *Mémoires de Madame de Rémusat, 1802–1808*, 3 vols (Paris: Calmann Levy, 1880).
40 Jan Herman, Kris Peeters, and Paul Pelckmans, eds. *Mme Riccoboni, romancière, épistolière, traductrice* (Louvain: Éditions Peeters, 2007).
41 Laure Adler, *À l'aube du féminisme: les premières journalistes (1830–1850)* (Paris: Payot, 1979)

death two days later and committed suicide.⁴²

Amantine Lucile Aurore Dupin de Francueil, Baronne Dudevant [or **George Sand**] (1 July 1804–8 June 1876), born in Paris, wrote over seventy novels and fifty volumes of tales, plays, and political tracts. In 1822, she married François Casimir Dudevant. She moved to Paris in 1831, where she caused scandal: masculine dress, a male pseudonym. Famous by 1832, Sand began a liaison with Mérimée. In 1833, she met Marie Dorval and Musset. Her liaison with Chopin began in 1838; it lasted ten years. At Nohant, she welcomed Liszt, Chopin, d'Agoult, Balzac, Flaubert, and Delacroix. Lamennais, Pierre Leroux, and Louis Blanc helped shape her move toward socialism; Sand inspired Ledru-Rollin and helped found three newspapers. She also wrote autobiography—*Histoire de ma vie*, 1855.⁴³

Virginie de Senancour, née **Agathe Eulalie Ursule Pivert de Sénancourt** (8 September 1791–11 March 1876), born in Fribourg, began her writing career in 1814 with articles in the *Mercure de France*. She contributed to the *Gazette de France*, the *Diable boiteux*, the *Bonhomme Richard*, and other periodicals, in 1820–1835. Senancour also published short stories and novels from 1820–1827, largely comic and satirical, and the *Réplique à un mal avisé* in 1858.⁴⁴

Adélaïde-Emilie [or **Émilie-Adélaïde**] **Filleul, Marquise de Souza-Botelho** (14 May 1761–19 April 1836), born in Paris, was perhaps the daughter of Louis XV. When her mother died in 1767, Adélaïde was put in a convent, leaving it in 1779 to marry Charles François, Comte de Flahaut de la Billarderie. Talleyrand presided at her salon from 1783–1792; they had a son in 1785. The salon drew Gouverneur Morris, Lavoisier, Condorcet, d'Holbach, Suard, and Marmontel. During the Terror, Flahaut left her husband for London. He was guillotined that year. In 1794, she published *Adèle de Sénange*. In Hamburg, she met Dom José Maria de Sousa Botelho Mourão e Vasconcelos. De Souza returned to France in 1797, publishing *Émilie et Alphonse* in 1799 and *Charles et Marie* in 1802, the year she

---

42 Siân Reynolds, *Marriage & Revolution. Monsieur and Madame Roland* (Oxford: Oxford University Press, 2012).
43 Elizabeth Harlan, *George Sand* (New Haven, CT: Yale University Press, 2004).
44 Philippe Gariel, *Deux Études chinoises: Senancour et sa fille Eulalie; Les leçons du voyage extraordinaire d'un jeune Chinois* (Fribourg: Imprimerie de l'Œuvre de Saint-Paul, 1933).

remarried.⁴⁵

Anne-Louise-Germaine Necker, Baronne de Staël-Holstein, known as **Germaine de Staël** (22 April 1766–14 July 1817) was born in Paris, daughter of Jacques Necker, minister of Finance for Louis XVI, and Suzanne Necker, in whose salon she met Buffon, Grimm, Gibbon, and Raynal. In 1786, she married Erik Magnus, Baron Staël von Holstein. Staël found fame with her *Lettres sur les ouvrages et le caractère de Jean-Jacques Rousseau*, 1788. Her lover Narbonne was Minister for War in 1791–1792. She left Paris in 1792, returning as a republican in 1795. Exiled by Bonaparte in 1803, Staël continued to publish with European success: the novels *Delphine*, 1802, and *Corinne ou l'Italie*, 1807, and the treatise *De l'Allemagne*, 1810/1813. Her home became a meeting-place for Europe's Romantics, from A.W. Schlegel to Byron, and her great love, Benjamin Constant. Staël also wrote a history of the French Revolution, 1818.⁴⁶

Flore Célestine Thérèse Henriette Tristán y Moscoso [or **Flora Tristan**] (7 April 1803–14 November 1844), born in Paris, was the daughter of a Peruvian aristocrat who died in 1807; the family's home was seized by the state. Hardship helped precipitate Flora's own marriage at seventeen to André Chazal, a mediocre and violent man. Flora escaped in 1825 while pregnant with Aline, future mother of Paul Gauguin. When her family sided with Chazal, Flora left for Peru, where her uncle granted her one fifth of the estate. Flora published *Pérégrinations d'une paria* in 1838. Meanwhile, Chazal abducted Aline. Released from prison, he punctured Flora's lung with a pistol shot and returned to prison for twenty years. Flora committed herself to organizing the working classes, publishing *L'Union ouvrière* in 1843.⁴⁷

Marie Louise Élisabeth Vigée Le Brun (16 April 1755–30 March 1842), born in Paris, was given to a wet nurse until she was six, then put in a convent until 1766. In 1776, she married Jean Baptiste Pierre Lebrun and was admitted to paint for the court of Louis XVI. Her portraits sold

---

45 André de Maricourt, *Madame de Souza et sa famille. Les Marigny, les Flahaut, Auguste de Morny (1761–1836)* (Paris: Émile-Paul, 1907).
46 John Claiborne Isbell, *Staël, Romanticism and Revolution. The Life and Times of the First European* (Cambridge: Cambridge University Press, 2023).
47 Stéphane Michaud, *Flora Tristan: La paria et son rêve* (Paris: Sorbonne nouvelle, 2003).

for 12,000 francs, of which she saw just six, the rest pocketed by her husband. Vigée Le Brun painted mainly portraits. In 1789, a *sans-culotte* crowd sacked her home; Vigée Le Brun fled the capital with twenty francs, leaving a million to her husband. She toured Europe's absolutist courts in triumph. Finding Napoleonic France unpleasant, Vigée Le Brun went to England for three years, meeting Byron, Benjamin West, and Lady Hamilton.[48]

---

48   Françoise Pitt-Rivers, *Madame Vigée Le Brun* (Paris: Gallimard, 2001).

3. Writers from German Lands

German history, 1776–1848, can be divided somewhat neatly in two: the last three decades of the Holy Roman Empire, followed in 1806 by Francis II's abdication and then the remapping of the entire region after 1815 as the German Confederation. The term "German Lands" reflects the fact that Germany, as much as Italy, was a geographical concept prior to Bismarck's work to create a unified Prussian state after 1862. But like Italy, indeed like almost every national territory retraced in this volume, German lands were also unified by language, and indeed, the German national tradition has recovered thirty-one women writing and publishing in German for the period 1776–1848, a number surpassed only by writers speaking French and English.

Germany (31 writers)

Annette von Droste-Hülshoff

Die Judenbuche. Ein Sittengemälde aus dem gebirgigten Westfalen (1842)

> Friedrich Mergel, geboren 1738, war der einzige Sohn eines sogenannten Halbmeiers oder Grundeigentümers geringerer Klasse im Dorfe B., das, so schlecht gebaut und rauchig es sein mag, doch das Auge jedes Reisenden fesselt durch die überaus malerische Schönheit seiner Lage in der grünen Waldschlucht eines bedeutenden und geschichtlich merkwürdigen Gebirges. Das Ländchen, dem es angehörte, war damals einer jener abgeschlossenen Erdwinkel ohne Fabriken und Handel, ohne Heerstraßen, wo noch ein fremdes Gesicht Aufsehen erregte, und eine Reise von dreißig Meilen selbst den Vornehmeren zum Ulysses seiner Gegend machte—kurz, ein Fleck, wie es deren sonst so viele in Deutschland gab, mit all den Mängeln und Tugenden, all der Originalität und Beschränktheit, wie sie nur in solchen Zuständen gedeihen. Unter höchst einfachen und häufig unzulänglichen Gesetzen waren die Begriffe

der Einwohner von Recht und Unrecht einigermaßen in Verwirrung geraten, oder vielmehr, es hatte sich neben dem gesetzlichen ein zweites Recht gebildet, ein Recht der öffentlichen Meinung, der Gewohnheit und der durch Vernachlässigung entstandenen Verjährung. Die Gutsbesitzer, denen die niedere Gerichtsbarkeit zustand, straften und belohnten nach ihrer in den meisten Fällen redlichen Einsicht; der Untergebene tat, was ihm ausführbar und mit einem etwas weiten Gewissen verträglich schien, und nur dem Verlierenden fiel es zuweilen ein, in alten staubigten Urkunden nachzuschlagen.—Es ist schwer, jene Zeit unparteiisch ins Auge zu fassen; sie ist seit ihrem Verschwinden entweder hochmütig getadelt oder albern gelobt worden, da den, der sie erlebte, zu viel teure Erinnerungen blenden und der Spätergeborene sie nicht begreift. So viel darf man indessen behaupten, daß die Form schwächer, der Kern fester, Vergehen häufiger, Gewissenlosigkeit seltener waren. Denn wer nach seiner Überzeugung handelt, und sei sie noch so mangelhaft, kann nie ganz zu Grunde gehen, wogegen nichts seelentötender wirkt, als gegen das innere Rechtsgefühl das äußere Recht in Anspruch nehmen.[1]

Friedrich Mergel, born in 1738, was the only son of a so-called Halbmeier or lower-class landowner in the village of B., which, poorly built and smoky as it may be, still catches the eye of every traveler by the extremely picturesque beauty of its location in the green forest gorge of an important and historically remarkable mountain range. The little territory to which it belonged was, at that time, one of those isolated corners of the earth without factories or trade, without military roads, where a foreign face still caused a stir and a journey of thirty leagues made even the most distinguished people the Ulysses of their region—in short, a spot like so many others in Germany, with all the shortcomings and virtues, all the originality and limitations that only thrive in such conditions. Under extremely simple and often inadequate laws, the inhabitants' concepts of right and wrong had become somewhat confused, or rather, a second law had formed in addition to the legal one, a law of public opinion, custom and the statute of limitations arising from neglect. The landowners, to whom jurisdiction over the lower courts was given, punished and rewarded according to their honest understanding in most cases; those subject to them did what seemed feasible and acceptable to them with a somewhat broad conscience, and only the loser sometimes thought of looking up old, dusty documents.—It is difficult to look at that time impartially; since its disappearance it has either been arrogantly blamed or foolishly praised, because those who experienced it are blinded by too many dear memories and those born later do not understand them. However, one can say that the form was weaker, the core was stronger, offenses were more frequent, and lack of conscience was rarer.

---

1 Annette von Droste-Hülsoff, *Die Judenbuche. Ein Sittengemälde aus dem gebirgten Westfalen* [The Jews' Tree. A Painting of Customs from the Hills of Westphalia], ed. Walter Huge (Ditzingen: Reclam, 2014), pp. 3–4.

For anyone who acts according to his conviction, no matter how flawed it may be, can never completely perish, and nothing is more soul-killing than invoking external law against the inner sense of justice.[2]

German writing in the mid-nineteenth century saw the flowering of a characteristic genre, the *Novelle*. Formally, it is a long short story; typically, its world is realistic or believable, though often with a window on the supernatural. That is the case in Droste-Hülshoff's famous example of the genre, *Die Judenbuche* or *The Jews' Tree*, 1842, a beautifully written meditation on justice and the law. The *Novelle* is based on a true story, published by Droste-Hülshoff's uncle in 1818: in 1783, a man on her grandfather's Westphalian lands had murdered a Jewish man, fled, spent years in Algerian slavery, then returned in 1805 and hanged himself (p. 68). Droste-Hülshoff chooses to push these events back two decades, and she builds the beech tree of her title into an emblem of fate or almost magical justice: the Jew's body is found beneath the beech tree, and on it, twenty-eight years later, the murderer hangs himself. The short *Novelle* contains one line of Hebrew, carved into the tree after the murder by the area's Jewish community: "When you approach this place, it will befall you as you did me" (pp. 46, 58). One may think of the German Romantic *Schicksalstragödie* or tragedy of fate exemplified by Zacharias Werner's *Der 24. Februar*, 1810, in which the element of the fantastic is more clearly foregrounded.

Droste-Hülshoff's opening paragraph follows a short prefatory poem. We begin in 1738—a century in the past—and the tale ends in 1788, a year before the seismic event that was the Fall of the Bastille, within a Holy Roman Empire still defined by its *Kleinstaaterei*: German lands had been splintered since the 1648 Peace of Westphalia into over 300 separate principalities. This *Novelle*, for instance, takes place in a hilly and relentlessly Catholic setting, though Catholic Westphalia is in largely flat and Protestant North Germany. The two highest peaks in Westphalia are just over 2,760 feet high. Droste-Hülshoff prefers local color to painting with a broad brush; but if local color is a Romantic preoccupation, as is her contrast of inner spirit with external law, Droste-Hülshoff's emphasis on how laws affect social norms directly echoes Charles de Montesquieu's *De l'esprit des lois* of 1748. The entire criminal

---

2   Translation reviewed by Roger Paulin.

narrative in fact takes place in a setting where forest laws are routinely broken, with the state either impotent or complicit.

The opening paragraph unfolds elegantly. We move from the birth of Friedrich Mergel, the murderer's father, to his village, to its picturesque setting (a *Waldschlucht* somewhat akin to that of Carl Maria von Weber's 1819 *Der Freischütz*), to the laws and customs that governed the area in that vanished age. People, it appears, are anchored both in topography and in social norms: Droste-Hülshoff's main characters thus have individual traits that define them, even from childhood, but nurture plays an equal part in their development.

The *Novelle* is informed by the Catholic faith: crosses, rosaries, the Hail Mary, confession. The murderer returns (and dies) because he does not want to end his days among heretics in nearby Holland; meanwhile his mother, like the villagers, is casually antisemitic (p. 10). The tale presents as gospel the reported deathbed confession of another Jew to the murder (p. 47), before the conclusion posits that that was a convenient fiction; indeed, justice comes not from any of the murderer's Catholic compatriots, but from the beech tree the region's wronged Jews carved anathema into. The narrator here is limited, compiling data to the best of their ability, which makes for a subtle story. But what of the victim? He is barely seen, though his wife makes an appearance. The justice he receives is strangely impersonal, in keeping perhaps with the word 'dog' (*Hund*) thrown in his direction and then reused by the murderer to describe how his Turkish captors viewed Christians. The three Abrahamic religions coexist here in mutual incomprehension and dislike, a world far removed from Gotthold Ephraim Lessing's enlightened dream of tolerance in *Nathan der Weise*, 1783. Nor, amid this wealth of context, is any context provided as to why Droste-Hülshoff's victim might have become a moneylender. His Jewish universe, in short, remains occluded in the *Novelle*—a glaring lacuna in her narrator's storytelling, and resonant today.

Bettina von Arnim, née **Elisabeth Catharina Ludovica Magdalena Brentano** (4 April 1785–20 January 1859), born in Frankfurt-am-Main, was the granddaughter of Sophie von La Roche and the sister of the poet Clemens Brentano. Bettina knew Karoline von Günderrode before the latter's suicide in 1806 and published their fictionalized correspondence in 1840. From 1806–1808, she helped her brother and Achim von Arnim collect the songs in *Des Knaben Wunderhorn*. She met Goethe in 1807, a friendship he ended somewhat acrimoniously in 1811; in 1835, she published their fictionalized correspondence as *Goethes Briefwechsel mit einem Kinde*. She met Beethoven in 1810, later publishing a fictitious letter from him. She married Arnim in 1811 and published some few art songs before his death in 1831, when she resumed publishing, including social criticism.[3]

Charlotte Birch-Pfeiffer (23 June 1800–25 August 1868), born in Stuttgart, made her stage debut in 1813, appearing across Germany from 1818–1826. In 1825, she married Christian Andreas Birch. From 1827–1839, she directed the Theater an der Wien, then the Stadttheater in Zürich from 1837–1842, moving to Berlin after 1844. She wrote over 100 plays and libretti, later collected, along with three volumes of tales in 1863–1865, specializing in adapting popular novels for the stage: Wilkie Collins, Victor Hugo, George Sand, Charlotte Brontë.[4]

Helmina von Chézy, née **Wilhelmine Christiane von Klencke** (26 January 1783–28 January 1856), born in Berlin, married in 1799, then divorced in 1800 and moved to Paris, editing her *Französische Miszellen* from 1803–1807. Dorothea Schlegel there introduced her to Antoine-Léonard de Chézy, whom she married in 1805. Around 1810, Chézy parted from her husband and had a brief liaison with Adalbert von Chamisso, with whom she worked for a time on translating Staël's *De l'Allemagne*. In Germany after 1810, Chézy moved to Dresden in 1817, writing the libretto for Carl Maria von Weber's *Euryanthe*. In 1823, Franz Schubert wrote the music for her play *Rosamunde*; Chézy moved to Vienna, growing close to Beethoven. She published extensively from 1804–1833. Nearly blind in later years, Chézy retired to Geneva after 1848.[5]

Anna Elisabeth "Annette" Franziska Adolphine Wilhelmine Louise Maria, Baroness von Droste zu Hülshoff, known as **Annette von Droste-Hülshoff** (10 January 1797–25 May 1848), born in the Hülshoff chateau in Westphalia, gave her first singing concert in 1820, later composing seventy-four *lieder* for voice and piano. Corresponding with

---

3   Helmut Hirsch, *Bettine von Arnim*, 6th edition (Hamburg: Rowohlt,1987).
4   Katharina M. Wilson, ed. *An Encyclopedia of Continental Women Writers*, 2 vols (New York & London: Garland Publishing, 1991).
5   Ibid..

the brothers Grimm, A.W. Schlegel, and Clara and Robert Schumann, Droste-Hülshoff published books of poems in 1838 and 1844, *Die Judenbuche* in 1842, and a poem cycle *Das geistliche Jahr*, 1830–1840. She retired to Lake Constance near her sister and mother. Droste-Hülshoff was discovered as a composer posthumously in 1877, though Robert Schumann had set one of her poems to music.[6]

Magdalene Philippine Engelhard, née **Gatterer** (21 October 1756– 28 September 1831), born in Nuremberg, was one of the five Göttingen University *Universitätsmamsellen*, along with Meta Forkel-Liebeskind, Caroline Schelling, Therese Huber, and Dorothea Schlözer. Gatterer published occasional pieces in the *Göttinger Musenalmanach* and elsewhere from 1781–1787, a book of poems in 1821, and a translation of Béranger in 1830. Her correspondence with the poet Gottfried August Bürger appeared posthumously.[7]

Caroline Auguste Fischer, née **Venturini** (9 August 1764–26 May 1842), born in Brunswick, married Cristoph Johann Rudolph Christiani before 1791, moving to Copenhagen with him by 1793, where she met Jens Immanuel Baggesen. The couple divorced in 1801 and she moved to Dresden, marrying Christian August Fischer in 1808 and divorcing in 1809. Fischer published her first novel in 1801, but after 1820, hardship meant less time for writing: she ran a reform school in Heidelberg and sold books in Frankfurt, where she died penniless in 1842. Her novels called for equality and women's right to independence: *Gustavs Verirrungen*, 1801; the anonymous *Die Honigmonathe*, 1802–1804; *Der Günstling*, 1809; *William der Neger*, 1819.[8]

Sophie Dorothea Margarete "Meta" Forkel-Liebeskind (22 February 1765–1853), born in Göttingen, was one of the five Göttingen *Universitätsmamsellen*, along with Philippine Gatterer, Caroline Schelling, Therese Huber, and Dorothea Schlözer. She was a writer and translator.[9]

Karoline Friederike Louise Maximiliane von Günderrode [or

---

6   Clemens Heselhaus, *Annette von Droste-Hülshoff. Werk und Leben* (Düsseldorf: Bagel, 1971).
7   Ruth P. Dawson, *The Contested Quill. Literature by Women in Germany 1770–1800* (Newark, DE: University of Delaware Press, 2002).
8   Clementine Kügler, *Caroline Auguste Fischer (1764–1842). Eine Werkbiographie*, Diss. (Berlin: Freie Universität Berlin, 1989).
9   Eckart Kleßmann, *Universitätsmamsellen. Fünf aufgeklärte Frauen zwischen Rokoko, Revolution und Romantik* (Frankfurt am Main: Eichborn, 2008).

Tian] (11 February 1780–26 July 1806), born in Karlsruhe, lost her father aged six, moving to Frankfurt in 1797. There, she met the Brentanos and Friedrich Carl von Savigny, her first love. Günderrode published her first work, *Gedichte und Phantasien*, in 1804, combining poems and a philosophical text. Her *Geschichte eines Braminen* followed in 1805, her *Nikator. Eine dramatische Skizze* in 1806. In 1804, Günderrode met Georg Friedrich Creuzer, married and ten years older, who introduced her to Indian civilization. In 1806, he informed her that he would not leave his wife, and Günderrode committed suicide. Her friend Bettina von Arnim published their correspondence in 1840 as an epistolary novel. Günderrode's collected works appeared in 1920.[10]

Ida, Countess von Hahn-Hahn (22 June 1805–12 January 1880), born in Tressow, married her cousin Friedrich Wilhelm Adolph Graf von Hahn in 1826. They divorced in 1829, and she lived unmarried with Baron Adolf von Bystram until 1849, defying convention. After his death and the 1848 revolutions, Hahn-Hahn embraced Catholicism, retiring to a convent in Mainz after 1852. Her novels about female autonomy (*Ulrich* and *Gräfin Faustine*, 1841, *Sigismund Forster*, *Cecil*, and *Sibylle*, 1843–1846) were popular, her later Catholic proselytizing less so. Her collected works appeared in forty-five volumes in 1903–1904.[11]

Luise Hensel (30 March 1798–18 December 1876), born in Linum, moved with her family to Berlin at her father's death in 1809. Around 1816, she met Clemens Brentano, whom she influenced; Wilhelm Müller's love for her may be reflected in the two song cycles of his that Schubert set to music, *Winterreise* and *Die schöne Müllerin*. In 1818, she joined the Catholic Church, taking a vow of virginity in 1820. In 1821–1823, she taught the widow of the poet Count Friedrich Leopold zu Stolberg, moving to Aachen in 1827, then Berlin and Paderborn after 1833. Her *Gedichte* appeared in 1858, her *Lieder* in 1869.[12]

Henriette Julie Herz, née **de Lemos** (5 September 1764–22 October 1847), born in Berlin, was descended from a Portuguese Jewish family and shared tutors with Moses Mendelssohn's daughters. At fifteen, she

---

10 Doris Hopp, *Karoline von Günderrode* (Frankfurt am Main: Freies Deutsches Hochstift, 2006).
11 Carol Diethe, *Towards Emancipation: German Women Writers of the Nineteenth Century* (New York: Berghahn Books, 1998).
12 Barbara Stambolis, *Luise Hensel (1798–1876). Frauenleben in historischen Umbruchszeiten* (Cologne: SH-Verlag, 1999).

married Markus Herz, a physician seventeen years her senior. After a few years, their salon split in two, Markus hosting a science salon and Henriette, a literary one. Her circle included Jean Paul, Friedrich Schiller, Mirabeau, Friedrich Rückert, Barthold Georg Niebuhr, Johannes von Müller, Friedrich von Gentz, Madame de Genlis, Dorothea and Friedrich Schlegel, and Wilhelm von Humboldt. Alexander von Humboldt visited and studied Hebrew with her. Friedrich Schleiermacher, a frequent guest, encouraged Henriette's conversion to Protestantism after her husband's death.[13]

Therese Huber (7 May 1764–15 June 1829), born in Göttingen to the classical philologist Christian Gottlob Heyne, was one of the five Göttingen *Universitätsmamsellen*. She married traveler and ethnologist Georg Forster in 1785. He left for Paris in 1792 and Forster moved with her lover Ludwig Ferdinand Huber to Neuchâtel. Georg died in 1794 and the Hubers married, though Ludwig died in 1804. Huber wrote novels, novellas, and travel journals, at first under Forster's name; she also edited the *Morgenblatt für gebildete Stände*, translated, and composed essays. She wrote over 4,500 letters and edited the works of both her husbands. Her novel *Abentheuer auf einer Reise nach Neu-Holland*, drawing on Georg's travels, appeared in 1793–1794.[14]

Anna Louisa Karsch (1 December 1722–12 October 1791), born on a dairy farm in Hammer, Silesia, was hit as a child for her *Lesesucht*, her reading compulsion. In 1738, she married a weaver, winning the first divorce in Prussia in 1745. Penniless, she married a tailor, Karsch, who moved them to Fraustadt. Here, Karsch began composing occasional poems for celebrations, appearing in the Silesian press. A Prussian general took her to Berlin in 1761 and she visited the salons, meeting Johann Wilhelm Ludwig Gleim, who published two volumes of her poetry in 1764–1772. Frederick II gave her a pension; Friedrich Wilhelm II had a house built for her. Helmina von Chézy was her granddaughter.[15]

Johanna Kinkel, née **Maria Johanna Mockel** (8 July 1810–15 November 1858), born in Bonn, composed her first piece of music in 1829; it was published in 1838. In Berlin, she continued composing,

---

13 Hertz, Deborah, *Jewish High Society in Old Regime Berlin* (New Haven and London: Yale University Press, 1988).
14 Katharina M. Wilson, ed., *An Encyclopedia of Continental Women Writers* (1991).
15 Ibid.

attending salons and making friends: Bettina von Arnim, Fanny Mendelssohn Hensel. In 1832, she married the abusive Johann Paul Matthieux; they divorced in 1840. In 1843, she married Gottfried Kinkel. Following the 1848 revolutions, Kinkel fled to London. She was found dead in her garden in 1858; suicide was suspected but never proven. Kinkel reviewed music for the *Bonner Zeitung* that she and her husband edited; her autobiographical novel, *Hans Ibeles in London*, appeared in 1860. She also composed for the *Maikäfer* group of poets she directed, 1840–1848.[16]

Caroline Philippine von Briest [or **Caroline de la Motte Fouqué**] (7 October 1773–20 July 1831), born in Nennhausen, married Friedrich Ehrenreich Adolf Ludwig Rochus von Rochow, whom she divorced in 1798. He committed suicide in 1799. She then married the writer Friedrich de La Motte Fouqué in 1803. She published about twenty novels and sixty short stories between 1806–1829, as well as poems, fairy tales, essays, travelogues, romances, and comedies.[17]

Marie Sophie von La Roche, née **Gutermann von Gutershofen** (6 December 1730–18 February 1807), born in Kaufbeuren, became engaged to Christoph Martin Wieland but married Georg Michael Anton Frank Maria von La Roche, to Wieland's surprise. From 1761–1768, Sophie was a lady of the court at her father-in-law's palace near Biberach, with a large library. Moving to Bönningheim, she composed the sentimental novel *Geschichte des Fräuleins von Sternheim*, published by Wieland in 1771. That year, the couple moved again to Koblenz: their salon hosted Heinse, Lavater, and Jacobi. Georg was fired in 1780 and died in 1788; French occupation of the Rhineland ended her widow's pension. La Roche then relied on her writing for income, traveling in Europe and the British Isles. She was grandmother to the Brentanos.[18]

Fanny Lewald (21 March 1811–5 August 1889), born in Königsberg, converted from Judaism to Christianity for a marriage canceled when the fiancé died. She traveled in the German Confederation, France, and Italy, first publishing a letter in her cousin's Stuttgart periodical, *Europa*, then

---

16 Monica Klaus, *Johanna Kinkel. Romantik und Revolution*. (Cologne: Böhlau, 2008).
17 Petra Kabus, ed., *Caroline de la Motte Fouqué: Ausgewählte Werke* (Hildesheim: Olms, 2003–2005).
18 Barbara Becker-Cantarino, *Meine Liebe zu Büchern. Sophie von La Roche als professionelle Schriftstellerin* (Heidelberg: Universitätsverlag Winter, 2008).

her first novel there in 1841: *Der Stellvertreter*. Lewald settled in Berlin in 1845, marrying Adolf Stahr in 1854 and publishing several novels advocating for women's rights, 1843–1883, alongside two broadsides on the emancipation of women. Her autobiography appeared in 1861–1862. She moved to Dresden at her husband's death in 1876.[19]

Sophie Friederike Mereau, née **Schubart** (27 March 1770–31 October 1806), born in Altenburg, studied Spanish, French, English, and Italian, and in 1791 was the only female student in Johann Gottlieb Fichte's private seminars. She married Karl Mereau in 1793, moving to Jena with him where she met Schiller and published her first novel, *Das Blüthenalter der Empfindung*, but divorced Karl after the death of their first child. In 1800, while editing three literary journals, Mereau published her *Gedichte* [Poems] and wrote another novel, *Amanda und Eduard*. Parts appeared in Schiller's *Die Horen*, with whom she also published poetry. Mereau also translated from French and Italian. In 1802, she resumed a relationship with Clemens Brentano, marrying him in 1803. She died in childbirth in 1806.[20]

Clara Mundt, née **Clara Maria Regina Müller** [or **Luise Mühlbach**] (2 January 1814–26 September 1873), born in Neubrandenburg, married the writer Theodor Mundt in 1839. She wrote historical fiction, on Frederick the Great, on Andreas Hofer, on Napoleon, on the Empress Josephine, on Goethe and Schiller, on Henry VIII, to some contemporary success.[21]

Benedikte Naubert, née **Christiana Benedicta Hebenstreit** (13 September 1756–12 January 1819), born in Leipzig, studied Latin, Greek, English, French and Italian. Naubert anonymously published more than fifty historical novels to considerable praise, publishing a novel a year or more after *Heerfort und Klärchen* in 1779. Several men were suspected as authors. In 1797, she married Lorenz Holderieder; he died in 1800 and she married Johann Georg Naubert. A newspaper revealed her identity in 1817, against her will, and her reviews abruptly became more negative.[22]

---

19 Margaret E. Ward, *Fanny Lewald. Between Rebellion and Renunciation* (New York: Peter Lang, 2006).
20 Kontje, Todd Curtis, *Women, the Novel, and the German Nation, 1771–1871: Domestic Fiction in the Fatherland* (Cambridge: Cambridge University Press, 1998).
21 Cornelia Tönnesen, *Die Vormärz-Autorin Luise Mühlbach. Vom sozialkritischen Frühwerk zum historischen Roman; mit einem Anhang unbekannter Briefe an Gustav Kühne* (Neuss: Ahasvera-Verlag, 1997).
22 Nikolaus Dorsch, ed. *Sich rettend aus der kalten Würklichkeit. Die Briefe Benedikte Nauberts* (Frankfurt am Main: Lang, 1986).

Louise Otto-Peters [or **Otto Stern**] (26 March 1819–13 March 1895), born in Meissen, published several novels, 1843–1887 (*Schloss und Fabrik*, 1846–1847), volumes of poetry and political articles. She wrote two opera libretti. In 1843, she became a staff member for the democratic periodicals *Der Wandelstern* and *Sächsische Vaterlandsblätter*. Her *Frauen-Zeitung*, founded in 1848 specifically for women, resulted in a new law banning women newspaper editors in Saxony. She moved the paper outside Leipzig until it folded in 1853. Otto-Peters then founded *Neue Bahnen* in 1855, which she edited until her death. She became engaged to August Peters in 1849, but his imprisonment delayed the marriage until 1858. In 1865, Otto-Peters co-founded the Allgemeiner Deutscher Frauenverein or General German Women's Association.[23]

Luise von Ploennies, née **Leisler** (7 November 1803–22 January 1872), born in Hanau, married August von Ploennies in 1824. After his death in 1847, she traveled to Belgium for some years, then settling in Darmstadt. She published several volumes of poetry, 1844–1870, and two biblical dramas, *Maria Magdalena*, 1870, and *David*, 1873. Ploennies also published two collections of poems translated from the English, in 1843 and 1863.[24]

Elisabeth Charlotte Constanzia "Elisa" von der Recke (20 May 1754–13 April 1833), born in Schönberg, Duchy of Courland (now Latvia), was forbidden by her grandmother to read books as a child. She married Georg Magnus von der Recke in 1771, divorcing in 1781. In 1787, she published a critical assessment of Cagliostro's visit to Mitau that earned her a lifetime pension from Catherine the Great. Von der Recke traveled across Europe to meet enlightened aristocrats and intellectuals: Nicolai, Klopstock, Gleim, Kant, Hamann, Goethe, Schiller, and others. In 1798, she settled in Dresden, with her companion Christoph August Tiedge from 1804 until her death. Her works include Pietistic poems and memoirs.[25]

---

23 Carol Diethe, *The Life and Work of Germany's Founding Feminist Louise Otto-Peters (1819–1895)* (Lewiston, NY: Edwin Mellen Press, 2002).
24 Gabriele Käfer-Dittmar, *Luise von Ploennies 1803–1872. Annäherung an eine vergessene Dichterin* (Darmstadt: Schlapp, 1999).
25 Valérie Leyh, Adelheid Müller, and Vera Viehöver, eds. *Elisa von der Recke: Aufklärerische Kontexte und lebensweltliche Perspektiven. Germanisch-romanische Monatsschrift. Beiheft 90* (Heidelberg: Universitätsverlag Winter, 2018).

Dorothea Friederike von Schlegel, née **Brendel Mendelssohn** (24 October 1764–3 August 1839), born in Berlin, Moses Mendelssohn's daughter married Simon Veit in 1783. Their son became a Nazarene painter, while the composer Felix Mendelssohn was her nephew. After her 1797 meeting with Friedrich Schlegel, the Veits divorced in 1799. Her salon was frequented by Tieck, Schelling, the Schlegel brothers, and Novalis; Friedrich published her novel *Florentin* anonymously in 1801, and the two moved to Paris from 1802–1804. Dorothea translated Staël's *Corinne ou l'Italie* in 1807. She and Friedrich, married as Protestants, converted to Catholicism in 1808, though still frequenting Rahel Levin's and Henriette Herz's salons. After Friedrich's death in 1829, Dorothea moved from Vienna to Frankfurt-am-Main.[26]

Caroline Schlegel-Schelling, née **Michaelis** (2 September 1763–7 September 1809), born in Göttingen, was one of the five Göttingen *Universitätsmamsellen*. Caroline married Johann Böhmer in 1784. He died in 1788 and Caroline settled in Mainz in 1792. Here, she was friendly with Georg Forster and his wife Therese Huber. In 1793, Prussian troops recaptured Mainz and Caroline was briefly imprisoned. She married A.W. Schlegel in 1796, moving to Jena with him. Caroline is credited with help in her husband's translation of Shakespeare and his 300 reviews for the Jena *Allgemeine Literaturzeitung*, 1796–1799. In 1803, she divorced to marry the philosopher Friedrich Wilhelm Joseph Schelling. The couple moved to Würzburg, then Munich. From 1805–1807, Caroline published several reviews in her name and assisted in her husband's reviews. She maintained an extensive correspondence.[27]

Johanna Schopenhauer, née **Trosiener** (9 July 1766–17 April 1838), born in Danzig (then Poland), knew German, Polish, French, and English by the age of ten. In 1784, she married Heinrich Floris Schopenhauer; their son was the philosopher Arthur Schopenhauer. In 1793, the family moved to Hamburg, then Weimar in 1805 after her husband's death. Her Weimar salon hosted Wieland, the Schlegel brothers, Tieck, and Goethe. Arthur came in 1809, though mother and son never met again after 1814. Schopenhauer was the first German woman to publish books

---

26 Carola Stern, *'Ich möchte mir Flügel wünschen'. Das Leben der Dorothea Schlegel* (Reinbek bei Hamburg: Rowohlt, 1995).
27 Sabine Appel, *Caroline Schlegel-Schelling: Das Wagnis der Freiheit* (Munich: C.H. Beck, 2013).

without a pseudonym; in the 1820s, she was arguably the most famous woman writer in Germany. After her first book, a biography in 1810, Schopenhauer published travelogues, fiction (*Gabriele*, 1819; *Die Tante*, 1823), and a two-volume study of Jan van Eyck in 1822.[28]

Charlotte Albertine Ernestine [or **Charlotta Ernestina Bernadina**] **von Stein**, née **von Schardt** (25 December 1742–6 January 1827), born in Eisenach, moved to Weimar as a child, where she became a lady-in-waiting from 1758 to 1807. In 1764, she married Baron Gottlob Ernst Josias Friedrich von Stein; of their seven children, four daughters died, three sons survived. She met Goethe in 1774; their friendship lasted twelve years, Goethe raising her son Fritz after 1783. The friendship ended when he departed for Italy in 1786 without informing her, though it rekindled in 1800. Stein wrote four plays, one published anonymously but with Schiller's name on the cover: *Die zwey Emilien*, 1800. The others are lost, including her 1794 drama *Dido*, echoing the Goethe affair.[29]

Rahel Antonie Friederike Varnhagen, née **Levin** (19 May 1771–7 March 1833), born in Berlin, became friends with Moses Mendelssohn's daughters, through whom she met Henriette Herz. Her salon hosted the Schlegel brothers, Schelling, Schleiermacher, the Humboldt brothers, La Motte Fouqué, Tieck, Jean Paul, and Gentz. She met Goethe in 1795 and in 1815. After 1806, she lived in Paris, Frankfurt-am-Main, Hamburg, Prague, and Dresden. In 1814, she converted from Judaism to Christianity and married the Prussian diplomat Karl August Varnhagen von Ense in Berlin, joining him in Vienna in 1815, then Karlsruhe, before returning to Berlin in 1819. Varnhagen published essays in the press; her *Denkblätter einer Berlinerin* appeared in 1830, and after her death, her husband edited her 6,000-letter correspondence along with two memorial volumes.[30]

Ottilie Wildermuth, née **Rooschüz** (22 February 1817–12 July 1877), born in Rottenburg am Neckar, married Wilhelm David Wildermuth in 1843. The couple settled in Tübingen, where Wildermuth's salon drew Ludwig Uhland and Karl Mayer. In 1847, she sent her first story to the

---

28 Ulrike Bergmann, *Johanna Schopenhauer. 'Lebe und sei so glücklich als du kannst'*. (Leipzig: Reclam, 2002).
29 Doris Maurer, *Charlotte von Stein. Eine Biographie*, 5th edition (Frankfurt am Main: Insel, 2009).
30 Heidi Thomann Tewarson, *Rahel Levin Varnhagen* (Hamburg: Rowohlt, 1988).

press: *Die alte Jungfer*. Stories, biographies, family books, memoirs of Swabian life, and children's history books followed. In 1870, Wildermuth founded the children's periodical *Jugendgarten*.[31]

Caroline von Wolzogen, née **von Lengefeld** (3 February 1763–11 January 1847), born in Rudolstadt, married Friedrich Wilhelm Ludwig von Beulwitz in 1784. Caroline met Friedrich Schiller in 1785; he married her sister in 1790. Caroline's dramatic fragment *Der leukadische Fels* appeared in 1792, and she began her novel *Agnes von Lilien* in 1793; it featured anonymously in Schiller's *Die Horen* in 1796–1797, amid speculation as to authorship. Caroline's other works appeared much later, notably her life of Schiller in 1830. Caroline had left von Beulwitz in 1794 to marry Wilhelm von Wolzogen, though her family and Schiller disapproved. The couple left Weimar, returning in 1796. In 1802, von Wolzogen was contacted by Germaine de Staël, who had admired her novel. Her final novel, *Cordelia*, appeared in 1840. Von Wolzogen's literary remains appeared in 1849.[32]

Kathinka Zitz-Halein, née **Halein** (4 November 1801–8 March 1877), born in Mainz, lost her mother in 1825 and was given power of attorney to run the family business. After three years as a governess, she returned to Mainz to support her sister. In 1833–1835, she translated three plays by Victor Hugo; in 1837, she married the 1848 revolutionary Dr. Franz Heinrich Zitz, living together for two years. Zitz wrote for the *Mannheimer Abendzeitung* against censorship and in favor of divorce; in 1848, she founded the revolutionary women's Humania Association. Her fictionalized biographies of Goethe, Heine, Rahel Varnhagen, and Byron appeared in 1863–1867.[33]

---

31 Maria Pfadt, *Ottilie Wildermuth. Profile ihrer Kinder- und Jugendliteratur*. Diss. (Ludwigsburg: Pädagogische Hochschule Ludwigsburg, 1994).
32 Jochen Golz, ed. *Caroline von Wolzogen 1763–1847* (Marbach: Deutsche Schillergesellschaft, 1998).
33 Oliver Bock, *Kathinka Zitz-Halein, Leben und Werk—'Nur was das Herz mich lehrt, das hauch' ich aus in Tönen'* (Hamburg: Igel, 2010).

4. Writers from Habsburg Territories

The Austrian Empire came into existence in 1806, when Francis II abdicated as Holy Roman Emperor and proclaimed himself Emperor of Austria in its stead. This moment, brought about by Napoleon's redrawing of Germany's map, permanently recentered Habsburg ambitions away from Germany and toward Italy and Eastern Europe, from Poland to the Balkans. Austria briefly rejoined Germany in 1938, with the *Anschluss*, and has been its modern shape since 1945. The Habsburgs are departed. There is, then, an Austrian national tradition, independent of Germany, featuring just four women writing in German for our period, and other Habsburg territories are also listed here: not the former Austrian Netherlands, nor Italy, nor Poland, but modern Croatia, with three women writers, 1776–1848, Czechia, with one, Hungary, with two, and Slovenia, with zero. There is perhaps no better illustration of the existential risk emergent nationalism posed to the European political order than the Habsburg story, in which a heterogeneous empire speaking at least nine languages fought tooth and nail against reform for decades before its eventual collapse into nation states, many of them still splintering today.

Austria (4 writers)

Ida Laura Pfeiffer (14 October 1797–27 October 1858), born in Vienna, married Dr. Mark Anton Pfeiffer in 1820. In 1842, Pfeiffer traveled to Istanbul and Jerusalem, publishing an account in 1844. In 1845, she traveled to Scandinavia and Iceland, publishing in 1846. She traveled around the world from 1846–1848, visiting South America, Tahiti, China, India, Persia, and Greece, and publishing an account in 1850. In 1851–1855, she began a second round the world trip in Berlin, meeting Alexander von Humboldt, then London, South Africa, Malaysia, Borneo, Sumatra, California, Central and South America, New Orleans and the Great Lakes, meeting Washington Irving and Louis Agassiz. Her account appeared in 1856. Traveling to Madagascar and Mauritius in 1857–1858, Pfeiffer contracted malaria, dying in Vienna. Her account appeared in 1861.[1]

Caroline [or **Karoline**] **Pichler** (7 September 1769–9 July 1843), born in Vienna, met Haydn and was taught by Mozart, along with Latin, French, Italian, and English. In 1796, she married Andreas Pichler, founding a salon frequented by Beethoven, Schubert, Friedrich Schlegel, and Grillparzer. Her *Gleichnisse* appeared in 1800, *Lenore* and *Ruth* in 1804–1805. She moved to historical romance in 1808 with *Agathokles*, publishing for instance *Biblische Idyllen*, 1812, *Die Belagerung Wiens*, 1824, *Die Schweden in Prag*, 1827, and *Henriette von England* in 1832. Pichler's autobiography appeared in 1844. Her complete works fill sixty volumes.[2]

Theresa Pulszky, née **Walter** (7 January 1819–4 September 1866), born in Vienna, married Ferenc Pulszky and moved to London with him in 1845 before they could return to their manor near Pest. Pulszky chronicled the 1848 revolution and her flight to Belgium in her 1850 *Memoirs of a Hungarian Lady*. The couple met Lajos Kossuth in Southampton in 1851, after his refusal of the throne of Hungary, traveling with him to the United States, then London. Pulszky published a book of Hungarian myths and legends in 1852, then an account of her American tour in 1853. She translated Lermontov's *Hero of Our Time* from Russian in 1854.[3]

Sophie Ritter von Scherer, née **Sockl** (5 February 1817–29 May 1876), born in Vienna, married Anton Ritter von Scherer in 1841. In 1848, she published a three-volume educational work, presented as letters opposing the 1848 Revolution but in support of social reform. Two open letters followed in 1848 concerning reforms in the Catholic Church, suggesting for instance the use of the vernacular in the liturgy and the abolition of priestly celibacy.[4]

---

1 Gabriele Habinger, *Eine Wiener Biedermeierdame erobert die Welt. Die Lebensgeschichte der Ida Pfeiffer (1797–1858)* (Vienna: Promedia Verlag, 1997).
2 Donald G. Daviau, ed. *Major Figures of Nineteenth-Century Austrian Literature* (Riverside, CA: Ariadne Press, 1998).
3 Constant Wurzbach, *Biographische Lexikon des Kaiserthums Oesterreich*, 60 vols (Vienna: Kaiserlich-königliche Hof- und Staatsdruckerei, 1856–1891).
4 Constant Wurzbach, *Biographische Lexikon* (1856–1891).

Croatia (3 writers)

Anica Bošković (1714–1804)

"Na čast Prisvetoga Djetešca Jezusa Pjesan"

Sobom dare ponesoše
    Kad Pastiri otidoše,
Poklonit se u veselju
    Porođenu Spasitelju,
Nu njihovi dari njemu
    Priprosti su bili u svemu.
Kralji opeta, kad dodoše,
    Prid noge mu donesoše
Druge u sebi zlamenite
    Izabrane, plemenite,
I s ljubavi primio je
    On jednakom dare oboje.
A ja s huda moga udesa
    Poklonit mu nejmam česa.
Nesvjestan sam tako bio,
    Da sam sasvjem istratio
Sve što imah, sva godišta,
    U ispraznos, i u ništa,
Ali ja ću, kako svoje,
    Poklonit mu srce moje
I ako stečem milos taku,
    Da on primi čast ovaku,
Ne zavidim ni ja veće
    Tad njihove česti i sreće![5]

---

5   Slavica Stojan, *Anica Bošković* (Dubrovnik: Hazu, 1998), p. 251.

Song in Honor of the Holy Child Jesus

They brought gifts with them
    When the Shepherds left,
To bow in great joy
    To the Savior Born.
But their gifts to him
    Proved plain one and all.
The kings again, when they came,
    At his feet they laid
Others more renowned
    The chosen, noble ones,
And with love he received
    All of them equally.
But I in my foul calamity
    Have nothing to offer him.
In my heedless ways
    I completely wasted
All that I had, all years,
    In nothing, and in vain,
But I will, as my own,
    Give him my heart,
And if I gain such grace
    That he receives this honor,
I will not envy them
    Their greater fortune and honor![6]

A look through Bošković's published works reveals that religious poems are not atypical for her. Bošković was active by 1758, the year of her prose work *The Dialogue*, and she died in 1804. Her poems are often undated but fall within this timeframe, which may seem early for a South Slavic publication until one observes that the first Croatian printed book was published in 1483, being the first non-Latin printed missal in Europe. A manuscript in Serbian similarly is recorded as early as the twelfth century. Bošković's contemporary Lukrecija Budmani was also publishing well before 1800, by which time literary Croatian was well established.

---

6   Translation reviewed by Vladislav Beronja.

Like much religious poetry, this piece is not particularly characterized by the period in which it was produced; one must look hard to find in it evidence of revolutionary or Romantic sentiment. Bošković was writing in the aristocratic Republic of Ragusa, which governed the southern Dalmatian coast from 1358–1808, when it was absorbed by the Napoleonic Kingdom of Italy. Bošković died shortly before the republic's pillage by the French and Russians (after 1806) and subsequent dissolution; there is no hint in this poem of the old republic's forthcoming fate. The poem is instead concerned with the relation between the narrator and the Christ Child, contrasting the shepherds and kings who were received equally when visiting Christ's manger in Bethlehem, then turning to the narrator, who is without a gift. Interest quickens here with mention of the narrator's "foul calamity;" all humans are imperfect and sinners, from a Christian perspective, but evidently the narrator has a particular trauma to remember in writing this piece. One may recall at this point Ivan Gundulić's long poem "Suze sina razmetnoga" [Tears of the Prodigal Son] (1622), which stands among the literary achievements of the Ragusan Baroque. Bošković would have been familiar with this work and seems here to be paying homage to it. This information was provided by Vladislav Beronja.

Anica Bošković (3 November or 3 December 1714–13 August 1804), born in Dubrovnik (Republic of Ragusa), was the sister of the scientist and polymath Roger Joseph Boscovich. She wrote a pastoral song and translated from the Italian. Her 1758 work, *The Dialogue*, is the first known literary work by a woman in the literature of Ragusa.[7]

Lukrecija Bogašinović Budmani (26 October 1710–8 June 1784), born in Dubrovnik (Republic of Ragusa), was the daughter of a government clerk banished from Dubrovnik for corruption. In 1752, she married Simone Budmani, who died ten years later. Budmani was a popular poet, though only four works of hers survive as manuscripts.[8]

Dragojla Jarnević [or **Jarnjević**] (4 January 1812–12 March 1875), born in Habsburg Karlovac, was a Croatian poet and teacher who joined the pan-South-Slavic Illyrian Movement in the 1830s, writing on women's rights. She was also an early mountaineer and rock-climber.[9]

---

7   *Književstvo—Theory and History of Women›s Writing in Serbian until 1915.* http://knjizenstvo.etf.bg.ac.rs/en
8   Katharina M. Wilson, Paul Schlueter, and June Schlueter, eds. *Women Writers of Great Britain and Europe: An Encyclopedia* (London: Garland, 1997).
9   Francisca de Haan, Krassimira Daskalova, and Anna Loutfi, eds. *A Biographical*

Czechia (1 writer)

Božena Němcová

Národní báchorky a pověsti (1845)
O zlatém kolovrátku

Jedna chudá vdova měla dvě dcery, dvojčata. Byly si v tváři tak podobny, že je nebylo možná rozeznati. Tím rozdílnější byly ale jejich povahy. Dobrunka byla děvče poslušné, pracovité, přívětivé a rozumné, zkrátka děvče nad obyčej dobré. Zlobohá naproti tomu byla zlá, mstivá, neposlušná, lenivá a hrdá, ba měla všecky nectnosti, které jen vedle sebe býti mohou. A matka přece jen Zlobohu ráda měla, a kde jen mohla, jí nadlehčovala. Bydlely v lese v malé chaloupce, kam člověk málokdy zabloudil, ačkoli to nedaleko města bylo. Aby se Zlobohá něčemu naučila, dovedla ji matka do města do jedné služby, kde se jí dosti dobře vedlo. Dobrunka musela zatím doma malé hospodářství spravovat. Když ráno kozu nakrmila, skromné, ale chutné jídlo přistrojila, sedničku a kuchyňku čistě vymetla a uspořádala, musela ještě, neměla-li právě potřebnější práci před rukama, ke kolovrátku zasednout a pilně přísti. Tenounké její předivo matka potom v městě prodala a začasté z výdělku Zloboze na šaty koupila; ubohá Dobrunka ale z toho nikdy ani za vlas nedostala. Proto však přece matku milovala, a ač od ní za celý den ani vlídného oka neviděla, ani dobrého slova neslyšela, přece ji vždycky bez škaredění a bez odmluvy poslouchala, takže ani Pánbůh od ní reptavého slova neslyšel.[10]

National Gossip and Rumors
About the Golden Wheel

A poor widow had two daughters, twins. Their faces were so similar that it was impossible to tell them apart. But their personalities were all the more different. Dobrunka [Good girl] was an obedient, hard-working, friendly, and reasonable girl, in short, a very good girl. Zlobohá [Nasty girl], on the other hand, was evil, vengeful, disobedient, lazy, and proud, indeed she had all the vices that can only exist side by side. And mother liked Zlobohá after all, and whenever she could, she made it easy for her. They lived in a small cottage in the forest, where one rarely wandered, although it was not far from the city. In order for Zlobohá to learn something, her mother took her to service in the city, where she did quite

---

Dictionary of Women's Movements and Feminisms: Central, Eastern and South Eastern Europe, 19th and 20th Centuries (Budapest: Central European University Press, 2006).

10 Božena Němcová, *Národní báchorky a pověsti* (Prague: Československý spisovatel, 1950), p. 9.

well. For the time being, Dobrunka had to manage a small farm at home. In the morning, when she had fed the goat, prepared a modest but tasty meal, swept, and tidied up the sitting room and the kitchen, she still had to sit down at the spinning wheel and work diligently, unless she had more important work to do. Her mother then sold her thin yarn in the city and often used the earnings to buy Zloboha clothes; but poor Dobrunka never got a hair's breadth from it. But that's why she loved her mother, and even though she didn't see a kind eye or hear a good word from her during the whole day, she always listened to her without nagging and without excuses, so even the Lord God didn't hear a grumbling word from her.[11]

Three things about this text of Němcová's catch the eye at once. First, it is in Czech, some eighty years before Czech independence; second, her collection's title opens with the word "národní" or *national*; and third, this is a folk tale, in the tradition of the elegant Charles Perrault, 1697, or the less elegant Brothers Grimm, 1812–1815. Across nineteenth-century Eastern and Northern Europe, following on eighteenth-century British figures like Bishop Percy or James MacPherson, linguists and compilers repeatedly played a key role in national Romantic movements, and Němcová is no exception. There is a self-deprecating wit about her collection's title, "National Gossip and Rumors," which depends in part for its effect on the author's gender; she here offers us old wives' tales, but these are "national" and thus public creations, they belong simultaneously to public and private spheres and are in that sense androgynous. In those terms, the whole thing has a certain revolutionary thrill.

As for this extract, it is an interesting artifact. Diligent and lazy twins have a long history in folk tales, they are not new; and the opposition Němcová establishes between the twins is somewhat simplistic. But that is not where the extract's interest lies. Instead, it lies in the author's choice of the Grimm brothers over Perrault as a model, her resolutely rustic narrative. The text is a world away from sophisticated Romantic productions like the opening to George Sand's *Indiana*, but it is not the less Romantic for that; the embrace of folk elements is indeed a quintessential Romantic gesture. Furthermore, a hermeneutic pattern emerges in this brief text, starting with the very names—Dobrunka and Zloboha, Goodie and Nasty—which trace an absolute system of meaning behind the day's local occurrences. "There is another world, and it is this

---

11   Translation reviewed by Naděžda Salmhoferová.

one," wrote Paul Éluard, they say, and Dobrunka and Zloboha inhabit a world in which their nature is proclaimed incontrovertibly from birth. This is a world in which cottagers encounter golden wheels; it is the world of fairy tale.[12]

Božena Němcová, née **Barbara Pankel** (4 February 1820–21 January 1862), born in Vienna, grew up in Bohemia. In 1837, aged seventeen, she married Josef Němec. It was an unhappy marriage. Němcová may later have been involved with the poet Václav Bolemir Nebeský, a fellow member of the Czech National Revival Movement. There is also some speculation about her birth. Němcová published two novels in 1855, *Babička* [The Grandmother], inspired by her own childhood with her grandmother, and *Pohorská vesnice* [The Village under the Mountains]. She also published collections of fairy tales and legends, notably *Národní báchorky a pověsti* in 1845.[13]

Hungary (2 writers)

Teréz Karacs (1808–1892)

Történetem

Apám szegény napszámos volt, de nem azon nappalók közül, kik ezreken vásárolják napi örömeiket; hanem azok egyike, kik néhány garasért árulgatják fáradságuk verejtékétől csillogó napjaikat. Mély szegénység vala sorsa, és örök vágyódás jobb után, de mellynek elérhetésére lépéseket sem tehete a csupán taligatolásra, favágásra oktatott pór. Anyám hasonlón szegény kofa volt, de csak czimjénél fogva rokon azokkal, kik e mesterséget szabadon, helypénz-fizetés nélkül űzik; ezek embertársaik boldogságán nyerekednek, anyám csak egy-két garasáru gyümölcsön; s mig ezek pompásan világított palotáikban a városi történeteket és nem történteket szövögeték, addig anyám—fösvényen világító mécsénél gyermeke s férje rongyait foltozgatá, azon elégüléssel dölve az álom karjába, hogy vasárnapra kijavított öltönyt adhat családjára.

Mint látható, szülőim körülményei a leghomályosbak valának, s következőleg sorsom sem igen rózsaszínű.[14]

---

12 The Éluard quotation is apocryphal.
13 Wilma Abeles Iggers, *Women of Prague: Ethnic Diversity and Social Change from the Eighteenth Century to the Present* (Providence, RI: Berghahn Books, 1995).
14 In *Karacs Teréz összes munkái* [All the Works of Teréz Karacs] ed. Ádám Takács, 2

My Story

My father was a poor day laborer, but not one of those day laborers who buy their daily pleasures by the thousands; but one of those who sell their days shining with the sweat of their labor for a few pennies. Deep poverty was his destiny, and an eternal longing for better things, but which he could not even take steps to achieve, being trained only to push a wheelbarrow and cut wood. My mother was similarly a poor costermonger, but only related by name to those who practice this craft freely, without paying local money; these gain from the happiness of their fellow men, my mother only from a fruit for a penny or two; and while these in their magnificently lit palaces were weaving the stories of the city and what had not happened, my mother was patching the rags of her child and husband at the miserly lit candle, contentedly falling into the arms of the dream that she could give her family a repaired suit for Sunday.

As you can see, my parents' circumstances were the gloomiest, and consequently my fate is not very rosy either.[15]

Teréz Karacs's short prose narrative *Történetem*, or *My Story*, opens with a description of the extreme poverty that circumscribed the narrator's childhood. It does this, not by reviewing the family's possessions, in the sort of scene-setting one might find to open a fairy tale, but by precisely indicating the parents' socioeconomic status: day laborer and costermonger, they are perched at the precarious end of proletarian existence, patching their family's rags by a "miserly lit candle." And from this opening scene, two immediate conclusions emerge. First, it matters that we have traveled on from the ringing words "We the people" which open 1787's United States Constitution, indeed from the taking of the Bastille in 1789, a time when "the people" could still mean first and foremost the Third Estate—the urban bourgeoisie. Just as France's bourgeois elected representatives found their actions to some extent determined by the more proletarian *sans-culotte* crowd they admitted to their deliberations—just as the Terror and the great *journées* saw proletarian emergence into the light of national politics—so here, we have come to a popular art in which 'the people' no longer means the bourgeoisie, let alone the minor nobility: it means the proletariat. This new focus on workers and on the economic circumstances that determine their existence becomes common after the 1830s and helps

---

vols (Miskolcz: Lajos Tóth, 1853), I pp. 179–180.
15 Translation reviewed by Márta Csire.

to determine the Europe-wide revolutions of 1848. Second, it matters that the grinding proletarian existence here described evidently in no way characterized the childhood of Teréz Karacs, whose father was an engraver and engineer and no day laborer, and whose mother was an advocate for women's rights. What then are we to make of her *My Story*? We might perhaps begin by stating that the author's heart is clearly with the urban poor, like, say, Flora Tristan in the same period. Does her own economic background matter? Only in that this text is presented as autobiography. But then, fairy tales can begin thus, from Bohemia to Norway. Robespierre, who certainly spoke for the poor, was a lawyer by profession. Karacs may have been invited to tutor royalty; here, in the age of Marx and Hugo, she speaks for the day laborer, and she deserves credit for that. Hers is an art shaped and conditioned by the different revolutions of the age, from 1776 to 1848; it is, in that sense, a quintessentially Romantic production.

Teréz Karacs (18 April 1808–2 October 1892), born in Budapest, was the daughter of an advocate for women's rights and an engraver and engineer. Their Protestant home was a meeting place for intellectuals. After 1822, Karacs published poems, novels, and contributions to literary journals. From 1838 to 1844, she worked as a housekeeper while continuing to write. From 1846 to 1859, Karacs managed a school for girls in Miskolc, publishing a collection of romantic stories in 1853. In 1865–1877, she worked in Budapest as a private teacher, though invited to tutor King Louis Philippe's grandchild. In 1877, Karacs moved to Kiskunhalas, living with relatives. Her memoirs appeared to critical acclaim in the 1880s.[16]

Judit Dukai Takách [or **Malvina**] (1795–1836), born in Duka, was a Hungarian poet. She was known under her pseudonym 'Malvina.'[17]

Slovenia (0 writers)

I have identified zero Slovenian women authors in this period. Further research clearly remains to be done.

---

16 Francisca de Haan et al., eds. *A Biographical Dictionary of Women's Movements* (2006).
17 Vadász Norbert, *Dukai Takács Judit élete és munkái* (Budapest: Franklin-Társ, 1909).

5. Writers from Latin America and the Caribbean

Following on the United States *Declaration of Independence* in 1776, and Napoleon's invasion of the Iberian Peninsula in 1808, Spain and Portugal lost all Latin America to Bolívar's and San Martín's armies in the years 1810–1826. In the Caribbean, Spain retained Cuba and Puerto Rico. A survey of women writers in these emergent nation states, in the period 1776–1848, reveals some disparities: whereas my English sources identify two Argentinian, two Brazilian, and two Chilean women writers, I found just one apiece in Bolivia, Colombia, Cuba, Ecuador, Peru, and Uruguay, and none in Haiti, Paraguay, Venezuela, all Central America, or even Mexico. It seemed unlikely that no Mexican woman picked up a pen in the seven decades bracketing Mexican independence, and further research indeed identified potential leads for Mexican women writers during this period. Finally, let us note that movement across borders within Latin America seems to have been common at the time; writers are thus listed under the national tradition to which their major works belong, but the underlying fluidity of national identification deserves separate mention.

This project began with English-language sources. Subsequent research in Spanish and Portuguese revealed some interesting finds, notably José Domingo Cortés, ed. *Poetisas Americanas: Ramillete Poético del Bello Sexo Hispano-Americano* (Paris: Bouret, 1896), which anthologizes no less than forty-eight Latin American women poets, of whom just one, Gertrudis Gómez de Avellaneda, appears in Commire and Klezmer, *Women in World History: A Biographical Encyclopedia*, 17 vols (1999–2002), and just seven in Foster, *Handbook of Latin American Literature* (1992), whose 2,500-name index lists roughly 200 women. Four of Cortés's forty-eight writers are reviewed in this volume: **Josefa**

Acevedo (Colombia); **Gertrudis Gómez de Avellaneda** (Cuba); **Maria Josefa Mujía** (Bolivia); and **Dolores Veintemilla** (Ecuador). Cortés lists a nationality for each.

Cortés's remaining forty-four writers are **Mercedes Belzu de Dorado** (Bolivia, 1835–1879); **Ema A. Berdier** (Argentina, fictitious); **Leonor Blander** (Colombia); **Isabel Bunch de Cortés** (Colombia, 1845–1921); **Carlota Joaquina Bustamante** (Chile); **Ángela Caamaño de Vivero** (Ecuador, 1830–1879); **Maria Natividad Cortés** (Peru); **Úrsula Céspedes de Escanaverino** (Cuba, 1832–1874); **Ubaldina Dávila de Ponte** (Colombia); **Amelia Dénis de Icaza** (Colombia, 1836–1911); **Edda** (Colombia); **Carolina Freire** or **Freyre** (Peru, 1844–1916); **Elena F. Lince** (Colombia); **Carmen Febres-Cordero de Ballén** (Colombia, 1829–1893); **Julia Gaona** (Argentina); **Carolina García** (Peru); **Justa García Robledo** (Peru); **Dolores Guerrero** (Mexico, 1833–1858); **Dolores Haro** (New Granada); **Juana Lazo de Eléspuru** (Peru, 1819–1905); **Rita Lecumberri** (Ecuador, 1836–1910); **Juana Manso de Noronha** (Argentina, 1819–1875); **Manuela Antonia Márquez** (Peru, 1844–1890); **Mercedes Marín de Solar** (Chile, 1804–1866); **Luisa Molina** (Cuba); **Agripina Montes del Valle** (Colombia, 1844–1912); **Rosario Orrego** (Chile, 1834–1879): **Mercedes Parraga de Quijano** (Colombia); **Josefina Pelliza de Sagasta** (Argentina, 1848–1888); **Luisa Pérez de Zambrana** (Cuba, 1837–1922); **Carmen Pérez de Rodríguez** (Ecuador); **Julia Pérez de Montes de Oca** (Cuba, 1839–1875); **Carmen Potts** (Peru); **Isabel A. Prieto de Landázuri** (Mexico, 1833–1876); **María Ignacia Rojas** (Chile); **Mercedes Salazar de Cámara** (Mexico, fictitious); **Agripina Samper de Ancízar** (Colombia, 1833–1892); **Jésus Sánchez** (Peru); **Leonor Sauri Santisteban** (Peru, 1840–1890); **Mercedes Suárez** (Colombia); **Dolores Sucre y Lavayen** (Ecuador, 1837–1917); **Ester Tapia de Castellanos** (Mexico, 1842–1897); **Mercedes Valdés Mendoza** (Cuba, 1820–1896); **Manuela Varela** (Peru); **Quiteria Varas Marín** (Chile, 1838–1886); and **Manuela Villarán** (Peru, 1840–1888). I have determined dates for just twenty-nine of these anthologized writers; four were born early enough to be active by 1848; two are demonstrably fictitious.

The discovery of Cortés's 1896 *Ramillete* brings some insights to the project at hand. In immediate terms, it adds to our somewhat curt Latin American list from 1776–1848 not forty-eight, but four new women writers: **Juana Laso de Eléspuru** (Peru, 1819–1905), a dramaturge and contributor to the press; **Juana Paula Manso de Noronha** (Argentina, 1819–1875), a writer and newspaper editor who fled to Brazil in 1841; **Mercedes Marín de Solar** (Chile, 1804–1866), a poet and school reformer; and **Mercedes Valdés Mendoza** (Cuba, 1820–1896), a poet and writer. In broader terms, the discovery illustrates a central thesis governing this project: that women wrote across the Eurosphere in the Romantic epoch, and that their unequal presence in an array of global surveys reflects not an unchanging truth but a field yet to be thoroughly investigated.

Schuma Schumaher and Erico Vital Brazil, *Dicionário mulheres do Brasil: de 1500 até a atualidade* (Rio de Janeiro: Jorge Zahar, 2000) is in turn an excellent first resource for Brazil, listing Brazilian women from empresses to coffee-makers, nuns to revolutionaries, including about forty women active between 1776 and 1848, of whom nine are writers. Two, **Beatriz Francisca de Assis Brandão** (1779–1868) and **Nisia Floresta Brasileira Augusta** (1810–1885), are reviewed below. The other seven are **Bárbara Eliodora Guilhiermina da Silveira** (1759–1819), a poet; **Delfina Benigna da Cunha** (1791–1857), a poet; **Margarida Teresa da Silva e Orta** (1711–1793), Portugal's first woman novelist in 1752 (having left Brazil aged six); **Ana Euridice Eufrosina de Barandas** (1806? -), a poet; **Juana Paula Manso de Noronha** (1819–1875), listed above as Argentinian; **Maria Firmina dos Reis** (1825–1917), a novelist (*Úrsula* in 1859 is considered the first novel by a Brazilian woman); and **Violante Atabalipa Ximenes Bivar e Velasco** (1817–1875), a translator of Dumas and newspaper editor.

Our bibliography lists various other Latin American resources. Rogério Budasz, *Opera in the Tropics: Music and Theater in Early Modern Brazil* (Oxford: Oxford University Press, 2019) notes an 1818 eulogy addressed to the public by the opera performer **Estella Joaquina de Moraes** and nothing further by women writers. Sara Beatriz Guardia, *Mujeres que escriben en América Latina* (Lima: Centro de Estudios La Mujer en la Historia de América Latina, CEMHAL, 2007), we were unable to consult, but the *Primer congreso internacional, las mujeres en los procesos de independencia de América Latina* (Lima: CEMHAL, 2014) offers 400 pages of useful essays including on Brazil. **Gloria María Hintze**, *Escritura femenina: diversidad y género en América Latina* (Mendoza: Universidad Nacional de Cuyo, Facultad de Filsofía y Letras, 2004), has articles on **Sor Josefa de los Dolores Peña y Lillo** and **Juana Manuela Gorriti**, both reviewed in this volume, and some general topics such as the female press. Asunción Lavrín and Rosalva Loreto López, *Diálogos espirituales: manuscritos femeninos hispanoamericanos siglos XVI-XIX* (Mexico City: Instituto de Ciencias Sociales y Humanidades de la Benemérita Universidad Autónoma de Puebla, 2006), offers 500 pages of spiritual extracts by Latin American women, 1500–1900. Iona MacIntyre, *Women and Print Culture in Post-Independence Buenos Aires* (Rochester, NY: Tamesis, 2010), reviews six texts, 1820–1830, five written by men and one, the journal *La Aljaba*, by **Petrona Rosende de Sierra** who is reviewed in this volume. Diane E. Marting, *Spanish American Women Writers: A Bio-Bibliographical Source Book* (Westport, CT: Greenwood Press, 1990), has detail on fifty Latin American women writers, of whom only two, **Gertrudis Gómez de Avellaneda** and **Juana Manuela Gorriti**, wrote in the Romantic period. Both are reviewed in this volume. Finally, Sonia Montecino Aguirre, *Mujeres chilenas: fragmentos de una historia* (Santiago: Editorial Catalonia, 2008), offers a 600-page overview including for instance the article "Imágenes y escritura de mujeres en la literatura colonial chilena" (pp. 77–86), which is focused on the period before 1780.

To conclude: our search in Spanish and Portuguese has yielded four new Spanish-language writers, from Peru, from Argentina (though later from Brazil), from Chile, and from Cuba, and seven new Portuguese-language writers, all from Brazil. Brief indices to their biographies are given above. However, compiling our global list of 650 women writers was made possible by imposing strict parameters on the field, those being the initial English-language search terms we applied, since this is after all an English-language study. As our subsequent non-English research has revealed, one may anticipate adding to the list by pursuing further research in a variety of languages represented. We think of the various Slavic languages. But that after all is the point of this book: it is conceived and designed primarily as a spur to further research, in hope that the unequal field it has identified may over time become more equal, and the true shape of women's writing across the field may emerge at last from the legacy of shadow that envelops it.

Argentina (2 writers)

María Guadalupe Cuenca de Moreno (1790–1 September 1854), born in Chuquisaca (now Bolivia), spent her childhood in a convent after her father's death. In 1804, she married the Argentine patriot Mariano Moreno and moved to Buenos Aires. In 1811, some days after her husband's departure for England, she received a box containing black gloves, a black fan, and a mourning veil, though never informed of her husband's death at sea. She wrote him a dozen love letters which were returned to the sender, later published as *Cartas que nunca llegaron* [Letters That Never Arrived]. She died in Buenos Aires.[1]

María Sáez Pérez de Vernet (19 November 1800–20 October 1858), born in Montevideo (now Uruguay), married Luis Vernet in 1819, settling with him in Puerto Luis in the Falkland Islands, where she sang and played the piano, favoring Rossini. Vernet kept a diary, now in the Argentine National Archive, first published in 1989.[2]

Bolivia (1 writer)

María Josefa Mujía (1812–30 July 1888), born in Sucre, grew up during the Bolivian War of Independence. She went blind at age fourteen following her father's death; her brother read to her and transcribed her writing. Despite his promise to keep her works secret, he shared her poem "La Ciega" [The Blind Woman] with a friend, and it appeared in the press in 1850. She may later have participated in a national competition for an inscription for the tomb of Simón Bolívar. In 1854, her brother died, then her mother and two other brothers. She ceased composing until her nephew resumed transcription. Mujía authored over 320 poems, wrote a novel, and translated from French and Italian. Considered independent Bolivia's first woman writer, she is known as "La Alondra del dolor" [The Lark of Pain].[3]

---

1. Enrique Williams Alzaga, *Cartas que nunca llegaron: María Guadalupe Cuenca y la muerte de Mariano Moreno* (Buenos Aires: Emecé Editores, 1967).
2. Seymour Menton, *Latin America's New Historical Novel* (Austin, TX: University of Texas Press, 2010).
3. Gustavo Jordán Ríos, *María Josefa Mujía: Obra Completa: Poesía-prosa traducciones epistolario a Gabriel René Moreno* (La Paz: Proyecto Sucre Ciudad Universitaria, 2009).

Brazil (2 writers)

Nísia Floresta

Conselhos à minha filha (1842)

Tu vás completar teus doze annos! eu escrevo pois para minha innocente Livia, que nada mais conhece do mundo senão os cuidados, com que sua terna mãy lhe tem dirigido na infancia, e nestas circumstancias procurando amoldar a minha lingoagem á tua infantil comprehensão, eu começarei por insinuar-te aqui em um estylo simples e claro os deveres e virtudes filiaes. Não quero, nem desejo antecipar tuas idéas em conhecimentos mais profundos, em que os annos, e o estudo far-te-hão meditar: possam a ternura e a experiencia de tua triste mãy servir-te então de guia na escabrosa senda da vida. Por ora fallo à minha pequena Livia. Possa ella, a despeito de sua idade, ouvir-me com a attenção de uma filha, por cuja felicidade jurei viver sobre o tumulo de seu Pai.[4]

Advice to my Daughter

You will soon reach thirteen years of age! I therefore write for my innocent Livia, who knows nothing of the world but the cares with which her tender mother has directed her in her childhood, and in these circumstances, seeking to shape my language to fit your childish understanding, I will begin by instilling in you here in a simple and clear style a daughter's duties and virtues. I do not want, nor do I wish to anticipate your ideas in deeper knowledge, on which years and study will make you meditate; may the tenderness and experience of your sad mother then serve you as a guide on the harsh path of life. For now I speak to my little Livia. May she, despite her age, listen to me with the attention of a daughter, for whose happiness I swore upon her Father's tomb to live.[5]

After some prefatory material, Floresta's readers in 1842 came to a text that opens thus. Nisia Floresta published a variety of works, including a translation of Wollstonecraft's 1792 *Vindication of the Rights of Woman*; here, she chooses to address her pre-teenage daughter in a public discourse. One may speculate on what led to this publication: is this text opposed to the Wollstonecraft text, or do the two works stand in a continuum? The question remains pertinent. Certainly, there is an element of *captatio benevolentiae* for a nineteenth-century woman writer

---

4 Nísia Floresta, *Conselhos à minha filha*, 2nd edn (Rio de Janeiro: F. de Paula Brito, 1845).
5 Translation reviewed by Luiza Duarte Caetano.

in presenting herself to the public as a widow and mother; and yet, what could be more feminist than to assert her daughter's right to self-determination, to agency, as exemplified in the advice her mother offers her as a sort of spiritual dowry? Her daughter, Floresta suggests, will be the captain of her soul, in William Ernest Henley's famous words. And Floresta asserts this early. For readers other than her daughter, Floresta thus offers a variety of things: a brief domestic idyll; traditional women's roles played out, rather interestingly, in public; and antithetically, an empowerment of mother and daughter in dialogue, independent of any patriarchal gaze, in which a matrilineal succession is established and celebrated. The inheritance is immaterial—since the text, both dowry and testament, leaves only words to the daughter—but perhaps all the more powerful for that.

What is Floresta's daughter to make of this text? She is after all its uniquely privileged reader. Let us begin with the Father's place in this extract, and the fact that the Father is dead. The fact itself might be happenstance, but its function in the text is not; while the father is definitionally and irrecoverably absent, he determines Floresta's mother's discourse, as the conclusion of the opening paragraph makes explicit. The entire text is thus situated under his paternal aegis; his dead hand, in a sense, starts the motor of this plot. And yet, just as the goddess Athena's aegis sheltered Odysseus without limiting his free will, so both mother and daughter—two women—are autonomous agents here. The father's only wish, after all, is evidently for his daughter's happiness. As to the mother's status, it is somewhat complex. Unlike the father, she is prescriptive: she is like Solon a lawgiver, communicating "a child's duties and virtues." She is also, by virtue of circumstance, both mother and father, both public and private, a sort of doubled being. And lastly, she has her own story, one of "the tenderness and experience of your sad mother." If her daughter is a *tabula rasa*, Floresta is not; and one reason for her writing, as the word "sad" indicates, is to transmit to the girl what she as a woman has learned the hard way.

Beatriz Francisca de Assis Brandão (29 July 1779–5 February 1868) was born in Vila Rica (now Ouro Preto), then the largest city in Brazil and a center of agitation for Brazilian independence. The Brandãos had close ties to the Brazilian imperial family. In 1816, Brandão married Vicente Batista Rodrigues Alvarenga, divorcing in 1839 and moving to

Rio de Janeiro. She was the lover of the poet Tomás António Gonzaga, publishing her poems in the Brazilian press and in collected volumes. In 1852–1857, *Marmota Fluminense* alone published thirty-eight of her poems. Much of her work is lost, and about 500 pages of poetry remains in manuscript. She also translated several plays by Pietro Metastasio, many now lost, and worked throughout her life as an educator in girls' schools to support herself.[6]

Nísia Floresta Brasileira Augusta [pseudonym of **Dionísia Gonçalves Pinto**] (12 October 1810–24 April 1885), born in Papari, married Manuel Augusto de Faria Rocha in 1828; he died in 1831. Floresta published her *Direitos das mulheres e injustiça dos homens* in 1832, freely inspired by Mary Wollstonecraft—perhaps the first feminist text in Latin America. Moving in 1838 to Rio de Janeiro, she founded the radical Augusto College school for girls, directing it until 1849. Her *Conselhos a minha filha* appeared in 1842. Floresta left in 1849 for Paris, returning to Brazil in 1852. Her progressive newspaper articles were collected before her return to Europe in 1856–1872; she also published poetry, novels, travel memoirs, and essays. *A Mulher* [The Woman] appeared in 1859. After returning to Brazil in 1872–1875, Floresta then sailed back to Europe, publishing her last work in French in 1878.[7]

Chile (2 writers)

María del Carmen Thomasa del Rosario Arriagada García (1807–12 January 1888), born in Chillán Viejo, married the German Eduardo Gutike in 1825, moving with him to Linares, then Talca in 1836. Her sixteen-year correspondence with the painter Mauricio Rugendas, whom she met in 1835, is considered the first women's writing in independent Chile. In it, she militates for better education for women and observes Chilean society.[8]

Josefa de los Dolores Peña y Lillo Barbosa [or **Sister Josefa de los Dolores** or **Sister Dolores Peña y Lillo**] (25 March or 25 May

---

6   Rogério Budasz, *Opera in the Tropics: Music and Theater in Early Modern Brazil* (Oxford: Oxford University Press, 2019).
7   Schuma Schumaher and Erico Vital Brazil, *Dicionário mulheres do Brasil: de 1500 até a atualidade: com 270 ilustrações*, 2nd edition (Rio de Janeiro: Jorge Zahar Editor, 2001).
8   *Memoria Chilena* (https://www.memoriachilena.gob.cl/602/w3-channel.html).

1739-August 1822/1823), born in Santiago, joined a Dominican convent in 1751 (becoming a nun in 1756) and began writing in 1763, both letters and poetry. She had some political influence in the early republic. Her writings are among the first women's writings in Chile, alongside the autobiography of the nun Ursula Suarez and the poems of Juana López and the nun Tadea de San Joaquín. Other texts by colonial nuns have likely been lost: spiritual instructions, diaries, autobiographies, letters. Sister Josefa's over a hundred letters to her Jesuit confessor from 1763–1769 were rediscovered in 1923 and partially published in 2008.[9]

Colombia (1 writer)

María Josefa Acevedo Sánchez de Gómez [or **Josefa Acevedo** or **Josefa Acevedo de Gómez**] (23 January 1803–19 January 1861), born in Bogotá, married Diego Fernándo Gómez in 1822. Her first work, the marriage manual *Ensayo sobre los deberes de los casados*, appeared anonymously. Acevedo published formal verse, 1854–1856, more essays on marriage in 1848, and biographies of various famous contemporaries in 1850–1860, leaving a manuscript two-act play called *La coqueta burlada*, a novel, and an autobiography. Other works were lost, and her *Cuadros de la vida privada de algunos granadinos* appeared posthumously.[10]

Cuba (1 writer)

Gertrudis Gómez de Avellaneda

Sab (1841)

Veinte años hace, poco más o menos, que al declinar una tarde del mes de junio un joven de hermosa presencia atravesaba a caballo los campos pintorescos que riega el Tínima, y dirigía a paso corto su brioso alazán por la senda conocida en el país con el nombre de camino de Cubitas, por conducir a las aldeas de este nombre, llamadas también tierras

---

9   Alejandra Araya Espinoza, Ximena Azúa Ríos et Lucía Invernizzi, *Diálogos espirituales: manuscritos femeninos hispanoamericanos siglos XVI-XIX* (Puebla: Instituto de Ciencias Sociales y Humanidades de la Benemérita Universidad Autónoma de Puebla, 2006).

10   José Domingo Cortés, ed. *Poetisas Americanas: Ramillete Poético del Bello Sexo Hispano-Americano* (Paris: Vida de Charles Bouret, 1896).

rojas. Hallábase el joven de quien hablamos a distancia de cuatro leguas de Cubitas, de donde al parecer venía, y a tres de la ciudad de Puerto Príncipe, capital de la provincia central de la isla de Cuba en aquella época, como al presente, pero que hacía entonces muy pocos años había dejado su humilde dictado de villa.

Fuese efecto de poco conocimiento del camino que seguia, fuese por complacencia de contemplar detenidamente los paisajes que se ofrecían a su vista, el viajero acortaba cada vez más el paso de su caballo y le paraba a trechos como para examinar los sitios por donde pasaba. A la verdad, era harto probable que sus repetidas detenciones sólo tuvieran por objeto admirar más a su sabor los campos fertilísimos de aquel país privilegiado, y que debían tener mayor atractivo para él si como lo indicaban su tez blanca y sonrosada, sus ojos azules, y su cabello de oro había venido al mundo en una región del Norte.[11]

Chapter One

Twenty years ago, or thereabouts, late on a June afternoon a young man of handsome bearing journeyed on horseback through the picturesque country watered by the Tinima River and in leisurely fashion guided his spirited sorrel along the path known in these parts as the Cubitas Road, leading as it did to the villages of this name, which were also known as the red lands. The young man in question was four leagues from Cubitas, from whence he appeared to have come, and three from the city of Puerto Príncipe, at that time the capital of the central province of Cuba, though only a few years earlier it had been but a humble township.

Perhaps because of his scant knowledge of the road, perhaps because of the pleasure he took in appraising the landscape before him, the traveler gradually slackened his pace and from time to time reined in his horse as though to scrutinize the places through which he passed. Quite possibly his repeated stops had as their sole object the fuller savoring of the richly fertile earth of that privileged country, which most likely attracted him all the more if—as his fair, rosy skin, blue eyes, and golden hair seemed to indicate—he had been born in some northern region.[12]

Sab is a remarkably short title for a novel, and that in itself is a kind of manifesto. Tradition accorded established men in novel titles a first and last name (Tom Jones, Tristram Shandy, Jacopo Ortis) reserving first name alone for the young (Werther, Candide) or the female (Pamela, Julie, Corinne). Sab is neither young nor female, he is in fact very much

---

11 Gertrudis Gómez de Avellaneda, *Sab*, ed. José Servera (Madrid: Cátedra, 1997), pp. 101–102.
12 *Sab and Autobiography*, tr. Nina M. Scott (Austin: University of Texas Press, 1993), p. 27.

established; but he is also enslaved, and hence, his identity is summed up in the title's one three-letter word.

After a short preface, the opening scene focuses our gaze, and that bears investigation, because the young man we see on horseback is not Sab. What then do we learn in this opening extract? A variety of interconnected things. We learn both about this hero or protagonist, and about the island of Cuba. Let us begin with the hero. First, he is on horseback; since at least the three *Tours of Dr. Syntax in Search of the Picturesque*, 1809–1821, being on horseback indicates status much as being on foot indicates its absence. The hero is at ease with his "spirited sorrel" because he has had time and leisure and occasion to become so. Indeed, his ease defines him: he slows his horse to gaze at Cuba as he passes—again, he has the leisure and the inclination to do that. The young man may be single, and from a northern and thus non-African region, but he is an admirer of Cuba's "richly fertile earth," and a reader of novels may guess that he will not remain single throughout.

Sab, we have yet to see, but he already hovers over the text thanks to the title, much as the namesakes of Racine's plays tend only to surface later on. In brief, the novel features a love triangle in which the finally rather disappointing hero and the noble Sab love the same Cuban heiress, Carlota. It ends badly—the hero gets the girl—prefaced by Sab's mad ride across Cuba to save the day, which stands in sharp contrast to the hero's slow opening canter.

And what do we learn of Cuba in the opening? Cuba may be alien to the hero, but to everyone else here, it is home. *Sab* appeared in 1841, early in the story of Cuban literature as of Cuban abolitionism. The novel begins by situating events twenty years in the past; these were the latter years of Latin America's wars of independence, though the wars barely touched Cuba. One might note that Sab is no less at home in Cuba than Carlota. In the extract, we see Cuba's material progress—Puerto Principe is no longer a village—but political questions are elided. That is perhaps particularly evident in the remark about fertile fields, which require hands to tend them. The hero on his sorrel seems untroubled by such questions, but to Sab, who labors, they would be unavoidable. Cuba in 1821 as in 1841 ran a slave economy; it also happened that Spain, the colonial master, chose repression and torture to maintain its grip on the island, having already lost America south of the Rio Grande. *Sab* first appeared in Madrid, interestingly, after the author emigrated there from Cuba. But for the moment, Cuba is home, and that celebration of the local, of local color, is a fundamentally Romantic choice.

Gertrudis Gómez de Avellaneda (23 March or 11 December 1814–1 February 1873), born in Puerto Principe (now Camagüey), Cuba, moved to Spain in 1836, then composing the poem "Al partir." She published poetry in the press, meeting Ignacio de Cepeda y Alcalde in 1839, her great love. In 1841 appeared Avellaneda's first volume of poems and her abolitionist novel *Sab*. She published more novels, theater, and poetry, 1841–1867. In 1844, her play *Munio Alfonso* was staged in Madrid; she met the poet Gabriel Garcia Tessara and became pregnant. In 1846, Avellaneda married don Pedro Sabate, who died the following year. In 1858, she staged her drama *Baltasar*. Married in 1856 to don Domingo Verduro, Avellaneda traveled with him to Cuba in 1859. He died in 1863 and she left Cuba, traveling to the United States and back to Spain in 1864.[13]

Ecuador (1 writer)

Dolores Veintimilla de Galindo (1829–23 May 1857), born in Quito, married Dr. Sixto Antonio Galindo y Oroña in 1847, moving to Guayaquil. Her husband later left for Central America and Veintemilla took up literature. After witnessing the shooting of an indigenous friend, she wrote *Necrologia*, condemning the death penalty and the treatment of indigenous people. The work was attacked so vehemently that she couldn't leave the house. She committed suicide in 1857. Her other prose—*Fantasia, Recuerdos*—and poetry—"Quejas" [Complaints]— appeared after her death.[14]

---

13   Florinda Alzaga, *La Avellaneda: Intensidad y vanguardia* (Miami: Ediciones Universal, 1997).
14   María Helena Barrera Agarwal, *Dolores Veintimilla: más allá de los mitos* (Quito: Academia Nacional de Historia del Ecuador, 2015).

Peru (1 writer)

Juana Manuela Gorriti

La Quena (1845)

La Cita

Las doce de la noche acababan de sonar en el reloj de la catedral de Lima. Sus calles estaban lóbregas y desiertas como las avenidas de un cementerio ; sus casas, tan llenas de luz y de vida en las primeras horas de la noche, tenian entonces un aspecto sombrío y siniestro ; y la bella ciudad dormia sepultada en un profundo silencio, interrumpido solo á largos intérvalos por los sonidos melancólicos de la vihuela de algun amante, ó por el lejano murmullo del mar que la brisa de la noche traia mezclado con el perfume de los naranjos que forman embalsamados bosques al otro lado de las murallas.

Un hombre embozado en una ancha capa apareció á lo lejos entre las tinieblas. Adelantóse rápidamente, mirando con precaucion en torno suyo, y deteniéndose delante de una de las rejas doradas de un palacio, paseó suavemente sus dedos por la celosía de alambre.

La celosía se entreabrió.[15]

The Quena

The Meeting

Midnight had just sounded on the cathedral clock in Lima. The streets were dark and deserted, like the rows of a cemetery. The houses, so full of light and life earlier in the evening had, by then, a somber and sinister aspect to them. The beautiful city was asleep, buried in a deep silence interrupted only occasionally by the melancholic sounds of some lover playing the vihuela, or by the distant murmuring of the sea, which the night breeze brought along with the fragrance of the orange trees that form aromatic forests outside the city's walls.

A man appeared in the darkness, his face covered by his long cloak. He moved forward quickly, looking around him very carefully, and stopped before the golden railings of a palace window, where he ran his fingers softly over the latticework. The latticed window opened.[16]

A *quena* is an Andean wooden flute, as a *vihuela* is a viol, an old Spanish

---

15 In *Sueños y realidades. Obras completas de Señora Doña Juana Manuela Gorriti*, ed. Vicente G. Quesada (Buenos Aires: Casavalle, 1865), pp. 5–6.

16 *Dreams and Realities Selected Fiction of Juana Manuela Gorriti*, tr. Sergio Waisman (Oxford: Oxford University Press, 2003), p. 1.

stringed instrument. Gorriti has, rather nicely, used two musical instruments to locate and to date her story. As to the time of day, it is midnight, the witching hour, and our protagonist is caped like the heroes of the period's *romans de cape et d'épée*. The short text thus opens with several Romantic tropes: local color, both in space and time; a Gothic setting, complete with the mention of a cemetery; and a cloaked hero coming to an assignation. One might add the orange trees that recall Goethe's Mignon: "Kennst du das Land, wo die Zitronen blühn," Mignon sings, "Do you know the land where the lemon trees bloom?"[17] It is a highly charged opening scene.

What do we learn in this opening extract? We learn some elements of plot—a caped man approaches a palace at midnight and is met—but we learn more about Lima: its cathedral, its streets and houses, its soundtrack, its orange trees, its palaces. We learn that the city is old enough for someone to have played the viol in its streets. If Romantic creation valued the local, Gorriti seems happy to oblige; not only does she set her text in Latin America, it is in fact specific to the city of Lima, which must have gladdened Peruvian hearts. And just as Němcová chose to reduce her readership by writing in the language of Bohemia and Moravia, so Gorriti's text will remain, to a degree, alien to all who have not visited Peru. Who outside the Andes knows what a *quena* is? For a Peruvian, we find ourselves rather intimately at home; for the rest of the planet, we are confronted with the Other; and after all, these are two sides of the same coin, just as trash is packaging which has served its purpose. It is characteristic of Romantic thought, from Moscow to Montevideo, to value and empower what is individual and unique; Pope wrote that true wit was "What oft was thought, but ne'er so well express'd," and that statement is antithetical to Romantic aesthetics.[18] Lima is uniquely Lima, it is neither Paris nor Buenos Aires, and in that individuality, in that concert of unique identities, resides the polyphonic beauty of the world.

Finally, what does it mean to set a novel in the past? Europe's Romantics loved to do so, from at least the time of Walter Scott's *Waverley*

---

17 Johann Wolfgang von Goethe, *Wilhelm Meisters Lehrjahre: Roman* (Munich: Goldmann, [1979]), p. 149.
18 Alexander Pope, "An Essay on Criticism" (1711) in *Pope. Poetical Works* (Oxford: Oxford University Press, 1966), p. 72.

in 1814. If the Enlightenment project depends on a certain repudiation of the past—on a belief in progress and perfectibility—the historical novels typical of the Romantic period instead, or perhaps equally, find beauty and meaning in past societies and modes of life. It is the Romantic period that first found Racine anachronistic: A.W. Schlegel makes that reproach in the 1807 *Comparaison des deux Phèdres*, and what that anachronism represents is a failure of imagination, a failure in the end to allow other people to be Other, a narrowing of history. It matters to Gorriti that between the Inca Empire and independence lie three centuries of lived existence in Lima, as throughout Latin America, and she thus sets out to open a window onto them. In a sense, that insight matters more to this extract than the skeleton of plot it hangs on, whether the boy gets the girl. Boys get girls in countless stories; they do so less often in fictions set in colonial Peru.

Juana Manuela Gorriti (15 June 1818–6 November 1892), born in Rosario de la Frontera (Argentina), was exiled with her family in 1831. They went to Bolivia, where she married Manuel Isidro Belzú in 1833. President of Bolivia after 1848, he abandoned her after 1842, dying assassinated in 1865. In Bolivia, she founded a girls' school. Gorriti spent some years in Lima, where she hosted *tertulias* [gatherings] for Peruvian writers, men and women, to discuss literature and social progress, and published *La Quena*, 1845, and other stories in the press. When the Spanish Navy shelled Lima in 1866, Gorriti served as a battlefield nurse. She returned to Argentina in 1878, founding a newspaper, *La Alborada del Plata*, in which she published on women's rights and education. Her novels include *El Pozo de Yocci* [The Well of Yocci] in 1869 and *La Tierra natal* in 1889.[19]

Uruguay (1 writer)

Petrona Rosende (18 October 1787–28 January 1863), born in Montevideo (now Uruguay), moved to Buenos Aires during Montevideo's occupation by Brazil. In Buenos Aires, she edited the feminist periodical *La Aljaba* from 1830 to 1831, becoming the first female journalist in Argentina. In

---

19 Francine Masiello, ed. *Dreams and Realities: Selected Fiction of Juana Manuela Gorriti*, tr. Sergio Gabriel Waisman (New York: Oxford University Press, 2003).

1835, Rosende returned to Montevideo, publishing a patriotic sonnet titled *Al arribo de mi patria* that year and opening a *Casa de la Educación para Señoritas*. She was granted a Uruguayan state pension in 1861.[20]

Costa Rica (0 writers)

I have identified zero Costa Rican women authors in this period. Further research clearly remains to be done.

El Salvador (0 writers)

I have identified zero Salvadoran women authors in this period. Further research clearly remains to be done.

Guatemala (0 writers)

I have identified zero Guatemalan women authors in this period. Further research clearly remains to be done.

Haiti (0 writers)

I have identified zero Haitian women authors in this period. Further research clearly remains to be done.

Honduras (0 writers)

I have identified zero Honduran women authors in this period. Further research clearly remains to be done.

Mexico (0 writers)

My initial research identified zero Mexican women authors in this period, but two subsequent discoveries throw this conclusion into question. First, Mónica Díaz, *Indigenous Writings from the Convent:*

---

20 MacIntyre, Iona, *Women and Print Culture in Post-Independence Buenos Aires* (Rochester, NY: Tamesis, 2010).

Negotiating Ethnic Autonomy in Colonial Mexico (Tucson, AZ: University of Arizona Press, 2010). Díaz however indicates a single date after 1773: 1799, date of the first sermon eulogizing an indigenous nun, not a criolla. Reviewing her pre-1773 corpus, Díaz concludes that "most nuns' texts, if they were printed at all, did not appear as originally written but were instead published under the name of a man and in a greatly modified style" (p. 90). One might then wish to consult manuscript sources held in Mexican convents, that seems a promising avenue for research. Some prominent genres in Díaz's volume that one might look for include epistle and hagiography. Second, José Domingo Cortés, ed. *Poetisas Americanas: Ramillete Poético del Bello Sexo Hispano-Americano* (Paris: Bouret, 1896), which lists four Mexican women poets, as noted above, though none publishing prior to our cutoff date of 1848: **Dolores Guerrero** (1833–1858); **Isabel A. Prieto de Landázuri** (1833–1876); **Mercedes Salazar de Cámara** (who evidently did not exist); and **Ester Tapia de Castellanos** (1842–1897). In short, the absence of Mexican women writers in our initial search seems a function not of the field, but of the method adopted. This conclusion is likely to apply to all thirteen national traditions in this volume for which no names have been identified.

Nicaragua (0 writers)

I have identified zero Nicaraguan women authors in this period. Further research clearly remains to be done.

Paraguay (0 writers)

I have identified zero Paraguayan women authors in this period. Further research clearly remains to be done.

Venezuela (0 writers)

I have identified zero Venezuelan women authors in this period. Further research clearly remains to be done.

6. Writers from Ottoman Europe

As we have seen in Latin America, this study traces stories of national independence. The Ottomans took Constantinople in 1453, but they had occupied Bulgaria since 1396. Ottoman Europe was a reality into the twentieth century: the Greeks attained independence in 1821–1832, the Serbians in 1804–1835, the Romanians in 1877, the Bulgarians in 1878–1908, and the Albanians in 1912. In the period 1776–1848, only Serbia and Greece attained independence; it is perhaps indicative that my English-language sources revealed no Albanian or Bulgarian women writers during the period, and few elsewhere—one Greek, one Romanian, three Serbian. One would imagine that more are waiting to be rediscovered.

Greece (1 writer)

Elisavet Moutzan-Martinengou

Αυτοβιογραφία (1821)

Εἰς τοῦτον τὸν καιρόν, δηλαδὴ τῇ 25 Μαρτίου 1821 τὴν ἡμέραν τοῦ Εὐαγγελισμοῦ, ἔρχεται ὁ ποτὲ διδάσκαλός μου, Θεοδόσιος Δημάδης καὶ μᾶς κάμνει γνωστὸν μὲ πολλήν του χαράν, πῶς οἱ Γραικοὶ ἀνήγειραν τὰ ὅπλα ἐναντίον τῶν Ὀθωμανῶν, πῶς ἡ Πάτρα καὶ οἱ πλησίον της χώραις ἤδη εἶχον σείσει τὸν ζυγὸν τῆς σκλαβίας, καὶ πῶς οἱ ἐπίλοιπαις χώραις, κατὰ τὴν συμφωνίαν ἴσως, εἶχαν τότε καμωμένον τὸ ἴδιον, ἀλλὰ ὡς πλέον μακράν, ἀκόμη ἡ εἴδησις δὲν ἦτον φθασμένη εἰς τὴν Ζάκυνθον. Οὕτως εἶπεν ὁ μαῦρος, διότι τέτοια ἦτον ἡ φήμη ὁποῦ παρευθὺς ἔτρεξεν. Ἐγὼ εἰς τὰ λόγια του ἄκουσα τὸ αἷμα μου νὰ ζεσταίνη, ἐπεθύμησα ἀπὸ καρδίας νὰ ἤθελεν ἡμπορῶ νὰ ζωστῶ ἄρματα, ἐπεθύμησα ἀπὸ καρδίας νὰ ἤθελε ἡμπορῶ νὰ τρέξω διὰ νὰ δώσω βοήθειαν εἰς ἀνθρώπους, ὁποῦ δι' ἄλλο (καθὼς ἐφαίνετο) δὲν ἐπολεμοῦσαν, παρὰ διὰ θρησκείαν καὶ διὰ πατρίδα, καὶ διὰ ἐκείνην τὴν ποθητὴν ἐλευθερίαν ἡ ὁποία καλῶς μεταχειριζομένη, συνηθᾶ νὰ προξενῇ τὴν ἀθανασίαν, τὴν δόξαν, τὴν εὐτυχίαν τῶν λαῶν. Ἐπεθύμησα, εἶπα, ἀπὸ καρδίας, ἀλλὰ ἐκύτταξα τοὺς τοίχους τοῦ σπητιοῦ ὁποῦ μὲ ἐκρατοῦσαν κλεισμένην, ἐκύτταξα τὰ μακρὰ φορέματα τῆς γυναικείας σκλαβίας καὶ ἐνθυμήθηκα πως εἶμαι γυναῖκα, καὶ περιπλέον γυναῖκα Ζακυνθία καὶ ἀναστέναξα, ἀλλὰ δὲν ἔλειψα ὅμως ἀπὸ τὸ νὰ παρακαλέσω τὸν Οὐρανὸν διὰ νὰ ἤθελε τοὺς βοηθήσῃ νὰ νικήσουν, καὶ τοιούτης λογῆς νὰ ἀξιωθῶ καὶ ἐγὼ ἡ ταλαίπωρος νὰ ἰδῶ εἰς τὴν Ἑλλάδα ἐπιστρεμμένην τὴν ἐλευθερίαν καὶ μαζῒ μὲ αὐτὴν ἐπιστρεμμένας εἰς τὰς καθέδρας τους τὰς σεμνὰς Μούσας, ἀπὸ τὰς ὁποίας ἡ τυραννία τῶν Τούρκων τόσον καὶ τόσον καιρὸν τὰς ἐκρατοῦσε διωγμένας.[1]

My Story

At this time, that is, on the 25th of March, 1821, the day of the Annunciation, my teacher, Theodosios Dēmadēs, comes and with much joy makes it known to us that the Greeks had raised arms against the Ottomans, that Patras and the nearby towns already had shaken off the yoke of slavery, and that the remaining towns, perhaps according to an agreement, had done the same, but, since Zakynthos was far away, the news had not arrived here yet. This is how the poor man spoke, for that was the rumor, and, upon hearing it, he ran to tell us. Hearing his words, I felt my blood warming up, I wished in my heart that I could take up arms, I wished in my heart that I could run to give help to those people who (apparently) did not fight for anything else but for their religion and their country, and for that longed-for freedom which, when used well, brings immortality, glory, and happiness to people. I wished, as I said, in my heart, but then I looked at the walls of the house which kept me confined, I looked at the long dresses of women's slavery, and I remembered that I am a woman, and, furthermore, a woman of Zakynthos, and I sighed, but I did not fail to ask God to help them win and thus even I, miserable as I am, would be able to see freedom return to Greece and, along with it, the modest Muses, whom the tyranny of the Turks kept away for such a long time.[2]

It seems illustrative of the challenges facing women authors that Moutzan-Martinengou's more than fifteen plays, in addition to her autobiography, have been erased from the record. Her one surviving comedy is absent in the major libraries of Europe and America—Paris, London, Berlin, Washington D.C.; Oxford, Cambridge, Stanford, Berkeley, Harvard—and the fragmented autobiography that survives has been heavily edited by her son.

So, is her redacted autobiography any good? Well, this extract is

---

1 Elisavet Moutzan-Martinengou, *Αυτοβιογραφία*, ed. K. Porphyrēs (Athens: Keimena, 1983), pp. 59–60.
2 Elisavet Moutzan-Martinengou, *My Story*, tr. Helen Dendrinou Kolias (Athens, GA: University of Georgia Press, 1989), p. 30.

memorable for a couple of reasons. First, it relates a Greek's first reaction to news of the Greek uprising against the Turks—that quintessential Romantic struggle which Delacroix painted and for which Byron gave his life in 1824. Second, that Greek citizen is a woman, clad in "the long dresses of women's slavery." The text interests then both from a revolutionary and a feminist perspective. One might call it thrilling; based on this extract, it hardly seems to merit near-universal oblivion.

Let us look at the passage more closely. In it, Moutzan-Martinengou situates her narrative: she is off the west coast of the Peloponnese. Greece has 227 inhabited islands, to which news of necessity came more slowly than to the mainland—"since Zakynthos was far away, the news had not arrived here yet." The year is 1821, and the day, rather fittingly, that of the Annunciation; Turkey had occupied Greece since the fall of Constantinople, or some four hundred years, and now, freedom was coming. The male announcer of this news runs in, and the author focuses on her female reaction. Her blood warmed, she says, thinking of a people at war for religion, for country, for liberty, source of "happiness to people." In other words, the author, kept shut up in her island home in Turkish-occupied Greece, is at ease with Romantic talk of national self-determination. That in itself is newsworthy, as is the mention of the author's domestic prison and her opinion of it. Her conclusion is curious—her desire to see restored to their seats the modest Muses, to see Greek art flourish again. One may recall that the nine Muses are all female, and that writing has a preponderance among them.

Perhaps the most poignant aspect of this text is the contrast between the teacher, who runs in to give the news, and the female pupil, who cannot leave the house. She wished, she tells the page four times in this brief extract, to run help the cause. But she could not. She could only write about it. Moutzan-Martinengou, in conclusion, is the only Greek woman writer my initial search revealed for the Romantic period 1776–1848. There are surely others—other women who put pen to paper during those seventy years in which Greek independence was forged. One wonders what their texts might have to say.

Elisavet Moutzan-Martinengou (2 October 1801–9 November 1832), born in Zakynthos, was pressured by her aristocratic family to marry. After a failed attempt to leave the island, she accepted marriage to Nicholas Martinegos in 1831, after long negotiations about the dowry.

She died in childbirth the following year. Besides her autobiography, published heavily redacted by her son in 1881, Moutzan wrote more than fifteen plays in both Greek and Italian, also translating from *The Odyssey*, *Prometheus Bound*, and *The Suppliants* and writing poetry, works on economics and on poetic theory. Of these, one comedy, some letters and poems, and various fragments have survived.[3]

Romania (1 writer)

Dora d'Istria [pen name of **Duchess Helena Koltsova-Massalskaya**, née **Elena Ghica** or **Gjika**] (22 January 1828–17 November 1888), born in Bucharest, was the niece of the then reigning Prince of Wallachia. She was educated in Vienna, Venice, and Berlin. Returning to Wallachia in 1849, she married the Russian Duke Alexander Koltsov-Massalski. After some years in Russia, Dora d'Istria traveled to Switzerland, Greece, then Florence where she settled. After 1855, her voluminous writings—on monastic orders, on the emancipation of women, on Ottoman poetry, on her travels—showed her proficiency in French, German, Romanian, Italian, Ancient and Modern Greek, Latin, and Russian as well as her grasp of science and her progressive views. After 1866, she was also a leading spokesperson for the Albanian nationalist cause.[4]

Serbia (3 writers)

Eustahija Arsić (14 March 1776–17 February 1843), born in Irig (then part of southern Hungary), spoke Serbian, Hungarian, German, Romanian, Church Slavonic, Italian, Latin, and some English. She was married and widowed three times: to a Mr. Lacković, to Toma Radovanović, then to Sava Arsić, at which point she began her literary activity. Her salon in Arad welcomed Dositej Obradović, Joakim Vukić, Vuk Karadžić and other Serbian nationalist writers; she also translated the Enlightenment writers Voltaire, Wieland, and James Thomson. Arsić was the first female member of Matica srpska and contributed to its

---

3   Elisavet Moutzan-Martinengou, *My Story*, tr. Helen Dendrinou Kolias (Athens, GA: University of Georgia Press, 1989).
4   Antonio D'Alessandri, *Il pensiero e l'opera di Dora d'Istria fra Oriente europeo e Italia* (Roma: Gangemi, 2008).

periodical *Letopis*. Her works appeared in 1814–1816 and 1829.[5]

Ana Marija Marović (7 February 1815–3 October 1887), who lived in Italy and Montenegro, was a Serbian writer and painter. She spoke Serbian and Italian. In 1952, a cause for her beatification was opened by the Catholic Church, and she was declared a Servant of God.[6]

Princess Anka Obrenović, later **Anka Konstantinović** (1 April 1821–10 June 1868), born in Belgrade, was the niece of Serbia's first Obrenović ruler. Known as *Anka pomodarka* [Anka the fashionable], she played the piano and did not wear Turkish garb. Obrenović published in periodicals including *Danica ilirska*; her volume of translations in 1836 was the first literary work published by a woman in Serbia. The Croatian poet Antun Mihanović asked for her hand but was denied. In 1842, she married Alexander Konstantinović, establishing a salon in 1860. That year, her cousin became Prince Michael III of Serbia; Obrenović lived at court. The two were assassinated together in 1868. The modern pretender to the Montenegrin throne is her descendant.[7]

Albania (0 writers)

I have identified zero Albanian women authors in this period. Further research clearly remains to be done.

Bulgaria (0 writers)

I have identified zero Bulgarian women authors in this period. Further research clearly remains to be done.

---

5   Živan Milisavac, ed. *Jugoslovenski književni leksikon* [Yugoslav Literary Lexicon], 2nd edition (Novi Sad: Matica Srpska, 1984).
6   Vlatko Perčin, *Ana Marija Marović - Monografski prikaz života i rada* (Zagreb: Bogdan Malešević, 1997).
7   Celia Hawkesworth. *Voices in the Shadows: Women and Verbal Art in Serbia and Bosnia* (Budapest: Central European University Press, 2000).

7. Writers from Romanov Territories

This section is headed Romanov Territories, and central to its narrative is the emergence of national traditions upon that polyglot empire's extensive western flank. From Saint Petersburg to Vladivostok, across modern Russia, people largely speak Russian; but this section also traces the western language communities around which national sentiment in this period played out. Modern Estonia and Latvia were ceded by Sweden to Russia in 1721; Lithuania was acquired in 1795 at the Third Partition of Poland. Estonia, Lithuania, and Latvia regained independence in 1918–1921. Russo-German occupation of Poland began in 1772–1795 and ended in 1918. In short, these territories were in 1776 either independent or recent acquisitions, though occupied throughout most of our period. Ukraine's case is somewhat different; most of Ukraine had passed from Polish to Tsarist control in 1667, more being absorbed in the Partitions of Poland; and after brief independence in 1917–1921, Ukraine regained independence in 1991 with the fall of the Soviet Union. Polish territory alone was independent and sovereign during this period, both prior to 1795 and briefly under Napoleon as the Grand-Duchy of Warsaw. In today's Baltic states, my English-language search has identified just one Latvian and one Lithuanian woman writer (both writing in French) and as yet no Estonian woman writer in the period. In occupied Poland, I have found eight women writing in Polish, with one woman in Ukraine writing in Ukrainian. In Russia proper, during this period 1776–1848, I have found thirteen women writers.

Latvia (1 writer)

Beate Barbara Juliane Freifrau von Krüdener [or **Julie de Krüdener**], née **Freiin von Vietinghoff genannt Scheel** (22 November 1764–25 December 1824), born in Riga, married Baron Burkhardt Alexis Constantine Krüdener in 1782. Their son's godfather was the future Tsar Paul. In 1784, Krüdener's husband became ambassador in Venice, then Munich, then Copenhagen in 1787. Krüdener traveled to Paris in 1789; she fell in love, but the baron refused a divorce. She traveled in Europe, joining the baron in Berlin in 1800; he died in 1802. Krüdener published her novel *Valérie* in 1803, then fell under the influence of the Moravian Brethren in Riga. She met Tsar Alexander in 1815, helping him found the Holy Alliance. Chateaubriand, Duras, Benjamin Constant, Juliette Récamier attended their Paris prayer meetings. Krüdener's later appeal for Alexander to liberate Greece was rebuffed.[1]

Lithuania (1 writer)

Sophie de Choiseul-Gouffier, née **Zofia Tyzenhauz** (1790–28 May 1878), born in Lithuania, married Antoine Louis Octave de Choiseul-Gouffier in 1818, a French count whose father had emigrated during the French Revolution. Her first historical novel appeared in Warsaw in 1818: *Le Polonois à St. Domingue ou La jeune Créole*. Later novels appeared in Paris, mostly concerning Polish and Lithuanian history and all in French: *Barbe Radziwill. Roman historique*, 1820; *Vladislas Jagellon et Hedwige, ou la réunion de la Lithuanie à la Pologne. Nouvelle historique*, 1824; *Le Nain politique. Roman historique*, 1827; and *Halina Ogińska ou les Suédois en Pologne*, 1839. Choiseul-Gouffier also published two volumes of reminiscences: *Mémoires historiques sur l'empereur Alexandre et la cour de Russie*, 1829, and *Réminiscences sur l'empereur Alexandre Ier et sur l'empereur Napoléon Ier*, 1862.[2]

---

1   Francis Ley, *Madame de Krüdener et son temps, 1764–1824* (Paris: Plon, 1961).
2   Mme la Comtesse de Choiseul-Gouffier, née Comtesse de Tisenhaus, *Réminiscences sur l'empereur Alexandre Ier et sur l'empereur Napoléon Ier* (Besançon: Bonvalot, 1862).

Poland (8 writers)

Klementyna z Tańskich Hoffmanowa

Dziennik Franciszki Krasińskiej w Ostatnich Latach Panowiana Augusta III Pisany (1825)

1 stycznia 1759 r. w Maleszowskim zamku, w poniedziałek

Tydzień temu, w samo święto Bożego Narodzenia, Jmć Dobrodziej Ojciec mój kazał przynieść sobie ogromną księgę, w którą już od lat kilkunastu, obyczajem wszystkich niemal panów polskich, wpisuje własną ręką rozmaite publiczne i prywatne pisma; są w niej mowy, manifesta, uniwersały, listy, paszkwile, wiersze, wszystko porządkiem dat ułożone; pokazywał nam ów zbiór szacowny, czytał niektóre kawałki. Bardzo mi się podobała ta myśl zapisywania ciekawszych zdarzeń i okoliczności, a ponieważ już od lat kilku i po francusku, i po polsku dosyć gładko pisać umiem i niezmiernie pisać lubię, ponieważ i we Francji wiele białych głów podobne rzeczy pisze— przyszło mi na myśl, czybym i ja też coś takiego według możności mojej rozpocząć nie mogła? Uszyłam sobie zatem duży sekstern, umieszczę w nim jak najdokładniej, cokolwiek się mnie i bliskiej mojej rodziny tycze, wspomnę, jak potrafię, o rzeczach publicznych.—Jmć Dobrodziej, jako mężczyzna i człowiek stateczny, niemi wyłącznie swoją księgę zajmuje; on ją układa dla wszystkich, i sposobem poważnym; ja, jako panna nie uczona i młoda, moją ramotę jedynie dla własnej zabawy pisać będę, ale z głowy, szczerze i bez pretensji: będzie to prawdziwy dziennik, bo go prawie co dzień pisać zamyślam. Dziś właśnie Nowy Rok i poniedziałek, wyborna pora do zaczęcia porządnie jakowej rzeczy; już tydzień jak ją w umyśle układam, trzeba raz z nią wystąpić; zaczynam więc: mam czas wolny, nabożeństwo odbyte rano, pacierze pozostałe odmówię na nieszporach; jużem ubrana i ufryzowana; właśnie dziesiąta bije na zamkowym zegarze, dwie godziny mam jeszcze do obiadu—napiszę dziś, co tylko wiem o sobie, o rodzinie mojej, o domu naszym, o Rzeczypospolitej, a potem pisać będę kolejno, cokolwiek nam wszystkim ciekawego się przydarzy.[3]

The Journal of Countess Franciszka Krasinska in the Eighteenth Century [*in the Last Years of Augustus III Pisana*]

In the Castle of Maleszow, Monday, January 1, 1759.

One week ago—it was Christmas Day—my honored father ordered to be brought to him a huge book, in which for many years he had written in his

---

[3] In Klementyna Tańska, *Dziennik Franciszki Krasińskiej w Ostatnich Latach Panowiana Augusta III Pisany*, ed. Ida Kotowa (Kraków: W.L. Anczyca i Spółki, 1929), pp. 3–4.

own hand all the important things which have happened in our country [as is the custom of almost all Polish gentlemen]; also copies of the notable pamphlets, speeches, manifestoes, public and private letters, occasional poems, etc., and having placed everything in the order of its date, he showed us this precious collection and showed us some extracts. I was much pleased with his idea of recording interesting facts and circumstances; and as I know how to write pretty well in Polish and in French, and have heard that in France some women have written their memoirs, I thought, "Why should I not try to do something of the kind?"

So I have made a big copy-book by fastening together many sheets of paper, and I shall note down, as accurately as I am able, everything which may happen to me and to my family, and I shall also mention public affairs as they happen, as far as I may be acquainted with them.

[My father the Benefactor, as a man and a stable person, deals exclusively with them in his book; he arranges it for everyone, and in a serious way; I, as an uneducated and young lady, will write my rubbish just for my own fun, but from my head, honestly and without pretense: it will be a real diary, because I plan to write it almost every day.] Today is New Year's Day and Monday, a very proper season to begin something new. I am at leisure; the morning Service is finished, I am dressed and my hair is curled; ten is just striking on the castle clock, so I have two hours till dinner time. Well, I begin. [today I will write what I know about myself, about my family, about our house, about the Polish-Lithuanian Commonwealth, and then I will write, one by one, whatever interesting things happen to us all.][4]

The most striking thing about this fictitious diary entry is the opening date: January 1, 1759, a good decade before the First Partition of Poland. Hoffmanowa in 1825, some sixty years later, was writing in a Poland that had been erased from the map in three bites by the greed of its Russian and German neighbors, two of whose three leaders, Frederick and Catherine, history has somewhat conveniently labeled great. One might think of Thucydides and his Melian Dialogue, in which the Athenian envoys tell the citizens of Melos that the strong will oppress the weak because they are able to, after which Athens does exactly that. But unlike the Russians and the Germans, the Athenians were honest about it. A brief Napoleonic interlude brought back a Grand-Duchy of Warsaw; otherwise, Poland waited until 1918 to recover its centuries-old

---

4   *The Journal of Countess Françoise Krasinska Great Grandmother of Victor Emmanuel*, tr. Kasimir Dziekonska, 7th edition (Chicago, A.C. McClurg & Co., 1899), pp. 7–8. Text in square brackets is absent in the published translation.

independence. Hoffmanowa published anonymously in a Polish magazine, where her opening date's political subtext was surely patent to every Polish reader.

In this first diary entry, one or two things occur. First, we learn something of the customs and habits of a Polish gentleman in the reign of Augustus III: he keeps a day-book full of miscellaneous written texts, from poems to lampoons and manifestoes. Second, we learn of his unmarried daughter's accomplishments—she writes fluent French, though she calls herself "uneducated;" she is devout, going from morning prayers to Vespers; she is modest, referring to her planned diary entries as "rubbish;" and her thoughts are not limited to the private sphere, they extend to the doomed "Polish-Lithuanian Commonwealth."

Whereas Němcová in Bohemia puts cottagers onstage, Hoffmanowa in Warsaw chooses a countess. This matters, if Romanticism is indeed the people's voice; how can Hoffmanowa present the Polish nation in the person of a young countess? The answer is to some extent specific to Poland. Just as Adam Mickiewicz peopled 1834's *Pan Tadeusz* with the minor nobility, so the cause of Polish independence, it seems possible to say, was prior to the 1840s primarily an aristocratic movement; the peasantry, unlike the nobility, had little affection for the Commonwealth that had been swallowed. Both Němcová and Hoffmanowa, in short, are symptomatic of their unique sociohistorical context, of their different national traditions.

Let us add as a final note that the male translator of this text deleted at least two topical political remarks in the novel's opening page. I have reinserted the deleted text [in square brackets], but readers looking for the novel, apparently untranslated in the past century, will of necessity encounter it in versions having their own agendas, like this one, and may in consequence find the author rather brusquely removed from the public sphere to the private. This is not atypical for women authors interpreted by men prior to 1900 or thereabouts. A word of caution thus seems in order.

Elżbieta "Izabela" Dorota Czartoryska, née **Flemming** (3 March 1746–15 July 1835), born in Warsaw, married Prince Adam Kazimierz Czartoryski in 1761. In Paris in 1772, she met Benjamin Franklin, Rousseau, and Voltaire, opening a salon after 1775 at the Czartoryski

Palace at Puławy. In 1784, she joined the Patriotic Party; after the Kościuszko Uprising, Tsarina Catherine II took her two sons as hostages. Czartoryska opened a Polish museum at the Czartoryski Palace in 1796, which subsists in Kraków today. Her works include *Myśli różne o sposobie zakładania ogrodów* [Different Thoughts About How to Create Gardens], 1805, and *Pielgrzym w Dobromilu, czyli nauki wiejskie* [Pilgrim in Dobromil, or Rural Teachings], c. 1818.[5]

Princess Maria Czartoryska [formerly **Duchess Maria of Württemberg**] (15 March 1768–21 October 1854), born in Warsaw, was the daughter of Izabela Czartoryska. She married Duke Louis of Württemberg in 1784, brother of the tsarina and Hetman of the Lithuanian Army in the 1792 war against Russia; she divorced him when his betrayal of the Polish-Lithuanian Commonwealth became known. Their son was raised by his father. Maria lived mainly in Warsaw, hosting a salon and in 1816 publishing Poland's first known psychological novel, *Malvina, or the Heart's Intuition*. Following the November Uprising of 1830–1831, she moved to Sieniawa in Galicia, then to Paris in 1837. She also composed chamber and vocal music.[6]

Wirydianna Fiszerowa, née **Wirydianna Radolińska**, later **Wirydianna Kwilecka** (1761–1826), born in Wyszyny, married Antoni Kwilecki in 1786, helping to write his speeches at the Four-Year Sejm. Kwilecki divorced Fiszerowa after falling for a fourteen-year-old, and in 1806 she married Stanisław Fiszer, a general who fought in Napoleon's Russian campaign. Her wit earned her the nickname "the Voltaire in skirts;" she wrote in French, her memoirs first appearing in Polish in 1975. They mention her wide circle of acquaintances, from Frederick II of Prussia to Józef Poniatowski, Izabela Czartoryska, or Tadeusz Kościuszko, whom she adored.[7]

Klementyna Hoffmanowa, née **Klementyna Tańska** (23 November 1798–21 September 1845), born in Warsaw, published her first treatise in 1819, *A Souvenir After a Good Mother*, also editing a children's magazine. Her several novels include *The Letters of Elżbieta Rzeczycka to*

---

5 Gabriela Pauszer-Klonowska, *Pani na Puławach* [Lady in Puławy] (Warsaw: Inicjal, 2010).
6 Aaron I. Cohen. *International Encyclopedia of Women Composers*, 2nd edition, 2 vols (New York: Books & Music, 1987).
7 Wirydianna Fiszerowa. *Dzieje moje własne* [My Own Story] (Warsaw: Świat Książki, 1998).

her friend Urszula, 1824, and *The Diary of Countess Françoise Krasinska*, 1825, arguing for women's education and self-empowerment. She taught in girls' schools and at the Warsaw Governess's Institute, 1826–1831. Hoffmanowa married Karol Boromeusz Hoffman in 1829; after the November Uprising, the couple left for exile in Paris. There, she joined Prince Adam Czartoryski's literary society as well as the Benevolent Society of Polish Ladies presided by Adam's wife. She was a friend of Chopin and Mickiewicz.[8]

Anna Nakwaska, née **Krajewska** (28 March 1781–21 October 1851), born in Warsaw, was raised entirely in French. She married the politician Franciszek Salezy Nakwaski; their son later became a political activist. The couple lived in Lipnice but often visited Warsaw, where Nakwaska joined the society in the Copper-Roof Palace. During the Grand-Duchy, she was an inspector of girls' schools. In 1816, Nakwaska opened a salon; after 1821, she also published novels, children's stories, and fiction based on the November Uprising, in French and Polish. She left for Switzerland in 1837, returning to visit Lower Silesia in 1844. In 1852, an extract from her memoirs appeared in the Warsaw press; the memoirs have yet to appear in their entirety.[9]

Tekla Teresa Łubieńska (6 June 1767–August 1810), born in Warsaw, lost her mother at eleven and was then raised in French by her grandmother. She married Feliks Łubieński, a future Minister of Justice, and they had ten children. During the Targowica Confederation, Łubieńska left for Prague, returning in 1785 to the family estate to write and raise her children. During the Four-Year Sejm of 1788–1792, she wrote patriotic verse, but she wrote chiefly comedies before her historical dramas *Wanda, Queen of Poland*, 1806, and *Charlemagne and Wedekind*, 1807, produced in Warsaw in 1807–1808. She also translated plays by Racine (*Andromaque*) and Metastasio (*Siroe*), and Voltaire's *Candide*, though these and other writings remain unpublished. Zacharias Werner published his own *Wanda, Königin der Sarmaten* in 1810.[10]

Barbara Urszula Sanguszko, née **Dunin** (4 February 1718–2 October 1791), orphaned early, was brought up by her stepmother. She was married

---

[8] Joanna E. Dąbrowska: *Klementyna* (Białystok: Trans Humana Wydawnictwo Uniwersyteckie, 2008).
[9] *Bibliografia Literatury Polskiej—Nowy Korbut*, 12 vols (Warsaw: Państwowy Instytut Wydawniczy, 1967).
[10] *Ibid.*

off in 1735 to the much older Duke Paweł Karol Sanguszko, Grand-Marshal of Lithuania. The couple had ten children. Widowed in 1750, Sanguszko thereafter ran the considerable household, moving to Warsaw after 1763. Every two years, she hosted an enlightenment salon in Poddębice, her guests including Stanisław August Poniatowski, the future king, and Ignacy Krasicki. Sanguszko was known for her philanthropy, restoring churches and founding new religious houses. In 1743, she translated into Polish two religious tracts in French and Italian, then a medical manual, and in 1788, an anti-Voltairean novel, *Le Comte de Valmont*. She published a *Guide for Mothers* in 1755 and left some manuscript poetry and correspondence.[11]

Narcyza Żmichowska [Gabryella] (4 March 1819–24 December 1876), born in Warsaw, became governess to the Zamoyski children in 1838 and went with them to Paris, where her exiled brother helped to radicalize her political and social views. She returned to Poland smoking cigars, finding employment as a governess to the Kisielecki children. In Warsaw, she met other intellectuals, debuting in the magazine *Pierwiosnek* and writing for other magazines: *Pielgrzym, Przegląd Naukowy*. She founded a group of suffragettes who took part in anti-Tsarist activities, 1842–1849. In 1849, arrested by the Russians, she was sentenced to three years in prison. Żmichowska's first novel, *Poganka* [The Heathen], appeared in 1846, others following. Her correspondence was published in 1960.[12]

Russia (13 writers)

Evdokiya Petrovna Rostopchina

Насильный брак (1845)

Баллада и аллегория

Посвящается мысленно Мицкевичу

Lascia ch'io piango mia cruda sorte,
E che sospiri la libertà

[...]

---

11 Jakuboszczak Agnieszka, *Sarmacka dama Barbara Sanguszkowa (1718–1791) i jej salon towarzyski* (Poznań: Wydawnictwo Poznańskie, 2008).

12 Barbara Winklowa, *Narcyza Żmichowska i Wanda Żeleńska* (Kraków: Literackie, 2004).

Жена

Раба ли я или подруга—
То знает Бог! ... Я ль избрала
Себе жестокого супруга?
Сама ли клятву я дала?
Жила я вольно и счастливо,
Свою любила волю я;
Но победил, пленил меня
Соседей злых набег хищливый.
Я предана, я продана—
Я узница, я не жена!

Напрасно иго роковое
Властитель мнит озолотить;
Напрасно мщенье, мне святое,
В любовь он хочет превратить!
Не нужны мне его щедроты!
Его я стражи не хочу!
Сама строптивых научу
Платить мне честно дань почета.
Лишь им одним унижена,
Я враг ему, я не жена!

Он говорить мне запрещает
На языке моем родном,
Знаменоваться мне мешает
Моим наследственным гербом;
Не смею перед ним гордиться
Старинным именем моим
И предков храмам вековым,
Как предки славные, молиться ...
Иной устав принуждена
Принять несчастная жена.

Послал он в ссылку, в заточенье
Всех верных, лучших слуг моих;
Меня же предал притесненью
Рабов—лазутчиков своих.
Позор, гоненье и неволю
Мне в брачный дар приносит он -
И мне ли ропот запрещен?
Еще ль, терпя такую долю,
Таить от всех ее должна

Насильно взятая жена?[13]

Forced Marriage
Ballad and Allegory
Dedicated mentally to Mickiewicz

> *Let me mourn my hard fate,*
> *And let me long for freedom*

[...]

Wife

Am I a slave or a girlfriend?
God knows! ... Did I choose
An abusive spouse?
Did I take the oath myself?
I lived freely and happily,
I loved my free will;
But the evil neighbors' attack
Won and captured me.
I'm betrayed, I'm sold –
I'm a prisoner, I'm not a wife!

The ruler thinks to enrich
The fatal yoke in vain;
In vain he wants to convert into love
The revenge which is sacred to me!
I don't need his generosity!
I don't want his guarding!
I'll teach the obstinate person myself
To pay me an honest tribute of honor.
Humiliated only by him alone,
I am his enemy, not his wife!

He forbids me to speak

---

13 *Ростопчина, Е.П. Талисман (Москва: Московский рабочий*, 1987) [Rostopchina, E.P., *Talisman* (Moscow, Moskovskiy rabochiy, 1987)], pp. 109–111. See also: https://litrika.ru/evdokiya-rastopchina-nasilnyj-brak/#sbirajtes-slugi-i.a1

In my native language,
He doesn't let me celebrate
My hereditary coat of arms;
In front of him I don't dare be proud
Of my ancient name
And pray like my noble ancestors
to centuries-old temples ...
And the unhappy wife is forced
To adopt a different charter.

He sent into exile, into captivity,
All my faithful, best servants;
Meanwhile, he betrayed me,
leaving me to slaves—his spies.
Shame, persecution, and bondage
He brings me as a marriage gift—
And am I forbidden to lament?
Still, enduring such a fate,
Must a forcibly taken wife
Hide it from everyone?[14]

Countess Rostopchina's poem is a good lesson in how to make oneself unpopular. Dedicated to the Polish patriot Adam Mickiewicz, it is, as it says, "an allegory" about Poland's ongoing subjugation to its Russian masters, in eight nine-syllable rhymed stanzas of ten lines apiece (Alexander Pushkin's longer *Evgenii Onegin* stanzas, 1825–1832, alternate nine- and eight-syllable lines). The tsar was furious. It's a shame not to cite the whole poem: the wife's four stanzas, given here, respond to four from the old baron complaining about his troublesome wife in their "forced marriage." The Italian epigraph about longing for freedom is from Georg Friedrich Händel's London opera *Rinaldo*, composed in 1711 (it is absent in our cited Soviet edition). Rostopchina has clearly put some thought into her subject.

What then is the wife's argument? "Am I a slave or a girlfriend," she opens. She contrasts her, or Poland's, past freedom and happiness with her new status—betrayed, sold, prisoner. Each stanza ends with a

---

14 Translation reviewed by Margarita Madanova Isbell.

rhetorical flourish: a prisoner, not a wife; an enemy, not a wife; an unhappy wife; a forcibly taken wife. Rostopchina calls the baron "abusive;" she refers to "the evil neighbors' attack;" she speaks of sacred revenge; she even notes being forbidden to speak in her native language, and adds that her spouse sent "into exile, into captivity, / All my faithful, best servants, leaving me to [...] his spies." One grasps the tsar's displeasure. Indeed, the allegory, though vivid, is somewhat thinly stretched over the generous indignation Rostopchina puts on the page; signposts like the dedication to Mickiewicz simply provide her highly charged text with an allegorical bullhorn.

One might wonder whether Rostopchina's gender made this text easier to write. Perhaps so: a woman writing about an abusive marriage has some latitude for indignation, and it is possible that the tsar's anger would have taken a more punitive turn had the poem's author been male. As it was, Nicholas I banned her from St Petersburg, the capital, and she spent the rest of his reign in Moscow.

Elizaveta Niklaevna Akhmatova [or **Leila**] (2 December 1820–12 April 1904), born in Nachalovo, lost her father aged five. In 1842, she sent an unpublished translation to the journalist Osip Senkovsky, and he replied favorably; in 1848, she moved to Saint Petersburg, writing for his journal *Library for Reading*. In 1856, Akhmatova created her own periodical, *Collected Foreign Novels, Novellas, and Stories Translated into Russian*, which lasted over twenty years, publishing Charles Dickens, Wilkie Collins, Anthony Trollope, George Sand, and Emile Zola.[15]

Varvara Nikolaevna Annenkova (1795–1866), born in Nizhny Novgorod, was the sister of General Nicholas Annenkov and of the poet Ivan Annenkov. Her writing was influenced by her close friend and mentor, Mikhail Lermontov. Her publications include *For the Chosen Few*, 1844, *Poems*, 1854–1856, and *Charlotte Corday*, 1866.[16]

Yekaterina Alekseyevna Avdeyeva, née **Polevaya** (16 August 1788–21 July 1865), born in Kursk, was the sister of Nikolai Polevoy and Ksenofont Polevoy. Avdeyeva was known for her books on homemaking and her collections of Russian folk tales. In 1837, she published her *Notes*

---

15 Marina Ledkovsky, Charlotte Rosenthal, and Mary Fleming Zirin. *Dictionary of Russian Women Writers* (Westport, CT: Greenwood Press, 1994).

16 Marina Ledkovsky et al. *Dictionary of Russian Women Writers* (1994).

and Remarks about Siberia. She died in Derpt, now Tartu, Estonia.[17]

Countess Antonina Dmitrievna Bludova (25 April 1813–9 April 1891), born in Stockholm, early met Alexander Pushkin, Vasily Zhukovsky, Nikolai Gogol, Mikhail Lermontov, and other leading writers. Her Saint Petersburg salon was a vital link between the imperial court and Slavophile circles; but after her father's death in 1864, Bludova left the capital and devoted herself to Christian philanthropy. Her memoirs were published in 1889.[18]

Anna Petrovna Bunina (18 January 1774–16 December 1829), born in the village of Urusovo, lost her mother in childbirth and received a rudimentary education. In 1802, Bunina moved to Saint Petersburg and devoted herself to writing. In 1807–1810, she was part of Gavrila Derzhavin's and Alexander Shishkov's literary circle; Shishkov became a mentor. The imperial family awarded her pensions in 1809, 1810, and 1813. Burina published her first work in 1809: *The Inexperienced Muse*, with a second volume in 1812. In 1811, she was made an honorary member of the Lovers of the Russian Word. Burina traveled to Britain in 1815–1817 for breast cancer treatment, without success. Her collected works appeared in 1819; she left the capital in 1824 due to continuing illness, dying in 1829.[19]

Dorothea "Dolly" de Ficquelmont, née **Countess Dorothea von Tiesenhausen** (14 October 1804–10 April 1863), born in Saint Petersburg, was the granddaughter of General Prince Kutuzov. From 1815–1821, Ficquelmont lived in Reval (now Tallinn) and Florence. In 1821, she married Count Charles-Louis de Ficquelmont, who was then appointed Austrian Ambassador to the Kingdom of Two Sicilies in Naples. In 1829, Charles-Louis was appointed Austrian Ambassador to Russia; Ficquelmont opened a salon, featuring Turgenev, Vyazemsky, and Alexander Pushkin. The Ficquelmonts left for Vienna in 1839. In 1848, Charles-Louis, Minister-President of the Habsburg Empire, was

---

17   A.A. Polovtsov, *Русский биографический словарь* [Russian Biographical Dictionary], 25 vols (St Petersburg: Imperial Russian Historical Society, 1896–1918).

18   *Энциклопедический словарь Брокгауза и Ефрона* [Brockhaus and Efron Encyclopedic Dictionary], 86 volumes (St. Petersburg and Leipzig: Brockhaus and Efron, 1890–1907).

19   Smith, Bonnie, ed. *The Oxford Encyclopedia of Women in World History*, 4 vols (Oxford: Oxford University Press, 2008).

accused of supporting Russia; Ficquelmont in Venice was twice arrested. Her French diary appeared in 1950, while her many letters remain unpublished.[20]

Aleksandra Ishimova (6 January 1805–16 June 1881), born in Kostroma, studied in private boarding schools in Saint Petersburg until a scandal involving her father made the family relocate to the northern provinces. Tsar Alexander I pardoned her father in 1825 and they returned to the capital. Ishimova there opened a small school, meeting Vyazemsky, Zhukovsky, and Pushkin. Ishimova received Pushkin's final letter, written the day of his duel. She published two monthly journals for young ladies: *Little Star*, 1842–1863, and *Rays of Light*, 1850–1860. Her 1841 book *History of Russia in Stories for Children* received the Demidov Prize in 1852. Ishimova also translated and printed several narratives for children, focused on religious and moral education.[21]

Nadezhda Dmitryevna Khvoshchinskaya [or **V. Krestovsky**] (20 May 1821?–8 June 1889) was born in Ryazan, where her father was accused of embezzlement; it took him ten years to clear his name, while the family sank into poverty. Khvoshchinskaya was educated at home by private tutors. She published her first poems in 1842, writing over a hundred poems in her lifetime, mostly unpublished. Her first novel, *Anna Mikhailovna* appeared in 1850 in *Notes of the Fatherland*, using her pen name. Several further novels and stories followed, including *The Boarding School Girl*, 1861, and *Ursa Major*, 1871. Khvoshchinskaya also translated several of George Sand's novels. She spent most of her life in Ryazan, moving to Saint Petersburg after her mother's death in 1884.[22]

Yekaterina Aleksandrovna Kniazhnina (1746–6 June 1797), born in Saint Petersburg, married Yakov Knyazhnin in 1770. Kniazhnina hosted an important salon, published poetry in Russian journals, and was also the first known Russian woman to write an elegy. Ivan Krylov wrote a parody about the couple in 1787, *Prokazniki* [The Troublemakers].[23]

Yevdokiya Petrovna Rostopchina (23 December 1811–3 December

---

20 Dolly Ficquelmont, *Дневник 1829–1837. Весь пушкинский Петербург* [Diary 1829–1837. All Pushkin's Petersburg] (Moscow: Minuvshee, 2009).

21 Andrew Kahn, *The Cambridge Companion to Pushkin* (Cambridge: Cambridge University Press, 2006); Marina Ledkovsky et al. *Dictionary of Russian Women Writers* (Westport, CT: Greenwood Press, 1994).

22 Jehanne M. Gheith, *Finding the Middle Ground: Krestovskii, Tur, and the Power of Ambivalence in Nineteenth-Century Russian Women's Prose* (Evanston, IL: Northwestern University Press, 2004).

23 Marina Ledkovsky et al., *Dictionary of Russian Women Writers* (1994).

1858), born in Moscow, lost her mother at six. She learned German, French, Italian, and English. Her friend Vyazemsky published her first poem, "Talisman," in his almanac in 1831; in 1833, she married Count Andrey Fedorovich Rostopchin. The family moved in 1836 to Saint Petersburg; Lermontov, Pushkin, Zhukovsky supported her work; her salon featured Vyazemsky, Gogol, and others. Rostopchina wrote poetry, prose, and comedy. During her trip abroad in 1845, she wrote the poem "Forced Marriage," about Russia's occupation of Poland. The furious tsar banned her from the capital. She continued to write poems, plays, and translations, living in Moscow until the tsar's death.[24]

Alexandra Osipovna Smirnova, née **Rosset** (6 March 1809–7 June 1882), born in Odessa, lost her father in 1814 to the plague. In 1826, she became lady-in-waiting to the Dowager Empress, then the Empress after 1828. She also shone in the Karamzin salon, counting Pushkin, Vyazemsky, and Zhukovsky as admirers. In 1832, she married Nikolai Mikhailovich Smirnov, traveling in Europe in 1833–1837 for her health, then again in 1842–1844, when she spent time with Gogol. After 1845 and an interval in Kaluga, the couple moved between Saint Petersburg and Europe, notably Paris where Smirnova visited Mickiewicz. She died there, leaving both actual memoirs and 'posthumous notes' which appear to have been largely fabricated by her daughter.[25]

Princess Yekaterina Romanovna Dashkova, née **Countess Vorontsova** (28 March 1743–15 January 1810), learned Russian, French, Italian, and German, studying mathematics at university and becoming a maid-of-honor to the tsarina in her teens. At court, she grew close to Grand Duchess Yekaterina Alexeyevna [Catherine]. In 1759, she married Prince Mikhail Dashkov. When Peter became tsar in 1762, Catherine led a *coup d'État*. In 1764, Dashkov died; Dashkova left for Europe from 1768–1782. In France, she became friends with Diderot, Voltaire, and Benjamin Franklin. Back in Russia, Catherine appointed Dashkova director of the Imperial Academy of Arts and Sciences, the first woman in the world to lead a national academy. She edited a six-volume Russian dictionary and a monthly magazine, writing at least two novels and

---

24 Diana Greene, *Reinventing Romantic Poetry: Russian Women Poets of the Mid-Nineteenth Century* (Madison, WI: University of Wisconsin Press, 2004).
25 A.O. Smirnova-Rosset, *Воспоминания, письма* [Memories, Letters] (Moscow: Pravda, 1990).

her memoirs, published in French in 1804. She also composed music.[26]

Maria Semyonovna Zhukova (1805–26 April 1855), born in Arzamas, spent her childhood in the provinces. She married a local landowner at seventeen or eighteen. Zhukova moved to Saint Petersburg around 1830, writing to support herself and pay her husband's gambling debts. Her first story appeared in 1837, her first real success with the story collection *Evenings on the Karpovka* in 1838–1839. Zhukova published frequently, both novels and travel accounts. *Tales* followed in 1840, and *Sketches of Southern France and Nice* in 1844.[27]

Ukraine (1 writer)

Hanna Barvinok

Лихо не без добра (1857)

Як ішла я заміж, дак свого жениха й не бачила. Я осталась п›яти год од матері, да ще було в мене дві сестри да брат жонатий; у його ми й жили. Невістка нами орудувала. Нікого ми не знали, нікуди не ходили. Хто ходить, тому як у себе в оселі, а я було боюсь і за тин вийти: неволя була; тільки по воду до колодязя ходила.

От один раз, якось так случилось, у сусідстві весілля було. Я й пішла. Як біжить невістчин хлопець:—Іди додому!

Я зараз і йду. Звісно, не рідна мати кличе. Ідемо, аж бачу: недалеко від хати ходить шкапа. Я питаю хлопця:—Чия то шкапа? Де вона взялася?

Бо до нас ніхто ніколи не ходив, таких злючих собак держала невістка, і ми нікого не проводили, то й людей не бачили.

—А то,—каже,—хтось до нас приїхав.

Прийшли в хату, аж дивлюсь—такого багато людей! Ну, сказано —багато. Да все локшу кришять. Аж тут невістка мені назустріч:— Одягайся: підеш вінчатись.

Як мені сказано *одягайся*, так я й отетеріла й отерпла: ходю по хаті, нічого перед собою не бачу: завертілось—завертілось у голові... Я нічого не знаю. Ну, і на весілля прохала—як дерев›яна була. Сказано —не знаю.[28]

---

26 A. Woronzoff-Dashkoff, *Dashkova: A Life of Influence and Exile* (Philadelphia: American Philosophical Society, 2008).

27 Victor Terras, *A History of Russian Literature* (New Haven, CT: Yale University Press, 1991).

28 Hanna Barvinok, *Твори у двох томах* [Works in two volumes] (Lviv: BaK, 2011), I p. 20.

A Blessing in Disguise

I met my fiancé only at the wedding. I was five years old when my mother passed away; I had two sisters and a married brother; we lived in his house. Our sister-in-law ordered us around. We didn't know anyone, we didn't go anywhere. In your home, you do whatever you like, but I was scared to step even beyond the fence: It was my bondage; I would only go to the well to get some water.

Once, our neighbors had a wedding. So, I went. And then my sister-in-law's boy ran up:—Go home!

I went right away, of course. You know, it is not your mother who sends for you. We were walking, and then I saw an old horse near the house. I asked the boy:—Whose horse is that? Where did it come from?

No one ever visited us, our sister-in-law kept vicious dogs. And we didn't invite anyone, so we didn't see people.

—We've got some guests—he said.

We entered the house, and I saw a lot of people! Yes, many people. They were talking and cooking. Then my sister-in-law came up to me and said:—Get dressed: you are going to get married.

As I was told "Get dressed," I became dazed and numb. I was walking around the house and I couldn't see anything in front of me: my head was spinning– everything was spinning around me. I don't know anything. Well, I invited everyone to the wedding—I was numb. I told you—I don't know.[29]

Hanna Barvinok was writing by the 1840s; this story is dated 1857, but finding Barvinok proved complicated, and the Harvard library copy here cited begins with this tale. I am told that Barvinok is still read in Ukrainian schools, and this writing is popular, true to its designation—*narodny*—in this modern L'viv edition. As in the Czech and Hungarian extracts from Němcová and Karacs, this is a simple story, describing a young woman's imprisonment in her brother's house, her subjection to her sister-in-law, and her eventual freedom through marriage, reflecting the title's premise that there is no evil without good. Class markers here are infrequent but present: the first-person narrator goes to the well for water, no servant performs that task. The tone in this dialogue-heavy extract is immediate and chatty; Barvinok has a gift for storytelling, with a focus on plot and dialogue in the place of description and character development. One thinks of the French neoclassical maxim, "Parler c'est agir," to speak is to act. Were it not for the first-person narration, this might be one of the Grimm Brothers' fairy tales: the scene is deftly set in

---

29   Translation reviewed by Nataliya Shpylova-Saeed.

the narrow space that a three-page short story occupies.

Beyond the class setting, this extract also tells us more than a little about the situation of women in mid-nineteenth-century Ukraine, at least of women who draw their own water. The narrator and protagonist, on her mother's disappearance, is not free to act; she is imprisoned in her married brother's house and subject to his wife's caprices: "We didn't know anyone, we didn't go anywhere." This is a society in which unmarried women answer to their male family members; freedom, per the title, comes with marriage, and that is not so very different from the imprisonment described by the rather wealthier Elisavet Moutzan-Martinengou on contemporary Zakynthos, as class distinctions bow to the dead hand of patriarchy. Indeed, it is worth pointing out that the liberating marriage here is an arranged one: "I met my fiancé only at the wedding," writes Barvinok. The narrator is in no way master of her fate; she is traded from one household to another much as a piece of furniture might be.

Is Romanticism to be found in this short tale of marriage and liberation? We have argued that a defining characteristic of women's writing in the age is empathy for the oppressed, and that certainly seems to be the case here. We are squarely in the shoes of the protagonist, a person endowed with sentience if not free will, who seems relatively resigned to her lot and yet finds meaning in the liberation an arranged marriage grants her. If Barvinok found this situation appalling, she does not shout it from the rooftops, she instead chooses to let us note the details—the vicious dogs that keep visitors away—and draw our own conclusions. There is tact in this approach, and even kindness. So, from a populist or folk tale perspective, as from a woman's perspective, the story has typical Romantic elements. But further, the very choice of idiom is itself a Romantic manifesto: Ukraine was occupied in 1857, but Barvinok elects not to write in the language of the occupier. She writes in Ukrainian, indeed in dialectal Ukrainian. This appeal to the living speech of the nation—a national or *narodny* discourse—is fundamental to the history of Romanticism, from the ballad to the fairy tale to the dictionary, and from the 1760s—Bishop Percy in England—to at least the 1850s—Asbjørnsen and Moe in Norway, collectors of fairy tales. It is a revolutionary act, and part of a tradition stretching, like the present volume, from St Petersburg to Lima. Barvinok's choice of language is, in short, a quintessentially Romantic decision. She is in good company, and it is entirely fitting that she should be read today by the schoolchildren of Ukraine.

Oleksandra Mikhailovna Bilozerska-Kulish [or **Hanna Barvinok**] (5 May 1828–6 July 1911), born into a literary family in the Chernigov Governorate (Ukraine), married Panteleimon Kulish in 1847. The couple traveled to Warsaw, where Panteleimon was arrested, sent to Saint Petersburg, and tried for writing *The Tale of the Ukrainian People*. Barvinok suffered a miscarriage and became unable to have children. From 1854, the couple lived in Saint Petersburg, returning to Motronivka in 1883. When Panteleimon died, Barvinok published his writings. She wrote more than thirty stories, beginning in the 1840s; her first work was *The Jewish Serf*. She began publishing in 1858: *House Disaster*, 1861, *Women's Poverty* and *Victory*, 1887, *Father's Mistake*, 1902. Barvinok's works appeared in *Khata, First Wreath, Osnova, Pravda*, and elsewhere, her complete works in 2002.[30]

Estonia (0 writers)

I have identified zero Estonian women authors in this period. Further research clearly remains to be done.

---

30 Kubijovyč, Volodymyr, and Arkadii Zhukovsky, eds. *Encyclopedia of Ukraine*, 2 vols (Toronto: University of Toronto Press, 1984–1988).

8. Writers from Scandinavia

Scandinavia was a relatively stable region in the period 1776–1848, marked however by the assassination of Sweden's King Gustav III in 1792, by Sweden's loss of Finland to Russia in 1809 after the Finnish War, and by Sweden's acquisition of Norway from Denmark in 1814 under Bernadotte, a consequence of the Danish alliance with Napoleon. Denmark kept Iceland (until 1944), Greenland, and the Faroe Islands. This entire region has also done work to reclaim women writers in the period: my English-language sources identify seventeen Danish women writers, eight Finnish (writing mostly in Swedish), one Icelandic, five Norwegian, and seventeen Swedish.

Denmark (17 writers)

Clara Elisabeth Andersen [or **Paul Winter**] (13 May 1826–28 August 1895), born in Copenhagen, sent her play *En Evadatter* to the poet Henrik Hertz in 1848, who encouraged her. It was published and then staged by Frederik Høedt in 1855. Her 1862 play *Rosa og Rosita* was staged in Copenhagen, Vienna, Berlin, Breslau, and Christiania (now Oslo). However, Andersen left her plays unsigned, while her short stories—*Noveller*, 1855—and her novel—*Kastaniebaandet* [The Chestnut Band], 1861—appeared under the pen name 'Paul Winter.' She died still unknown as a playwright.[1]

Charlotte Baden (21 November 1740–6 June 1824) was raised by her relative Anna Susanne von der Osten, head lady-in-waiting to Princess Charlotte Amalie of Denmark. In 1763, she married a Copenhagen professor, Jacob Baden. She published a novel, *Den fortsatte Grandison*

---

[1] Jytte Larsen, Grethe Ilsøe, and Hanne Rimmen Nielsen, eds. *Dansk Kvindebiografisk Leksikon*, 4 vols (Copenhagen: Rosinante, 2000).

[The Continued Grandison], after Richardson's 1753 novel, in 1784. Baden also left correspondence.[2]

Charlotta Dorothea Biehl (2 June 1731–17 May 1788), born in Copenhagen, learned to read and write in German and Danish from her grandfather, after whose death her parents forbade her to read, making her a maid in 1747. In 1755, her father joined the Royal Danish Academy of Fine Arts. In 1761, Biehl began translating plays from French, German, and Italian for the Royal Danish Theater. In 1762, her *Poète campagnard* had its first performance; she continued as a comedic playwright until 1783. *Den kierlige Mand* [The Loving Man] in 1764 was a success; *Den listige Optrækkerske* [The Cunning Winding Machine] in 1765, about sexuality, caused a scandal. In 1771, Biehl met Johan Bülow, who inspired her to write historical letters about Danish kings. Their correspondence was published in 1783. She also translated *Don Quixote* into Danish in 1776–1777.[3]

Friederike Brun, née **Münther** (3 June 1765–25 March 1835), born in Gräfentonna (now Germany), soon moved to Copenhagen where her father became pastor. Visitors included Klopstock, Cramer, and Johannes Ewald. Brun's father published her first verses and a travel memoir in 1782; poems followed in 1795, 1812, and 1820, travel memoirs in 1799–1801, 1818, and 1833. In 1783, she married Constantin Brun, traveling in Europe from 1789–1810, hosting salons and meeting Goethe, Schiller, A.W. Schlegel, Herder, Wilhelm Grimm, and Germaine de Staël. With the poet Matthisson and the historian Johannes von Müller, she spent time in the Bern home of Charles Victor de Bonstetten, with whom she corresponded thereafter. After a long stay in Italy, she returned to Denmark. Her poem "Chamouny at Sunrise" inspired Coleridge.[4]

Baroness Thomasine Christine Gyllembourg-Ehrensvärd (9 November 1773–2 July 1856), born in Copenhagen, married the writer Peter Andreas Heiberg in 1789. In 1800, he was exiled for political activity, and she obtained a divorce, marrying the Swedish Baron Carl Fredrik Ehrensvärd in 1801. The baron was himself a fugitive, implicated in the

---

2 Carl Frederik Bricka, *Dansk biografisk Leksikon*, 27 vols (Copenhagen: J.H. Schulz, 1933–1944); Jytte Larsen et al, eds. *Dansk Kvindebiografisk Leksikon* (2000).
3 Jytte Larsen et al, eds. *Dansk Kvindebiografisk Leksikon* (2000); Katharina M. Wilson, ed. *An Encyclopedia of Continental Women Writers* (1991).
4 Jytte Larsen et al, eds. *Dansk Kvindebiografisk Leksikon* (2000); Katharina M. Wilson, ed. *An Encyclopedia of Continental Women Writers* (1991).

1792 assassination of King Gustav III. He died in 1815. From 1822–1825, Gyllembourg joined her son in Kiel, returning then to Copenhagen. In 1827, she published the romance *Familien Polonius* [The Polonius Family] anonymously in her son's newspaper. In 1828 appeared her *Den Magiske Nøgle* [The Magic Key] and *En Hverdags-Historie* [An Everyday Story], then *Old and New Novels* in 1833–1834, *New Stories* in 1835–1836, and so forth. In 1849–1851, she brought out a library edition of her collected works. Her authorship became known only after her death.[5]

Marie Kirstine Henriette Hanck (19 July 1807–1846), born in Odense, was a childhood friend of Hans Christian Andersen, corresponding with him from 1830 until her death. She spent her life in her childhood home. Hanck's first published poem appeared in her grandfather's local newspaper in 1830. Other poetry followed, some posthumous, and two novels: *Tante Anna* in 1838 and *En Skribentindes Datter* [A Writer's Daughter] in 1842. Hanck translated both novels into German; they appeared in 1845–1846 with a foreword by Andersen.[6]

Mette Louise Christiane Frederikke Hegermann-Lindencrone (4 December 1778–18 June 1853), born in Copenhagen, was the only one of six siblings to reach adulthood. She married Johan Hendrik Hegermann-Lindencrone in 1797, with whom she had nine children. Hegermann-Lindencrone first published poetry at fifteen. Her three main works, all with strong female leads, appeared under her own name: the two dramas *Eleonora Christa Uhlfeldt*, 1817, and *Troubadouren*, 1820, and *Danske Fortellinger*, 1825, a collection of short stories. The playwright Adam Oehlenschläger attended the couple's Copenhagen salon.[7]

Johanne Luise Heiberg, née **Pätges** (22 November 1812–21 December 1890), was born to German emigrants: a Catholic father and a Jewish mother. She entered ballet school in 1820, making her acting debut in 1827. In 1831, she married the playwright Johan Ludvig Heiberg; their home became a cultural center. He died in 1860, and in 1864 she retired from the theater. Heiberg starred at Copenhagen in plays by Shakespeare, Holberg, Oehlenschläger, Henrik Hertz, and her husband, writing some vaudevilles herself, notably *En Søndag paa Amager* [A

---

5   Elisabeth Hude, *Thomasine Gyllembourg og Hverdagshistorierne* (Copenhagen: Rosenkilde og Bagger, 1951).
6   Carl Frederik Bricka, *Dansk biografisk Leksikon* (1933–1944).
7   Ibid.

Sunday at Amager]. Søren Kierkegaard wrote a tribute to her in 1847; her autobiography appeared in 1891–1892.[8]

Anna Christiane Lauterup Ludvigsen (14 June 1794–28 June 1884), born in Aabenraa, was blessed in her cradle by Johann Kaspar Lavater and felt it her vocation to write poetry. The family moved to Brede in 1796, where her father taught her French, German, and Latin. In 1819, she married Jürgen Simon Jessen, who died in 1842; with him, she spent some years in southern Jutland. In 1844, she married the farmer Laurenz Paulsen Lauterup, settling in Vollum. Lauterup died in 1864, and in 1867 Ludvigsen returned to southern Jutland, now under German rule. In 1840, she published several poems in the local newspaper. After corresponding with Oehlenschläger and Ingemann, in 1852 she published *Markblomster af Anna* [Wildflowers by Anna]. Her poems had special significance in Jutland under German rule.[9]

Birgitte Dorothea Henriette Nielsen [or **Theodora**] (23 January 1815–17 January 1900) was born in Strandgården in northern Jutland. Her vaudevillean *Slægtningene* [The Relatives] was staged at Copenhagen's Royal Danish Theater, featuring local costumes from Fanø and songs she had composed herself. It ran to seventy-eight performances in 1849. Her 1862 novel *Esberhs Skolehistorier* [Esberh's School Stories] calls for female emancipation.[10]

Elise Charlotte Otté (30 September 1818–20 December 1903), born in Copenhagen, moved with her parents in 1820 to Saint Croix in the Danish West Indies, returning when her father died, first to Denmark, then England when her English mother remarried an Englishman, the philologist Benjamin Thorpe. Thorpe taught Otté several languages, old and new, to assist his grammatical work. In 1840, she escaped to study physiology at Harvard University, returning to assist in translating the *Elder Edda*. In 1849, she left again for Scotland, translating for George Edward Day, with whom she remained until 1872. Her monograph *Scandinavian History* appeared in 1874, to lasting impact. She translated Alexander von Humboldt and Quatrefages de Bréau and published grammars of Danish and of Swedish in 1883–1884.[11]

---

8   Ibid.; Jytte Larsen et al., eds. *Dansk Kvindebiografisk Leksikon* (2000).
9   Carl Frederik Bricka, *Dansk biografisk Leksikon* (1933–1944).
10 Ibid.
11 *Dictionary of National Biography* [DNB].

Louise Scheel von Plessen, née **Countess Louise von Berckentin** (26 April 1725–14 September 1799), born in Vienna to the Danish Ambassador, spent her childhood in that town. From 1740–1744, she was maid of honor to Christian VI's queen consort. In 1744, she married Major Christian Sigfred Scheel von Plessen, becoming a childless widow in 1755 and retiring to the countryside. In 1766, she became head lady-in-waiting at the court of the new queen. The queen grew very attached to her, but she was blamed for separating the royal couple; in 1768, von Plessen was exiled with six hours' notice, first to her home, then Germany. There, von Plessen wrote her *Mémoires de la cour de Danemark*, which were later published.[12]

Julie Reventlow, née **Schimmelmann** (16 February 1763–28 December 1816), married Count Frederik Reventlow in 1779. Reventlow hosted a literary salon at the couple's Holstein estate and published two works in German about education: *Sonntagsfreuden des Landmannes* [Sunday Joys of the Countryman], 1791, and *Kinderfreuden oder Unterricht in Gesprächen* [Children's Joys or Teaching in Conversations], 1793.[13]

Sophie Frederikke Louise Charlotte Reventlow, née **von Beulwitz** or **von Beulwiz** (1 June 1747–26 July 1822), was born in Oldenburg and raised in Sorø, receiving a German education. In 1774, she married Lengreve Christian Ditlev Frederik Reventlow; they had twelve children, nine reaching adulthood. The family spent summers in Pederstrup and winters in Copenhagen. In the late 1770s and early 1780s, Frederikke Charlotte kept a diary about their children, translated from German to Danish and published in 1990. Her manuscript correspondence survives.[14]

Maria Engelbrecht Stokkenbech [also **E.M. Stokkenbeck**] (1759-after 1806), born in Hamburg, lost her father aged one; her mother raised her on the island of Ærø. From age twelve, she worked as a waitress, then a maid. Married to a drunk, she left but could not find work; she had a tailor sew her a man's suit, calling herself Gotfried Jacob Eichstedt, and found work as a tailor's apprentice. She smoked, drank, and played cards with her coworkers, urinating with the help

---

12   August Fjelstrup, *Damerne ved Karoline Mathildes Hof* (Copenhagen: Hermann-Petersens Forlag, 1909); Jytte Larsen et al, eds. *Dansk Kvindebiografisk Leksikon* (2000).
13   Jytte Larsen et al., eds. *Dansk Kvindebiografisk Leksikon* (2000).
14   *The History of Nordic Women's Literature* (https://www.kau.se/en/node/37172).

of a horn, working in Poland, then Germany, then Spain. In 1784, returning to Copenhagen, she was recognized as a woman and arrested. Stokkenbech explained herself in court and was released on condition she wear women's clothes, but with permission to practice her trade. Her short autobiography appeared in German in Copenhagen in 1784; Danish editions followed in 1787 and 1806.[15]

Anna Magdalene Thoresen, née **Kragh** (3 June 1819–28 March 1903), born in Fredericia, had an illegitimate child who was put out to nurse. In 1842, she married Hans Conrad Thoresen and moved with him to Bergen. Their home became a meeting place for writers and actors; in 1850, Ole Bull founded a theater in Bergen, Det Norske Theater, for which Thoresen wrote four anonymous plays. Her stepdaughter was married to Henrik Ibsen. A volume of her poems appeared in 1860; her novels include *Studenten*, 1862, *Signes Historie*, 1864, and *Solen i Siljedalen* [The Sun in Siljedalen] in 1868. After her husband's death in 1858, Thoresen moved to Copenhagen. Her play *Et rigt Parti* [A Rich Party] was staged at the Royal Danish Theater in 1870, then in Stockholm and Christiania (now Oslo); *Inden Døre* [Indoors] followed in 1877. She also published travel memoirs in 1872 and 1882.[16]

Pauline Frederikke Worm (29 November 1825–13 December 1883), born in Hyllested, tried aged nine to persuade her uncle (a politician) to give women the vote. In 1838, Worm was sent to a girls' school in Randers, staying on to become a teacher before working as a private tutor from 1847. Her poem for the 1848 coronation of Frederick VII appeared in the press. In Præstø, she wrote the poetry volume *En Krands af ni Blade* [A Wreath of Nine Leaves] in 1850 and a novel, *De Fornuftige* [The Sensible], first published in 1857. In 1853, after a year studying in Copenhagen, she opened a girls' school in Randers as headmistress. It failed and she resumed tutoring, also speaking in public after 1864 about women's emancipation and Danish patriotism. She moved to Copenhagen in 1881.[17]

---

15 Inger Wiene, *En historie om kvindelige håndværkere i 200 år* (Copenhagen: SFAH, 1991).
16 Knut Helle, ed. *Norsk biografisk leksikon*, 10 vols (Oslo: Kunnskapsforlaget, 1999–2005).
17 Jytte Larsen et al., eds. *Dansk Kvindebiografisk Leksikon* (2000).

Finland (8 writers)

Fredrika Wilhelmina Carstens

Murgrönan (1840)

N. 28. Maji 18..

Ännu en hälsning! En så kär så varm.
Jag dig, o hulda Fosterbygd! vill sända;
Tag den emot, den går ur trofast barm;
Och huru än mitt öde sig må vända.
Är du den tanke först och sist likväl,
Som smyger sig utur min sorgsna själ.

Jag har uppvaknat, älskade Emilia, ifrån en ganska god sömn; mina själssåväl som kroppskrafter äro styrkte af den hvila jag erfarit. Vid mitt lilla kammarfönster har jag njutit af den milda vårluften, hvilken fritt spelar in genom det öppnade fönstret, O! hvilken herrlig morgon, detta ställe är långt trefligare än jag i går vid min ankomst fann det, skymningen såväl som tröttheten hindrade mig att då urskilja dess högst trefliga läge; ån som löper alldeles under mitt fönster kröker sig i behagliga bugter framåt, och på dess stränder resa sig björkar, så vackra, så raka, som voro de af den vårdsammaste mästares hand ditplanterade. Men, hvad säger jag, som voro de? Hvilken hand kunde i förmåga öfverträffa *dens*, som dit sat dem? Ack, Emilia! hvilkens kunde mera vårdande hvila öfver och beskydda sitt verk? Hvad den är vacker, denna vårens färg; denna unga, friska, gröna; jag fruktar att förtrampa ett enda grässtrå, så obeskrifligen skön och ljuflig förefaller mig naturen.

Denna dag förer mig åter längre ifrån dig, och likväl tycker jag mig aldrig varit dig närmare än just nu; mina tårar blanda sig med dem på bladen af den daggfriska syrenqvist jag nyss brutit ur den lilla häcken under mitt fönster. Det skall följa mig, detta minne ifrån mitt hemlands nejder, och ännu der borta, ehuru vissnadt, för mig utgöra ett vanligt fridens budskap.

Min glada men något nyfikna värdinna har redan bestyrsamt inburit min varma morgondryck; hon står ännu med frågande blick, och tyckes afbida något uppdrag. Lef väl, Emilia! lef väl![18]

---

18 Fredrika Wilhelmina Carstens, *Murgrönan* (Helsingfors: G. O. Wasenius, 1840), pp. 4–5.

The Ivy

N. 28 May 18..

> *Another greeting! One so dear so warm,*
> *O esteemed Foster town! I want to send you;*
> *Receive it, it proceeds from faithful bosom;*
> *And however my fate may turn,*
> *You are that thought, first and last anyway,*
> *That sneaks out of my sad soul.*

I have awakened, dear Emilia, from a rather good sleep; my mental and physical powers are strengthened by the rest I have experienced. At my little chamber window, I have enjoyed the mild spring air, which freely enters through the open window. O! what a glorious morning, this place is far more beautiful than I found it yesterday on my arrival, the twilight as well as fatigue prevented me from then distinguishing its most beautiful situation; the river that runs right below my windows curves forward in pleasant bays, and on its banks rise birches, as beautiful, as straight, as if they had been planted there by the hand of the most careful master. But what do I say, who were they? What hand could surpass in ability that which set them there? Alas, Emilia! whose hand could more care rest on and protect his work? How beautiful it is, this color of spring; this young, healthy, green; I fear to step on a single blade of grass, so indescribably beautiful and lovely does nature seem to me.

This day brings me further away from you again, and yet I think I have never been closer to you than right now; my tears mix with those on the leaves of the dewy lilac I have just plucked from the little hedge under my window. This memory will follow me from the depths of my homeland, and still over there, although withered, constitute a common message of peace for me.

My cheerful but somewhat curious hostess has already bewilderingly brought in my warm morning drink; she still stands with a questioning look and seems to refuse some mission. Live well, Emilia! live well!

Russia took Finland from Sweden following the Finnish War of 1808–1809 and held it as a grand duchy until Finnish independence in 1918. In Helsinki today, Swedish is much spoken, but in 1840, writing in Swedish was a political act: it partakes of the *polis*, not the *oikos*, in contrast to the resolutely domestic and female tone of this opening extract.

What we have here is a letter, dated "May 18..," that follows the introduction and opens an epistolary novel apparently about ivy. One might expect the chooser of such a title to be alert to the natural world, and that seems to be the case in this extract which speaks of a chamber window, mild spring air, a river, birches, grass blades, dewy lilac, a hedge, and a warm morning drink. The scene invites illustration, and that is worthy of remark: the nineteenth century was the great age of the illustrated novel, a project dependent on the sort of novelistic description that a Voltaire or a Fielding, with their emphasis on swiftly moving plot, essentially bypass. Can this then be called a Romantic urge? I believe it can. First, the world is full of books on the Romantics and nature. Second, description matters to Romantic writers, as we saw already in the opening to Sand's *Indiana*, or indeed in Gorriti's *La Quena*. It matters because to a Romantic mind, the self is fundamentally integrated within the context it inhabits. This may be traced back to Kant, who argues that we cannot distinguish *Phainomena* inside and outside our brain: all we have is the matter of our senses, since *Noumena* or things in themselves are forever unknowable. If Fichte argues that all is mind, or Schelling argues that all is nature, both inhabit a post-Kantian space, as does European society by 1840 when this book appeared. What to Voltaire is brute and undynamic matter can thus take on for Carstens a vibrant and interdependent life; her speaker reflects her surroundings as was almost impossible for writers prior to perhaps Rousseau with his periwinkle—"je pousse un cri de joie: *ah! voilà de la pervenche!*", he writes in his posthumous *Confessions*, 1782–1789.[19] Two other strands here seem worth teasing out: first, Linnaeus, the father of botanic taxonomy, had died in Sweden in 1778; and second, the role of electricity in living organisms had been increasingly evident since Galvani published his work on frogs in 1791. Carstens's attention to nature is thus rooted in contemporary philosophy and science; it is rather typically Romantic. "I fear to step on a single blade of grass," she writes.

Is there more to be said? One might add that Carstens opens the letter with six rhymed lines of iambic pentameter, the meter of Shakespeare, that romantic bard; she also sees in nature "the hand of the most careful master," a natural theology akin to that popularized by William Paley's book of that title in 1802. There is, in short, a considerable amount going on in this domestic letter with its description of the bucolic scene outside the speaker's window; the letter shares in the great European debates of the age, it is not isolated from them. One awaits with interest the ivy the novel will present.

---

19 *Les Confessions de J.-J. Rousseau*. Nouvelle édition précédée d'une notice par George Sand (Paris: Charpentier, 1841), p. 236.

Fredrika Wilhelmina Carstens, née **Stichaeus** [or **R**] (5 June 1808–13 April 1888), was born in Naantali during the Finnish War. In 1829, she married Carl Adolf Otto Carstens; the couple had seven children. In the 1830s, Carstens began writing for newspapers about women's education under the pen name 'R.' She published the Swedish-language novel *Murgrönan* [The Ivy] anonymously in 1840. It was criticized for its "female" sprawling language, and Carstens published only a few poems in the press thereafter. After her husband's death in 1842, the estate briefly went bankrupt. In the 1850s, she announced her charity work under her own name, which was disapproved of.[20]

Gustafva Sofia Hjärne, née **Rosenborg** (4 July 1780–6 March 1860), born in Kloster (Sweden), married Captain Gustaf Hjärne in 1801. Hjärne held one of Finland's earliest salons. During the Finnish War, Hjärne may have averted a battle by arranging the peaceful handover of Sveaborg to the Russians in 1808. She translated two plays and wrote poems for the press anonymously. In 1831, she published the Swedish-language novel *Tavastehus slott* [Tavastehus Castle], about the medieval Häme Castle.[21]

Agatha Lovisa de la Myle, née **Brumengeber** or **Brunnengräber** (30 August 1724–1 September 1787), born in Courland (now Latvia), married her nephew Carl Johan de la Myle in 1750, moving to Finland with him in 1762. She wrote poetry in German and Latvian and corresponded with Christian Furchegott Gellert in Leipzig. She composed the poem "Lofqväden" in 1771 for Gustav III of Sweden's coronation. She died on her estate outside Åbo (now Turku).[22]

Fredrika Lovisa Lindqvist (22 February 1786–14 April 1841), born in Åbo (now Turku), moved to Sweden after the Great Fire of Turku in 1827. In 1838, she published *Poems in Prose* in Swedish. *Thoughts on Several Subjects*, also in Swedish, followed in 1842.[23]

Barbara Catharina Mjödh (8 November 1738–1776), born to the politician Abraham Mjödh and Magdalena Ross, wrote occasional

---

20 Päivi Lappalainen and Lea Rojola, *Women›s Voices. Female Authors and Feminist Criticism in the Finnish Literary Tradition* (Helsinki: Finnish Literature Society, 2007).
21 *The History of Nordic Women's Literature*.
22 P.G. Berg and Wilhelmina Stålberg, eds. *Anteckningar om svenska qvinnor* (Stockholm: P.G. Berg, 1864).
23 *Suomen kansallisbiografia* [National Biography of Finland] (https://openlibrary.org/books/OL16394345M/Suomen_kansallisbiografia).

poems for weddings and funerals. In 1754, she published a funeral poem for Anna Gerdzlovia. Her marriage severely restricted her career.[24]

Fredrika Charlotta Runeberg, née **Tengström** (2 September 1807–27 May 1879), born in Jakobstad, spent her youth in Turku, then capital of Finland. In 1828, she moved to Helsinki, marrying the national poet Johan Ludvig Runeberg in 1831. The couple settled in Porvoo. Runeberg wrote two Swedish-language historical novels about the status of women: *Fru Catharina Boije och hennes döttrar* [Mrs Catharina Boije and Her Daughters], 1858, set in Finland during the Great Northern War, and *Sigrid Liljeholm*, 1862, set in the Cudgel War. She also wrote for the press and translated from French, German, and English into Swedish. She may have created the Runeberg torte.[25]

Catharina Charlotta Swedenmarck (29 January 1744–1813), born in Stockholm, first married Lieutenant Carl Johan Hastfer, who died in 1771. In 1773, she married Major Carl Fredrik Toll, a Finnish landowner. She published Swedish-language poems for Gustav III's 1771 coronation, and the play *Dianas fest* [The Feast of Diana] in 1775.[26]

Sara Elizabeth Wacklin (26 May 1790–28 January 1846), born in Uleåborg, lost her father early and her three brothers emigrated. Wacklin worked as a schoolteacher until the Finnish War. In 1813, Wacklin moved to Turku to work as a governess, notably for Gustafva Hjärne. In 1819, she studied in Sweden, opening a girls' school in Uleåborg which burned down in the fire of 1822. From 1823–1827, Wacklin ran a school in Turku; it burned in the fire of 1827, and she opened a school in Helsinki, then Uleåborg again after 1830. Wacklin also taught French and traveled in Denmark, Germany, and Sweden. In 1835, she left for the Sorbonne, becoming the first female university graduate in Finland. She returned to Helsinki to found her sixth girls' school. In 1843, Wacklin retired to Stockholm, publishing *Hundrade minnen från Österbotten* [A Hundred Memories of Ostrobothnia] in 1844–1845.[27]

---

24 *Suomen kansallisbiografia* [National Biography of Finland].
25 *Svenska Litteratursällskapet i Finland* (https://www.sls.fi/sv/); *Suomen kansallisbiografia* [National Biography of Finland].
26 Carina Burman, *Den finländska Sapfo. Catharina Charlotta Swedenmarcks liv och verk* (Uppsala: Lunne böcker, 2004).
27 Henrik Knif et al., eds. *Biografiskt lexikon för Finland*, 4 vols (Helsingfors and Stockholm: Adantis, 2008–2011).

Iceland (1 writer)

Rósa Guðmundsdóttir [or **Vatnsenda-Rósa**] (23 December 1795–28 September 1855), born in Ásgerðarstaðir ín Hörgárdal, lost her mother aged twelve. A farmer's daughter, she received no formal schooling, though there were books in the house. In 1818, she married Olaf Ásmundason; they had five children before divorcing in 1837. Guðmundsdóttir (a patronymic) then married the sailor Gísli Gíslason, twenty years her junior. Both marriages were unhappy; she was also involved with a man named Natan Ketilsson, who was murdered in 1828. As far as is known, none of Guðmundsdóttir's works were published prior to her death in 1855, and some attributions may be apocryphal. Singers including Björk have set her songs and poems to music. Her most famous poem is likely "Augað mitt og augað sítt" [My eye and your eye].[28]

Norway (5 writers)

Gustava Kielland (1800–1889)

"O Jul Med Din Glede"

1. O jul med din glede og barnlige lyst
   vi ønsker deg alle velkommen;
   vi hilser deg alle med jublende røst
   titusinde gange velkommen!

   Refreng
   Vi klapper i hendene,
   vi synger og vi ler,
   så gladerlig, så gladerlig.
   Vi svinger oss i kretsen og neier og bukker.

2. I Østerlands vise, I tre vise menn,
   vi vide hvorhen I vil drage;
   thi vi ville også så gjerne derhen
   og eder på reisen ledsage. *Refreng*

---

28   *The History of Nordic Women's Literature* (https://www.kau.se/en/node/37172).

3. Så rekker jeg deg nå med glede min hånd,
   kom skynd deg og gi meg den annen,
   så knytter vi kjærlighets hellige bånd
   og lover at elske hinannen. *Refreng*

4. Om stormen den tuter og sneen vi ser
   det kan oss dog slet ikke skade
   thi våren og julen oss alltid er nær
   blot vi ere fromme og glade. *Refreng*

5. Når en gang vi samles i himlenes sal
   og synger om jul med sin glede
   vi takker og jubler i tusinde tal
   for tronen i himlen at trede. *Refreng*[29]

1. *O Christmas with your joy and childlike desire*
   we all wish you welcome;
   we all greet you with cheering voices
   ten thousand times welcome!

   Chorus
   We clap hands,
   we sing and we laugh,
   so happy, so happy.
   We swing in circles and curtsey and bow.

2. *You sages of the East, you three wise men,*
   we know where you want to go;
   because we wanted to go there too
   and accompany you on your journey. Chorus

3. *So now I gladly extend my hand to you,*
   come hurry give me the other,
   then we tie the sacred bond of love
   and promise to love each other. Chorus

---

[29] Gustava Kielland, "O Jul Med Din Glede," in Tove Valmot, ed. *Julens stemninger. Dikt, sanger og fortellinger* (Oslo: Bestselgerforlaget, 2012), p. 133. Words and music in http://www.julesanger.no/o_jul_med_din_glede_tekst.shtml.

> 4. *As for the storm that blows and the snow we see*
> *it still can't hurt us at all*
> *because spring and Christmas are always close to us*
> *when we are pious and happy. Chorus*
>
> 5. *When once we gather in heaven's hall*
> *and sing of Christmas with its joy*
> *we give thanks and rejoice in a thousand ways*
> *to tread the throne in heaven. Chorus*

This is a well-known Norwegian Christmas carol. The present anthology of 650 women authors features several hymn writers; certain genres lent themselves relatively unproblematically to female writers prior to 1848, and religious verse is an example of that. The text seems fairly simple, but it bears review. For instance, it opens with the word "barnlige," childlike. Childhood, as Dickens or the Grimm brothers or Andersen bear witness, is one of the nineteenth century's great discoveries; if child protagonists are rare prior to 1800, they are common thereafter, from Philip Pirrip to Hansel and Gretel. And just as the text names childhood, so it speaks to childhood in its performative chorus: we clap hands, we sing, we laugh, we swing in circles and bow and curtsey. Verse three adds that all hold hands—this is uncommon in hymns, but common enough in children's song. I have seen it in Sweden. The other verses celebrate Christmas in somewhat unsurprising fashion—"You sages of the East"—except for verse four, which focuses on the storm and snow, powerless to hurt. One thinks, as perhaps Kielland did, of children bundled against the cold. The verses' song meter is four alternating eleven-syllable and nine-syllable lines with an ABAB rhyme scheme. It takes skill to make such a format sing across five verses as Kielland has done. The chorus is in essence free verse.

What then are we to make of such a text? It is both unpretentious and very successful; indeed, few women composers of the period have had more success. And one reason for this success is certainly its limpidity. It does not clutter the mind; it is well-suited to being sung in Yuletide gatherings in unproblematic fashion by people of all ages. It does presume belief—we are, it says, "pious and happy"—but this is Christmas after all, and Norway is a Catholic country. Few texts in this anthology have a clearer function or fulfill that function more ably.

Magdalene Sophie Buchholm (15 March 1758–12 August 1825), born in Skien, lost her father in 1770 and was raised by a cousin. In 1777, she married Peter Leganger Castberg; in 1781, the couple moved to Flekkefjord, where he died in 1784. She then married Joachim Frederik Buchholm in 1785, moving to Stavanger in 1798 and Kragerø in 1806 and being the center of social life there. Buchholm made frequent long trips to Copenhagen; in 1778, she became the first female member of the academic society Det Norske Selskab, receiving a prize for her poetry in 1783. She published her collected works in 1793.[30]

Jacobine Camilla Collett, née **Wergeland** (23 January 1813–6 March 1895), born in Kristiansand, was the daughter of Nicolai Wergeland and the sister of Henrik Wergeland. In 1816, the family moved to Eidsvoll; as a teen, Collett was sent to finishing school in Denmark. In Christiania (now Oslo), she fell in love with the poet Johan Sebastian Welhaven, her brother's nemesis; in any event, in 1841, she married the politician Peter Jonas Collett and began writing for publication. He died in 1851 and Collett was left with four young sons; she struggled financially thereafter. In 1854–1855, she published *Amtmandens Døtre* [The District Governor's Daughters], among the first realist novels in Norway. Collett grew more radical with age, publishing anonymous articles on women's rights which appeared in collected volumes between 1868–1885. Her diary appeared in 1862.[31]

Conradine Birgitte Dunker, née **Hansteen** (25 August 1780–11 September 1866), born in Christiania (now Oslo), married Captain Ulrik Anton Nicolai Blix Aamodt in 1796 and in 1807, the businessman Johan Friedrich Wilhelm Dunker. In Christiania, Dunker served in the Dramatic Society from 1796–1831 as both translator and actress. From 1814–1831, she ran a fashionable finishing school in her home; the family moved to Trondheim in 1831. Dunker was widowed (again) in 1844 and taught in her daughter's girls' school from 1849–1857 before moving back to Christiania. Dunker's posthumous memoirs *Gamle Dage: Erindringer og Tidsbilleder* [Old Days: Memories and Time Pictures] appeared in 1871.[32]

---

30 *Store norske leksikon* (https://snl.no/); Knut Helle, ed. *Norsk biografisk leksikon* (2005).
31 Katharina M. Wilson, ed. *An Encyclopedia of Continental Women Writers* (1991).
32 *Store norske leksikon*; Knut Helle, ed. *Norsk biografisk leksikon* (2005).

Susanne Sophie Catharina Gustava Kielland, née **Blom**, known as **Gustava Kielland** (6 March 1800–28 February 1889), born in Kongsberg, married the minister Gabriel Kirsebom Kielland in 1824; the couple had eight children. In 1840, Kielland attended a lecture in Stavanger which spurred her to missionary work: back in Lyngdal, she founded a Christian-social women's association, considered Norway's first women's association. Kielland's songs include "O, Jul med din Glæde" and the children's song "Liden Ekorn" [Suffering Squirrel]. Later, she dictated memoirs, *Erindringer fra mitt liv* [Reminiscence from my Life], which appeared in 1882.[33]

Christiane Koren (27 July 1764–28 January 1815), born in Kastrup (Denmark), frequented the academic society Det Norske Selskab in Copenhagen and grew close to the Swede Carl Frederik Dichmann. In 1787, she married the Norwegian Johan Randulf Clausen Koren, leaving Denmark for Østfold, Norway, where her husband was appointed judge. The couple had eight children. Koren published a volume of poetry in 1803; she also wrote plays. Her manuscript diaries were published in 1915, her manuscript description of an 1802 trip to Denmark in 1945.[34]

Sweden (17 writers)

Emilie Flygare-Carlén

Rosen på Tistelön. Berättelse från skärgården (1842)

Första Kapitlet.

> I oron, som beständigt väckes
> Och sjelf sitt gift begärligt när,
> Vår tanke ut på hafvet sträckes
> Och skeppen ser, som krossas der.
>
> Gyllenborg.
> Min son, tag läran af min mun!
> Leopold.

---

[33] Knut Helle, ed. *Norsk biografisk leksikon* (2005).
[34] *Store norske leksikon*; Knut Helle, ed. *Norsk biografisk leksikon* (2005).

Omkring en half mil inom de i nordvest från Marstrand belägna Pater-Noster-skären, hvilka—än i dag ryktbara för de ofta der inträffande skepps-brott—troligen fått sitt namn af de många pater-noster, forntida sjöfarare der uppsändt för sina lifs räddning, ligger en liten grupp af ofruktbara öar, hvaribland dock en är bebodd och den vi i vår berättelse vilja kalla Tistelön. All vegetation på denna fläck af jorden är nästan utdöd, ocla de buskar och andra växter, som här och der visa sig, hafva ett tvinande utseende, liksom för öfrigt hela naturen på dessa klippmassor bär pregeln af en ödslig tomhet.

Vestra kusten af ön består endast af rödaktiga berg, emellan hvilkas öppningar hafvet, nästan ständigt i raseri, vräker sina fradgande vågor. Stenarne, som betäcka stranden, under årtusenden rullade fram och tillbaka af de rastlösa böljorna, hafva alla erhållit en nästan klotrund form. I sjelfva bergen äro bildade runda, genombrutna hålor, der hafsvattnet oupphörligt rusar in och åter fradgande utströmmar, så att dess klagande, entoniga ljud sammansmälter med de hemska skri, sjöfoglarne låta höra, antingen de uppstämma sina liksånger öfver de ovigda menniskoben, hvilka, jemte spillror af vrak, ligga spridda omkring kusten, eller de för strandbons vanda öra förkunna sin väntan på ett nytt skeppsbrott.[35]

Chapter I.

[In the worries, which are constantly awakened
And greedily eat themselves,
Our thought is stretched out to sea
And we see the ships that are broken there.

Gyllenborg.
My son, learn from my mouth!
Leopold.]

On the western coast of Sweden, to the north of Marstrand, and about three miles from the Paternoster rocks [which probably got their name from the many paternosters ancient sailors sent there for saving their lives], well known as the scene of many a fatal shipwreck, lies a little group of barren islands; one only is inhabited, which, in the following narration, we shall call Tistelon. This desolate spot is nearly bare of vegetation, and the few shrubs and plants here and there visible look dry and withered; all nature among those masses of stone presenting only one uniform aspect of dreary sterility.

---

35 Emilie Flygare-Carlén, *Rosen på Tistelön. Berättelse från skärgården* [The Rose on Thistle Island. Story from the Archipelago] (Stockholm: N.H. Thomson, 1842), pp. 5–6.

> *The western shore of the island consists entirely of a range of gray rocks, between the openings of which the ocean, in an almost constant agitation, dashes its foaming waters; the stones that cover the beach, rolled for centuries to and fro by the restless billows, are for the most part rounded; even in the rocks, themselves, circular holes have been formed, through which the waters for ever pour, and then, rushing back, unite their sullen monotonous sound with the dismal scream of the sea-birds, when they uplift their death-cry over the human bones which, mingled with pieces of wreck, lie scattered on the shore, or announce to the experienced ear of the solitary fisherman their anticipation of an approaching shipwreck.*[36]

Sweden, though largely mainland, has 984 inhabited islands, mostly in the Baltic, out of some 267,000 total; Stockholm for instance is on an archipelago. Emilie Carlén grew up a sea captain's daughter in the archipelago of Bohuslän, and the sea recurs in her novels, though she moved from there to Stockholm and remarried in 1841. This extract opens 1842's *Rosen på Tistelön* [The Rose on Thistle Island], set on a desolate island lost in a shipwreck-prone Baltic archipelago.

The extract opens with two epigraphs, from the recent Swedish poets Gustaf Fredrik Gyllenborg and Carl Gustaf af Leopold (both missing in the 1844 translation). The two subsequent paragraphs of text contain no human protagonist: they are somewhat akin to a landscape painting with no human figure, such as Caspar David Friedrich began to paint after about 1820 (earlier Dutch landscapes, by comparison, generally feature people). This is not to say the human element is entirely absent in these opening pages: beyond the poetry, sailors named the shoals; someone named the island of Marstrand, a few leagues away; human bones and debris dot the shore; finally, the island is inhabited. And yet, it is so desolate that the narrator feels compelled to coin a name for it as they begin the tale. There is, in short, a curious sort of waltz here from pristine nature to the human and back again, from what is hidden to what lies in plain sight just off the coast of Sweden. A Freud might call the result *uncanny*.

While a significant Romantic preoccupation, the uncanny is relatively uncommon in European literature before the late eighteenth century. One thinks of Horace Walpole's *The Castle of Otranto*, 1764, and the Gothic tradition he helped launch across Europe. It is hard for the uncanny to

---

36 *The Rose of Tistelon. A Tale of the Swedish Coast* (New York: William H. Colyer, 1844), p. 3. Text in square brackets is omitted in the published translation.

exist without a human element, which makes this opening extract all the more interesting: screaming seabirds and crashing waves are not *per se* uncanny, they become so when combined with unconsecrated human bones—the exposure of what is hidden, indeed we might say the return of the repressed. Nevertheless, and despite her play with what is human, Carlén is unique in this anthology in not putting a living human protagonist in her opening pages. She thereby builds suspense: this *mondo sanza gente* or world without people is a strange place for anyone to live, and we await the eventual protagonist with interest.

The game Carlén is playing might well have been impossible a half-century earlier. I have argued that as late as the mid-eighteenth century, novels tend to begin *in medias res*, in the middle of things; in this anthology's extracts, an opening description is common, and in itself fairly new, but to eliminate a human protagonist altogether seems unique to Carlén. It brings a certain frisson of pleasure and excitement— oddly enough, because in terms of plot, nothing happens. There is a mastery to it all. It seems no surprise that Carlén sold well in her lifetime and did so beyond her Swedish ambit.

Catharina Ahlgren (1734–c. 1800), born in Östergötland, married Bengt Edvard Eckerman but divorced in 1770. She then married Anders Bark, moving to Finland c. 1775 and again divorcing. She settled in Linköping in 1796. Ahlgren became known as an unpublished translator from English, French, and German in the 1750s; she was a friend of Hedvig Charlotta Nordenflycht, and their letters survive. In 1764, Ahlgren published a poem on the queen's birthday. She later acquired a printing press, publishing Nordenflycht, a Wieland translation in 1772, and a 1772 periodical, *Brefwäxling emellan twänne fruntimmer* ... [Correspondence between Two Ladies ...] arguing for gender equality. Ahlgren may also have published the periodical *De Nymodiga Fruntimren* ... [Modern Women ...], promoting women's education. She published the first periodical in Finland in 1782.[37]

Christina Charlotta Ulrika Berger, née **Cronhielm af Hakunge** (21 August 1784–25 May 1852), born in Linköping, married the composer

---

37 Margareta Björkman, *Catharina Ahlgren: ett skrivande fruntimmer i 1700-talets Sverige* [Catharina Ahlgren: a writing woman in eighteenth-century Sweden] (Stockholm: Atlantis, 2006).

Johan Göran Berger in 1817. Berger began as a translator of French poetry; she then started publishing her own poems in the press, sometimes with music by her husband. "Korset på Idas grav" [The Cross on Ida's Grave] in 1816, a ballad with music, was popular. She also published several serial novels, in *Aftonbladet* and elsewhere, and poems in the *Magasin för konst, nyheter och moder*, 1823–1844. Berger's poems often described historical events and her novels, such as *Lustresan* [The Desire Trip] in 1841, echoed Richardson and Radcliffe. Her two plays, 1842, were not performed.[38]

Sophie Christina Mathilda Bolander (28 January 1807–2 June 1869), born in Gothenburg, lost her mother early and lived with her brother in Gothenburg after her father's death. She worked as a governess in 1838–1844, then as a music teacher from 1845–1855, publishing her antiaristocratic novel *Trolldomstecknet* [The Magic Sign] in 1845, then serializing several historical romances in the press (*Aftonbladet*). Her novel *Qvinnan med förmyndare* [Woman with Guardian], in 1842, was a conservative and parodic response to the novel *Qvinnan utan förmyndare* [Woman without Guardian] by Amelie von Strussenfelt, part of the debate regarding female legal minority at the time. Bolander believed women's education should be improved; however, she viewed marriage and motherhood as woman's true goal, though herself unmarried and childless.[39]

Fredrika Bremer (17 August 1801–31 December 1865), born outside Åbo (now Turku) in Finland, moved to Stockholm aged three with her family, spending the next two decades in the area. Forbidden to exercise outside, she jumped up and down holding onto chairs. Bremer published *Sketches of Everyday Life* in 1828–1831 to an academy prize. *The President's Daughters* appeared in 1834; five years in Norway saw *The Neighbors* and *The Home*, 1837–1839, and the 1840 play *The Thrall*. In 1842, *Morning Watches* appeared under Bremer's name, winning another prize. Bremer then traveled, on the Rhine in 1846, then across the United States, Cuba, and Britain, meeting Emerson, Hawthorne, Irving, George Eliot. Returning in 1851, Bremer founded two charitable societies and published *Hertha*, 1856, the novel that ended Swedish women's legal minority. She traveled south to the Levant in 1856–1861.[40]

---

38 *Svenskt kvinnobiografiskt lexikon* (SKBL) [Biographical Dictionary of Swedish Women] (https://skbl.se/en).
39 *Svenskt kvinnobiografiskt lexikon* (SKBL) [Biographical Dictionary of Swedish Women].
40 Carina Burman, *Bremer—en biografi* [Bremer: A Biography] (Stockholm: Albert Bonniers Förlag, 2001).

Ulrica Charlotta Falkman (18 March 1795–24 May 1882), born in Sweden, moved to Helsinki as a child. Speaking French, Swedish, and Finnish, Falkman worked as a governess until hearing loss led her to take up writing. Her Swedish-language novels appeared serialized in Finnish magazines and in book form, 1847–1864.[41]

Emilie Flygare-Carlén, née **Smith** (8 August 1807–5 February 1892), born in Strömstad, grew up in the Bohuslän archipelago. In 1827, she married Axel Flygare; he died in 1833, and she decided to write. Her first novel, *Waldemar Klein*, followed in 1838. Moving to Stockholm, she married Johan Gabriel Carlén in 1841. Their house became a meeting place for writers, and she published one or two novels a year until her son's death in 1853, followed by six years of silence. Flygare-Carlén then resumed writing until 1884. *Rosen på Tistelön* [The Rose of Thistle Island], 1842, or *Jungfrutornet* [The Maiden's Tower], 1848, feature life in the archipelago. Other novels—*Fosterbröderna* [The Foster Brothers], 1840, *Vindskuporna* [The Wind Domes], 1845—take place among the wealthy. Her collected works appeared in 1869–1875, an autobiography in 1878. She was translated into eleven languages.[42]

Wilhelmina Carolina Gravallius, née **Isaksson** (7 September 1807–22 November 1884), born in Mogata, supported herself as a governess until 1846. In 1844, her first novel *Högadals prostgård* [Högadal's Rectory] was a success, but she stopped writing after marrying the Thoresund vicar Christian Gravallius, 1846–1861. She then moved to Stockholm and resumed her career, publishing popular if somewhat simplistic serialized novels.[43]

Abela Maria Gullbransson, née **Berglund** (18 March 1775–1822), born in Varberg, married Laurentius Gulbransson in 1795. Some of her influential correspondence or "själavårdsbrev" [letters of spiritual welfare] survives, along with a collection of her songs, published posthumously in 1823 as *Några andeliga sånger jemte ett bref till ett barn* [Some Spiritual Songs together with a Letter to a Child] and often republished.[44]

---

41 Heidi Grönstrand, *Naiskirjailija, romaani ja kirjallisuuden merkitys 1840-luvulla* (Helsinki: SKS, 2005).
42 Herman Hofberg, Frithiof Heurlin, Viktor Millqvist, and Olof Rubenson, eds. *Svenskt Biografiskt Handlexikon...* [Swedish Biographical Dictionary], 2nd edition (Stockholm: Bonnier, 1906).
43 *Svenskt kvinnobiografiskt lexikon* (SKBL) [Biographical Dictionary of Swedish Women], https://www.skbl.se/en/article
44 *Ibid.*; *The History of Nordic Women's Literature.*

Sophie Margareta von Knorring, née **Zelow** (28 September 1797–13 February 1848), born in Gräfsnäs manor, learned German, English, French, and Italian as a child. She lived in Stockholm after 1810, debuting in the 1812 season and meeting Germaine de Staël. In 1814, her family was ruined; she married Baron Sebastian von Knorring in 1820, living after 1834 in Axevalla. Von Knorring contracted consumption in 1827; she was however able to visit Denmark in 1838 and Germany in 1846. Her first novel *Cousinerna* [The Cousins] appeared anonymously in 1834, opposing love to duty, as often in her work. *Torparen* [The Crofter], 1843, was set among the poor. Her novels were translated into four languages, though Fredrika Bremer and Emilie Flygare-Carlén, for instance, found her morals questionable.[45]

Thekla Levinia Andrietta Knös (17 July 1815–10 March 1880) was born in Uppsala, where her mother hosted a salon. Her friends included Fredrika Bremer and Pontus Wikner. Knös's poems combine descriptions of Uppsala, heroic pieces, and songs for children in the style of the late German Romantics; in 1846, the Swedish Academy read them aloud, and on their publication in 1851 as *Ragnar Lodbrok*, awarded them prizes. Knös also wrote children's books. Her mother died in 1855 and Knös was forced to support herself via translations and language lessons. In 1870, she contracted a mental illness and was placed in an asylum in Växjö, where she spent her remaining years.[46]

Aurora Lovisa Ljungstedt, née **Hjort** [or **Claude Gérard**] (2 September 1821–21 February 1908), born in Karlskrona, married Samuel Viktor Ljungstedt in 1846 and settled in Stockholm. Free to write after marriage, Ljungstedt debuted in the 1840s, publishing her sensational crime novels anonymously (often in serial form in the press) until her pen name was exposed in the 1870s. Inspired by Eugène Sue and Edward Bulwer-Lytton, her novels also often have supernatural elements.[47]

Julia Kristina Nyberg, née **Svärdström** [or **Euphrosyne**] (17 November 1784–16 April 1854), born in the parish of Skultuna, lost both parents as a child and was fostered. In 1809, she moved to Stockholm and was influenced by the Aurora League, a society led by

---

45 Bertil Boëthius, *Svenskt biografiskt lexikon* [Dictionary of Swedish Biography], 33 vols (Stockholm: Bonnier, 1918–).
46 Ibid.
47 Ibid.

the Romantic Per Daniel Amadeus Atterbom, in whose journal *Poetisk kalender* she later published much of her poetry. Back in Skultuna in 1822, she married Anders Wilhelm Nyberg. Nyberg's songs for the Walpurgis Night holiday are still sung today: "Vårvindar friska" [Fresh Spring Winds], "Fruktmånglerskan med tapperhetsmedalj" [The Fruit Shopper with a Bravery Medal]. Nyberg avoided epic, preferring short lyric pieces inspired by nature. The Swedish Academy awarded her a prize.[48]

Märta Helena Reenstierna [married name **von Schnell**] (16 September 1753–12 January 1841), married Captain Christian Henrik von Schnell in 1775. The couple had eight children, though only one reached adulthood. In 1793, she began a diary; widowed in 1811, she lost her surviving son in a riding accident the following year. Reenstierna went blind in 1839 and ceased both writing and managing the Årsta estate. Her diary, published in 1946–1953, describes the daily life of the entire estate, 1793–1839, alongside Stockholm events such as the 1794 Armfelt Conspiracy.[49]

Marie Sophie Schwartz, née **Birath** [or **Fru M.S.S.**] (4 July 1819–7 May 1894), born in Borås, was the illegitimate daughter of a maidservant, though her own account differs. She was adopted by a Stockholm customs official but the family went bankrupt after his death. Schwartz was educated at a girls' school and by private tutors; from 1840–1858, she lived openly with Gustaf Magnus Schwartz, though he was still married to a Catholic and could not divorce. They had two sons. Schwartz wrote early but was not allowed to publish until her 1851 debut under the pen name 'Fru M.S.S.' She was employed by the newspaper *Svenska Tidningen Dagligt Allehanda* from 1851–1859. After her husband's death in 1858, Schwartz lived with her lady's companion, writing prolifically about social injustice, both books and serialized novels, until moving in with her married son in 1876. Her works were translated into eight languages.[50]

Magdalena Sofia "Malla" Silfverstolpe, née **Montgomery** (8 February 1782–17 January 1861), born in the county of Nyland and

---

48 *Svenskt kvinnobiografiskt lexikon* (SKBL) [Biographical Dictionary of Swedish Women].
49 Bertil Boëthius. *Svenskt biografiskt lexikon* [Dictionary of Swedish Biography] (1918–).
50 Carin Österberg, Inga Lewenhaupt, and Anna Greta Wahlberg, *Svenska kvinnor: föregångare, nyskapare* (Lund: Signum, 1990).

Tavastehus (Finland), lost her mother after childbirth; father and daughter returned to Sweden. In 1789, he was sentenced to death after the Anjala Conspiracy but was released from prison in 1793. Silfverstolpe was raised by her grandmother in Edsberg. In 1807, she married Colonel David Gudmund Silfverstolpe, an unhappy union. Her husband suffered from "mjältsjuka," spleen or depression; they moved to Uppsala in 1812 and he died in 1819. In 1820, Silfverstolpe opened a salon that was for two decades a center for Sweden's Romantic movement, open to writers, scientists, and foreign visitors. She began writing memoirs in 1822, first published in 1908–1911. Almqvist, Tegnér, Atterbom and others appear in them.[51]

Constantina Carolina Amalia "Amelie" von Strussenfelt (16 May 1803–24 February 1847), born in Arrie parish, was the sister of the writer Ulrika von Strussenfelt. Her mother died in childbirth and her father remarried and left the country, leaving the two sisters with their different grandparents. The sisters did not get on. Amelie worked as a governess from 1831, then set up a school in 1845. She debuted as a poet in 1828 and as a novelist in 1829. In her 1841 novel *Qvinnan utan förmyndare* [Woman without Guardian], she joined the debate about female legal minority; Sophie Bolander published a parodic conservative reply in 1842.[52]

Ulrika "Ulla" Sophia von Strussenfelt (9 May 1801–16 January 1873), born in Hilleshög, was the older sister of Amelie von Strussenfelt, though raised separately. Like her sister, she never married, supporting herself first as a governess, then from 1834–1859 managing a girls' school. Active as a translator for periodicals, Ulla started publishing novels in the 1840s and 1850s, to popular if not critical success; they were translated into several languages. Her novels were mostly historical and nationalistic but progressive.[53]

---

51 Carin Österberg et al. *Svenska kvinnor* (1990).
52 Bertil Boëthius, *Svenskt biografiskt lexikon* [Dictionary of Swedish Biography] (1918–).
53 Ibid.

9. Writers from Spain and Portugal

The Spanish and Portuguese regimes—in Iberia, if not overseas—were fairly calm in the period before Napoleon's invasion in 1808, but the following years of French occupation and guerilla war left their trace on the peninsula. Spain broadly chose repression, rather as Austria did, after the return of their Bourbon dynasty in 1814; Restoration Portugal witnessed a struggle between conservatives and liberals that played out over a decade or more and from Lisbon to Rio de Janeiro, capital after 1822 of the new Empire of Brazil. My English-language research has found five Portuguese women writers in this period, with eleven in Spain.

Portugal (5 writers)

Maria da Felicidade do Couto Browne, known as **Maria Browne** (10 January 1797–8 or 9 November 1861), born in Porto, married Manuel Clamouse Browne, a port wine merchant. Browne published pseudonymously as 'Sóror Dolores' and 'A Coruja Trovador' [The Troubadour Owl], which were also the titles of her first two known books, in 1849–1854. In that year, she also published *Virações da Madrugada* [Dawn Turns] and *Sonetos e Poesias Líricas*. Her writings met with some success. Browne also hosted a literary salon and wrote for the periodicals *O Nacional*, *Miscelânea Política* and *Almanaque de Lembranças Luso-Brasileiro*.[1]

Margarida Teresa da Silva e Orta (1711–24 October 1793), born in São Paulo, Brazil, moved with her parents to Lisbon at the age of six

---

1 Anne Commire and Deborah Klezmer, eds. *Dictionary of Women Worldwide: 25,000 Women Through the Ages*, 3 vols (Farmington Hills, MI: Thomson Gale, 2007).

and remained there. Convent-educated and destined for a religious order, da Silva e Orta instead married Pedro Jansen Moller van Praet; they had twelve children. After her husband's death, the Marquis of Pombal imprisoned her for seven years in the Monastery of Ferreira de Aves; she was released in 1777. Da Silva e Orta published under a perfect anagrammatic pseudonym, 'Dorotéia Engrassia Tavareda Dalmira,' leaving works misattributed: for instance, *Maximas de Virtude e Formosura*, 1752, reissued in 1777 as *Aventuras de Diófanes*. In Ferreira de Aves, she also wrote unpublished texts: an 'epic-tragic poem,' the *Novena of the Patriarch São Bento*, and the *Petition that the Prey Makes to Queen N. Senhora*. Da Silva e Orta was fluent in Portuguese, French, and Italian.[2]

Catarina Micaela de Sousa César e Lencastre, known as **Catarina de Lencastre** (29 September 1749–4 January 1824), born in Guimarães, was married by proxy in 1767 to Luís Pinto de Sousa Coutinho, Viscount of Balsemão and Governor of Mato Grosso in Brazil. In 1774, he was named envoy to Great Britain and Lencastre accompanied him to London, where she opened a salon. Returning to Portugal, she became famous as the 'Portuguese Sappho' because of her love poetry. Lencastre also wrote for the theater, though most of her work remains unpublished.[3]

Leonor de Almeida Portugal, 4th Marquise of Alorna, 8th Countess of Assumar [or **Alcipe**] (31 October 1750–11 October 1839), born in Lisbon, spent nineteen years in a convent from age eight because of the Távora affair, resulting in executions and prison for her family. Here, she wrote poetry, discovered by the writer Francisco Manuel do Nascimento: her *Poemas de Chelas* appeared in 1772. Released in 1777, she married Carlos Pedro Maria José Augusto, Count of Oyenhausen-Grevenburg, in 1779, following him to Vienna in 1780, where he became minister plenipotentiary. She continued to write poetry and to paint, meeting kings, popes, and emperors. They returned home in 1785, and she opened a salon. Carlos died in 1793. Portugal stayed in England from 1801 to 1813, translating Chateaubriand's brochure *De Buonaparte* ... in 1814 and returning to live in retirement until 1826. Her *Obras poeticas* appeared in 1844.[4]

---

2   C.R. Boxer, *Women in Iberian Expansion Overseas: Some Facts, Fancies and Personalities* (Oxford: Oxford University Press, 1975).
3   João Esteves Pereira, *Portugal - Dicionário Histórico, Corográfico, Heráldico, Biográfico, Bibliográfico, Numismático e Artístico*, 7 vols (Lisbon: João Romano Torres, 1904).
4   Maria João Lopo de Carvalho, *Marquesa de Alorna: do Cativeiro de Chelas á Corte de Viena* (Lisbon: Oficina do Livro, 2011).

Antónia Gertrudes Pusich (1 October 1805–6 October 1883), born on São Nicolau in Portuguese Cape Verde to the island's Ragusa-born governor, married João Cardoso de Almeida Amado Viana Coelho in 1820. She later married Francisco Teixeira Henriques, and in 1836, José Roberto de Melo Fernandes e Almeida, having eleven children in all. Pusich published extensively under her own name: poems, elegies, novels, theater, biography. She wrote for several periodicals including *Paquete do Tejo, Revista universal lisbonense: jornal dos interesses physicos, moraes e litterarios por uma sociedade estudiosa*, and *Almanach*, and directed the periodicals *A assemblea literaria, A Beneficiência* and *A Cruzada*. Pusich also composed and played the piano. She died in Lisbon.[5]

Spain (11 writers)

Fernán Caballero

La Gaviota (1849)

Capítulo I

En noviembre del año de 1836, el paquebote de vapor *Royal Sovereign* se alejaba de las costas nebulosas de Falmouth, azotando las olas con sus brazos, y desplegando sus velas pardas y húmedas en la neblina, aún más parda y más húmeda que ellas.

El interior del buque presentaba el triste espectáculo del principio de un viaje marítimo. Los pasajeros apiñados en él luchaban con las fatigas del mareo. Veíanse mujeres desmayadas, desordenados los caballeros, ajados los camisolines, chafados los sombreros. Los hombres, pálidos y de mal humor; los niños, abandonados y llorosos; los criados, atravesando con angulosos pasos la cámara, para llevar a los pacientes té, café y otros remedios imaginarios, mientras que el buque, rey y señor de las aguas, sin cuidarse de los males que ocasionaba, luchaba a brazo partido con las olas, dominándolas cuando le ponían resistencia, y persiguiéndolas de cerca cuando cedían.

Paseábanse sobre cubierta los hombres que se habían preservado del azote común, por una complexión especial, o por la costumbre de viajar. Entre ellos se hallaba el gobernador de una colonia inglesa, de noble

---

5 *Portuguese Women Writers (16th-19th centuries)* (http://www.womenwriters.nl/index.php/Portuguese_Women_Writers); Silvia Bermúdez and Roberta Johnson. *A New History of Iberian Feminisms* (Toronto: University of Toronto Press, 2018).

rostro y de alta estatura, acompañado de dos ayudantes. Algunos otros estaban envueltos en sus *mackintosh*, metidas las manos en los bolsillos, los rostros encendidos, azulados o muy pálidos, y generalmente desconcertados. En fin, aquel hermoso bajel parecía haberse convertido en el alcázar de la displicencia y del malestar.[6]

La Gaviota
Chapter 1

In November, in the year 1836, the steamer "Royal Sovereign" took her departure from the foggy coast of Falmouth, lashing the waves with her paddle-wheels, and spreading her sails, gray and wet, in the mist still grayer and more wet than they.

The interior of the hull presented the uncheerful spectacle of the commencement of a sea voyage. The passengers, crowded together, were struggling with the fatigue of sea-sickness. Women were seen in extraordinary attitudes, with hair disordered, crinolines disarranged, hats crushed; the men pale, and in bad-humor; the children neglected and crying; the servants traversing the cabin with unsteady steps, carrying to their patients tea, coffee, and other imaginary remedies; while the ship, queen and mistress of the waters, without heeding the ills she occasioned, wrestled powerfully with the waves, triumphing over resistance, and pursuing the retreating billows.

The men who had escaped the common scourge were enabled to walk the deck, either by being so constituted as to withstand the ship's motion, or by being accustomed to travel.

Among them was the governor of an English colony, a tall, fine-looking fellow, accompanied by two of his staff officers. There were several who wore their mackintoshes, thrusting their hands into their pockets; some had flushed countenances, others blue, or very pale, and, generally, all were discontented. In fine, that beautiful vessel seemed to be converted into a palace of discontent.[7]

The Seagull opens with two epigraphs, from G. de Molene—perhaps G. Tirso de Molina—and from Alexandre Dumas, who writes: "It is undeniable that simple things are those which most move deep hearts and large understandings." And we open with a relatively simple thing, a description of a steamship off the coast of England. After a brief mention of the waves, the paddles, and the damp sails in the damp brown mist, we move inside the ship for a vignette: men, women, children in all attitudes as they confront seasickness. Nightgowns are torn, hats are

---

6   Fernán Caballero, *La Gaviota* [The Seagull], ed. Juan Alcina Franch (Barcelona: Bosch, 1974), pp. 57–60.
7   Fernán Caballero, tr. J. Leander Starr, *La Gaviota: A Spanish Novel* (New York: John Bradburn, 1864), pp. 9–10.

flattened, servants are serving tea and coffee, hoping to help. The ship sails on apace. And now we pan in on one face among the sturdier men on deck—the tall governor of an English colony, with his two assistants. Others in their mackintoshes are flushed, bluish, or pale.

This is a masterful description. Caballero—a pseudonym, meaning *gentleman*—moves like a film director from a view of the ship amid the waves, inside to the huddled crowd, back to the waves and the men on deck, and in close-up to her protagonist, before pulling finally back to his neighbors' flushed or bluish faces. The governor's mastery of the weather associates him to the ship and parts him dramatically from the mass of travelers around and behind him. Caballero does not tell us about this distinction; she shows it to us. One thinks of the rather similar opening to Gustave Flaubert's 1869 *L'Éducation sentimentale*, another journey by water.

Once again, one may ask whether this scene is inherently Romantic. We have argued above, more than once, as to how description is a characteristically Romantic novelistic activity. It also bears saying that Northern nations, and England in particular, played an outsize part in Romantic narrative, as we saw in the opening to Avellaneda's *Sab*; ever since Ossian emerged in the 1760s as a Northern counterweight to Homer, European culture had found in the British Isles a model of various things, starting with constitutional government, continuing with melancholy and introspection, and concluding perhaps with an art—in Ossian, in Shakespeare—to oppose to neoclassical hegemony. We set sail here from Falmouth for good reason. England is also the home of both the Industrial Revolution and the steam engine, and in that sense, the steamship is as English as the governor aboard it. This is, in short, a topical novel extract, as its opening date—November 1836— might suggest.

Concepción Arenal Ponte (31 January 1820–4 February 1893), born in Ferrol, lost her father aged eight, a political prisoner. The family then moved to Madrid. A year after her mother's death, in 1842, Arenal dressed as a man to enroll in Law at Madrid's University of Alcalá. In 1847, she married the writer Fernando García Carrasco; the two collaborated at *La Iberia*. In 1848, Arenal published the libretto of *Los hijos de Pelayo*; her first novel was *Historia de un corazón* in 1850. Widowed in 1857, Arenal retired to Santander, then to Galicia. In 1862, she wrote her *Prisoner Visitor's*

Manual, translated into many languages. She worked visiting prisons and for women's education, founding the periodical *La Voz de la Caridad* in 1870, writing tirelessly on just war theory, prison reform, education, and state intervention.⁸

Cecilia Francisca Josefa Böhl de Faber y Ruiz de Larrea [or **Fernán Caballero**] (24 December 1796–7 April 1877), born at Morges in Switzerland, was educated in Hamburg, her father's hometown, visiting Spain in 1815. In 1816, she married Captain Antonio Planells y Bardaxi. He was killed in action in 1817, and in 1822 she married Francisco Ruiz del Arco, Marqués de Arco Hermoso. When Arco Hermoso died in 1835, Caballero married Antonio Arrom de Ayala, who committed suicide in 1859. Caballero anonymously published the novel *Sole* in German in 1840, then *La Gaviota* in 1849, serialized in *El Heraldo* and translated into several languages. Other novels and short stories preceded her posthumous *Obras completas*.⁹

Dolores Cabrera y Heredia (15 September 1828–1 December 1899), born in Tamarite de Litera, followed her family to Pamplona, Madrid, and Jaca. She published her first poem in 1847, contributing verse from then on to *La Velada, La Reforma, El Correo de la Moda*, and other journals. For the latter, she also wrote historical articles, biographies of women, and her novel *Una perla y una lágrima* in 1853. Cabrera also published the novel *Quien bien ama nunca olvida* and a poetry collection, *Las violetas*, in 1850, as well as occasional pieces for the royal family. In 1856, she married army officer Joaquín María Miranda, moving with him to Valencia, Granada, and Saragossa. Cabrera was a member of the Hermandad lirica and earned various honors from 1860 onward. She went blind in later life.¹⁰

María Rosa de Gálvez (14 August 1768–2 October 1806), born in Malaga to unknown parents, was adopted by a colonel and married a distant cousin, Captain José Cabrera Ramarez, settling with him in Madrid. There, she became close to Manuel José Quintana, for whose *Variedades de Ciencias, Literatura y Artes* she wrote in 1803–1805, and to the minister Manuel Godoy, who helped her publish. Gálvez wrote

---

8   Anna Caballé, *Concepción Arenal. La caminante y su sombra* (Barcelona: Taurus, 2018).
9   Milagros Fernández Poza, *Cecilia Böhl de Faber: Fernán Caballero (1796–1877)* (Madrid: Ediciones del Orto, 2003).
10 Maria Soledad Catalán Marín, "Dolores Cabrera y Heredia, una poetisa literana," in Centro de Estudios Literanos, *Revista Littera* (2009), 1: 87–106.

seventeen tragedies and comedies, a *zarzuela* or musical play, and various lyric poems—heroic and Anacreontic odes, descriptive and philosophical pieces. To neoclassical form, Gálvez married Romantic content: liberty of peoples, denunciation of slavery and oppression, rights of women. Her *Obras poéticas* appeared in 1804.[11]

María Gertrudis Hore (5 December 1742–9 August 1801), born to Irish immigrant parents in Spain, married in 1762 and became a nun sixteen years later. In the convent, she wrote poetry, with friendship among women as a theme. Her work is occasionally erotic.[12]

Inés Joyes y Blake (27 December 1731–1808), born in Madrid to a French mother and an Irish father, spoke English, French, and Spanish, and married Agustín Blake in 1752. The couple settled in Málaga, having nine children. In 1798, Joyes translated Samuel Johnson's short philosophical novel *A History of Rasselas, Prince of Abyssinia*, including in it the *Apología de las mujeres* [Apology of Women], dedicated to her daughters, which is both among Spain's first feminist essays and Joyes's only surviving work. The text focuses on inequality and on the education of women. However, it was not reissued until 2009, and subsequent Spanish translators of *Rasselas*, in 1813, 1831, and 1860, did not mention it.[13]

Enriqueta Lozano y Velázquez de Vilchez (18 August 1829/1830–5 May 1895), born in Granada, entered the beguinage of Santo Domingo from the age of seven to thirteen. In 1846, she published her first poem; her first play, *Una actriz por amor*, followed in 1847, starring her. Lozano wrote more than 200 works, all Catholic and moral, including novels, legends, poetry, dramas, comedies, lives of women and saints, devotional books, essays, epistles, and opera and zarzuela librettos. She published in various journals, local and national. In 1859, she married Antonio Vílchez; the couple had twelve children. Her plays include *Dios es el rey de reyes*, 1852, and *Don Juan de Austria*, 1854; her poetry includes *Poesías de la señorita doña Enriqueta Lozano*, 1848, and *La lira cristiana*, 1857; and her novels include *Juan, hermano de los pobres*, 1848, *El secreto de*

---

11 Françoise Etienvre, *Regards sur les Espagnoles créatrices (XVIIIe-XXe siècle)* (Paris: Presses Sorbonne Nouvelle, 2006).
12 Ulrich L. Lehner, *Women, Enlightenment and Catholicism. A Transnational Biographical History* (London: Routledge, 2018).
13 Rosa Capel, ed. *Mujeres para la Historia. Figuras destacadas del primer feminismo* (Madrid: Abada Editores, 2004).

una muerta, Consuelo, and *Juicio de Dios,* 1860.[14]

Maria Josepa Massanés i Dalmau [or **Josepa Massanés** or **Josefa Massanés**] (19 March 1811–1 July 1887) moved to Barcelona at two months old. Her mother died when she was five, leaving her in her grandparents' care. She learned embroidery, French, Latin, and Italian. In 1830, Massanés helped her father flee to French exile, from which he returned in 1833. Her first three poems appeared in the press in 1834 above the initials 'D.B.C.A.;' her own initials followed in 1835 under her "Himno Guerrero," then her full name in 1836. From 1837–1840, more poems appeared in other newspapers; in 1843, she married Captain Fernando González de Ortega, moving to Madrid in 1843–1844, writing and becoming known at court. Massanés's *Poesías* appeared in 1841, *Flores marchitas* in 1850, then a religious drama in 1862, and a *Garlanda poética* in 1881. Massanés also published in Catalan from 1858–1881.[15]

Victòria Peña i Nicolau [or **Victoria Peña de Amer**] (28 March 1827–1898) was born in Palma, Mallorca. At about twenty, Amer published her first poems in the Palma press, followed by a collection of religious poems in 1855. Amer then began work with the group that published *El Plantel*, where she met Miquel Amer, marrying him in 1859 and settling in Barcelona. His role in the Barcelona Floral Games helped Amer to take part in poetic contests, winning several awards. Much of her poetry, largely written in Catalan, was collected posthumously in 1909.[16]

Mariana de Silva-Bazán y Sarmiento [or **Mariana de Silva-Meneses** or **Sarmiento de Sotomayor**] (14 October 1739–17 January 1784), born in Madrid, married Francisco de Paula de Silva y Álvarez de Toledo, 10th Duke of Huescar, in 1757. They had one child before the duke's death in 1770. In 1775, Mariana married Joaquin Atanasio Pignatelli de Aragón y Moncayo, XVI Count of Fuentes and so forth. He died in 1776. In 1778, she married Antonio Ponce de León, 11th Duke of Arcos and so forth. She was widowed again in 1780. Mariana wrote lyric verse and translated some French tragedies, also painting with merit, it is claimed, though neither texts nor paintings have survived. She was a member of the Madrid royal

---

14   Juan Rodríguez Titos, *Enriqueta Lozano* (Granada: DMC, 2010).
15   Angela Esterhammer, ed. *Romantic Poetry* (Amsterdam and Philadelphia: John Benjamins Publishing, 2002).
16   Simón Palmer, María Carmendel (1991). *Escritoras españolas del siglo XIX: manual bio-bibliográfico* (Buenos Aires: Clásico Castalia, 1991).

academy of arts and the Saint Petersburg imperial academy of arts.[17]

Xosefa de Xovellanos y Xove Ramírez (4 June 1745–2 June 1807), born in Gijón, became a nun against the strong wishes of her brother. Her poetry, or some of it, is preserved in an 1839 anthology, *Colección de poesías en dialecto asturiano*, compiled by Xosé Caveda y Nava.[18]

---

17 Vicent Ibiza i Osca, *Les dones al món de l'art. Pintores i escultores valencianes (1500–1950)* (Valencia: Institució Alfons el Magnànim, Centre Valencià d'Estudis i d'Investigació, 2017).

18 *Actos de la XIX Selmana de les Lletres Asturianes dedicada a Xosefa Xovellanos, 1745–1807* (Uviéu: Serviciu de Publicaciones del Principáu d'Asturies, 1998).

10. Writers from the British Isles

The British Isles were and are a complex thing. This anthology follows 2024's national borders, giving the islands two national traditions, British and Irish; but Ireland beyond the Pale of Settlement was occupied by the English Crown from 1649 (or indeed 1541) until 1921, firmly bracketing this period marked by the United Irishmen's uprising in 1798 and the Act of Union in 1800. Scottish, Welsh, and Manx women writers are here listed with the English (though their nation is identified) under the heading British Writers, of whom I have identified 167, far more than any tradition outside the United States. But the fifty-eight Irish women writers here identified continue to outpace all continental traditions, including France, Germany, and all Latin America. I count thirty-three Scottish writers in the British tally.

Great Britain: The Eighteenth Century (67 writers)

Lady Christian Henrietta Caroline Acland [or **Lady Harriet Acland**], née **Fox-Strangways** (3 January 1750–21 July 1815), born in Kilmington, was a cousin of Charles James Fox. In 1770, she married John Dyke Acland, accompanying him to the Thirteen Colonies during the Revolutionary War. When he was captured and wounded at the Battle of Saratoga, the pregnant Acland crossed the Hudson River to nurse him back to health, as later celebrated in the British press. He died in 1778. Acland co-authored *The Acland Journal* (perhaps with the help of a chaplain or military valet), which narrates this expedition.[1]

Anna Laetitia Barbauld, née **Aikin** (20 June 1743–9 March 1825), born in Kibworth Harcourt to a Dissenting family, learned Latin, Greek,

---

1   Lady Harriet Acland, *The Acland Journal: Lady Harriet Acland and the American Revolution* (Winchester: Hampshire County Council, 1993).

French, and Italian. In 1773, Barbauld published *Poems*, with four editions in a year. She married Rochemont Barbauld in 1774, teaching with him in Suffolk, 1774–1785, and publishing *Lessons for Children* in 1778–1779 and *Hymns in Prose for Children* in 1781. In London after 1787, Barbauld became close to Joanna Baillie. She published against the Test Act, the slave trade, and the French War in 1790–1793. The couple moved to Stoke Newington in 1802. Barbauld edited. Rochemont drowned himself in 1808. In 1812, Barbauld published her radical and anti-war poem, *Eighteen Hundred and Eleven*, her last publication, to very negative reviews. Also attacked by the older Wordsworth and Coleridge, Barbauld was remembered for a century only as a children's writer.[2]

Maria Barrell, née **Weylar** (?–1803), born in England or the West Indies, moved to Grenada in 1763, marrying Theodore Barrell in 1773. Accused of loyalism in revolutionary Boston, Barrell was allowed to depart without her husband. In London in 1782, she published in the press as 'Maria.' Barrell was imprisoned for debt in the 1780s, with two compensation claims for American losses both failing. From the King's Bench Prison in 1788, Barrell published *British Liberty Vindicated*, describing the futility of imprisonment for debt. Her play *The Captive* appeared in 1790, dedicated to the Prince of Wales and comparing her situation to the storming of the Bastille. Barrell briefly married James Makitterick Adair in 1791. In 1801, she was convicted of passing counterfeit coin; convicted again in 1803, she was spared death by a royal pardon. She died in Newgate Prison awaiting transportation to New South Wales.[3]

Frances Burney [or **Fanny Burney** or **Madame d'Arblay**] (13 June 1752–6 January 1840), born in Lynn Regis (now King's Lynn), married Alexandre d'Arblay in 1793. He died in 1818. Burney wrote four satirical novels, eight tragedies and comedies, one biography, and twenty-five volumes of journals and letters. After burning her first novel, Burney published *Evelina* anonymously in 1778, to immediate success; *Cecilia* followed in 1782, *Camilla* in 1796, and *The Wanderer* in 1814. Her one staged play, *Edwy and Elgiva*, did poorly in 1795. Jane Austen's title *Pride and Prejudice* is taken from *Cecilia*; Thackeray's *Vanity Fair* borrows from her first-hand description of the Battle of Waterloo. Burney's journal begins in

---

2   Betsy Rodgers, *Georgian Chronicle: Mrs. Barbauld and Her Family* (London: Methuen, 1958).
3   Janet M. Todd, ed. *British and American Women Writers* (1985).

1768 and extends over seventy-two years, describing acquaintances from Hester Thrale to Germaine de Staël. She survived breast cancer surgery, publishing a memoir of her father, Dr. Charles Burney, in 1832.[4]

Sophia, Lady Burrell (11 April 1753–20 June 1802), born in Valentines, Essex, married William Burrell, MP in 1773. From 1773–1784, Burrell wrote mostly *vers de société*, with an imitation of Ossian, *Comala*, in 1784. She published her collected poems in 1793, alongside Xenophon's *Thymriad* and a *Telemachus*. Burrell also wrote two tragedies, *Maximian* and *Theodora*, the latter republished in 1814 in *The New British Theatre*. In 1796, William died, and in 1797 Burrell remarried William Clay, retiring to the Isle of Wight.[5]

Rebekah Carmichael [or **Rebecca**], later, **Hay** (1766?–1823), a Scottish writer born in London (or Edinburgh, say some sources), was baptized at Saint Martin-in-the-Fields, London, on 24 May 1766. She lost both parents early and married John Hay in Edinburgh in 1793. In 1787, Robert Burns gave an inscribed book of Scottish poems to "Miss R. Carmichael, poetess." In 1790, she published by subscription her *Poems* in Edinburgh, signed 'Carmichael;' Burns received a copy. In 1806, she published a broadsheet poem under her married name. Her poetry has been recently anthologized.[6]

Elizabeth Carter [or **Eliza**] (16 December 1717–19 February 1806), born in Deal, lost her mother aged ten; her father taught her Greek, Latin, and Hebrew. Carter later learned French, Italian, Spanish, German, Portuguese, and some Arabic. At sixteen, she published poems in *The Gentleman's Magazine*, meeting Samuel Johnson in 1737. In 1738, Carter published a volume of her poems anonymously, translating two works from French and Italian in 1739. In 1749, Carter began translating Epictetus; the work appeared in 1758. Johnson wrote "My old friend Mrs. Carter could make a pudding as well as translate Epictetus from the Greek." Her correspondence followed, alongside religious tracts, poems in 1762, and *Essays and Poems* after 1770. An abolitionist and Bluestocking, Carter also edited some issues of Johnson's *The Rambler*.[7]

---

4   Margaret Anne Doody, *Frances Burney: The Life in The Works* (New Brunswick, NJ: Rutgers University Press, 1988).
5   *Dictionary of National Biography* [DNB].
6   Daniel Cook, ed. *Scottish Poetry, 1730–1830* (Oxford: Oxford University Press, 2023).
7   Elizabeth Eger, *Bluestockings Displayed: Portraiture, Performance and Patronage, 1730–1830* (Cambridge, UK: Cambridge University Press, 2013).

Mrs H. Cartwright (fl. 1777–1785) in her first known publication, *Letters on Female Education, Addressed to a Married Lady*, 1777, claims that Elizabeth Montagu encouraged her. Her 1785 novel *The Duped Guardian, or, The Amant Malade* earned some compliments from *The Monthly Review*, while her novel *The Platonic Marriage* in 1785 is mocked in Mary Wollstonecraft's own novel *Mary*. Cartwright also published *The Memoirs of Lady Eliza Audley*, 1779, *Letters Moral and Entertaining*, 1780, and *The Generous Sister*, 1780. *The Vale of Glendor, or, Memoirs of Emily Westbrook*, 1785, has been attributed to her, but the title page gives Emily Westbrook's name as author. A note from "the editor" follows.[8]

Emily Frederick Clark (fl. 1798–1833) was the daughter of a customs official; her title pages claim that she was the great-granddaughter of King Theodore of Corsica. Two of Clark's known novels are set in Wales. She received little press attention and faced lifelong financial hardship; twenty-four of her forty-two applications to the Royal Literary Fund were unsuccessful, the last being in 1833. Her novels include *Ianthé, or the Flower of Caernarvon*, 1798, *Ermina Montrose or The Cottage of the Vale*, 1800, *The Banks of the Douro, or, The Maid of Portugal*, 1805, *Tales at the Fireside*, 1817, and *The Esquimaux*, 1819. Clark also published *Poems* in 1810.[9]

Elizabeth Cobbold, née **Knipe** [or **Carolina Petty Pasty**] (1767–17 October 1824), born in London, married William Clarke in 1790. He died in 1791; Cobbold published her first novel that year, *The Sword, or Father Bertrand's History of his own Times*, influenced by her friend Clara Reeve. Her *Poems on Various Subjects* had appeared in 1783, further poems in 1787. In 1791, she married the Ipswich brewer John Cobbold and became stepmother to fifteen children, with seven of her own. The family settled in Ipswich, where Cobbold published *The Mince Pie, an Heroic Epistle* in 1800. From 1806, Cobbold was known for Valentine's Day verses; she published these on cards in 1813–1814. Cobbold was also an early geologist, with a fossil and a species of shellfish named after her. *Poems, with a Memoir of the Author* appeared posthumously in 1825.[10]

---

8   Peter Garside and Karen O›Brien, eds. *English and British Fiction 1750–1820* (Oxford: Oxford University Press, 2018).
9   *Dictionary of National Biography* [DNB].
10 Ibid.

Alison Cockburn [or **Alison Rutherford** or **Alicia Cockburn**] (8 October 1712–22 November 1794), a Scottish writer, was born at Fairnilee House in the Scottish Borders. In 1731, she married Patrick Cockburn; at his father's death, the couple moved to Edinburgh, where Cockburn mixed in society. During the Jacobite Rising in 1745, her Whig squib on Bonnie Prince Charlie almost got her arrested. Patrick died in 1753, their only son in infancy. In 1765, Cockburn published her lyrics to the Border Ballad, "The Flowers of the Forest." In 1777, she met the young Walter Scott; in 1786, Robert Burns. Cockburn composed letters, parodies, squibs, toasts, and character sketches, mostly forgotten. At her Edinburgh home, she received Henry Mackenzie, William Robertson, Lord Monboddo, and her great friend David Hume.[11]

Janet Colquhoun, née **Sinclair** [or **Lady Colquhoun of Luss**] (17 April 1781–21 October 1846), born in London, was brought up at Thurso Castle. In 1799, she married Sir James Colquhoun of Luss. She founded a girls' school at their Edinburgh house and worked for several causes: the Scottish Gaelic Society, the local Bible society, the Irish Home mission, the local Free Church, education in India. After an illness in 1820, Colquhoun wrote anonymous books with religious themes: *Despair and Hope* in 1822, a conversation with a dying cottager; *Thoughts on the Religious Profession*, 1823; *Impressions of the Heart*, 1825; *The Kingdom of God*, 1836. She first used her name after her husband's death in 1836. Colquhoun believed in justification by faith but resisted antinomianism. The Colquhouns were perhaps the model for the Colwans in Hogg's *The Private Memoirs and Confessions of a Justified Sinner*.[12]

Helen Craik (c. 1751–11 June 1825), a Scottish writer born at Arbigland near Dumfries, was sister to James Craik, who became George Washington's personal physician. John Paul Jones, also born at Arbigland, may have been a second illegitimate brother. Robert Burns wrote to Craik praising her poetry, long thought lost but rediscovered and published in 2023. Thirty-nine poems feature. In 1792, Craik left Arbigland abruptly for Cumberland, perhaps as her father transferred

---

11 H.G. Graham, *The Social Life of Scotland in the Eighteenth Century* (London: A.& C. Black, 1899).

12 *Dictionary of National Biography* [DNB]; Elizabeth L. Ewan, Sue Innes, Sian Reynolds, Rose Pipes. *Biographical Dictionary of Scottish Women* (Edinburgh: Edinburgh University Press, 2007).

the estate to his grandson, who married that year. Craik now turned to fiction, publishing five anonymous novels from 1796–1805 with the Minerva Press. *Adelaide de Narbonne*, 1800, has received praise. The novels often involve contemporary French events, as in *Julia de Saint Pierre* in 1796. *Henry of Northumberland, or The Hermit's Cell*, also 1800, uniquely has a medieval setting.[13]

Elizabeth, Princess Berkeley [or unofficially **Margravine of Brandenburg-Ansbach**], née **Lady Elizabeth Berkeley**, previously **Elizabeth Craven, Baroness Craven** (17 December 1750–13 January 1828), born in Mayfair, married William Craven, 6th Baron Craven in 1767. The couple parted in 1780. After their spouses' deaths in 1791, Craven married Charles Alexander, Margrave of Brandenburg-Anspach; she did not share his German title but was granted the morganatic title 'Princess Berkeley' by the last Holy Roman Emperor in 1801. Charles Alexander died in 1806 and Craven settled in Naples. She wrote farces, pantomimes, and fables between 1778 and 1802, three of them produced on the London stage in 1780–1799. Craven knew Samuel Johnson and became a close friend of Horace Walpole, who published her early works. She also published travelogues and memoirs in 1789–1791, 1814, and 1826.[14]

Ann Batten Cristall (1769?–9 February 1848), whose date of birth is unknown, was baptized in Penzance in 1769. The family moved to London during her childhood. Cristall became a schoolteacher, publishing her *Poetical Sketches* in 1795 by a subscription featuring Mary Wollstonecraft, Anna Letitia Barbauld, Mary Hays, Ann Jebb, and others. In 1797, Cristall met Robert Southey, who praised her genius in a letter to the publisher Joseph Cottle that year. Little is known of her later life. Her grave bears her maiden name, and other publications are unknown.[15]

Margaret Sarah Croker (1773?-after 1820), whose date of birth is unknown, was baptized in Holbeton, Devon in 1773. In 1817, Croker published *A Monody on the Lamented Death of Princess Charlotte Augusta*, in hope of a female monarch after a disappointing series of male ones.

---

13 *Dictionary of National Biography* [DNB]; Elizabeth L. Ewan et al. *Scottish Women* (2007).
14 Julia Gasper, *Elizabeth Craven: Writer, Feminist and European* (Wilmington, DE: Vernon Press, 2017).
15 Frederick Burwick, ed. *Encyclopedia of Romantic Literature* (Oxford: Blackwell, 2012).

In 1818, she published her novel *The Question, Who Is Anna?* The main character is born to unmarried parents.[16]

Mary Deverell (4 February 1731-September 1805), born near Minchinhampton, was self-educated. She published a volume of sermons in 1774, her subscribers including aristocracy and clergy; a third edition was dedicated to Charlotte, Princess Royal. In 1781, Deverell published *Miscellanies in Prose and Verse*, speaking out against assigned gender roles and on behalf of poor authors. Samuel Johnson was a subscriber, though Hannah More was unimpressed. Deverell's 1792 play *Mary, Queen of Scots* seems never to have been staged; *The Critical Review* condemned it. A book of essays addressed to women appeared that same year. Deverell seems not to have published thereafter.[17]

Catherine Maria Fanshawe (6 July 1765–17 April 1834), born at Shabden in Surrey, wrote occasional verses; Joanna Baillie published some of them in 1823. Fanshawe's best-known poem is the "Riddle on the Letter H" which begins, "'Twas whispered in heaven, 'twas muttered in hell," often attributed to Byron; she also wrote a fragment in imitation of Wordsworth. Walter Scott thought her poetry "quite beautiful." In 1829, Fanshawe and her sister published the memoirs of Ann, Lady Fanshawe. Fanshawe's own diary has not been found.[18]

Ellenor Fenn, née **Frere** [or **Mrs. Teachwell**, or **Mrs. Lovechild**] (12 March 1743–1 November 1813), born in Westhorpe, was the aunt of John Hookham Frere. In 1766, she married John Fenn and moved with him to Dereham. Inspired by Anna Laetitia Barbauld's *Lessons for Children*, 1778–1779, Fenn wrote children's books for her nieces and nephews. In 1782, Fenn contacted John Marshall who published her works, mostly anonymously or pseudonymously. *Cobwebs to Catch Flies*, a 1783 reading primer, was republished into the 1870s; *The Child's Grammar*, 1798, saw sixty editions by the 1860s. In 1785, Fenn established a Sunday school in Dereham which by 1788 had over 100 pupils. In 1787, her husband was knighted, and she became Lady Fenn. He died in 1794. Fenn and Marshall fell out in 1795, and Fenn moved to Elizabeth Newbery. Fenn never received royalties for her work, only free copies.[19]

---

16 *Dictionary of National Biography* [DNB].
17 Virginia Blain et al. *The Feminist Companion to Literature in English* (1990).
18 *Dictionary of National Biography* [DNB].
19 Ibid.

Charlotte Forman [or **Probus**] (1715–1787), daughter of an Irish Jacobite who fled to France in 1715, was born that year in France or England. She lived most of her life in London in poverty, going briefly into debtors' prison in 1767. As 'Probus,' Forman wrote about 200 essays on European politics for the *Gazetteer* and *London Daily Advertiser* in 1756–1760, during the Seven Years' War, then carried in the *Public Ledger* in 1760; both newspapers were for London merchants and shopkeepers and focused on international trade. Forman exchanged letters with the radical politician John Wilkes but is not known to have published anything under her own name. She was one of the few women of the time to publish on politics, giving her essays additional interest.[20]

Jane Arden Gardiner (26 August 1758–1840) was a childhood friend of Mary Wollstonecraft, whom her father taught. In her mid-teens, Gardiner took a position as governess in Norfolk; in 1780, she moved to Somerset, later opening a girls' school in Beverley in 1784, which she ran for thirteen years. Gardiner married a friend of her brother in 1797, and the couple moved with her pupils to Elsham Hall in Lincolnshire. Gardiner ran her school for another thirty years. In 1799, Gardiner published her *Young Ladies' Grammar*, using French as a model. *English Exercises* followed in 1801, then a travelogue to Dover in 1806 and *An Easy French Grammar* in 1808. Gardiner's daughter published a memoir by subscription drawing on letters and diary entries, mostly religious in tone.[21]

Jean Glover [or **Jennifer Glover**] (31 October 1758–1801), a Scottish writer and singer born in Kilmarnock, was a weaver's daughter. She eloped at an early age with a performer named Richard, performing at public houses given the dearth of theaters. Robert Burns, who admired her voice, copied down her song "O'er the moor amang the heather" in 1792; he called her "not only a whore but also a thief," though another witness called her "the bravest woman I had ever seen step in leather shoon." She was spotted performing at Letterkenny in County Donegal, Ireland, shortly before her death.[22]

---

20 Lorna Sage et al., eds. *The Cambridge Guide to Women's Writing in English* (1999).
21 Janet Todd, *Mary Wollstonecraft: A Revolutionary Life* (New York: Columbia University Press, 2002).
22 James Mackay, *A Biography of Robert Burns* (Edinburgh: Mainstream Publishing, 1992); *Dictionary of National Biography* [DNB].

Ann Gomersall, née **Richardson** (24 January 1750–17 June 1835), likely born in Portsmouth, lived for some years in Leeds. Gomersall began writing to raise money for her husband after a setback. Widowed after thirty-five years of marriage, she worked for eight years at manual labor; from 1818, she applied for relief to the Royal Literary Fund. With failing vision, she turned to writing again, publishing *Creation, A Poem* by subscription in 1824. All 500 copies were sold. She died a parish pauper in 1835. *Eleonora*, Gomersall's first novel, was published anonymously in 1789. It earned favorable notices from the press, and she signed her works thereafter. Gomersall writes about women's economic precarity. Her *The Disappointed Heir*, in 1796, has episodes in revolutionary America and in the West Indies. *The Citizen*, 1790, was republished in 2016.[23]

Emma Jane Greenland [after marriage, **Hooker**] (1760/1761–9 September 1838), born in London, was baptized in 1761. From 1772–1782, she studied painting at the Incorporated Society of Artists, then in Rome and Florence in 1783–1785. In London after 1786, she published *Curious Discovery of the Ancient Grecian Method of Painting on Wax* (encaustic painting) in 1787. In 1801, Greenland opened a school for the aristocracy in Sussex with her husband. She may have been a pupil of Johann Christian Bach, who dedicated six sonatas to her.[24]

Elizabeth Gunning (1769–20 July 1823), daughter of Susannah Gunning, married Major James Plunkett in 1803. She published four translations from the French in 1795–1810, including a Pixérécourt tragicomedy in 1803, Fontenelle's *Plurality of Worlds* in 1808, and Sophie Cottin's *Malvina* in 1810. Gunning also published several novels in 1794–1815, among them *The Packet* in 1794, *The Foresters* in 1796, *The Village Library* and *Family Stories* in 1802, and *The Exile of Erin* in 1808.[25]

Susannah Gunning, née **Minifie** (c. 1740–28 August 1800) was the sister of Margaret Minifie, with whom she published her first novel in 1763. Gunning wrote thirteen novels in all, also a long poem and a defense of her daughter: *Family Pictures* in 1764, *Barford Abbey* in 1768, *The Cottage* in 1769, *The Hermit* in 1770 and so forth, often concerning

---

23 Edward Copeland, *Women Writing about Money: Women's Fiction in England, 1790–1820* (Cambridge, UK: Cambridge University Press, 1995).
24 John Ingamells, *A Dictionary of British and Irish Travellers in Italy 1701–1800* (New Haven, CT: Yale University Press, 1997).
25 *Dictionary of National Biography* [DNB].

young women marrying into aristocracy. In 1768, she married Captain John Gunning, who distinguished himself at the Battle of Bunker Hill, and her production slowed: *The Count de Poland* in 1780 may be her sister's. A scandal involving her daughter Elizabeth led mother and daughter to retreat to France in 1791; John meanwhile was fined for 'criminal conversation' with the wife of his tailor. He left for Naples, dying in 1797. Susannah Gunning, whose novels in 1783–1793 seem to reflect family events, is buried in Westminster Abbey.[26]

Elizabeth Hamilton (25 July 1756 or 1758–23 July 1816), a Scottish writer born in Belfast, lost her father in 1759, her mother in 1767. In 1762, she was sent to live with her aunt near Stirling, then later near Bannockburn. She settled in Edinburgh. Hamilton began writing in support of her brother's orientalist studies, continuing after his death in 1792. She revisited Belfast in 1793. In 1796, her *Translation of the Letters of the Hindoo Rajah* followed the adventures of an Indian prince in England, meeting slave owners and philosophers and growing disillusioned. In 1800, she published her novel *Memoirs of Modern Philosophers*, a pointed response to the 1790s Revolution Controversy: Hamilton wanted women's education but focused on the domestic sphere. Works on education followed, in 1801, 1806, and 1815. In 1808, she published *The Cottagers of Glenburnie*, a novel focused on inequities in women's domestic life.[27]

Lady Mary Hamilton, née **Leslie** [or **Lady Mary Walker**] (8 May 1736–29 February 1821), a Scottish writer born in Fife, married Dr. James Walker in 1762. James moved to Jamaica in the 1770s and Hamilton wrote to support her family. Her novel *Letters from the Duchesse de Crui* appeared in 1777. *Munster Village* in 1778 describes a utopian city for those escaping disastrous marriages. Jane Austen's names Bennet and Bingley echo Hamilton, whose utopianism may also have influenced Wollstonecraft. Hamilton had two children with George Musgrave MP, born in 1768–1769. She seems to have married George Robinson Hamilton, settling in Lille in 1782. He died in 1797; but his will suggests

---

26 *Dictionary of National Biography* [DNB]; Janet M. Todd, ed. *British and American Women Writers* (1985).
27 Matthew Grenby, *The Anti-Jacobin Novel: British Conservatism and the French Revolution* (Cambridge, UK: Cambridge University Press, 2001); *Dictionary of National Biography* [DNB].

they were unmarried, and Walker was still alive in 1786. Hamilton met Charles Nodier who translated *Munster Village* and helped with her French *Duc de Popoli* in 1810. Her daughter may have had a child by Ugo Foscolo.[28]

Mary Ann Hanway (fl. 1798–1814) published three novels with the Minerva Press: *Ellinor, or, The World as It Is*, 1798, *Andrew Stuart, or the Northern Wanderer*, 1800, and *Falconbridge Abbey. A Devonshire Story*, 1809. Her *Christabelle, The Maid of Rouen. A Novel, Founded on Facts* appeared in 1814, in which Christabelle's father loses their fortune and she becomes a nun. It has been conjectured that Hanway wrote *A Journey to the Highlands of Scotland. With Occasional Remarks on Dr. Johnson's Tour: By a Lady*, published in London in 1776.[29]

Martha Harley [later **Hugill**] (fl. 1786–1797) published two novels with the Minerva Press: a first novel "by a young lady," printed privately and sold by subscription in 1786, *St. Bernard's Priory. An Old English Tale*, whose second edition was with Lane in 1789; then *The Countess of Hennebon, an Historical Novel*, 1789. Harley's four other Gothic novels appeared elsewhere: *The Castle of Mowbray, an English Romance*, 1788, and *Juliana Ormeston: or, the Fraternal Victim*, 1793, both with Irish editions, the second credited for the first time to Mrs. Harley; *The Prince of Leon. A Spanish Romance*, 1794; and *Isidora of Gallicia: A Novel*, 1797, credited to Mrs. Hugill. She seems to have lived in London and married between 1794–1797. After Harley's first novel, she moved to professional publishers, with some success and some notice in the press. *Isidora of Gallicia* was translated into French.[30]

Mary Hays (4 May 1759–20 February 1843), born in London, was the daughter of Rational Dissenters. In 1777, she fell in love with John Eccles, who died in 1780. Her first novel was based on her letters to him; her first poem appeared in 1781, with more publications in 1785–1786. In 1791, she began a passionate correspondence with William Frend.

---

28 Alessa Johns, *Women's Utopias of the Eighteenth Century* (Champaign, IL: University of Illinois Press, 2003); *Dictionary of National Biography* [DNB].

29 Edward Copeland, *Women Writing about Money* (1995); Pamela Clemit, *The Cambridge Companion to British Literature of the French Revolution in the 1790s* (Cambridge, UK: Cambridge University Press, 2011).

30 *Orlando: Women's Writing in the British Isles from the Beginnings to the Present* (Cambridge: Cambridge University Press, https://orlando.cambridge.org/); Janet M. Todd, ed. *British and American Women Writers* (1985).

In 1792, she read Wollstonecraft's *Vindication of the Rights of Woman*, meeting the author and London's Jacobin circle. For her 1793 *Letters and Essays*, she invited Wollstonecraft to comment. William Godwin became a friend and mentor; Hays meanwhile moved out of her mother's home. In 1796, Hays published *Memoirs of Emma Courtney*, about Frend and her own experiment in freedom; her use of actual letters from Frend and Godwin shocked London and alienated Godwin. She published *Female Biography*, listing 294 women, in 1803. Her later years were difficult.[31]

Elizabeth Hervey, née **March** (1748–1820) lost her father early and her mother remarried the planter William Beckford; Hervey was thus the half-sister of William Beckford the writer, whose novel *Azemia* in 1797 satirized her writing. She married Alexander Harvie but was widowed at seventeen in 1765. In 1774, she married Colonel William Thomas Hervey, having two sons before his death (or divorce) in 1778. She was in Brussels in 1789 with the poet and radical Robert Merry. Hervey published her first five novels anonymously: *Melissa and Marcia; or the Sisters*, 1788, with the Minerva Press; *Louisa*, 1790; *The History of Ned Evans*, 1796; *The Church of St. Siffrid*, 1797; and *The Mourtray Family*, 1800. Her 1814 *Amabel; or, Memoirs of a Woman of Fashion* was signed. Her novels saw multiple editions and at least four were translated into French. A seventh novel exists in manuscript form.[32]

Harriett Hesketh [or **Harriett Cowper**] (1733–5 January 1807), baptized in Hertingfordbury, was a cousin of William Cowper. The two had a long correspondence—despite a nineteen-year gap at her insistence—which served as a basis for his biography.[33]

Fanny Margaretta Holcroft (21 February 1780–7 October 1844), daughter of the British Jacobin writer Thomas Holcroft, lost her mother shortly after birth. In 1797, Holcroft published three poems in the *Monthly Magazine*, including the abolitionist "The Negro." In 1805–1806, she translated seven plays—Alfieri, Lessing, Calderón, Moratin—for her father's *Theatrical Recorder*, also providing the music for his 1805 *The Lady of the Rock* and writing her own unpublished melodrama. She lost

---

31   Gina Luria Walker, *Mary Hays, (1759–1843): The Growth of a Woman's Mind* (Aldershot: Ashgate, 2006).
32   Virginia Blain et al., *The Feminist Companion to Literature in English* (1990); Janet M. Todd, ed. *British and American Women Writers* (1985).
33   *Dictionary of National Biography* [DNB].

a position as governess due to reports her father was a French spy; as he aged, she became his amanuensis. Holcroft's writing was driven by economic necessity. She later published two novels dedicated to her late father and reflecting his reformist politics, *The Wife and the Lover*, 1813, and *Fortitude and Frailty*, 1817.³⁴

Margaret Holford [known as **"the elder"**] (1757–1834), born in Chester, married Allen Holford and died in Chester. Her daughter, also Margaret Holford and an author, is sometimes confused with her. Holford—a novelist, poet, and dramatist—published *Fanny: A Novel: In a Series of Letters* anonymously in 1785, then *Gresford Vale; and Other Poems* in 1798, and *The Way to Win Her* in *The New British Theatre*, 1814.³⁵

Anne Hunter, née **Home** (13 March 1742–7 January 1821), a Scottish writer born in Berwickshire, published her first poem in Edinburgh in 1765. She married John Hunter, creator of Glasgow's Hunterian Museum, in 1771; her salon hosted the Bluestockings Elizabeth Carter, Mary Delany, and Elizabeth Montagu. Hunter inspired the young Joanna Baillie. John died in 1793, leaving Hunter poorly provided for; she published a volume of poems in 1802 which was reprinted the following year. Haydn set nine of her songs to music, including "My Mother Bids Me Bind My Hair," "The Mermaid's Song," "Fidelity," "Pleasing Pain," and "The Spirit's Song." Hunter also wrote the libretto for *The Creation*. Their relationship is ambiguous, though she was a widow when he visited.³⁶

Elizabeth Inchbald, née **Simpson** (15 October 1753–1 August 1821), born at Stanningfield, overcame a stammer to act. In London in 1772, she married the older Joseph Inchbald; the couple appeared onstage that year in *King Lear*, then toured until 1776. In Liverpool, Inchbald met Sarah Siddons and John Philip Kemble; Joseph died in 1779. Inchbald acted for another decade but was better known as a playwright and author. From 1784–1805, nineteen of her comedies, sentimental dramas, and farces (many translated from French and German) were staged in London theaters; two more went unperformed and two are unpublished.

---

34 Virginia Blain et al., *The Feminist Companion to Literature in English* (1990); *Dictionary of National Biography* [DNB].
35 *Orlando: Women's Writing in the British Isles*.
36 Caroline Grigson, *The Life and Poems of Anne Hunter: Haydn's Tuneful Voice* (Liverpool: Liverpool University Press, 2009).

Inchbald published two novels, *A Simple Story*, 1791, and *Nature and Art*, 1796, to some acclaim; a friend of Godwin and Holcroft, her radicalism is clearer here than onstage. She wrote ample criticism and destroyed a four-volume autobiography. She did not remarry.[37]

Ann Jebb, née **Torkington** (9 November 1735–20 January 1812), born in Ripton-Kings, grew up in Huntingdonshire, marrying the reformer John Jebb in 1764. He was lecturing at Cambridge, where Jebb held reformist gatherings. Anne Plumptre was a friend. Jebb often wrote in epistolary form, signed 'Priscilla;' thus, her 1772–1774 series on abolishing the required subscription to the Thirty-Nine Articles. John resigned his church living in 1775 and the couple moved to London, involved in reformist causes from the American and French Revolutions to the franchise and abolitionism. Widowed in 1786, Jebb remained in London and politically active. Her writing appeared in the *London Chronicle*, the *Whitehall Evening Post*, and the *Monthly Repository*, as well as in pamphlet form.[38]

Susanna Keir, née **Harvey** (1747–20 November 1802), married the chemist and poet James Keir, a friend of Erasmus Darwin and Joseph Priestley. Keir published her two known novels while living in Edinburgh, both of them epistolary and anonymous: *Interesting Memoirs* in 1785 and *The History of Miss Greville* in 1787. She died in 1802.[39]

Anne Ker, née **Phillips** (17 November 1766-c. 5 December 1821), born in London, married John Ker in 1788. Ker published six Gothic novels, to more commercial than critical success: *The Heiress di Montalde; or, the Castle of Bezanto*, 1799; *Adeline St Julian; or, the Midnight Hour*, 1800; *Emmeline; or, the Happy Discovery*, 1801; *The Mysterious Count; or, Montville Castle*, 1803; *Modem Faults, a Novel, Founded on Facts*, 1804; and *Edric, the Forester: Or, the Mysteries of the Haunted Chamber. An Historical Romance*, 1817. She had a good number of subscribers, including Caroline, Princess of Wales, a tribute perhaps to her moral ambiguity (promiscuity, prostitution), her debts to Radcliffe, or her portrayal of poorer characters. Ker later appealed six times to the Royal Literary Fund, receiving ten pounds total.[40]

---

37 Roger Manvell, *Elizabeth Inchbald: England's Principal Woman Dramatist and Independent Woman of Letters in 18th Century London: A Biographical Study* (Lanham, MD: University of America, 1987).
38 Virginia Blain et al., *The Feminist Companion to Literature in English* (1990).
39 Janet M. Todd, ed. *British and American Women Writers* (1985).
40 Virginia Blain et al., *The Feminist Companion to Literature in English* (1990).

Mary Ann Kilner, née **Maze** (14 December 1753–1 December 1831), born in London to a Huguenot silk throwster, grew up bilingual in French and English. In 1774, she married her childhood friend Thomas Kilner. When Thomas's sister Dorothy published with John Marshall in 1780, Kilner proposed to him *Familiar Dialogues for the Instruction and Amusement of Children of Four and Five Years Old*, which he published in 1781. More children's books followed: *Memoirs of a Peg Top* and *Jemima Placid* in 1782, *The Adventures of a Whipping Top* and *William Sedley* in 1783 along with *A Course of Lectures, for Sunday Evenings*. In 1783 or 1784, *The Adventures of a Pincushion* appeared and was republished until the 1830s. When Dorothy abandoned anonymity for the initials 'M.P.' (referring to Maryland Point), Kilner adopted 'S.S.' (for Spital Square, London).[41]

Charlotte Lennox, née **Ramsay** (c. 1729–4 January 1804), a Scottish writer born in Gibraltar, lived in England until her father moved the family to Albany, New York in 1738. He died in 1742. Back in London by 1746, Lennox married Alexander Lennox and appeared onstage. *Poems on Several Occasions* followed in 1747, then in 1750, *The Life of Harriot Stuart*; her 1752 novel *The Female Quixote* was praised by Johnson, Richardson, and Fielding, though the Bluestockings faulted her. From 1756–1774, Lennox translated the Duke de Sully's memoirs, the Greek theater of Brumoy, and the meditations of the Duchesse de La Vallière. She published three plays, 1758–1775, *Philander, The Sister*, and *Old City Manners*, staged by Garrick; more poems; a magazine, *The Lady's Museum*; and five more novels, 1758–1791. Her *Shakespear Illustrated* (1753–1754) remains relevant. She died in penury.[42]

Agnes Lyon (1762–14 September 1840), a Scottish comic poet born in Dundee, married Rev. Dr James Lyon in 1780. At her death, Lyon's poems filled four manuscript volumes; she directed that they remain unprinted unless her family needed the money. Subjects include "Glammis Castle," 1821, about a drunken episode involving Sir Walter Scott, and the song beginning "You've surely heard of famous Neil," about Neil Gow and set to his air "Farewell to Whisky."[43]

---

41 *Dictionary of National Biography* [DNB].
42 Susan Carlile, *Charlotte Lennox: An Independent Mind* (Toronto: University of Toronto Press, 2018).
43 *Dictionary of National Biography* [DNB].

Jean Marishall [or **Jane Marshall**] (fl. 1765–1788), a Scottish novelist and dramatist, published for children with John Newbery. Her novels were influenced by Samuel Richardson: *The History of Miss Clarinda Cathcart and Miss Fanny Kenton*, 1765, a sentimental epistolary novel; *The History of Alicia Montagu, by the Author of Clarinda Cathcart*, 1767; the play *Sir Harry Gaylove, or Comedy in Embryo*, 1772, with a prologue by Thomas Blacklock and an epilogue by Hugh Downman; and *A Series of Letters for the Improvement of Youth*, 1788.[44]

Margaret Minifie (15 July 1734–11 May 1803), born in Staplegrove, was the sister of Susannah Gunning, to whom some of her own works have been attributed, notably *The Count de Poland*, 1780, and *Coombe Wood*, 1783. The two collaborated on at least two novels, *The Histories of Lady Frances S— and Lady Caroline S—*, 1763, which went into a second edition, and *The Picture*, 1766. Both ceased writing for a time, Minifie for twenty years from 1783 before her final novel, *The Union*, 1801. No extant portraits of Minifie are known, but there are several caricatures of her as a spinster (with cats) by Isaac Cruikshank and James Gilray, thanks to the 1791 scandal involving her niece, the novelist Elizabeth Gunning, dubbed the "Gunninghiad" by Horace Walpole. Minifie's other novels include *Barford Abbey*, 1768, with the Minerva Press; *The Cottage*, 1769; and *The Hermit*, 1770.[45]

Jane Elizabeth Moore (30 September 1738–1796?), born in London, lost her mother aged three and was raised by relatives. She began work in the leather trade in 1753; in 1761, she married a Thomas Moore, working in his and her father's firms. She negotiated a dowry from her father, who then left her out of his will, resulting in a lawsuit. Moore moved to Ireland before 1795; in 1796, she wrote of her displeasure at being "obligated to any man breathing." In 1786, she published her *Genuine Memoirs of Jane Elizabeth Moore*, volume three being a treatise on British industry. *Miscellaneous Poems* followed in 1796, with over 300 subscribers including Mary Tighe. It contains her challenge to the Dublin Freemasons to admit women, and it saw a second edition. As a loyalist Tory in Ireland, Moore has been neglected; she is now enjoying rediscovery.[46]

---

44 *Dictionary of National Biography* [DNB].
45 Debbie McVitty, *Familiar Collaboration and Women Writers in Eighteenth-Century Britain: Elizabeth Griffith, Sarah Fielding and Susannah and Margaret Minifie* (D. Phil. University of Oxford, 2008).
46 Stephen C. Behrendt, *British Women Poets and the Romantic Writing Community* (Baltimore: The Johns Hopkins University Press, 2009).

Hannah More (2 February 1745–7 September 1833), born near Bristol, attended her father's girls' school and later taught there. In 1767, she became engaged to William Turner. In 1773, he broke off the engagement but created an annuity which enabled her independence. More's first play, *The Search after Happiness*, appeared in 1762. More met Samuel Johnson, Edmund Burke, Horace Walpole, and Elizabeth Montagu, at whose salon she met Elizabeth Carter and others. Her 1784 poem *The Bas Bleu, or, Conversation* celebrates that circle. More's tragedy *Percy*, with prologue by Garrick, was staged in 1777 and again in 1785. Mozart owned a copy. More gave up drama from 1779–1818, except for *Sacred Dramas*, 1782; an abolitionist and evangelical moralist, she attacked Thomas Paine in *Village Politics*, 1792, and in the *Cheap Repository Tracts*, 1795–1798, which sold over two million copies.[47]

Amelia Opie, née **Alderson** (12 November 1769–2 December 1853), born in Norwich, lost her mother in 1784. She married John Opie in 1798, who died in 1807. Opie became close to Walter Scott, Richard Brinsley Sheridan, William Godwin, and Mary Wollstonecraft, among others. She published *Dangers of Coquetry* in 1790, *Father and Daughter* in 1801. *Adeline Mowbray* followed in 1804, and other novels, with a hiatus after 1828 until the twelve-volume *Miscellaneous Tales* in 1845–1847. Opie published two biographies, 1809–1814; travel memoirs in 1831 and 1840; and poetry from 1801 to 1834, including *The Black Man's Lament, Or, How to Make Sugar* in 1826. Her 1802 *Poems* went through six editions. Opie's was the first of 187,000 names on an abolitionist petition to Parliament. She joined the Society of Friends in 1825.[48]

Eliza Parsons, née **Phelp** (1739?–5 February 1811), born in Plymouth, was baptized in 1739. She married James Parsons in 1760. The couple had eight children, moving to London in 1778–1779. In 1782, the Parsons lost their eldest in Jamaica and James's turpentine business in a fire. He died in 1790. Parsons then wrote to support the family, producing nineteen Gothic novels and one play from 1790–1807, in sixty volumes. *The Castle of Wolfenbach*, 1793, and *The Mysterious Warning*, 1796, are two of seven

---

[47] Anne Stott, *Hannah More: The First Victorian* (Oxford: Oxford University Press, 2003).
[48] Eleanor Ty, *Empowering the Feminine: The Narratives of Mary Robinson, Jane West, and Amelia Opie, 1796–1812* (Toronto: University of Toronto Press, 1998); Bradford K. Mudge, ed. *British Romantic Novelists, 1789–1832* (Detroit: Gale Research, 1992).

titles recommended as "horrid" novels in Jane Austen's *Northanger Abbey*; Parsons believed good should be rewarded and evil punished, as seen in her work. Besides her play *The Intrigues of a Morning; or an Hour in Paris*, 1792, Parsons also wrote two undated novels, *The Wise Ones Bubbled; or Lovers Triumphant* and *Rosetta* [as 'A Lady']. She received forty-five guineas from the Royal Literary Fund, 1793–1803.[49]

Lucy Peacock (fl. 1785–1816) published her first known work in London in 1785, anonymously and by subscription: *The Adventures of the Six Princesses of Babylon*, an adaptation for children of Edmund Spenser's *Faerie Queene*. It saw five editions and a German translation. *The Rambles of Fancy*, 1786, which includes the tale "The Creole," was also published "for the author." From 1788, Peacock edited *The Juvenile Magazine*, contributors including herself and Dorothy and Mary Ann Kilner. *Martin & James or the Reward of Integrity*, 1791, also appeared in Dublin and Philadelphia; *The Visit for a Week*, 1794, had ten editions by 1823. Peacock may have been married, since 'R. and L. Peacock' published at the Juvenile Library from 1796–1810. She also translated Ducray-Duminil and La Croze from the French in 1796 and 1802–1807.[50]

Anne Plumptre (22 February 1760–20 October 1818), born in Norwich, spoke French, Italian, Spanish, and German. Her first novel, *Antoinette*, appeared anonymously, though a second edition printed her name. In 1798–1799, Plumptre translated several plays by Kotzebue, then also a *Life and Literary Career of Kotzebue* in 1801. Living in France from 1802–1805, Plumptre published her experiences in 1810, stating that she would welcome Napoleon invading England to improve its government. In 1814–1815, she visited Ireland, recording her experiences in 1817—a work ridiculed in *The Quarterly Review*. Plumptre also published travel memoirs translated from French and German and some political enquiry, sometimes collaborating with her sister Annabella Plumptre. Helen Maria Williams and Amelia Opie were friends of hers.[51]

Agnes Porter (c. 18 June 1752–1814) was born in Edinburgh; the date is uncertain, but we know her birthday. She was fluent in French. Her diaries and correspondence survive for the period 1788–1814: in

---

49 Virginia Blain et al., *The Feminist Companion to Literature in English* (1990).
50 Janet M. Todd, ed. *British and American women writers* (1985); *Dictionary of National Biography* [DNB].
51 *Dictionary of National Biography* [DNB].

1788, Porter moved to Great Yarmouth as a governess for the children of Ambrose Goddard, M.P.; she later cared for the children of the 2nd Earl of Ilchester, retiring in 1806. Her manuscripts were discovered in Penrice Castle in the 1970s.[52]

Elizabeth Purbeck and **Jane Purbeck** (fl. 1789–1802) were daughters of the Mayor of Southampton; Elizabeth was baptized in 1746. The two lived together and remained unmarried, publishing six anonymous novels between 1798–1802: *Honoria Sommerville*, 1789, *Raynsford Park*, 1790, *William Thornborough, the Benevolent Quixote*, 1791, *Matilda and Elizabeth*, 1796, *The History of Sir George Warrington; or the Political Quixote*, 1797, and *Neville Castle; or, The Generous Cambrians*, 1802. Three of the novels are epistolary and somewhat Richardsonian; in *Neville Castle*, a discussion of writers prefers Frances Burney and Sophia Lee to Richardson and Henry Fielding. *Neville Castle* may have appeared after Elizabeth's death; *Honoria Sommerville* in particular drew considerable press attention. *The Gentleman's Magazine* was still citing the sisters in 1822.[53]

Ann Radcliffe, née **Ward** (9 July 1764–7 February 1823), born in London, was childhood friends with Josiah Wedgwood's daughter. In 1787, she married William Radcliffe, whose newspaper celebrated the French Revolution and freedom of the press. Radcliffe published her first novel anonymously in 1789, *The Castles of Athlin and Dunblayne*; *A Sicilian Romance* followed in 1790, *The Romance of the Forest* in 1791, *The Mysteries of Udolpho* in 1794, *The Italian* in 1797. In 1794, she visited the Netherlands and Germany, publishing a travelogue in 1795. Her payment for *The Italian* made her the highest-paid author in Britain in the 1790s. A final novel, *Gaston de Blondeville*, appeared posthumously in 1826, with her essay on terror versus horror in fiction. Radcliffe's readers included Jane Austen, Sir Walter Scott, Edgar Allan Poe, the Brontë sisters, Honoré de Balzac, Victor Hugo, and Fyodor Dostoyevsky.[54]

Eliza Roberts (fl. 1781–1788) may be the mother of the writer Emma Roberts. As 'Miss Roberts,' she published two poems, "Effusions of Melancholy" and "On a Supposed Slight from a Friend" in the *Lady's*

---

52 Joanna Martin, ed. *A Governess in the Age of Jane Austen. The Journals and Letters of Agnes Porter* (London: Hambledon Press, 1998).
53 Virginia Blain et al., *The Feminist Companion to Literature in English* (1990).
54 Robert Miles, *Ann Radcliffe: The Great Enchantress* (Manchester: Manchester University Press, 1995).

Poetical Magazine, London 1781. Both later appeared in the first known anthology of writing by women in English, *Poems by Eminent Ladies*, 1785. In London in 1788, she published *The Beauties of Rousseau. Selected by a Lady*, consisting of translations of excerpts from the works of Jean-Jacques Rousseau.[55]

Mary Robinson, née **Darby** (27 November 1757–26 December 1800), born in Bristol, attended Hannah More's school there. During her childhood, her father abandoned her mother, who then opened a girls' school in London in which Robinson taught. At fifteen, David Garrick tutored her; she married Thomas Robinson in 1773, living with him when he was imprisoned for debt. A volume of her poems appeared in 1775; the Duchess of Devonshire sponsored her second volume, *Captivity*. Robinson returned to the theater in 1776, supported by Richard Brinsley Sheridan and becoming the mistress of the Prince of Wales. Robinson influenced fashion, launching the flowing Perdita gown. She wrote eight volumes of poetry, eight novels (notably *Vancenza* in 1792), three plays, essays, sketches, and feminist treatises, besides a manuscript autobiography. Robinson, an ardent admirer of the French Revolution, died in poverty in 1800.[56]

Jane Marie Scott (1779–6 December 1839), baptized in 1779, founded the Sans Pareil Theatre in London with her father in 1806; he built the theater, and she wrote the texts for the opening. Scott wrote (and performed in) more than fifty stage pieces for the Sans Pareil: melodramas, pantomimes, farces, comic operettas, historical dramas, adaptations, from Maria Edgeworth and Walter Scott for instance, and translations. Most have not survived. The Sans Pareil played a role in the move away from theatrical monopoly at the time; it became the Adelphi Theatre in 1819, when Scott retired and married John Davies Middleton.[57]

Mary Scott [after marriage, **Mary Taylor**] (19 July 1751/1752–10 June 1793), born in Milborne Port, Somerset, was the daughter of a linen draper. Her first known work is *The Female Advocate*, 1774, 522 lines of rhyming couplets dedicated to her friend Mary Steele. She praises

---

55 Janet M. Todd, ed. *British and American women writers* (1985).
56 Paula Byrne, *Perdita: The Life of Mary Robinson* (London: HarperCollins, 2004).
57 Catherine Burroughs, ed. *Women in British Romantic Theatre: Drama, Performance, and Society, 1790–1840* (Cambridge: Cambridge University Press, 2000).

Anna Laetitia Barbauld, Helen Maria Williams, Phillis Wheatley, and others. Scott corresponded with Anna Seward, whose father is also praised, publishing verses to her in 1783. She cared for her mother until the latter's death in 1787; her father died in 1788 and she married John Taylor after a decade of courtship. That year, Scott published *The Messiah*, for the General Hospital at Bath. She was a Protestant Dissenter and found her husband's embrace of Quakerism difficult. A son founded *The Manchester Guardian*. Scott died in her third pregnancy.[58]

Anna Seward (12 December 1742–25 March 1809), born in Eyam in Derbyshire, moved to Lichfield in 1749. Her father, for whom she cared from 1780–1790, published *The Female Right to Literature* in 1748; their home in the Bishop's Palace welcomed Erasmus Darwin, Samuel Johnson, and James Boswell. Seward was outspoken against marriage and is cited, perhaps problematically, in the lesbian canon, which notes her attachment to Honora Sneyd. Seward wrote poetry after 1759, including elegies, sonnets, odes, and a verse novel, *Louisa*, 1784, which saw five editions; but she only published after 1780. Seward also wrote letters, six large volumes of them appearing in 1811. Samuel Johnson and Sir Walter Scott saw her as an authority, Scott somewhat freely editing her *Poetical Works* in 1810. Seward was a keen botanist, like her friend Erasmus Darwin.[59]

Eleanor Sleath, née **Carter** (15 October 1770–5 May 1847), born in Loughborough, married Joseph Barnabus Sleath in 1792. He died in 1794, leaving her in debt, and she returned to Leicester to care for her elderly mother. Sleath published *The Orphan of the Rhine* in 1798, one of the seven "horrid" novels listed in Jane Austen's *Northanger Abbey*. *Who's the Murderer?* followed in 1802. After rumors in 1807 involving Ann Dudley's husband, and the Dudleys' departure, Sleath wrote several more novels: *The Bristol Heiress* in 1809, *The Nocturnal Minstrel* in 1810, *Pyrenean Banditti* in 1811, and *Glenowen; or The Fairy Palace* in 1812. In 1813, her mother died, and Sleath moved to Loughborough. Ann Dudley died in 1823 and that year, Sleath married John Dudley.[60]

---

58 Roger Lonsdale, ed. *Eighteenth-Century Women Poets* (New York: Oxford University Press, 1989).
59 Teresa Barnard, *Anna Seward: A Constructed Life; a Critical Biography* (Farnham: Ashgate, 2009).
60 *Orlando: Women's Writing in the British Isles*.

Charlotte Smith (4 May 1749–28 October 1806), born in London, lost her mother early and was raised by an aunt—enrolled in girls' schools in Chichester, then London. In 1765, her father married her off to Benjamin Smith, a profligate, violent man. The couple had twelve children, to whom her planter father-in-law left a large inheritance in 1776; it was in chancery for forty years, Benjamin spending a third of it and going to debtor's prison in 1783. Smith there wrote her 1784 *Elegiac Sonnets*, launching that vogue. Their success paid for his release; he fled to France, where she joined him. She left Benjamin in 1787, though he maintained access to her finances. Smith published ten novels in ten years to dwindling critical and commercial success, condemning slavery and the exploitation of women, praising the French Revolution. She later wrote children's books and rural walks but died in poverty. Ann Radcliffe was a friend.[61]

Lady Louisa Stuart (12 August 1757–4 August 1851), born in London, was the daughter of the 3rd Earl of Bute, Tory prime minister 1762–1763 and thereafter retired. Stuart always published anonymously, though close to Sir Walter Scott from the 1790s to 1832. Manuscript memoirs and letters remain unpublished; selections appeared from 1895–1903. Stuart wrote a memoir of Lady Mary Coke in 1827, another in 1837 of her grandmother Lady Mary Wortley Montagu. She also wrote verses, including fables and a ballad.[62]

Susanna Whatman, née **Bosanquet** (23 January 1753–29 November 1814), born in Hamburg, married James Whatman in 1776. The couple settled in Kent. As head of household, Whatman kept detailed records of their household management over twenty-four years, receiving no attention until 1952 when the records were published.[63]

Helen Maria Williams (17 June 1759–15 December 1827), born in London, lost her father aged two, after which the family moved to Berwick-upon-Tweed. In 1781, the family returned to London; Williams published the novel *Edwin and Eltruda* in 1782, then the epic poem *Peru*, 1784, critiquing European colonialism. *Poems*, 1786, has an abolitionist poem; Williams published another in 1788. Williams's novel *Julia* in 1790

---

61 Bethan Roberts, *Charlotte Smith and the Sonnet: Form, Place and Tradition in the Late Eighteenth Century* (Liverpool: Liverpool University Press, 2019).
62 Devoney Looser, *British Women Writers and the Writing of History, 1670–1820* (Baltimore, MD: Johns Hopkins University Press, 2000).
63 *Dictionary of National Biography* [DNB].

favors the French Revolution; she then traveled to France, publishing the eight-volume *Letters Written in France*, 1790–1796, to record her experiences. In Paris, Williams hosted Mary Wollstonecraft and Thomas Paine. Imprisoned at the fall of the Girondins, Williams translated the novel *Paul et Virginie* and later Alexander von Humboldt. Her 1801 memoir of France opposes the First Consul. Williams acquired French citizenship in 1818.[64]

Mary Wollstonecraft (27 April 1759–10 September 1797), born in London to a spendthrift and violent father, became a lady's companion until her mother's death in 1780. She founded a school with a friend who died in 1785, returning thereafter to London, writing for the *Analytical Review* and translating from French and German. In 1790, Wollstonecraft published a novel, *Mary*, and her popular *Vindication of the Rights of Men*, to answer Burke, followed by *A Vindication of the Rights of Women* in 1792. Talleyrand visited her. She left for Paris in 1792–1795, avoiding arrest with the Girondins and having a child with Gilbert Imlay. Her *Historical and Moral View of the French Revolution* appeared in 1794. Wollstonecraft married William Godwin in 1797, giving birth that year to Mary Shelley and dying ten days later. Godwin's 1798 memoir of her compromised her reputation for the next century.[65]

Ann Yearsley, née **Cromartie** [or **Lactilla**] (8 July 1753–6 May 1806), born in Bristol, worked in childhood as a milkwoman and received no formal education. She married John Yearsley in 1774, being rescued from penury by Hannah More, who organized subscriptions for Yearsley's *Poems, on Several Occasions*, 1785. Its success led to a quarrel between the two about money and Yearsley's *Poems, on Various Subjects* in 1787 were instead supported by the 4th Earl of Bristol. An abolitionist poem followed in 1788, then *Earl Goodwin: an Historical Play* (performed in 1789; printed in 1791), and the novel *The Royal Captives: A Fragment of Secret History, Copied from an Old Manuscript*, 1795. Her last volume of poetry, *The Rural Lyre*, appeared in 1796. The poet Robert Southey published a memoir of Yearsley in 1831.[66]

---

64 Deborah Kennedy, *Helen Maria Williams and the Age of Revolution* (Lewisburg, PA: Bucknell University Press, 2002).
65 Janet Todd, *Mary Wollstonecraft: A Revolutionary Life* (London: Weidenfeld & Nicolson, 2000).
66 Mary Waldron, *Lactilla, Milkwoman of Clifton: The Life and Writings of Ann Yearsley, 1753–1806* (Athens, GA: University of Georgia Press, 1996).

Mary Julia Young (fl. 1788–1810) was a poet, translator, biographer, and novelist, sometimes with the Minerva Press. What little is known of her life comes from her 1808 application to the Royal Literary Fund. Young published the poetry collection *Genius and Fancy* in 1791, with a third edition tripled in length, and *Poems* in 1801. She published three translations from French and German, two of these from women writers. Young also published eight or nine novels: *Rose-Mount Castle; or, False Report*, 1798; *The East Indian, or Clifford Priory*, 1799; *Moss Cliff Abbey; or, The Sepulchral Harmonist*, 1803; *Right and Wrong; or, The Kinsmen of Naples*, 1803; *Donalda, or The Witches of Glenshiel*, 1805; *A Summer at Brighton* and *A Summer at Weymouth*, 1807–1808; and *The Heir of Drumcondra*, 1810. Young published a biography of Anna Maria Crouch in 1806.[67]

Great Britain: The Nineteenth Century (100 writers)

Jane Austen

Pride and Prejudice (1813)

It is a truth universally acknowledged, that a single man in possession of a good fortune, must be in want of a wife.

However little known the feelings or views of such a man may be on his first entering a neighbourhood, this truth is so well fixed in the minds of the surrounding families, that he is considered as the rightful property of some one or other of their daughters.

"My dear Mr. Bennet," said his lady to him one day, "have you heard that Netherfield Park is let at last?"

Mr. Bennet replied that he had not.

"But it is," returned she; "for Mrs. Long has just been here, and she told me all about it."

Mr. Bennet made no answer.

"Do not you want to know who has taken it?" cried his wife impatiently.

"*You* want to tell me, and I have no objection to hearing it."

This was invitation enough.[68]

---

67 *Orlando: Women's Writing in the British Isles*.
68 In *The Cambridge Edition of Jane Austen*, ed. Janet Todd: *Pride and Prejudice*, ed. Pat Rogers (Cambridge: Cambridge University Press, 2006), p. 3.

Jane Austen, who never married, is writing about marriage here, and at two levels. First, about her legendary man "in want of a wife" and second, about a man who has one; and the second man, Mr. Bennet, might lead us to wonder why the first would be so in want.

Austen's opening sentence is rightly famous. It begins grandly, like Jefferson's "We hold these truths to be self-evident," opening the American *Declaration of Independence* of 1776; and follows that claim to universal truth with an axiom tilted rather dramatically closer to the mind of Mrs. Bennet than to her husband's. The wit here is again twofold: Austen may be ribbing Mrs. Bennet and her ilk, but she is also ribbing the moral philosophers who announce the truths they have arrived at by sentiment or deduction. From the *incipit*, we are thus informed that Austen's narrator will be a slippery and partial creature, as are we all in the end, and rather like the narrator of Pushkin's *Evgenii Onegin* (1825–1832)—another very witty author.

Throughout this passage, Austen's pacing is superb. The second sentence, which is its own paragraph, contrasts the black box of the new neighbor's mind with the certainty regarding it that characterizes the surrounding families. As Fénelon writes, "Il y a des folies de diverses espèces," and this is folly, to believe we know another's mind.[69] The entire novel will play on this theme, with Darcy in particular, but also with Lydia and Wickham. The folly distinguishes Mrs. Bennet, but it does not spare Austen's heroine, the Bennets' daughter Elizabeth, who also believes she can read people when their mystery remains intact. Elizabeth is, in short, a victim of prejudice as much as of pride.

Having established an important axiom to open, Austen's narrator proceeds to pass to its practical application: a conversation between Mrs. Bennet and her husband. Mrs. Bennet launches what might be called a sneak attack, asking if he knows that a neighboring manor is let at last. The interest, of course, resides in who is letting it, but Mrs. Bennet prefers to beat around the bush. The argument may be made that with absolute power comes freedom from subterfuge and guile; one may simply proceed with one's plans, much as Russia, Prussia, and Austria did in carving Poland up between them in 1772–1795. By the same token, it is natural for the weak to use guile to achieve their ends,

---

[69] François de Salignac de La Mothe Fénelon, *Dialogues des morts; suivis de quelques dialogues de Boileau, Fontenelle et d'Alembert* (Paris: Hachette, 1862), p. 37.

since brute force cannot be relied on. Perhaps that is why Mrs. Bennet prefers to approach obliquely; in 1813, independently of any moral standing Mr. Bennet might have, he is also the *paterfamilias*, and more vested in rights than his spouse is. Or perhaps she simply wants more of a conversation than a bare announcement will get her: a question, for instance, solicits an answer.

Mr. Bennet now enters the scene. His speech is not given but reported—his mind is another black box—and it appears curt. One may again speculate. Perhaps he is distracted, or perhaps he has heard enough of Mrs. Bennet to know that she just requires the ball of conversation to clear the net in order to proceed. As the novel continues, one is often given the sense that they have been married many years and Mr. Bennet is, in his way, making the best of it, much as Mrs. Bennet is in hers. And Mrs. Bennet does return the ball—"returned she," writes Austen—in providing the source of her new gossip. One may wonder how Mr. Bennet is to react to that provincial authority, and indeed, he remains silent. And thus, Mrs. Bennet returns to the interrogative mode—but she does so "impatiently," she is seemingly unhappy with how her plan of attack has played out on the battlefield of marriage. Now Mr. Bennet, who as we will see is essentially a well-meaning person, at last somewhat condescendingly opens the door to his wife's entreaties. One has the sense that Mrs. Bennet finds gossip of consuming importance whereas Mr. Bennet prefers to avoid it.

What does all this tell us about marriage? A good deal in a short space. It reminds us how much of marriage is conversation, and how easy it is for two well-intentioned partners to find themselves in conflict. It is, like much that is funny, in the end somewhat sad as we reflect on it. Austen, we have said, never married; and though various Bennet daughters are married off in the end, this opening scene lingers, and it is not alone. Marriage, that universal end to comedy, is here not the panacea one might think it. To believe so is a prejudice, and as Austen implies, the freer we are from prejudice, the happier we may be.

Finally, is this a Romantic text? It requires a broad definition of Romanticism to find the Romantic in Austen's pages. One might see Darcy as somewhat Byronic, or a sort of proto-Heathcliff; but that reading may say more about the world Austen lived in than about her own priorities. What is true is that Austen's work, like that of Keats, would not have been possible a half-century earlier. She is in that sense reminiscent of George Crabbe, "Pope in worsted stockings," who represents a road not taken in nineteenth-century English verse.[70] Austen has her parallels, but she is not the immediate parent of Dickens, or Hardy, or Eliot, or the Brontës: she is in the end *sui generis*, which is perhaps just as well.

Mrs Meer Hassan Ali, née **Biddy Timms** (late 1700s–after 1832) married Meer Hassan Ali in London in 1817 and moved with him to Lucknow. Ali remained a Christian and wore Western clothing but spoke fluent Hindustani. After ten years, she returned to England, leaving her husband in India, for reasons unknown. Ali published her first-hand *Observations on the Mussulmauns of India* in 1832.[71]

Jane Austen (16 December 1775–18 July 1817), born in Steventon, was educated mostly at home. Austen gathered twenty-nine early works in three extant manuscript volumes, including *Love and Freindship* [sic] and *The History of England*, some of them reworked in later novels. Of her 3,000-odd letters, 160 have survived to be published. In 1800, the family moved to Bath, where her father died in 1805. In 1802, Harris Bigg-Wither proposed to her; Austen first accepted, then declined. The family moved to Chawton in 1809, where Austen published four anonymous novels: *Sense and Sensibility*, 1811, *Pride and Prejudice*, 1813, *Mansfield Park*, 1814, and *Emma*, published with John Murray in 1815. Her novels were pirated in France by Isabelle de Montolieu. In 1816, Austen repurchased *Northanger Abbey* from its dilatory publisher and completed *Persuasion* in manuscript, both appearing posthumously.[72]

Sarah Austin, née **Taylor** (1793–8 August 1867), born in Norwich, learned Latin, French, German, and Italian. She married John Austin in 1819; their London guests included John Stuart Mill and Jeremy Bentham. Austin published early in *The Edinburgh Review*; in 1833, she published *Selections from the Old Testament* and *Characteristics of Goethe*. The following year, she translated Carové's *The Story without an End* and Victor Cousin's report on education in Prussia promoting national education. From 1836–1848, the couple were in Germany and France; in

---

70 James and Horace Smith, *Rejected Addresses* (London: Methuen, 1904), p. 112.
71 *Dictionary of National Biography* [DNB].
72 Deirdre Le Faye, *Jane Austen: The World of Her Novels* (New York: Harry N. Abrams, 2002); Janet Todd, *The Cambridge Introduction to Jane Austen* (Cambridge, UK: Cambridge University Press, 2015).

1840, Austin translated Ranke's *History of the Reformation in Germany* and *History of the Popes*; in 1854 appeared her study *Germany from 1760 to 1814*. John died in 1859 and Austin published his *Lectures on Jurisprudence*. She also translated Pückler and Guizot and edited Sydney Smith's letters.[73]

Joanna Baillie (11 September 1762–23 February 1851), a Scottish writer born in Bothwell, saw no theater in childhood and learned to read aged ten. In 1802, the family moved to Hampstead. Through her aunt, Anne Hunter, Baillie met the Bluestocking circle; Anna Laetitia Barbauld was a friend, and she traded letters with Sir Walter Scott. In 1790, Baillie published *Poems* and completed an unpublished tragedy, *Arnold*. From 1798–1812, she published the three volumes of her *Plays on the Passions*, combining tragedy, comedy, and musical drama. Her name first appeared in 1800. That year, *De Montfort* was staged and did poorly, though revived in 1810 and 1821. Baillie wanted her plays staged. In 1804, Baillie published *Miscellaneous Plays*, with three further volumes in 1836. She also published poetry: *Metrical Legends* in 1821, *Dramatic Poetry* in 1836, and *Fugitive Verses* in 1840, with some Scots songs.[74]

Clara Lucas Balfour, née **Lucas** (21 December 1808–3 July 1878), born in the New Forest, was raised by her father until his death in 1818, when she moved to London with her mother. Needlework supported them. In 1824, she married James Balfour; the two took temperance pledges in 1837, and Balfour became a Baptist in 1840. She published *Common Sense versus Socialism* in 1840, followed by *Moral Heroism*, 1846, *Women of Scripture*, 1847, which saw nine editions, *Women and the Temperance Movement*, 1849, *Working Women*, 1854, and so forth. Harriet Beecher Stowe prefaced Balfour's *Morning Dew Drops* in 1853; *A Whisper to the Newly Married*, 1850, saw twenty-three editions. Many of her shorter temperance tales first appeared in the press—*British Workman*, *The Fireside, Home Words*. Balfour also gave public lectures on temperance and on women's roles in history.[75]

Anne Bannerman (31 October 1765–29 September 1829), a Scottish writer born in Edinburgh, published her early work often

---

73   *Dictionary of National Biography* [DNB].
74   Ibid.; Margaret S. Carhart, *The Life and Work of Joanna Baillie* (New Haven, CT: Yale University Press, 1923).
75   *Dictionary of National Biography* [DNB].

pseudonymously in periodicals: the *Monthly Magazine*, the *Poetical Register*, the *Edinburgh Magazine*. Bannerman's signed *Poems*, 1800, published to more critical than commercial success, contains odes and sonnets, including a sonnet series translated from Petrarch and another sonnet in imitation of Goethe's *Werther*. Her anonymous *Tales of Superstition and Chivalry*, 1802, contains ten Gothic ballads; a rare admirer was Sir Walter Scott. Struggling financially in later years, Bannerman became a governess. The 1800 "Epistle from the Marquis de Lafayette to General Washington" may be hers.[76]

Elizabeth "Eliza" Ann Ashurst Bardonneau, née **Ashurst** (8 July 1813–25 November 1850), born in London, attended the World Anti-Slavery Convention in London in 1840. After 1844, she became very close to the Italian revolutionary Giuseppe Mazzini, having already begun translating his friend George Sand with her friend Matilda Hays: *Spiridion*, 1842. Sand granted her blessing to this first English version of her work, despite misgivings on meeting Bardonneau. *The Mosaic Workers* and *The Orco* followed in 1844, *Letters of a Traveller*, *André*, and *The Works of George Sand* in 1847. Bardonneau married Jean Bardonneau Narcy in 1849 over family objections, dying in childbirth the next year.[77]

Frances Catherine Barnard [or **Mrs. Alfred Barnard**] (7 May 1796– 30 January 1869), born in Norwich, married Alfred Barnard in 1817; they had ten children. Barnard wrote mostly for children; her publications include the book of plays *Embroidered Facts*, 1836, *Doleful Death and the Flowery Funeral of Fancy*, 1837, *The Schoolfellows; Holidays at the Hall*, 1845, *The Cottage and the Hall*, 1840, and her adaptation of Charles Ball's 1837 memoir of American enslavement, *The Life of a Negro Slave*, 1846.[78]

Louisa Grace Bartolini, née **Grace** (14 February 1818–3 May 1865), born in Bristol to an Irish Catholic family, moved to Sorèze with them in 1818, writing her first poems in French and Italian. In 1841, she moved to Pistoia, contributing to various Italian periodicals such as *La Gioventù* and *La Rivista di Firenze*. She also translated contemporary

---

76   Adriana Craciun, *Fatal Women of Romanticism* (Cambridge: Cambridge University Press, 2003); *Dictionary of National Biography* [DNB].
77   *Dictionary of National Biography* [DNB].
78   Ray Desmond, *Dictionary* of *British and Irish Botanists and Horticulturalists Including Plant Collectors, Flower Painters and Garden Designers* (London: Taylor & Francis, 1977).

English and American authors into Italian, and her salon saw such leading Italian intellectuals as Giosuè Carducci. In 1860, she married Francesco Bartolini. Her paintings and manuscripts are preserved in Florence.[79]

Amelia Beauclerc (1 January 1790–1 March 1820) published eight Gothic novels, six with the Minerva Press. Little is known of her life and her works were for a long time attributed to the novelist Emma Parker. Her *Eva of Cambria; or, The Fugitive Daughter*, 1811, appeared under Emma Parker's pen name and other misattributions followed for *Ora and Juliet; or, Influence of First Principles*, 1811, *The Castle of Tariffa; or, The Self-Banished Man*, 1812, and *Alinda; or, The Child of Mystery*, 1812. *Montreithe; or, The Peer of Scotland*, 1814, and *Husband Hunters!!! A Novel*, 1816, appeared anonymously; only *The Deserter*, 1817, and *Disorder and Order*, 1820, credited her name (and listed her other works). All received mixed reviews. The tales are less thrilling than sentimental.[80]

Elizabeth Beverley [or **Mrs. R. Beverley**] (1792–19 November 1832), whose life is little known, was traveling about the West Country as an entertainer by 1814. Her first known pamphlet is *Modern Times*, 1818, prompted by the death in childbirth of Princess Charlotte of Wales. *A Poetical Olio* and *The Monmouth Street Cap* followed in 1819, then *The Actress's Ways and Means* in 1820, which allegedly saw twelve editions. Then came *The Coronation*, 1821, *The Book of Variety*, 1823, *The Indefatigable* and *Odd Thoughts on a Variety of Odd Subjects*, 1825, and *Useful Subjects in Prose and Verse*, 1828. *Veluti in speculum*, 1827, consists of prose letters on various subjects. *Entertaining and Moral Poems on Various Subjects*, around 1820, was a longer work. All Beverley's pamphlets were self-published.[81]

Rachel Charlotte Biggs (1763–1827) was an English spy in France during multiple visits between 1802–1816, corresponding with the British government about French military strength, industry, agriculture, and politics. Biggs was also in France during the French Revolution in 1792–1795 and wrote a narrative about her stay. A biography of her appeared in 2017.[82]

---

79   Jane Fortune and Linda Falcone, *Invisible Women: Forgotten Artists of Florence* (Florence: The Florentine Press, 2010).
80   *Dictionary of National Biography* [DNB]; *Orlando: Women's Writing in the British Isles*.
81   *Orlando: Women's Writing in the British Isles*.
82   Joanne Major and Sarah Murden, *A Georgian Heroine: The Intriguing Life of Rachel Charlotte William Biggs* (Barnsley: Pen and Sword, 2017).

Anne Brontë (17 January 1820–28 May 1849), born in Thornton, moved with her family to Haworth that same year. She lost her mother aged one and her two eldest sisters, Maria and Elizabeth, aged five. After Charlotte's departure for Roe Head School in 1831, Anne and Emily grew closer; in 1835, Anne went as pupil to Roe Head, where Charlotte now taught, and stayed two years. In 1839, she found work as a governess, a time retraced in her novel *Agnes Grey*, 1847. From 1840–1845, Anne found happier governess work near York, securing a position for her brother Branwell in 1843. In 1846, gathered at Haworth, the Brontë sisters published *Poems by Currer, Ellis, and Acton Bell*, keeping their initials, with twenty-one poems each from Anne and Emily and nineteen from Charlotte. *Agnes Grey* and Emily's *Wuthering Heights* appeared together in 1847; Anne's *The Tenant of Wildfell Hall*, on marriage law, in 1848.[83]

Charlotte Brontë (21 April 1816–31 March 1855), born in Thornton, was the eldest Brontë sister to survive into adulthood; Lowood School in *Jane Eyre* echoes the school where in 1825 the two eldest Brontë sisters died of tuberculosis. Charlotte enrolled in Roe Head School in 1831, leaving in 1832 to teach Anne and Emily at home, then returning in 1835–1838 as a teacher. From 1839–1841, Charlotte took work as a governess in various homes; from 1842–1844, she was in Brussels. In 1846, Charlotte published nineteen poems with her sisters. Her first novel, *The Professor*, was rejected, but *Jane Eyre* in 1847 met with immediate success. *Shirley*, 1849, was completed as her three siblings died; *Villette* followed in 1853. Charlotte wrote more than 200 known poems, many 'published' in *Branwell's Blackwood's Magazine*. She married Arthur Bell Nichols in 1854 and died in pregnancy the following year.[84]

Emily Jane Brontë (30 July 1818–19 December 1848), born in Thornton, wrote juvenilia with her siblings but withdrew with Anne from 'Angria' aged thirteen to create 'Gondal,' which still preoccupied her in her twenties. Emily joined the Roe Head Girls' School in 1835, leaving after a few months. In 1838, she became a teacher at Law Hill School in Halifax; she returned home in 1839, departing again with Charlotte to study French in Brussels in 1842–1844. Emily published twenty-one poems alongside her sisters in 1846 under gender-neutral

---

83 Edward Chitham, *A Life of Anne Brontë* (Oxford: Blackwell Publishers, 1991).
84 Rebecca Fraser, *Charlotte Brontë: A Writer's Life*, 2nd edition (New York: Pegasus Books, 2008).

names, then *Wuthering Heights* in 1847 with Anne's *Agnes Grey* completing the three-volume set. Emily's name was first attached in 1850. Some lost manuscript poems of Emily's were rediscovered in 2021; Emily's emergence from her myth (in which Charlotte played her part, as with Anne) has been a lengthy process.[85]

Mary Brunton, née **Balfour** (1 November 1778–7 December 1818), a Scottish writer born on Burray in the Orkney Islands, eloped with Rev. Alexander Brunton in 1798, moving to Edinburgh after 1803. Brunton's first novel, *Self-Control*, appeared in 1811; it saw a third edition in 1812, and a French translation in 1829. *Discipline*, 1814, had a Highland setting, like Sir Walter Scott's *Waverley* the same year. The couple were in London in 1815, and Brunton began to learn Gaelic. She died in 1818, five days after giving birth to a stillborn son. Brunton's manuscript *Emmeline*, describing a divorced woman, appeared in her husband's posthumous memoir of her in 1819, along with extracts from her travel diary. Her *Works* appeared in 1820, with reeditions to 1852.[86]

Hannah Dorothy Burdon [or later **Madame Wolfensberger** or **Lord B*********] (1800–1877) published her first historical novel *Seymour of Sudley; or, the Last of the Franciscans* in 1836, followed by *The Lost Evidence* in 1838, *The Thirst for Gold* in 1841, and so forth. In 1841, she married the Swiss painter Johan Jakob Wolfensberger, who died in 1850. After his death, Burdon turned to social problem novels, starting with *Masters and Workmen*, 1851, using the pen name 'Lord B*******.' These novels were for some time misattributed to the Earl of Belfast; others include *Wealth and Labour* and *The County Magistrate* in 1858, *The Fate of Folly* in 1859, and *Uncle Armstrong*, her final novel, in 1866. Burdon later married Jerome Schobinger in Switzerland, where she died in 1877.[87]

Catherine Ball [or **'Baroness de Calabrella'**] (c. 1788–6 October 1856), born in Lambourne, married Rev. Francis Lee in 1804; Francis disclaimed their second son, while Ball moved in with Captain George de Blaquière. In 1814, Francis sued unsuccessfully for divorce; he committed suicide in 1826, and George de Blaquière died the same year. Ball may later have married Thomas Jenkins, whose name she used. She also acquired property in southern Italy and began using the title

---

85 Steven Vine, *Emily Brontë* (New York: Twayne Publishers, 1998).
86 *Dictionary of National Biography* [DNB].
87 *Dictionary of National Biography* [DNB], "Burdon, William."

'Baroness de Calabrella.' From the 1840s, she owned the *Court Journal*. Ball's novels include *The Tempter and the Tempted*, 1842, *The Cousins*, 1843, *The Land of Promise*, 1844, and *The Double Oath*, 1850. She published stories—*The Prism of Thought* and *The Prism of Imagination*, two 1843 collections, and "The Old Man of Haarlem," also 1843—and *The Ladies' Science of Etiquette* in 1844, which saw multiple editions.[88]

Dorothea Primrose Campbell (4 May 1793–6 January 1863), a Scottish writer born in Lerwick on the Shetland Islands, lost her father at sixteen, becoming a teacher in 1812, then opening her own school. Campbell published her *Poems* in 1811 (reedited in London in 1816). She met Sir Walter Scott, who offered her financial support; but the school closed, and Campbell became a teacher again. She was in debt in 1822–1823 and 1835. Campbell published her one known novel, *Harley Radington: A Tale*, set in the Shetland Islands, with the Minerva Press in 1821. For some years (c. 1813–1853), she was also a member of the *Lady's Monthly Museum*, publishing fifty-three poems and tales under the name 'Ora from Thule.' In 1841, Campbell became a governess in England. That family went bankrupt. She applied to the Royal Literary Fund in 1844 and died in the London Aged Governesses' Asylum.[89]

Harriette Campbell (August 1817–15 February 1841), a Scottish writer born in Stirling, published her first novel, *The Only Daughter: A Domestic Story* in 1839. Her second, *The Cardinal Virtues, or, Morals and Manners Connected*, 1841, published after her arrival in London, made her reputation. Campbell traveled abroad to regain her health but died of influenza in Switzerland in 1841. Her third novel, *Self-Devotion: or, The History of Katherine Randolph*, appeared posthumously in 1842. Campbell also toured the Highlands of Scotland, publishing a travel account in the periodical press.[90]

Jane Baillie Carlyle, née **Welsh** (14 July 1801–21 April 1866), a Scottish writer born in Haddington, East Lothian, published nothing in her lifetime. She married Thomas Carlyle in 1826, moving to Edinburgh with him; in 1828, the couple moved to Craigenputtock, then London in 1834. Carlyle met Geraldine Jewsbury in 1841 and the two had a

---

88 William Bates, *The Maclise Portrait-Gallery of "Illustrious Literary Characters"* (London: Chatto & Windus, 1891).
89 *Dictionary of National Biography* [DNB]; *Orlando: Women's Writing in the British Isles*.
90 *Dictionary of National Biography* [DNB].

long correspondence, of which Jewsbury's letters survive, retracing a passionate friendship. Carlyle helped with two of Jewsbury's novels, *Zoe* and *The Half Sisters*. Carlyle's correspondence with her husband survives and has been published, along with other letters, on which her reputation rests. She may have inspired Leigh Hunt's poem "Jenny Kiss'd Me."[91]

Agnes Catlow (1806–10 May 1889), born in Mansfield, Nottinghamshire, found her greatest success with her first book, the illustrated *Popular Conchology*, in 1842. Her work as a popularizer of science continued in *The Conchologist's Nomenclator*, 1845, and *Popular Field Botany*, 1848. *Drops of Water: Their Marvellous and Beautiful Inhabitants Displayed by the Microscope* followed in 1851, reflecting a mid-century interest in microscopy, and two more botanical volumes, *Popular Garden Botany*, 1855, and *Popular Greenhouse Botany*, 1857. Catlow also wrote several books with her sister Maria, including *Sketching Rambles: Or, Nature in the Alps and Apennines*, 1861.[92]

Margaret Chalmers (12 December 1758–12 March 1827), a Scottish writer born in Lerwick, faced a life of penury like her fellow Lerwegian poet, Dorothea Primrose Campbell. Chalmers arranged to publish her poems by subscription; the process took so long that many subscribers lost interest. Chalmers sent copies of her poems to Sir Walter Scott in 1814, seemingly without reply. Her lone volume of poems, published in Newcastle in 1813, sold poorly, but did sell copies from the Shetlands to North Carolina.[93]

Catherine Davies (1773–after 1841), a Welsh writer born in Beaumaris, was brought up by a foster family in Liverpool until her sister in London took her in. In 1802, she left for Paris as a governess. Stranded there when hostilities resumed, Davies found work with Caroline Bonaparte, meeting Napoleon at least once. In 1808, the family moved to Naples as Queen and King; Davies raised Prince Achille Murat there, then Princess Louisa. When Queen Caroline of England visited in 1814, she befriended Davies. During the Hundred Days, the family evacuated to Gaeta, which was bombarded. Naples was captured and

---

91 Kathy Chamberlain, *Jane Welsh and Her Victorian World* (New York: Overlook Duckworth, 2017).
92 Jack Kramer, *Women of Flowers* (1996).
93 Elizabeth L. Ewan et al. *Scottish Women* (2007).

Queen Caroline exiled to Austria; Davies, in poor health, returned to England in 1816, then Wales two years later. In 1841, Davies published *Eleven Years' Residence in the Family of Murat, King of Naples*, with a foreword by Achille Murat. She was poor at the time and is thought to have died soon after.[94]

Ann Doherty, née **Holmes** (c. 1786–c. 1831/1832), aged fifteen married Hugh Doherty, but left him and their baby in 1806. He published a book containing her love letters and the statement that they had eloped after her parents confined her in a madhouse. In 1818, Doherty was going by the name Anne Attersoll and apparently cohabiting with John Attersoll, a former Whig MP. By 1820, Doherty was using the name St Anne Holmes in France, where she remained. Doherty published anonymously or as 'St Anne.' Her novels included *Ronaldsha*, 1808, *The Castles of Wolfnorth and Mont Eagle*, 1812, and *The Knight of the Glen. An Irish Romance*, 1815. While with Attersoll, Doherty began corresponding with the poet Robert Southey; in 1818, she sent him a copy of her play *Peter the Cruel King of Castile and Leon*, and he sent her a signed copy of his *Roderick the Last of the Goths* in French translation.[95]

Maria Edgeworth (1 January 1768–22 May 1849), born at Black Bourton, Oxfordshire, lost her mother aged five and moved with her father to his Irish estate. Edgeworth was schooled in Derby and London from 1775–1781, returning to care for the estate and for her many siblings. Edgeworth published *Letters for Literary Ladies* in 1795; *The Parent's Assistant* in 1796, a children's book; and *Practical Education* in 1798. She then published ten novels, from the Anglo-Irish *Castle Rackrent* in 1800 to *The Absentee* in 1812 and *Helen* in 1834, becoming the best-selling British novelist before Sir Walter Scott thanks to her *Tales of Fashionable Life* in 1809–1812. Edgeworth wrote the novel *Harrington* in 1817 to atone for anti-Semitism in *The Absentee*. She corresponded with Scott and with David Ricardo. During the Irish Famine, she provided her tenants with relief for the deserving poor.[96]

---

94 Jane Aaron, *Nineteenth-Century Women's Writing in Wales: Nation, Gender and Identity* (Cardiff: University of Wales Press, 2010).
95 Virginia Blain et al. *The Feminist Companion to Literature in English* (1990).
96 Marilyn Butler, *Maria Edgeworth: A Literary Biography* (Oxford: Oxford University Press, 1972).

Mary Ann Evans [or **George Eliot**] (22 November 1819–22 December 1880), born in Nuneaton, had little formal education beyond age sixteen, when her mother died, and she returned home. Moving near Coventry in 1830, Eliot met Robert Owen, Herbert Spencer, and Ralph Waldo Emerson; she also published reviews in the local press. In 1846, she published her translation of Strauss's then-scandalous life of Jesus; her translation of Spinoza remained in manuscript. Eliot settled in London in 1850, becoming assistant editor of *The Westminster Review* from 1851–1854. That year, she moved in with the married George Henry Lewes. Eliot published *Scenes of Clerical Life* in 1858 and seven novels from 1859–1876: *Adam Bede; The Mill on the Floss; Silas Marner; Romola; Felix Holt, the Radical; Middlemarch*; and *Daniel Deronda*. She also wrote poetry and non-fiction.[97]

Anne Elwood, née **Curteis** (1796–24 February 1873), born near Battle, married Major Charles William Elwood in 1824. The couple set off overland for India in 1825, she being perhaps the first British woman to make that journey. Elwood published her *Narrative of a Journey Overland from England to India* in 1830, which also describes their return by sea in 1828. Elwood's second book, *Memoirs of the Literary Ladies of England from the Commencement of the Last Century*, 1841, describes the lives of twenty-nine women, of whom Elwood knew several.[98]

Eliza Fay (1755 or 1756–9 September 1816), born probably in Rotherhithe, married Anthony Fay in London in 1772. The couple set out for India in 1779, where he ran into debt and fathered an illegitimate child. They separated in 1781. Fay's letters begin in Paris; then the Alps, Egypt, and imprisonment in Calicut before reaching Calcutta (now Kolkata) in 1780. In Calcutta, Fay met Warren Hastings and observed society. She returned to England by way of St Helena in 1782, setting out again for India in 1784. Returning to England in 1794, Fay sailed to New York City in 1797, then again to Calcutta in 1804. She died insolvent in Calcutta, after two bankruptcies, on a final voyage there. A first edition of her letters—her remaining asset—appeared the next year.[99]

---

97 Kathryn Hughes, *George Eliot: The Last Victorian* (New York: Farrar Straus Giroux, 1999).
98 *Dictionary of National Biography* [DNB].
99 Virginia Blain et al. *The Feminist Companion to Literature in English* (1990).

Isabella Fenwick (1783–1856), born in Lemmington Hall, met William Wordsworth in her late forties. The friendship blossomed after her move to Ambleside in 1838 and was echoed by the Wordsworth household. Fenwick is remembered for the *Fenwick Notes*, dictated to her by Wordsworth in 1843 and in which he recorded the biographical context for many of his earlier poems. Wordsworth also dedicated two poems to Fenwick, "On a Portrait of I.F...." and the sonnet "To I.F."[100]

Susan Edmonstone Ferrier (7 September 1782–5 November 1854), a Scottish writer probably born in Edinburgh, was privately educated. She visited Sir Walter Scott in 1811, in 1829, and in 1831. Ferrier wrote three novels: *Marriage*, published in 1818, with a French translation in 1825; *The Inheritance* in 1824; and *Destiny* in 1831, moving from William Blackwood to Robert Cadell, two Edinburgh publishers. Richard Bentley reissued the three in 1841, and they sold throughout the nineteenth century, though little thereafter.[101]

Elizabeth "Eliza" Field [or **Elizabeth Jones** or **Elizabeth Jones Carey**, or **Kecheahgahmequa**] (1 June 1804–17 August 1890), born in London, married the Ojibwe Methodist minister Peter Jones in New York City in 1833, despite opposition from friends and parents, settling in a cabin on the Credit River Indian Reserve. Field there suffered two miscarriages and two stillbirths. In 1838, she published *Memoir of Elizabeth Jones, a Little Indian Girl*, an account of the life of her niece. In 1858, after Peter's death, she married John Carey, a New York farmer, separating from him some years later. Field arranged for the publication of Peter's diaries in 1860 and his *History of the Ojebway Indians* in 1861. Her *Sketch of the Life of Captain Joseph Brant, Thayendanagea* appeared in 1872. She lost her sight in 1880.[102]

Caroline Fry, later **Mrs Caroline Wilson** (31 December 1787–17 September 1846), born in Tunbridge Wells, married William Wilson in 1831. After a conversion experience in 1822, Fry began publishing in 1823 in a monthly periodical, the *Assistant of Education, Religious and Literary*, intended for the instruction of children. Fry wrote church theology, devotional meditations, prayers, poetry, and moral lessons. Her travels

---

100 Jared Curtis, ed. *The Fenwick Notes of William Wordsworth* (Tirril: Humanities Ebooks, 2007).
101 Lorna Sage et al., eds. *The Cambridge Guide to Women's Writing in English* (1999).
102 *Dictionary of Canadian Biography*.

through the English countryside she recorded in her book *The Listener*. *The Listener in Oxford* described the impact of John Henry Newman's Tractarian movement both on her and on the Anglican Church, a topic to which she returned in *The Table of the Lord*. Fry wrote numerous other Christian tracts.[103]

Elizabeth Fry, née **Gurney** (21 May 1780–12 October 1845), born in Norwich, lost her mother aged twelve. In 1800, she married fellow Quaker Joseph Fry and moved to London; they had eleven children. Fry visited Newgate Prison in 1813, founding a school and women's association there and speaking to parliament on the subject. She also visited 106 transport ships, reforming conditions aboard, and other prisons in Britain and Ireland. Fry influenced Queen Victoria, Florence Nightingale, Frederick William IV of Prussia, and Tsar Alexander. Her other causes included homelessness, nursing, and abolition. Besides her useful diary, Fry wrote *Observations on the Visiting, Superintendence and Government of Female Prisoners*, 1827; *Texts for Every Day in the Year, Principally Practical & Devotional, 1831*; and *An Address of Christian Counsel and Caution to Emigrants to Newly-Settled Colonies*, 1841.[104]

Catherine Grace Godwin, née **Garnett** (25 December 1798-May 1845), a Scottish writer born in Glasgow, lost her mother in childbirth and her father died in 1802. She was raised by a friend of her mother. Godwin began painting and writing poetry aged fifteen but first published in 1824: *The Night Before the Bridal and Other Poems*. She married Thomas Godwin in 1824. Her novel *Reine Canziani: A Tale of Modern Greece* followed in 1825, then *The Wanderer's Legacy and Other Poems*, dedicated to William Wordsworth, in 1828. Godwin was also an accomplished painter. Other poems of hers were published posthumously in 1854.[105]

Beatrice Grant, née **Campbell** (2 September 1761–20 February 1845), a Scottish writer born in Argyll, spent most of her life in the Highlands of Scotland. She lost her mother aged eight but had fifteen siblings in total. In 1784, Grant married the Rev. Patrick Grant, who died in 1809. She then moved to Inverness, publishing her first book in 1812: *Sketches*

---

103 *Dictionary of National Biography* [DNB].
104 Jean Hatton, *Betsy, the Dramatic Biography of a Prison Reformer* (Oxford: Monarch Books, 2005).
105 *Dictionary of National Biography* [DNB].

of Intellectual Education, and Hints on Domestic Economy, Addressed to Inexperienced Mothers. Grant dedicated her next three books to the Prince Regent, 1815–1816: *Popular Models and Impressive Warnings for the Sons and Daughters of Industry*, in three parts. She also published her moral tale, *The History of an Irish Family*, in 1822. Many of Grant's works are addressed to working-class readers; Grant used magazines as well as books to reach audiences, contributing often to *The Cheap Magazine* in Scotland and to more expensive London periodicals.[106]

Elizabeth Smith, née **Elizabeth Grant of Rothiemurchus** (7 May 1797–16 November 1885), a Scottish writer born in Edinburgh, moved with her family to Bombay (now Mumbai) in 1827. In 1829, she married Colonel Henry Smith. In France by the 1840s, the couple moved thereafter to Henry's Irish estate, where Grant died. Grant published in magazines anonymously, but she is remembered today for her *Memoirs of a Highland Lady*, written over the years as a private memoir for her family, which describes managing the estate during the Irish Famine. The memoir appeared in 1898, with subsequent editions.[107]

Mary Anne Everett Green, née **Wood** (19 July 1818–1 November 1895), born in Sheffield, moved to London with her family in 1841 and began research at the British Museum, private libraries, and archives, publishing her *Letters of Royal and Illustrious Ladies* in 1846 and *Lives of the Princesses of England: from the Norman Conquest* in 1849–1855. She married George Pycock Green in 1845 and they traveled to Paris and Antwerp. Sir Francis Palgrave had met Green; particularly impressed by her knowledge of languages, he recommended her to John Romilly, Master of the Rolls, who invited her to help edit Britain's external calendars of state papers in 1854. From 1857–1872, Green wrote 700 pages of prefaces for forty-one volumes, which amount to a history of seventeenth-century England. Her own volume *Elizabeth, Electress Palatine and Queen of Bohemia* appeared posthumously in 1909.[108]

Mary Leman Grimstone, née **Rede** [or **Oscar**] (12 June 1796–4 November 1869), born in Beccles, moved to Hamburg with her family

---

106 Elizabeth Ewan, Rose Pipes, Jane Rendall, and Siân Reynolds, *The New Biographical Dictionary of Scottish Women* (Edinburgh: Edinburgh University Press, 2018).
107 *Dictionary of National Biography* [DNB].
108 Philippa Levine, *The Amateur and the Professional: Antiquarians, Historians and Archaeologists in Victorian England, 1838–1886* (Cambridge, UK: Cambridge University Press, 1986).

in 1798, escaping her father's creditors. After his death in 1810, they moved to London. Grimstone published in *La Belle Assemblée* from 1815, marrying Richard Grimstone the following year. In 1820, she published the poem *Zayda, a Spanish Tale* to some attention, then *Cleone* in 1821, then a novel in 1825, *The Beauty of the British Alps*. Richard died that year and Grimstone moved to Hobart in Van Diemen's Land (now Tasmania). She returned in 1829, publishing *Louisa Egerton* in 1830, the first known Australian novel. *Character, or, Jew and Gentile* followed, then *Woman's Love*. In the 1830s, she wrote for Robert Owen's *New Moral World* newspaper and other periodicals. She married William Gillies in 1836.[109]

Maria Hack, née **Barton** (16 February 1777–4 January 1844), was born in Carlisle to a Quaker family, moving to London before her mother died. Her father married again, dying in 1789. Hack then lived with her stepmother, marrying Stephen Hack in 1800 and moving to Gloucester. From *First Lessons in English Grammar*, 1812, Hack published extensively for children: *Winter Evenings*, 1818, *Grecian Stories*, 1819, *English Stories*, 1820–1825. Hack also wrote on geology and optics. Her best-known work was *Harry Beaufoy, or, The Pupil of Nature*, 1821, arguing for God's hand in Nature. Reflecting Evangelical influence, Hack argued for Scripture, not Inner Light, as authority, and for the sacraments of baptism and communion, leaving the Society of Friends for the Anglican Church in 1837 and publishing on the question that year.[110]

Maria C. Hakewill, née **Browne** (?–1842), whose birth date is unknown, married James Hakewill, accompanying him to Italy for two years in 1816–1817. Her novel, *Coelebs Suited; or, The Stanley Letters*, appeared in 1812. Hakewill also painted portraits and scenes in oil, exhibiting at the Royal Academy and elsewhere between 1808 and 1838. She died in Calais in 1842.[111]

Agnes C. Hall, née **Scott** [or **Rosalia St Clair**] (1777–1 December 1846), a Scottish writer born in Roxburghshire, married Dr. Robert Hall, who died in 1824. Hall wrote on literary and scientific topics for

---

109 *Dictionary of National Biography* [DNB]; *Australian Dictionary of Biography*, 19 vols (Canberra: Australian National University, 1966–2021).
110 *Dictionary of National Biography* [DNB].
111 Sara Gray, *Dictionary of British Women Artists* (Havertown, PA: Casemate Publishers, 2009).

the *British Encyclopedia*, Rees's *Cyclopædia*, the *Old Monthly*, and other periodicals; later, she wrote for the *Annual Biography*, the *Westminster Review*, and *Fraser's Magazine*. She wrote the notes to Anton Zacharias Helms's *Buenos Ayres* in 1806; in 1807, she translated the *Travels* of F.R.J. De Pons. Other translations included Madame de Genlis's *La Duchesse de la Vallière*, 1804, Vittorio Alfieri's *Autobiography*, 1810, and novels by August Heinrich Lafontaine. Her own publications include *Rural Recreations*, 1802, and the novels *Obstinacy*, 1826; *First and Last Years of Wedded Life*, a story of Irish life in the reign of George IV; and a historical novel based on the massacre of Glencoe. John Stuart Mill was an acquaintance.[112]

Anne Raikes Harding, née **Orchard** (5 March 1781–28 April 1858), born in Bath, married Thomas Harding, who died intestate in 1805. Harding ran a school and worked as a governess while writing her six novels, all published anonymously: *Correction*, 1818; *Decision*, 1819; *The Refugees*, 1822; *Realities*, 1825; *Dissipation*, 1827; and *Experience*, 1828. She later wrote non-fiction: *Sketches of the Highlands*, 1832, *Little Sermons*, 1840, and *An Epitome of Universal History*, 1848. Harding also contributed to reviews and periodicals.[113]

Felicia Dorothea Hemans, née **Browne** (25 September 1793–16 May 1835), born in Liverpool, grew up in Wales. She spoke Welsh, French, German, Italian, Spanish, and Portuguese. Hemans published *Poems* in 1808, aged fourteen. Percy Bysshe Shelley expressed interest. *England and Spain* and *The Domestic Affections* followed in 1808–1812; she published nineteen individual books during her lifetime, including *The Restoration of the Works of Art to Italy* in 1816, *Modern Greece* in 1817, *The Forest Sanctuary* in 1825, *Records of Woman* in 1828, and *Songs of the Affections* in 1830. In 1812, Hemans married Captain Alfred Hemans; they separated in 1819. From 1831, she lived in Dublin. Hemans's death brought tributes from the great, though she was later regarded as a children's author. The term 'stately home' is her coinage, as is "The boy stood on the burning deck."[114]

---

112 *Dictionary of National Biography* [DNB].
113 Rachel Howard, *Domesticating the Novel: Moral-Domestic Fiction, 1820–1834* (Ph.D. thesis, Cardiff University, 2007).
114 Gary Kelly, ed. *Felicia Hemans: Selected Poems, Prose, and Letters* (Peterborough: Broadview Press, 2002).

Rose Ellen Hendriks, later **Rose Ellen Temple** (fl. 1845–1856) is known only from her works, published between 1845–1856. In her prefaces, Hendricks calls herself young and ambitious, describing herself as Jewish by heritage but raised Christian. Hendricks published the historical novel *The Astrologer's Daughter* in 1845; *Charlotte Corday* and *The Idler Reformed* appeared the next year. In 1847's *The Young Authoress*, the heroine Rosalie reads the famous author Rose Ellen Hendricks. The same year saw her book of essays, *Political Fame*, and *The Wild Rose and other Poems*. In her 1849 book *Chit-Chat*, Hendriks says she will marry; her last novel in 1851, *Ella, the Ballet Girl*, and her last published work, *The Poet's Souvenir of Amateur Artists* in 1856, use the last name 'Temple.' That final volume contains her portrait.[115]

Mary Hennell (23 May 1802–16 March 1843), born in Manchester, may with her sisters Sara and Caroline be the basis for the Meyrick family in George Eliot's *Daniel Deronda*, 1876. In 1836, Caroline married the sceptic, Charles Bray; Hennell prefaced his *The Philosophy of Necessity* in 1841, later published independently in 1844. She also wrote the entry "Ribbons" in the *Penny Cyclopædia*.[116]

Sarah Hoare (7 July 1777–1856), born in London, published her first known botanical poem in 1826. Her illustrated *Poems on Conchology and Botany*, based on contemporary scientific knowledge, followed in 1831. She had also published *The Brother, or, A Few Poems Intended for the Instruction of Very Young Persons* in 1827, and co-wrote a memoir of her father which appeared posthumously in 1911. Hoare's portrait of her father is reproduced in the National Portrait Gallery.[117]

Mary Hughes [or Hughs], née **Mary Robson** (fl. 1811–1850), born in Newcastle, began publishing children's books in 1811: *Aunt Mary's Tales for the Entertainment and Improvement of Little Girls: Addressed to her Nieces*. A sequel addressed to her nephews followed in 1813, and *The Ornaments Discovered* in 1815—all popular and republished in the United States, as she later discovered. Hughes also wrote pamphlets for the Christian Tract Society, becoming a member for life in 1813. She married Thomas Hughes in 1817, emigrating to Philadelphia

---

115 *Dictionary of National Biography* [DNB].
116 Ibid.
117 Fabienne Moine, *Women Poets in the Victorian Era. Cultural Practices and Nature Poetry* (London: Routledge, 2015).

in 1818, where she founded a girls' school. She closed the school in 1839. Hughes published two texts in 1818, six in 1820 (including three Christian tracts), nine in 1849, two in 1850, and so forth. Her publications are extensive.[118]

Anna Maria Hussey, née **Reed** (5 June 1805–26 August 1853), born in Leckhampstead, married Rev. Dr. Thomas John Hussey in 1831, but found mycology more interesting. She maintained correspondence with her mycological mentor, Rev. Miles Joseph Berkeley, with Charles Badham, and with M.C. Cooke. In the 1840s, she wrote for her husband's magazine *The Surplice*, and a story called "Matrimony" for *Frazer's Magazine*, all anonymous. Hussey knew Charles Darwin, whose sons her brother tutored. Several of her watercolors of fungi appeared uncredited in Badham's 1847 treatise on the topic; she also published the ambitious *Illustrations of British Mycology* in her own name, in two volumes, 1847–1855. A fungal genus, Husseia, bears her name.[119]

Frances "Fanny" Erskine Inglis, later **Marquesa of Calderón de la Barca** (23 December 1804–6 February 1882), a Scottish writer born in Edinburgh, moved to Boston with her mother after her father's death in 1831. In 1838, she married Ángel Calderón de la Barca in New York; when Ángel became Spanish minister to Mexico, the couple moved there from 1839–1841. Inglis's influential *Life in Mexico, during a Residence Of Two Years In That Country* appeared in 1843, containing fifty-four letters she wrote during that tumultuous time. Inglis also wrote *El agregado en Madrid o Bocetos de la Corte de Isabel II*, 1856, published under a male German pseudonym. She converted to Catholicism in 1847. Following her husband's death in 1861, she served as governess of the Infanta Isabel for two decades, earning the title 'Marquesa' in 1873. Inglis died in Madrid.[120]

Margaret Maxwell Inglis, née **Murray** (27 October 1774–21 December 1843), a Scottish writer born in Sanquhar, married a Mr. Finlay when young, who died in the West Indies. In 1803, she married John Inglis; on his death in 1826, the family depended on a small annuity he left. Inglis began writing, with her *Miscellaneous Collection of Poems, chiefly Scriptural Pieces* appearing in 1828. She was commended by Robert Burns for her

---

118 F.J. Harvey Darton and Brian Alderson, *Children's Books in England: Five Centuries of Social Life*, 3rd edition (New York: Cambridge University Press, 1982).
119 Ann B. Shteir, *Cultivating Women, Cultivating Science: Flora's Daughters and Botany in England, 1760–1860* (Baltimore, MD: Johns Hopkins University Press, 1996).
120 Adriana Méndez Rodenas, *Transatlantic Travels in Nineteenth-Century Latin America: European Women Pilgrims* (Lewisburg, PA: Bucknell University Press, 2014).

rendering of his songs.[121]

Maria Jane Jewsbury, later **Maria Jane Fletcher** (25 October 1800–4 October 1833), born in Measham, moved to Manchester in 1818 with her family when her father's cotton factory failed. Her mother died that year and Jewsbury took over the household for twelve years. She began publishing at this time, in the *Manchester Gazette* and in *The Literary Souvenir* alongside Coleridge, Southey, and William Wordsworth, with whom she corresponded. Her first book, *Phantasmagoria*, appeared in 1825; she also wrote for *The Poetical Album, The Literary Magnet, The Amulet*, and *The Athenæum*. Jewsbury visited Felicia Hemans in Wales in 1828. In 1830, she published *The Three Histories*, her best-known work. In 1832, Jewsbury married Rev. William K. Fletcher, traveling with him to India in 1832–1833, where she died that year. She left several manuscripts published after her death, including *Letters to the Young*, 1837.[122]

Christian Isobel Johnstone (12 June 1781–1857), a Scottish writer who may be the Christian Todd born in Edinburgh on 12 June 1781, married Thomas McLeish at age sixteen; they divorced in 1814, and she remarried John Johnstone in 1815. Johnstone wrote popular novels: *The Saxon and the Gaël*, 1814, *Clan-Albin: A National Tale*, 1815; *Elizabeth de Bruce*, 1827. She also wrote non-fiction: *Scenes of Industry Displayed in the Beehive and the Anthill*, 1827; *Lives and Voyages of Drake, Cavendish, and Dampier*, 1831. Johnstone mostly published anonymously, though *The Cook and Housewife's Manual*, 1826, appeared under the pseudonym Margaret Dods, a Walter Scott heroine, and she signed *The Edinburgh Tales* in 1846. The Johnstones ran several periodicals: *The Schoolmaster, The Edinburgh Weekly Magazine, Johnstone's Edinburgh Magazine*, which joined with *Tait's* in 1834, keeping Johnstone as editor.[123]

Hannah Maria Jones (1784?–1854) may have been born in 1784. She married a Mr. Jones. In the 1820s, she published *Gretna Green*, 1820; *The British Officer*, 1821; *The Wedding Ring* and *The Forged Note*, 1824, and *The Victim of Fashion*, 1825. About this time, she applied to the Royal Literary Fund, stating that her husband was ill. She later published a Romany trilogy, including *The Gypsy Mother*, 1835, and *The Gypsy Girl*, 1836. Jones lived at this time with a writer named John Lownes, using his last name although they

---

121 *Dictionary of National Biography* [DNB].
122 Ibid.
123 Douglas Gifford and Dorothy McMillan, eds. *A History of Scottish Women's Writing* (Edinburgh, Edinburgh University Press, 1997).

never married. The couple frequently applied to the Royal Literary Fund.[124]

Frances Anne Kemble (1809–1893), born in London and educated in France, was the niece of the actors Sarah Siddons and John Philip Kemble. She wrote her first five-act play, *Francis the First*, in 1827. In 1829, Kemble appeared on stage as Juliet at Covent Garden Theatre. In 1832, she accompanied her father on a tour of the United States. Kemble retired from acting while married from 1834–1849, then resumed until 1868, giving readings from twenty-five Shakespeare plays. She published a second play, *The Star of Seville*, in 1837. Kemble married a Georgia plantation owner and visited the plantations as recorded in her abolitionist *Journal of a Residence on a Georgian Plantation in 1838–1839*, which her husband forbade her to publish. In 1845, she returned to England, publishing in 1863. That year, she also published a volume of plays including translations from Dumas and Schiller. Other memoirs followed, along with *Notes on Some of Shakespeare's Plays*, 1882. Her *Poems* appeared in 1844.

Grace Kennedy (1782–28 February 1825), a Scottish writer born in Pinmore, moved to Edinburgh at an early age. Her first known work is an unstaged play in 1821, *The Decision; or Religion Must be All, or is Nothing*; later works include *Profession is not Principle* and *Jessy Allan, or The Lame Girl* in 1822; *Father Clement* in 1823; *Anna Ross, Andrew Campbell's Visit to his Irish Cousins,* and *The Word of God and the Word of Man* in 1824; *Dunallan* in 1825; and *Philip Colville*, a Covenanters' story she was working on when she died. Most of her work is religious; her anti-Catholic novel *Father Clement* saw some dozen editions and was translated into several languages, though today she is perhaps neglected. A six-volume collection of her works appeared in Edinburgh in 1827, with German translations in 1838–1842.[125]

Elizabeth "Bessy" Kent (1791–1861) was the younger sister of Marianne Kent, the future wife of the writer Leigh Hunt. Kent initially brought Leigh Hunt into the family circle; she acted as his agent and amanuensis, incurring some gossip until her breach with the household in 1822. Kent published mostly thereafter, including *New Tales for*

---

124 Hannah Maria Jones, *The Gypsy Mother or The Miseries of Enforced Marriage: A Tale of Mystery* (1833).
125 George Edwin Rines, ed. *The Encyclopedia Americana* [...], 16 vols (New York: Scientific American Compiling Dept., 1903–1905).

Young Readers in 1822 and *Sylvan Sketches* in 1825. Kent's best-known work appeared anonymously in 1823: *Flora Domestica*, which quotes extensively from Leigh Hunt and Keats. It was later incorrectly attributed to Henry Philips. Kent wrote for the *Magazine of Natural History*, taught botany and wrote books for children. She never married.[126]

Anne Knight, née **Waspe** (28 October 1792–11 December 1860), born in Woodbridge, married a fellow Quaker, James Knight, who died in 1820. By 1826, she was keeping a school. Knight wrote several children's books, sometimes attributed in error to her Quaker namesake Anne Knight (1786–1862), a campaigner for women's rights. They include *Poetic Gleanings*, 1827; *Mornings in the Library*, around 1828; *Mary Gray. A Tale for Little Girls*, 1831; and *School-Room Lyrics*, 1846. Charles Lamb mentions her. Knight died in Woodbridge.[127]

Letitia Elizabeth Landon [or **'L.E.L.'**] (14 August 1802–15 October 1838), born in London, helped pay for her brother's studies at Oxford; he spread rumors about her marriage and death. Landon first published in 1820. In 1821, she published *The Fate of Adelaide* under her full name, and more poems in *The Literary Gazette*, signed 'L.E.L.;' she also became the *Gazette*'s chief reviewer. In 1824, *The Improvisatrice; and Other Poems* appeared, then *The Troubadour* in 1825, and other volumes in 1827 and 1829. In 1831, Landon published her first novel, *Romance and Reality*, then more annual volumes of poetry in 1832–1836, alongside poetry and prose in *The New Monthly Magazine*. Her second novel appeared in 1834, the year she visited Paris. A third novel and a verse tragedy, *Castruccio Castracani*, followed in 1837. She married George Maclean on 7 June 1838, dying that October on the Gold Coast, where he was governor.[128]

Harriet Leveson-Gower, Countess Granville, née **Lady Henrietta Elizabeth Cavendish** (29 August 1785–25 November 1862), born in London to Lady Georgiana Spencer, married Granville Leveson-Gower, her aunt's former lover, in 1809. He became an earl in 1833. In 1824, after a brief stint at The Hague, the couple moved to Paris where Granville was named ambassador; he served from 1824–1828, 1830–1834, and

---

126 Jeffrey N. Cox, *Poetry and Politics in the Cockney School. Keats, Shelley, Hunt and their Circle* (Cambridge, UK: Cambridge University Press, 1998).
127 *Dictionary of National Biography* [DNB].
128 Serena Baiesi, *Letitia Elizabeth Landon and Metrical Romance. The Adventures of a Literary 'Genius'* (Bern: Peter Lang, 2009).

1835–1841. The couple returned to England in 1843, Granville dying in 1846. From 1801 onwards, Leveson-Gower had written to her sister almost daily; these and other letters make up her lively correspondence, published four times since her death between 1894 and 1990.[129]

Isabella Lickbarrow (5 November 1784–10 February 1847), born in Kendal, lost her mother aged five and her father at twenty, turning then to poetry to support the family, as she notes in her *Poetical Effusions*, 1814. Lickbarrow had begun publishing in the *Westmorland Advertiser* in 1811; that newspaper's publisher brought out her 1814 volume, funded by subscribers including William Wordsworth, Thomas De Quincey, and Robert Southey. It combines topography and politics. Lickbarrow followed it in 1818 with *A Lament upon the Death of Her Royal Highness the Princess Charlotte; and Alfred, a Vision*, reflecting some unease about Britain's future. She was first republished in 2004.[130]

Anne Manning (17 February 1807–14 September 1879), born in London, wrote over fifty books. These include *A Sister's Gift* in 1826 and *Stories from the History of Italy* in 1831, both non-fiction, followed by novels: *Village Belles*, 1833; *The Maiden and Married Life of Mary Powell, afterwards Mistress Milton*, 1849; *The Household of Sir Thomas More* and *The Colloquies of Edward Osborne*, 1852; *Cherry & Violet*, 1853; *The Adventures of Caliph Haroun Alraschid* and *The Old Chelsea Bun-House*, 1855, and so forth. Manning's works were at first printed serialized in *Sharpe's Magazine*, then in volume form. She published *Mary Powell* anonymously and later works listed her simply as its author, leading to misattributions. It and *Sir Thomas More* were reprinted into the 1930s.[131]

Jane Marcet, née **Haldimand** (1 January 1769–28 June 1858), born in London, ran the household from age fifteen at her mother's death, studying with Joshua Reynolds and Thomas Lawrence. In 1799, she married the fellow-Genevan Alexander John Gaspard Marcet, a fellow of the Royal Society. Their circle included Mary Somerville, Henry Hallam, Harriet Martineau, and Maria Edgeworth. Marcet wrote a series of *Conversations* on current science: on chemistry, 1805, with sixteen

---

129 Betty Askwith, *Piety and Wit: A Biography of Harriet Countess Granville 1785–1862* (Glasgow: William Collins Sons & Co, 1982).
130 Jonathan Wordsworth, *The Bright Work Grows: Women Writers of the Romantic Age* (Poole: Woodstock Books, 1997).
131 Sally Mitchell, ed. *Victorian Britain: an Encyclopedia* (1988. London: Routledge, 2011).

editions by 1840; on political economy, 1816, with fourteen editions; on natural philosophy, 1820; on the evidence of Christianity, 1826; and on vegetable physiology, 1839. Michael Faraday, Mary Somerville, and Harriet Martineau noted Marcet's impact. The couple moved to Geneva in 1820, but Alexander died in 1822 and Marcet returned to London. Her books were much-pirated in America and translated into German, French, Dutch, and Spanish.[132]

Elizabeth Penrose, née **Cartwright** [or **Mrs Markham**] (3 August 1780–24 January 1837), daughter of the inventor of the power loom, was born at Goadby Marwood in Leicestershire. Her mother died in 1785. In 1814, she married Rev. John Penrose. Penrose published two histories: *A History of England from the First Invasion by the Romans to the End of the Reign of George III* in 1823 and a *History of France* in 1828, both quite popular in America as in England. They are distinctive in removing all history's 'horrors' as unsuitable for children. Penrose published other children's books: *Amusements of Westernheath, or Moral Stories for Children* in 1824; *A Visit to the Zoological Gardens* in 1829; *The New Children's Friend* in 1832; *Historical Conversations for Young People* in 1836; and *Sermons for Children* in 1837.[133]

Emma Martin, née **Bullock** (1811/1812–8 October 1851), born in Bristol, lost her father when very young. In 1830, Martin set up a ladies' seminary and later school. In 1831, she married Isaac Luther Martin. She became editor of the *Bristol Literary Magazine* in 1835, and a follower of Robert Owen after 1839; by 1840, she had left her husband. In the 1840s, Martin toured the country, speaking to thousands and publishing: *Religion Superseded* and *Baptism, A Pagan Rite* in 1844, *The Bible No Revelation* in 1845. Opponents threw stones. She faced a real chance of being imprisoned for blasphemy; taken to court, she was never convicted. Martin withdrew from public speaking in 1845, becoming a midwife and cohabiting with Joshua Hopkins, who died in 1852. Her atheism denied her hospital positions, so she worked from home. George Jacob Holyoake published a posthumous memoir in 1852.[134]

Sarah Martin (June 1791–15 October 1843), born in Great Yarmouth,

---

132 Charles Coulston Gillispie, ed. *Dictionary of Scientific Biography*, 18 vols (New York: Charles Scribner's Sons, 1970–1990).
133 *Dictionary of National Biography* [DNB].
134 Ibid.

was orphaned young and raised by a grandmother. She earned her living by dressmaking. After a religious conversion at nineteen, Martin began teaching in the workhouse infirmary; she also took an interest in prisoners' welfare and began teaching in the Great Yarmouth jail in 1818. A collection of her poems, *Selections from the Poetical Remains of Miss S. Martin*, was published in 1845.[135]

Harriet Martineau (12 June 1802–27 June 1876), born in Norwich, England, lost her hearing from the age of twelve. In 1821, Martineau began writing for the Unitarian *Monthly Repository*. She published two novels in 1827–1829: *Principle and Practice* and *Five Years of Youth*. That year, the family's textile business failed, and Martineau began writing to earn a living, publishing her very successful *Illustrations of Political Economy* in 1834. She traveled in the United States from 1834–1836, publishing *Society in America* in 1837, then in 1839, the novel *Deerbrook* and the abolitionist article "The Martyr Age of the United States." Whig, feminist, and atheist, Martineau's circle stretched from Thomas Malthus to Charles Darwin. In 1841, she published *The Hour and the Man*, a novel about Toussaint L'Ouverture, followed in 1844 by *Life in the Sickroom*, a translation of Auguste Comte in 1853, and an autobiography in 1877.[136]

Mary Atkinson Maurice (1797–4 October 1858), born in Kirby Cane, Norfolk, moved with her family to Southampton in 1825, where Maurice opened a Pestalozzian school which ran until 1844. In 1829, Maurice anonymously published an educational manual, *Aids to Development*. *Conversations on the Human Frame, and the Five Senses* followed in 1837. In London after 1844, Maurice joined the Governesses' Benevolent Institution, publishing *Mothers and Governesses* in 1847 and *Governess Life: its Trials, Duties and Encouragements* in 1849. Maurice was an active patron of the Asylum for Aged Governesses, as of Queen's College, London, founded by her brother.[137]

Eliza Meteyard [or **Silverpen**] (21 June 1816–4 April 1879), born in Liverpool, settled in London in 1842. Meteyard began writing in 1833, helping to prepare her tithe commissioner brother's county reports, then later contributing fiction and social commentary to *Eliza Cook's*

---

135 *Dictionary of National Biography* [DNB].
136 Caroline Roberts, *The Woman and the Hour: Harriet Martineau and Victorian Ideologies* (Toronto: University of Toronto Press, 2002).
137 *Dictionary of National Biography* [DNB].

Journal, the *People's Journal, Tait's Magazine, Household Words*, and other periodicals. Douglas Jerrold gave her the pen name 'Silverpen.' Her first novel appeared in 1840 in *Tait's Magazine*, then in 1845 as *Struggles for Fame*. Others include *Mainstone's Housekeeper*, 1860, and *Lady Herbert's Gentle-Woman*, 1862. She wrote several stories and novels for children between 1850–1878: for instance, *Dora and Her Papa* in 1869. Meanwhile in *Howitt's Journal*, she advocated for small-scale social reform. Her *Life of Josiah Wedgwood* appeared in 1865–1866, followed by other Wedgwood monographs from 1871–1879.[138]

Lydia Mackenzie Falconer Miller [or **Mrs. Harriet Myrtle**] (1812– 11 March 1876), a Scottish children's writer, was baptized in 1812 and schooled in Inverness and Edinburgh. After some time in England, she set up a school in Cromarty, marrying Hugh Miller in 1837 and writing pieces for her husband's periodical, *The Witness*. Miller also wrote about twenty stories for children: *Adventure of a Kite*, which is in print today; *The Water Lily; Two Dear Friends; The Duck House*, and so forth. In 1847, Miller anonymously published *Passages in the Life of an English Heiress: or, Recollections of Disruption Times in Scotland*, her one adult novel. Her husband, unwell and possibly fearing insanity, shot himself in 1856. Miller published her husband's unfinished works and assisted in his biography.[139]

Judith, Lady Montefiore, née **Barent Cohen** (20 February 1784–24 September 1862), born in London, married Sir Moses Montefiore in 1812. The Portuguese Synagogue did not approve of marriages between Sephardim and Ashkenazim, but Moses (who was Sephardic) found this divisive. From 1812–1825, the couple lived next door to Nathan Mayer Rothschild in London, whom Montefiore's sister Hannah had married in 1806. A keen traveler, Montefiore accompanied her husband in all his foreign missions up to 1859, to the Holy Land, St Petersburg, and Rome, for instance; she was especially alert to Jewish conditions abroad, as her journals attest. Montefiore published the first English-language Jewish cookbook, *The Jewish Manual; or Practical Information in Jewish and Modern Cookery*, in 1846.[140]

---

138 Laurel Brake and Marysa Demoor, *Dictionary of Nineteenth-Century Journalism in Great Britain and Ireland* (Ghent: Academia Press, 2009).
139 *Dictionary of National Biography* [DNB].
140 Isidore Singer et al., eds. *The Jewish Encyclopedia* (1901–1906).

Esther Nelson (1810–21 March 1843), a Manx poet born in Jurby and baptized there on 6 June 1810, lived in Douglas in 1838 but was back in Bride the following year to dedicate her book of poems, *Island Minstrelsy*. Nelson traveled to Paris in 1841, perhaps for health reasons; returning to the Isle of Man, she died of tuberculosis in Bride in 1843. Nelson wrote under the pen names 'The Island Minstrel' or 'Hadassah.' *Island Minstrelsy* ranges from long narrative poems to short lyrics. Death is very present, as is the island itself.[141]

Alicia Tindal Palmer (1763–1822), born in Bath, lost her father in 1768. Palmer's first novel appeared in 1809: *The Husband and Lover*. Her next novel, *The Daughters of Isenberg: a Bavarian Romance*, appeared in 1810, to a negative review from John Gifford in the *Quarterly Review*, who alleged he had been given three pounds to write a good review. Palmer published another novel in 1811, then in 1815, a biography: *Authentic Memoirs of the Life of John Sobieski, King of Poland*.[142]

Fanny Parkes [or **Parks**], née **Frances Susanna Archer** (8 December 1794–1875), born in Conwy, married Charles Crawford Parks in 1822. The couple lived in India between 1822–1846, with some years in England and Cape Town, 1839–1844. Initially in Calcutta (now Kolkata), they moved to Allahabad ten years later. Parkes learned Persian, Hindustani, and Urdu. Her memoirs include controversial topics, like a death in *sati* she witnessed; they appeared in 1850 as *Wanderings of a Pilgrim in Search of the Picturesque During Four and Twenty Years in the East with Revelations of Life in the Zenana*, her authorship indicated by a signature in Urdu script. In 1851, Parkes organized and wrote the catalogue of the *Grand Moving Diorama of Hindostan, from Fort William, Bengal, to Gangoutri in the Himalaya*, which showed in London and in Hull. Her memoir was at length republished in 1970; a biography followed in 2018.[143]

Gertrude Parsons (19 March 1812–12 February 1891), born in Lanlivery in Cornwall, converted to Roman Catholicism in 1844 prior to marrying Daniel Parsons the following year; he had converted in 1843. The couple moved to Malvern Wells. Parsons wrote several novels with

---

141 John Belchem, ed. *A New History of the Isle of Man* (5 vols), *Vol. V: The Modern Period, 1830–1999* (Liverpool: Liverpool University Press, 2000).
142 *Dictionary of National Biography* [DNB]; *The Women's Print History Project* (https://womensprinthistoryproject.com/).
143 William Dalrymple, ed. *Begums, Thugs & Englishmen, the Journals of Fanny Parkes* (London: Sickle Moon Books, 2002).

Catholic themes: for instance, in *Thornberry Abbey: a Tale of the Established Church* in 1846, a couple convert and find happiness; in *Edith Mortimer* in 1857, a girl turns down her Protestant suitor. Parsons also published *The Life of St. Ignatius of Loyola* in 1860, and *Rhymes Gay and Grave* in 1864. The next year, she edited and largely wrote a magazine for Catholics called *Workman, or, Life and Leisure* and later the *Literary Workman*, which ceased publication the same year. Her later novels are less overtly Catholic.[144]

Jane Porter (3 December 1775–24 May 1850), born in Durham, moved with her family to Edinburgh after her father's death, where she met Sir Walter Scott. The Porters moved to London in the 1790s, meeting Hannah More, Elizabeth Inchbald, Anna Laetitia Barbauld, and others. Porter's best-selling historical novels precede Scott's 1814 *Waverley* and reflect the same nation-building exercise: *Thaddeus of Warsaw* in 1803, for which Porter saw barely a penny, and *The Scottish Chiefs* in 1810. Porter contributed to periodicals and wrote the play *Switzerland*, 1819, which seems to have been deliberately sabotaged by its lead, Edmund Kean. She also wrote *Tales Round a Winter Hearth*, 1826, and *Coming Out; and The Field of Forty Footsteps*, 1828, with her sister Anna Maria. Porter continued to write for periodicals in later years, often signing her work 'J.P.'[145]

Mary Prince (c. 1 October 1788-after 1833), born enslaved at Brackish Pond, Bermuda, was sold aged twelve to Captain John Ingham; her two sisters were sold the same day to other slave traders. Prince worked in the Bermuda salt pans. Sold before 1803 to Robert Darrell, she was physically abused. In 1815, Prince was sold to John Adams Wood of Antigua. In Antigua, Prince joined the Moravian Church, marrying the free Black man Daniel James in 1826. In 1828, the Woods traveled with Prince to England. Prince left for shelter in a Moravian church, working for the abolitionist Thomas Pringle; Wood in 1829 refused either to manumit Prince or to allow her to be purchased. Bills in Parliament failed until 1833. Prince dictated her life story to Susanna Strickland, published in 1831 as *The History of Mary Prince*. It sold out three printings that year, the first such first-person female account in British history.[146]

---

144 *Dictionary of National Biography* [DNB].
145 Devoney Looser, *Sister Novelists: the Trailblazing Porter Sisters, Who Paved the Way for Austen and the Brontës* (New York: Bloomsbury Publishing, 2022).
146 Kimberly Drake, ed. *The Slave Narrative* (Ipswich, MA: Salem Press, 2014).

Isabella Frances Romer (1798–27 April 1852), born in London, married Major Hamerton in 1818 but separated from him in 1827, reverting to her maiden name. Romer began in 1840 to contribute sketches and short stories to periodicals, including *Bentley's Miscellany* and the *New Monthly Magazine*. Romer's first book was a fictionalized account of mesmerism: *Sturmer: a Tale of Mesmerism*, published in 1841. Romer became famous as a travel writer: *The Rhone, the Darro, and the Guadalquivir. A Summer Ramble in 1842* appeared in 1843, *A Pilgrimage to the Temples and Tombs of Egypt, Nubia and Palestine in 1845–6* in 1846; *The Bird of Passage, or, Flying Glimpses of Many Lands* appeared in 1849. Her biography of Marie Thérèse Charlotte, Duchess of Angoulême, was completed after her death and published in 1852 as *Filia Dolorosa*.[147]

Margaret Roscoe, née **Lace** (c. 1786–1840), married Edward Roscoe in 1810. She illustrated her father-in-law William Roscoe's *Monandrian Plants of the Order Scitamineae: Chiefly Drawn from Living Specimens in the Botanical Gardens at Liverpool*, published in 1828, going on to write and illustrate her own *Floral Illustrations of the Seasons* in 1829–1831.[148]

Margaret Sandbach (28 April 1812–23 June 1852), born in Liverpool, was the daughter of Margaret Roscoe. Sandbach married Henry Robertson Sandbach in 1832, moving to his estate at Hafodunos in Denbighshire; in 1855, he became High Sheriff. Sandbach's first book was *Poems* in 1841. *Aurora and Other Poems* followed in 1850, as well as her novel *Hearts in Mortmain*. A second novel, *Spiritual Alchemy*, followed in 1851. A book based on her life appeared in 2013.[149]

Harriet Anne Scott, Lady Scott (24 March 1816–8 April 1894), born in Bombay (now Mumbai), married Sir James Sibbald David Scott in 1844. She had already published her first two novels, *The M.P.'s Wife and The Lady Geraldine*, 1838, and *The M.D.'s Daughter*, 1842. Seven more followed: *The Henpecked Husband*, 1847, *Percy, or the Old Love and the New*, 1848, *Hylton House and its Inmates*, 1850, *The Only Child: a Tale*, 1852, *The Pride of Life*, 1854, *The Skeleton in the Cupboard*, 1860, and *The Dream of a Life*, 1862. The first five were anonymous. Scott also contributed to the periodical press and published *Cottagers' Comforts, and other Recipes in Knitting and Crochet. By Grandmother*, 1887. She is sometimes confused

---

147 *Dictionary of National Biography* [DNB].
148 Ibid.
149 Linda H. Peterson, ed. *The Cambridge Companion to Victorian Women's Writing* (2015).

with her fellow novelist Caroline Lucy Scott, Lady Scott (1784–1857).[150]

Mary Wollstonecraft Shelley, née **Godwin** (30 August 1797–1 February 1851), born in London, lost her mother, Mary Wollstonecraft, eleven days after her birth. Her father, William Godwin, raised her as an anarchist. She eloped briefly to France with Percy Shelley in 1814, returning pregnant; in 1816, the couple traveled to Geneva, joining Byron there, a journey Shelley described in 1817. Here, Shelley wrote *Frankenstein; or, The Modern Prometheus*, 1818. The couple married in England in 1816, leaving for Italy in 1818, where Shelley lost two more children. She also wrote *Mathilda*, 1959, and *Valperga*, 1823, and two plays, *Proserpine* and *Midas*. Percy drowned in 1822; Shelley returned to England with their son, writing *The Last Man*, 1826, then *The Fortunes of Perkin Warbeck*, 1830, *Lodore*, 1835, *Falkner*, 1837, and five volumes of European *Lives* for an encyclopedia, and editing Percy's *Poetical Works*.[151]

Emily Anne Eliza Shirreff (3 November 1814–20 March 1897) spent the 1820s in France, moving to Gibraltar in 1831 with her family then returning to England in 1834. In 1835, Shirreff published *Letters from Spain and Barbary* with her sister Maria; a novel followed in 1841, *Passion and Principle*, and in 1850, *Thoughts on Self-Culture Addressed to Women*. Shirreff alone published her feminist *Intellectual Education and its Influence on the Character and Happiness of Women* in 1858; she became the second mistress of Girton College, Cambridge, and presided the Froebel Society from 1876 until her death. Shirreff founded the Women's Education Union and co-edited its journal. She supported women's suffrage and condemned American slavery in *The Chivalry of the South*, 1864. She published extensively on education and women's rights.[152]

Catherine Sinclair (17 April 1800–6 August 1864), a Scottish writer born in Edinburgh, was her father's secretary from the age of fourteen until his death in 1835. Her own first publication was *Modern Accomplishments, or the March of Intellect, a Study of Female Education*, in 1836, with a sequel in 1837. In 1838, she wrote *Hill and Valley; or, Hours in England and Wales*; she shone as a children's writer in 1839's anarchic

---

150 *Dictionary of National Biography* [DNB].
151 Betty T. Bennett, ed. *Mary Shelley in her Times* (Baltimore, MD: Johns Hopkins University Press, 2003).
152 Edward W. Ellsworth (1979). *Liberators of the Female Mind: The Shirreff Sisters, Educational Reform and the Women's Movement* (Westport, CT: Greenwood Press, 1979).

Holiday House: A Book for the Young. Sinclair wrote three books on Scotland and the Shetlands, in 1840–1859, and one on Wales in 1860. Other works include novels and children's books: *Modern Flirtations,* 1841; *Scotch Courtiers and the Court,* 1842; *Jane Bouverie, or Prosperity and Adversity,* 1846; *The Journey of Life,* 1847, and so forth, from *The Business of Life,* 1848, to *Anecdotes of the Cæsars,* 1858. Sinclair was active in Edinburgh charities.[153]

Jane Sinnett, née **Fry** (8 March 1804–14 November 1870), born in London, married Edward William Percy Sinnett in 1825. The couple moved to Hamburg, Germany, returning to England after 1835. Sinnett contributed to the *Dublin Review* and *The Athenæum.* Edward died in 1844, Sinnett then writing to support her family. Her translations and reviews appeared in the *Foreign and Quarterly Review, Bentley's Miscellany,* and *The Westminster Review,* where George Eliot described her as "tiresome," for uncertain reasons. Sinnett translated several travel memoirs, including Ida Pfeiffer's *A Lady's Voyage around the World.*[154]

Elizabeth Somerville, née **Helme** (1774–c. 1841), a Scottish writer born in Lanarkshire, began publishing in 1799 as 'Elizabeth Helme.' Being also her mother's name, this has caused confusion: *The Faithful Mirror,* 1799; *James Manners, Little John, and Their Dog Bluff,* 1799; *Flora: or the Deserted Child* and *Lessons for Children of Three Years Old,* 1800. After 1800, Somerville used her married name: *Lessons, or, Short Stories in Two and Three Syllables,* 1800; *The Village Maid, or, Dame Burton's Moral Stories,* 1801; *The Birth-Day, or, Moral Dialogues and Stories, Mabel Woodbine and her Sister Lydia,* and *The New Children in the Wood,* 1802; *Choice Tales, for the Improvement of Youth of Both Sexes, Sacred Lectures from the Holy Scriptures,* and *Preludes to Knowledge,* 1803; *The History of Little Charles, and his Friend Frank Wilful,* 1808; and so forth. Somerville appears in an 1841 census.[155]

Mary Somerville, née **Fairfax** [formerly **Greig**] (26 December 1780– 29 November 1872), a Scottish writer born in Jedburgh, had a desultory education, teaching herself Latin, Greek, and the sciences. She married Lieutenant Samuel Greig in 1804; he died in 1807 and Somerville returned from London to Scotland. In 1811, she published five solutions

---

153 *Dictionary of National Biography* [DNB].
154 Paul A. Olson, *The Kingdom of Science: Literary Utopianism and British Education, 1612–1870* (Lincoln, NE: University of Nebraska Press, 2002).
155 *Orlando: Women's Writing in the British Isles; The Women's Print History Project.*

in the *Mathematical Repository*. She married Dr. William Somerville in 1812, meeting Charles Babbage and Maria Edgeworth after returning to London in 1819. Somerville wrote on optics in 1826, then on photography, and translated and expounded Laplace's *Mécanique céleste* in 1831. The Somervilles settled in Italy after 1833. *On the Connexion of the Physical Sciences* in 1834—which predicted Neptune—sold 15,000 copies. *Physical Geography* followed in 1848, then *Molecular and Microscopic Science* in 1869. Somerville College, Oxford bears her name.[156]

Elizabeth Isabella Spence (12 January 1768–27 July 1832), a Scottish writer born in Dunkeld, was orphaned young and joined family in London. They also died and she began writing to subsist, both romances and British travel writing: *The Nobility of the Heart*, 1804; *The Wedding Day*, 1807; *Summer Excursions through Part of England and Wales*, 1809; *Sketches of the Present Manners, Custom, and Scenery of Scotland*, 1811; *Commemorative Feelings*, 1812; *The Curate and his Daughter: a Cornish Tale*, 1813; *The Spanish Guitar*, 1815; *A Traveller's Tale of the Last Century*, 1819; *Old Stories*, 1822; *How to Be Rid of a Wife*, 1823; *Dame Rebecca Berry* and *Tales of Welsh Society and Scenery*, 1827.[157]

Alicia Ann, Lady John Scott, née **Spottiswoode** (24 June 1810–12 March 1900), a Scottish songwriter born in Spottiswoode, married Lord John Scott in 1836. He died in 1860 and she resumed her maiden name in 1866. Spottiswoode composed many songs, among them "Annie Laurie," "Douglas Tender and True," "Durisdeer," "Etterick," "Farewell to Thee," "Foul Fords," "Katherine Logie," "Lammermoor," "Loch Lomond," "Mother, Oh Sing Me to Rest," "Shame on Ye, Gallants," "Think on Me," "When We First Rode Down to Ettrick," "Within the Garden of My Heart," and "Your Voices Are Not Hush'd." She is remembered especially for the tune "Annie Laurie," set to the words of the seventeenth-century poet William Douglas.[158]

Louisa Sidney Stanhope (fl. 1806–1827) is unknown outside her many historical and Gothic romances. She is sometimes identified with Louisa Grenville (1758–1829), wife of Charles Stanhope, 3rd Earl Stanhope. Stanhope's somewhat didactic novels include *Montbrasil*

---

156 Kathryn A. Neeley, *Mary Somerville: Science, Illumination, and the Female Mind* (Cambridge, UK: Cambridge University Press, 2001).
157 *Orlando: Women's Writing in the British Isles*; *Dictionary of National Biography* [DNB].
158 Aaron I. Cohen, *International Encyclopedia of Women Composers* (1987).

Abbey: or, Maternal Trials, 1806; *The Bandit's Bride: or, The Maid of Saxony*, 1807, translated into French in 1810; *Striking Likenesses; or, The Votaries of Fashion*, 1808; *The Age We Live In*, 1809; *Di Montranzo; or, The Novice of Corpus Domini*, 1810; *The Confessional of Valombre*, 1812; *Madelina. A Tale Founded on Facts*, 1814; *Treachery; or, The Grave of Antoinette. A Romance Interspersed with Poetry*, 1815; and so forth until *The Seer of Tiviotdale*, 1827. *Sydney Beresford. A Tale of the Day* is dated 1835.[159]

Arabella Jane Sullivan, née **Wilmot** (1 May 1796–27 January 1839) married Rev. Frederick Sullivan. She wrote *Recollections of a Chaperon*, 1831, and *Tales of the Peerage and Peasantry*, 1835, two collections of stories credited to her mother, Barbarina Wilmot, later Barbarina Brand, Lady Dacre. Both were in fact written by Sullivan and only edited by her mother.[160]

Anna Swanwick (22 June 1813–2 November 1899), born in Liverpool, went in 1839 to Berlin, where she studied German, Greek, and Hebrew. Swanwick returned to England in 1843, publishing *Selections from the Dramas of Goethe and Schiller* that year. A further volume appeared in 1850, including Goethe's *Faust I*; she published *Faust II* in 1878, to multiple reeditions. In 1865, Swanwick published Aeschylus's *Oresteia*, then his complete works in 1873, again often reedited. Swanwick was a council member for both Queen's College and Bedford College, London, serving as president of the latter; she assisted in founding Girton College, Cambridge, and Somerville College, Oxford. Her friends included Crabb Robinson, Tennyson, Browning, and Gladstone. In 1865, she signed John Stuart Mill's petition to parliament for women's enfranchisement.[161]

Ann Taylor [or **Ann Martin**] (20 June 1757–27 May 1830), born in London, lost her father as a child. In 1781, she married Isaac Taylor; they had eleven children, five surviving to become noted writers. Taylor's works include *Maternal Solicitude for a Daughter's Best Interests*, 1814; *Practical Hints to Young Females*, 1815; *The Present of a Mistress to a Young Servant*, 1816; *Reciprocal Duties of Parents and Children*, 1818;

---

159 Richard Maxwell and Katie Trumpener, eds. *The Cambridge Companion to Fiction in the Romantic Period* (Cambridge, UK: Cambridge University Press, 2008).
160 Lady Barbarina Charlotte Sullivan Grey, ed. Gertrude Lyster, *A Family Chronicle* (London: John Murray, 1908).
161 *Dictionary of National Biography* [DNB].

Correspondence between a Mother and her Daughter at School, 1817, written with her daughter Jane; *The Family Mansion*, 1819; *Retrospection: A Tale*, 1821; and *The Itinerary of a Traveller in the Wilderness*, 1825.[162]

Laura Sophia Temple (1763–?) married Samuel B. Sweetman, publishing her first book, *Poems*, in 1805. The next year, Temple published the novel *Ferdinand Fitzormond; or, The Fool of Nature*. She published a second volume of poetry in 1808, *Lyric and Other Poems*, and a third in 1812: *The Siege of Zaragosa, and Other Poems*, touching on the Peninsular War.[163]

Jane Tonge Thompson (17 February 1786–15 July 1851), born in Boston, Lincolnshire, married Pishey Thompson in 1807. In 1818, Thompson traveled to Washington, D.C.; Pishey came the following year. Here, Pishey fathered an illegitimate son in 1824, and Thompson published a book of poems, *Solitary Musings*, in 1826. The couple returned to England in 1846. Thompson may have contributed a chapter to *Change for American Notes*, a response to Dickens's *American Notes*. She also left several diaries, which survive.[164]

Katherine Thomson, née **Byerley** [or **Mrs. A.T. Thomson** or **Grace Wharton**] (1797–17 December 1862) married Anthony Todd Thomson in 1820; their friends included James Mackintosh, Francis Jeffrey, Thackeray, and Browning. Thomson published a *Life of Wolsey* in 1824; there followed memoirs of the court of Henry the Eighth, 1826; of Sir Walter Raleigh, 1830; of Sarah, Duchess of Marlborough, 1838; of the Jacobites of 1715 and 1745, 1845–1846; of Viscountess Sundon, 1847; and of George Villiers, Duke of Buckingham, 1860. Thomson also wrote *Constance*, a novel, in 1833; *Rosabel* in 1835; *Lady Annabella* in 1837; *Anne Boleyn* and *Widows and Widowers*, 1842, both seeing several editions; *Ragland Castle* in 1843; and so forth. With her son, Thomson wrote *The Queens of Society*, 1860, and other similar works. She pioneered anecdotal history. Thomson lived abroad for some years after 1849.[165]

Sarah Windsor Tomlinson (28 December 1809–17 October 1872), born in Salisbury, worked five years as a governess from age twenty-

---

162 Ann Taylor, *Reciprocal Duties of Parents and Children* (Cambridge, UK: Cambridge University Press, 2015).
163 Diego Saglia, *Poetic Castles in Spain: British Romanticism and Figurations of Iberia* (Amsterdam: Rodopi, 2000).
164 *Dictionary of National Biography* [DNB], "Thompson, Pishey (1785–1862), antiquary."
165 *Dictionary of National Biography* [DNB].

two. She married Charles Tomlinson in 1839 and the couple moved to London, publishing articles on science and technology in the *Saturday Magazine*. Tomlinson wrote several books for the Society for Promoting Christian Knowledge, including *Lessons Derived from the Animal World*, 1845, *First Steps in General Knowledge*, 1846, and *Sketches of Rural Affairs*, 1851. In 1866, Tomlinson became superintendent of a parochial mission in London and published a volume of pertinent short stories: *Tales For Mission Rooms, By a Lady Superintendent*, 1866.[166]

Mary Theresa Vidal, née **Johnson** (23 June 1815–19 November 1873), born in Devon, married Rev. Francis Vidal in 1840 and followed him to Penrith south of Sydney, Australia. In 1845, Vidal's first book, *Tales for the Bush*, was published in Sydney. Soon afterwards the couple returned to England, where Vidal published ten other volumes: *Winterton*, 1846; *Esther Merle and Other Tales*, 1847; *Cabramatta and Woodleigh Farm*, 1850; *Home Trials*, 1858; *Ellen Raymond*, 1859; *Bengala, or Some Time Ago*, 1860; *Florence Temple*, 1862; *Lucy Helmore*, 1863; *Trials of Rachel Charlcote*, 1864; and *Deb Clinton, The Smuggler's Daughter*, 1866. Vidal is sometimes called Australia's first woman novelist. *Bengala* returns to Australia in setting.[167]

Charlotte Williams-Wynn (16 January 1807–26 April 1869) spent her childhood at Dropmore Park. She traveled to Germany with her father, meeting Karl August Varnhagen von Ense, and on to Switzerland and Italy. Williams-Wynn was in Paris at the time of the 1851 *coup d'État*, recording events in detail. Her London circle included the Prussian ambassador and Thomas Carlyle. In 1866, she moved to Arcachon, where she died. Her surviving sister published her memoirs in 1877.[168]

Dorothy Mae Ann Wordsworth (25 December 1771–25 January 1855), born in Cockermouth, was the sister of William Wordsworth. She lost her mother early; her father died in 1781, and the children lived with relatives. Wordsworth did not publish; her 1803 *Recollections of a Tour Made in Scotland* found no publisher until 1874. Her 1818 description of climbing Scafell Pike appeared attributed to William; when he married in 1802, Wordsworth continued living with them. After an illness in 1829, she was an invalid. Wordsworth's *Grasmere Journal* appeared in

---

166 Sarah Tomlinson, *Tales for Mission Rooms, By a Lady Superintendent* (London: Society For Promoting Christian Knowledge, 1873).
167 *Australian Dictionary of Biography* (1966–2021).
168 *Dictionary of National Biography* [DNB].

1897, revealing how William borrowed from her texts—doing so in his poem "Daffodils" for instance, though he says he was "lonely as a cloud" at the time. Several other journals and collections of her letters have since appeared.[169]

Marianne Ridgway, later **Mrs. Thomas Postans** or **Marianne Young** (4 January 1811–6 October 1897), born in London, married Thomas Postans and followed him to India, publishing two books in 1839 after five years there: *Cutch; or, Random Sketches* and *Western India in 1838*, the latter extending to Bombay (now Mumbai). Young was by then fluent in Hindustani, and she illustrated her own texts. That year, Thomas was posted in Sindh in modern Pakistan. After five years in Sindh, Young published *Facts and Fictions*; Thomas died that year and Young returned to England and remarried. In 1853, she published "Persecution in Tuscany: a call for the protection of religious liberty throughout the world [...]," addressed to William Gladstone.[170]

Ireland (58 writers)

Sydney Lady Morgan

The Wild Irish Girl (1806)

LETTER I

TO J. D. ESQ., M. P.

Dublin, March, ——, 17——

I remember, when I was a boy, meeting somewhere with the quaintly-written travels of *Moryson* through Ireland, and being particularly struck with his assertion, that so late as the days of Elizabeth, an Irish chieftain and his family were frequently seen round their domestic fire in a state of perfect nudity. This singular anecdote (so illustrative of the barbarity of the Irish at a period when civilization had made such a wonderful progress even in its sister countries,) fastened so strongly on my boyish imagination, that whenever the *Irish* were mentioned in my presence, an *Esquimaux* group circling round the fire blazing to dress a dinner or broil an enemy, was the image which presented itself to my mind; and

---

169 Susan M. Levin, *Dorothy Wordsworth and Romanticism* (Jefferson, NC: McFarland & Co., 2009).
170 *Dictionary of National Biography* [DNB].

in this trivial source, I believe, originated, that early-formed opinion of Irish ferocity, which has since been nurtured into a *confirmed prejudice*. So true it is, that almost all errors which influence our later life, are to be traced to some fatal and early association. But, whatever maybe the *cause*, I feel the strongest objection to becoming a resident in the remote part of a country, which, for ever shaken by the convulsions of an anarchical spirit,—where for a series of ages the olive of peace has not been suffered to shoot forth *one* sweet blossom of national concord, which the sword of civil dissension has not cropt almost in the germ; and the natural character of whose factious sons, as we are still taught to believe, is turbulent, faithless, intemperate, and cruel; formerly destitute of arts, with all their boasted learning, or civilization, and still but slowly submitting to their salutary and ennobling influence.[171]

One hears so much about Walter Scott's *Waverley*, 1814, as the creator of a certain type of regional British novel that it is good to be reminded of Lady Morgan's *The Wild Irish Girl*, which preceded it by eight years. That in itself might guarantee her text a place in history; as to the actual aesthetic quality of her work, let us look at this opening extract. This is an epistolary novel, opening (like *Waverley*) in the eighteenth century, after several prefatory letters: the conceit in such novels is almost without exception that we are reading a found correspondence. Here, the opening letter's seventh word—*boy*—tells us that our opening narrator and protagonist is not female like the author; and though the narrator writes his missive from Dublin, he was not born there, again unlike Lady Morgan. He (Horatio) is a male visitor to this island, much like the opening protagonist of Avellaneda's *Sab*.

Why does Lady Morgan not have an Irish lady, like herself, narrating? Various reasons suggest themselves; or put another way, on reflection various effects of this choice become evident. First, it offers male English readers—a substantial potential market, including critics—a familiar spokesperson, while female or Irish readers were in 1806 accustomed to reading narratives in another voice. In Great Britain in 1806, after the Act of Union of 1801, male and English was perhaps the default setting for readers. Second, it allows us passage into a strange and characteristic land; Scott again does just this in *Waverley* eight years later, as Waverley vanishes into the Highlands. Third, it allows the wild Irish girl of the

---

[171] In Lady Morgan, *The Wild Irish Girl*, ed. Brigid Brophy (London: Pandora, 1986), p. 1.

title—the Prince of Inismore's daughter, Glorvina—a stage on which to make her entrance. If we looked through her eyes, she would be invisible to us; instead, she is seen and presented by our young Englishman in her otherness and wildness.

The wildness of the Irish is in fact the opening topic of conversation. There was indeed a Fynes Moryson who traveled beyond the Pale of Ireland in the 1590s, some decades before the Cromwellian conquest in which the narrator's English ancestors had their part. And Horatio's mind is, as he relates at length, subject to a *"confirmed prejudice"* where Ireland is concerned. Just as the English tell Irish jokes to this day, so Horatio compares this people his ancestors conquered to "Esquimaux" and details his vision of them sitting naked around the household fire, a vision acquired in childhood and shaping his thinking into the novel's present. Horatio has a long journey ahead to understanding the Irish, or at least to falling in love; and in that, he may well speak for a good fraction of the English public in 1806. The novel went through seven English editions in two years.

These are astute authorial choices, soon echoed as we have seen by Scott, and to massive success. That, the book's contemporary sales, and its place in the history of the regional novel all speak for its continued recuperation. Is anything more to be said? Perhaps so. Lady Morgan after this publication was put under surveillance by Dublin Castle, and the book, from the outset, is quite remarkably political, just five years after the Act of Union and eight years after the Irish Rebellion. Her talk here of national concord cropped in the germ by "the sword of civil dissension," her later talk of marriage between the old Irish nobility and the English heir, are reminiscent of Rostopchina's 1845 poem "Forced Marriage," on Russian-occupied Poland, which got Rostopchina banned from St Petersburg by the tsar. Indeed, this book has a constellation of Romantic themes, from national self-determination to ruined castles, which do a good deal to account for its immediate success, in England as in the United States.

Cecil Frances Alexander (April 1818–12 October 1895), born in Dublin, married Rev. William Alexander in 1850, later Archbishop of Armagh. Alexander was already known as a hymn writer, having published *Verses for Holy Seasons*, 1846, *The Lord of the Forest and His Vassals*, 1847, and *Hymns for Little Children*, 1848. By the century's end, *Hymns for Little*

Children had reached its sixty-ninth edition, and some of her hymns are often heard: "All Things Bright and Beautiful," "There Is a Green Hill Far Away," "Once in Royal David's City." Alexander did charitable work throughout her life; her book profits went to the Diocesan Institution for the Deaf and Dumb in Strabane, and she worked with the Derry Home for Fallen Women. Her husband published *Poems of the Late Mrs Alexander* in 1896. Alexander also published prose and verse pseudonymously in the *Dublin University Magazine*.[172]

Henrietta Battier, née **Fleming** (c.1751–1813), married William Battier in 1768. Visiting London in 1783–1784, she performed at the Drury Lane Theatre and met Samuel Johnson who encouraged her, though that book of her poems, *The Protected Fugitives*, waited until 1791 for publication, coming after her selected poems in 1789's *A Collection of Poems, Mostly Original, by Several Hands*. 1791 also saw Battier's gift for political lampoon emerge in *The Kirwanade*, signed 'Pat. Pindar.' Battier argued incisively for reform, religious tolerance, and Irish independence. In "Bitter Orange," she denounced the loyalist Orange Order; she protested the Act of Union in *An Address*, 1799, falling thereafter into poverty and oblivion. The writer Thomas Moore visited her in her final years.[173]

Louisa Catherine Beaufort (1781–1863) was the sister of Frances Anne Edgeworth. She presented a paper to the Royal Irish Academy in 1827 on Irish antiquities, with lithographs by the author; the essay was then published. Beaufort was the first woman to present a paper to this body; her father, Rev. Daniel Augustus Beaufort, was one of the founders of that institution and served as its librarian from 1788–1791. She wrote several manuscript journals which are now in the Library of Trinity College, Dublin.[174]

Marguerite Gardiner, Countess of Blessington, née **Power** (1 September 1789–4 June 1849), born near Clonmel in County Tipperary, married Captain Maurice St Leger Farmer at fifteen. He died in 1817. In 1818, she married Charles John Gardiner, 1st Earl of Blessington. In

---

172 *Orlando: Women's Writing in the British Isles*.
173 Ailbhe Darcy and David Wheatley, eds. *A History of Irish Women's Poetry* (Cambridge, UK: Cambridge University Press, 2021); Janet Todd, *Rebel Daughters: Ireland in Conflict 1798* (London: Viking, 2003).
174 Maria Edgeworth, *The Absentee*, ed. W.J. McCormack (Oxford: Oxford University Press, 1988).

1822, the couple began a continental tour; in Genoa, they frequented Byron, subject of Blessington's *Conversations of Lord Byron*, 1834. In 1827, Count d'Orsay married Blessington's stepdaughter Harriet, and the four proceeded to Paris, where the earl died of a stroke in 1829. D'Orsay and Harriet separated in England, d'Orsay then living with Blessington until her death. Disraeli stayed at their house; there, Hans Christian Andersen met Charles Dickens. Blessington wrote several novels, some poetry, the *Idler in Italy*, 1839–1840, and *Idler in France*, 1841, and edited *The Book of Beauty* and *The Keepsake*. She wrote a gossip column for Dickens.[175]

Charlotte Brooke (c. 1740–29 March 1793), born in Rantavan in County Cavan, was one of twenty-two children, of whom two survived childhood. Her family moved to County Kildare in 1758. Brooke cared for her father after her mother's death in 1773, the family returning to Rantavan. He died in 1783 and Brooke thereafter relied on her writing. Brooke's pioneering *Reliques of Irish Poetry*, 1788, had English on the facing page; she also published *Dialogue between a Lady and her Pupils* and *The School for Christians* in 1791. *Emma, or the Foundling of the Wood* and *Belisarius* appeared posthumously in 1803.[176]

Frances Browne (16 January 1816–21 August 1879), born at Stranorlar in County Donegal, lost her sight aged eighteen months. In 1841, Browne's first poems appeared in the *Irish Penny Journal* and the London *Athenæum*. A first volume of poems followed in 1844, a second in 1847. Her first contribution to *Chambers's Edinburgh Journal* appeared in 1845; she wrote for it for the next twenty-five years. Browne also contributed several stories to journals with female readers, for instance the *Ladies' Companion* in the 1850s. In 1847, Browne left Donegal for Edinburgh with a sister as reader and amanuensis. Here, she wrote essays, reviews, stories, and poems. In London in 1852, Browne published her first novel, *My Share of the World*. *Granny's Wonderful Chair*, a book of stories in print to this day, followed in 1856, along with a third volume of poetry, and later contributions to the Religious Tract Society.[177]

---

175 Virginia Blain et al., *The Feminist Companion to Literature in English* (1990).
176 Lesa Ní Mhunghaile, *Charlotte Brooke's Reliques of Irish Poetry* (Dublin: Irish Manuscripts Commission, 2009).
177 James McGuire and James Quinn, eds. *Dictionary of Irish Biography: from the Earliest Times to 2002*, 9 vols (Dublin and Cambridge: Royal Irish Academy and Cambridge University Press, 2009).

Selina Bunbury (1802–1882), born near Castlebellingham, County Louth, moved with her family to Dublin in 1819 and Liverpool about 1830. Bunbury kept house for her twin brother until he married in 1845. She wrote nearly 100 volumes of both fiction and non-fiction, beginning with *A Visit to My Birthplace* in 1821. Bunbury traveled from Stockholm to Rome in 1847–1848, witnessing revolution in various parts of Europe. Her travel writing includes *My Early Adventures During the Peninsular Campaign of Napoleon*, 1834; *A Visit to the Catacombs* [...] *and a Midnight Visit to Mount Vesuvius*, 1849; *Evelyn, or, A Journey from Stockholm to Rome in 1847–48*, 1849; *Russia After the War*, 1857; and *My First Travels*, 1859. Bunbury also wrote somewhat didactic fiction, from *Cabin Conversations and Castle Scenes* in 1827 to *Lady Flora* in 1870.[178]

Anne Burke (fl. 1787–1805) had been a governess and was widowed with a son. She took up writing to support her family, applying several times to the Royal Literary Fund, from which she received thirteen guineas in total. She wrote six known Gothic novels, to favorable reviews: *Ela; or, The Delusions of the Heart*, 1787, reprinted in Philadelphia and translated; *Emilia de St. Aubigne*, 1788; *Adela Northington*, 1796; *The Sorrows of Edith*, 1796; *Elliott; or, Vicissitudes of Early Life*, 1800; *The Secret of the Cavern*, 1805. *Ela* may have been an influence on Ann Radcliffe's *The Romance of the Forest*. It was reprinted several times.[179]

Margaret Callan, née **Hughes** [or **Thornton MacMahon**] (c. 1817–c. 1883), born in Newry, County Down, lost her father, a flax buyer, early and set up a school in Dublin with her sisters in 1835. It was advertised in *The Nation*, for which she wrote at least two articles in 1843: "A Day at Versailles" and "A Day in Paris." Callan had family connections to Charles Gavan Duffy and the Young Ireland movement. She married John B. Callan, a fellow contributor, editing *The Casket of Irish Pearls*, a collection of Irish prose and verse, in 1846 under the name 'Thornton MacMahon.' In 1848, Callan edited *The Nation* during Gavan Duffy's imprisonment in Newgate. The Callans emigrated to Australia in 1856, Callan dying in Melbourne.[180]

---

178 Patricia Coughlan and Tina O'Toole, eds. *Irish Literature: Feminist Perspectives* (Lausanne: Peter Lang, 2008).
179 Foster, John Wilson, *The Cambridge Companion to the Irish Novel* (Cambridge: Cambridge University Press, 2006).
180 James McGuire et al., eds. *Dictionary of Irish biography* (2009).

Mary Birkett Card (28 December 1774–1817), born in Liverpool, moved to Dublin with her Quaker family in 1784. Her uncle was the abolitionist George Harrison. Card married Nathaniel Card in 1801. She is perhaps best known for her abolitionist work, *A Poem on the African Slave Trade*, published when she was seventeen and arguing to boycott sugar in tea; Card wrote often on abolitionism, pushing for votes against the slave trade, but not exclusively, with a good portion of her work devoted to issues faced by a Quaker woman living in Dublin. Over time, Card turned toward prose; she raised funds for several charitable causes and served on various committees. Her son collected her writings in 1834, including her journal, letters, and over 220 poems.[181]

Anna Maria Chetwode [or **Miss Chetwode**] (fl. 1827–1829), daughter of Rev. John Chetwode of Glanmire, County Cork, and Elizabeth Chetwode, has been identified as Anna Maria by eliminating the couple's other daughters. Her father died in 1814. Chetwode was still in Glanmire in 1821; she traveled to Russia in the early 1800s, staying near Moscow with Yekaterina Vorontsova-Dashkova. Chetwode wrote at least two novels: *Blue-Stocking Hall*, 1827, set in County Kerry and advocating for women's education, and *Tales of My Time*, 1829, were first correctly attributed in 1839. A book called *Snugborough* has also been ascribed to Chetwode but is set in England and does not refer to Ireland. Several of Chetwode's poems are amongst the Wilmot papers in the Royal Irish Academy.[182]

Olivia, Lady Clarke, née **Owenson** (1785–24 April 1845), born in Dublin, was the sister of the novelist Lady Morgan. The two sisters lost their mother in 1789 and were sent away to school in Clontarf and Dublin. Clarke then became a governess. She wrote satirical verse for various periodicals: the *Metropolitan Magazine*, *The Comic Offering*, the London *Athenæum*. Clarke remained in touch with the theater—her father had been a professional actor—and in 1819 produced the comedy *The Irishwoman* at the Theatre Royal, Dublin. Her *Parodies on Popular Songs* appeared in 1836.[183]

---

181 Fionnghuala Sweeney, Fionnuala Dillane; and Maria Stuart, *Ireland, Slavery, Anti-Slavery, and Empire* (London: Routledge, 2018).
182 James McGuire et al., eds. *Dictionary of Irish Biography* (2009).
183 David O'Shaughnessy, *Ireland, Enlightenment and the English Stage, 1740–1820* (Cambridge, UK: Cambridge University Press, 2019).

Mary Downing, née **McCarthy** (c. 1815–1881), born in Kilgarvan, County Kerry, contributed poetry under the pen names 'Christabel' and 'Myrrha' to the *Freeholder* and the *Cork Southern Reporter*. She also contributed poems to the *Dublin Citizen* under the monikers 'M.F.D.' and 'C**I.' In the 1830s, she married Washington Downing, moving to London with him. A committed nationalist, Downing helped several participants in the Young Irelander Rebellion of 1848 to escape to France. Her best-known work, *Scraps from the Mountains, and Other Poems*, appeared in Dublin in 1840. Her papers are in the National Library of Ireland.[184]

Frances Anne "Fanny" Edgeworth, née **Beaufort** (1769–10 February 1865), born in Navan, County Meath, was the sister of Louisa Catherine Beaufort and the stepmother of Maria Edgeworth. Edgeworth studied art under Francis Robert West in Dublin and Raymond Deshouillères in London, where the family resided from 1789–1790. In 1788, Edgeworth joined her father for a tour of Ireland, illustrating his 1792 *A New Map of Ireland*. She married Richard Lovell Edgeworth in 1798, becoming his fourth wife. Maria was one year older, but the two became close. In 1813, James Hall attributed a novel to her: *What You Choose to Call It* or *The Good Wife*. But the family does not repeat this. Edgeworth did write a memoir of Maria, with selected letters; she also illustrated Maria's *The Parent's Assistant* for the third edition.[185]

Sarah Mary [or **Margaret**] **Fitton** (c. 1796–30 March 1874), born in Dublin, spent some years with her family following her brother William to Edinburgh, Northampton, and London. Her 1817 *Conversations on Botany*, written with her sister Elizabeth and explaining the Linnaean system, went through nine illustrated editions by 1840. Fitton's 1860 volume, *How I Became a Governess*, suggests she may have spent time as a governess in France; when she contributed short stories to Charles Dickens's *Household Words*, she was described as "long resident in Paris." Fitton's Paris circle included Eugène Sue and Elizabeth Barrett Browning. She also wrote on music: *Conversations on Harmony* in 1855 appeared in French and English; *Little by Little* in 1857 contains lessons in reading music. Fitton's *The Four Seasons: A Short Account of the Structure of Plants*,

---

184 James McGuire et al., eds. *Dictionary of Irish Biography* (2009).
185 Ray Desmond, *Dictionary of British and Irish Botanists and Horticulturalists* (1994).

in 1865, returns to botany. She died in Paris.[186]

Anne Fuller (?–1790), whose parents were from Tralee, County Kerry, wrote three Gothic novels which were reprinted several times: *The Convent; or, The History of Sophia Nelson* in 1786; *Alan Fitz-Osborne, an Historical Tale* in 1787; and *The Son of Ethelwolf: An Historical Tale* in 1789. She died of consumption in 1790.[187]

Catherine Rebecca Gray [or **Grey**], **Lady Manners**, later, **Lady Huntingtower** (1766–21 March 1852), born in Lehena, County Cork, married the Tory politician William Manners in 1790. The couple had twelve children. In 1821, the family name was changed from Manners to Tollemache. *Poems by Lady Manners* appeared in 1793; it was followed by *Review of Poetry, Ancient and Modern, A Poem, by Lady M***** in 1799.[188]

Sarah Green (fl. 1790–1825) was likely born in Ireland and later moved to London; eight of her works appeared with the London-based Minerva Press. Green was one of the ten most prolific novelists of the early nineteenth century, writing novels, tales, romances, mock romances, religious work, and conduct literature; she also translated and edited. Green published anonymously until 1810, when she began to publish under her own name. Her 1808 *Private History of the Court of England* is a fiction based on the life of writer Mary Robinson; her *Scotch Novel Reading* in 1824 mentions Burney, Byron, Dacre, Lennox, Owenson, Radcliffe, and Scott. Green's novels stretch from *Charles Henley* in 1790 to *Parents and Wives* in 1825; she also wrote *Mental Improvement for a Young Lady*, 1793; *A Letter to the Publisher of Brothers's Prophecies*, 1795; and *Raphael*, 1812, translated from Lafontaine's German.[189]

Frances Greville, née **Macartney** (c. 1724–1789), born in Longford, was in London by the 1740s with Sarah Lennox, Duchess of Richmond. She married Fulke Greville in 1748 after eloping, and may have contributed to his *Maxims, Characters, and Reflections* in 1756. Greville's poem "Prayer for Indifference," published in the *Edinburgh Chronicle* in 1759, attacks the cult of sensibility and was often reprinted in the

---

186 Ann B. Shteir, *Cultivating Women, Cultivating Science* (1996).
187 Jarlath Killeen, *The Emergence of Irish Gothic Fiction: History, Origins, Theories* (Edinburgh: Edinburgh University Press, 2014).
188 Backscheider, Paula R. *Eighteenth-Century Women Poets and Their Poetry: Inventing Agency, Inventing Genre* (Baltimore, MD: Johns Hopkins University Press, 2008)
189 Janet M. Todd, ed. *British and American Women Writers* (1985); *Dictionary of National Biography* [DNB].

next decades; otherwise, Greville wrote mostly *vers de société*. Her circle included Frances Burney and Richard Brinsley Sheridan, who dedicated *The Critic* to her. Greville is sometimes confused with her daughter, the Whig hostess Frances Anne Crewe (1748–1818).[190]

Elizabeth Griffith (1727–5 January 1793), born in Glamorgan, Wales, soon settled in Dublin with her family, where her father, a theater manager, died in 1744. Griffith debuted onstage as Juliet in 1749; she specialized in tragic roles. In 1751, she married Richard Griffith. In 1757–1770, Griffith published her first work, *A Series of Genuine Letters Between Henry and Frances*, in six volumes, an immediate success. Between 1764–1769, Griffith wrote four plays, with *The Double Mistake* staged at Covent Garden in 1766; she approached David Garrick for help staging her next comedy, *The School for Rakes*, in 1769, while Richard Brinsley Sheridan helped with her comedy *The Times* in 1779. In the years 1760–1779, Griffith staged five comedies, edited female dramatists, and published epistolary novels (*The Delicate Distress*, 1769), translations from the French, a dramatic poem, and a 500-page book on Shakespeare.[191]

Anna Maria Hall, née **Fielding** [or **Mrs S.C. Hall**] (6 January 1800–30 January 1881), born in Dublin, came to England with her mother in 1815. She married Samuel Carter Hall in 1824. Hall published *Sketches of Irish Character* in 1829, followed the next year by *Chronicles of a School-Room*. She published more Irish sketches in 1831, then nine novels, starting with *The Buccaneer*, 1832, which is set during the Protectorate. Her *Lights and Shadows of Irish Life* appeared in her husband's *New Monthly Magazine*, then in volume form in 1838. Hall's plays *The French Refugee*, 1836, and *Mabel's Curse*, 1837, were both staged at St James's Theatre. Her novel *Marian, or a Young Maid's Fortunes* appeared in 1840, followed by *Midsummer Eve, a Fairy Tale of Love* in 1848, then *Stories of the Irish Peasantry* in 1851. Hall edited the *St James's Magazine* in 1862–1863. She was also active in charity work.[192]

Marianne-Caroline Hamilton, née **Tighe** (1777–29 July 1861), cousin of Mary Tighe, born at Rossana, County Wicklow, spent much of her

---

190 Roger Lonsdale, *Eighteenth Century Women Poets* (1989).
191 Melinda C. Finberg, *Eighteenth-Century Women Dramatists* (Oxford: Oxford University Press, 2001).
192 Catherine Jane Hamilton, *Notable Irishwomen* (Dublin: Sealy, Bryers & Walker, 1900); *Dictionary of National Biography* [DNB].

youth in England and time on the continent before returning to Ireland in 1795. She married Charles Hamilton in 1801, Hamilton educating their six children. Hamilton in her writings satirized the Anglo-Irish ascendancy; these include *Domestic Happiness as Acted in the City: a Tragic Comic Farce*; *The Kingston to Holyhead Packet*; and *Society*. She wrote a family memoir later purchased by the National Library of Ireland and published in 2010: *Reminiscences of Marianne-Caroline Hamilton (1777–1861)*. Hamilton also drew and painted. Thomas Campbell wrote a poem about her, the "Stanzas to Painting."[193]

Elizabeth Hardy (16 December 1794–9 May 1854) published three known novels, all anonymous: *Michael Cassidy, or the Cottage Gardener* in 1845, *Owen Glendower or The Prince of Wales: A Historical Romance* in 1849 (republished with a modified title in 1851), and *The Confessor: a Jesuit Tale of the Times, Founded on Fact* in 1854. The latter two at least appeared in London, where Hardy died while imprisoned for debt in Queen's Bench Prison.[194]

Dorothea Herbert (c.1767–1829), born in Carrick-on-Suir, County Tipperary to Rev. Nicholas Herbert, withdrew from society after two unhappy amours and was barred from attending church because of her "profane conduct." Herbert suffered a nervous breakdown, followed by the deaths of her father and brother. She nevertheless wrote plays, novels, and an opera, all believed lost. Her *Poetical Eccentricities Written by an Oddity*, 1793, however, has survived, along with her *Retrospections of an Outcast, or the Reflections of Dorothea Herbert Written in Retirement*, first published in 1929–1930. These and her *Journal Notes*, which continue her retrospections, have been republished.[195]

Jane Emily Herbert (1821–26 May 1882) resided in Arklow, County Wicklow, in 1839, as *The Freeman's Journal* makes clear that year. Herbert's earliest known publication, *Poetical Recollections of Irish History* in 1842, earned warm reviews in the press, her long poem *The Bride of Imael; or Irish Love and Saxon Beauty* in 1847 likewise, as did *Ione's Dream, and Other Poems* in 1853. Herbert married Thomas

---

193 James McGuire et al., eds. *Dictionary of Irish Biography* (2009).
194 *Dictionary of National Biography* [DNB].
195 Barbara Hughes, *Between Literature and History: the Diaries and Memoirs of Mary Leadbeater and Dorothea Herbert* (Oxford: Peter Lang, 2010).

Mills in 1858 in Monkstown, and her production seems then to have diminished; *A Short History of Ireland from the Earliest Periods to the Year 1798*, attributed to Herbert, evidently first appeared posthumously in 1886.[196]

Mary Anne Holmes, née **Emmet** (10 October 1773–10 March 1805), born in Dublin, was the sister of the United Irishmen Thomas Addis and Robert Emmet. She married Robert Holmes in 1799. When Thomas was sent to Fort George in Scotland for his involvement, Holmes helped raise his children. In 1802, her father died; in 1803, her husband was arrested, and her brother Robert was executed. Holmes died soon after her husband's 1804 release. Holmes contributed prose and verse to the *Press*, a journal associated with the Society of United Irishmen. In 1799, she was active with her family in opposing the Act of Union; the pamphlet *An Address to the People of Ireland* was once attributed to her, though it is now thought Roger O'Connor's work. Her daughter's 1833 collection *The Dream and Other Poems* includes her poetry.[197]

Anna Brownell Jameson, née **Murphy** (17 May 1794–17 March 1860), born in Dublin, moved with the family to London in 1798. Aged sixteen, Jameson became a governess; in 1821, visiting Italy, she wrote *The Diary of an Ennuyée*, which appeared in 1826. She married Robert Jameson in 1825. In 1829, Robert went to Dominica and Jameson to Europe, publishing *Loves of the Poets*. Her Shakespeare volume, *Characteristics of Women: Moral, Poetical, and Historical*, in 1832, was reissued twenty-eight times by 1900; her German *Visits and Sketches at Home and Abroad* followed in 1834, then in 1838, *Winter Studies and Summer Rambles in Canada*. Several works on art, 1842–1846, culminated in her much-reissued six-volume *Sacred and Legendary Art*, published in 1845–1852 with two posthumous volumes in 1864. *Sisters of Charity* and *The Communion of Labour* in 1855–1856 retrace her philanthropy.[198]

Julia Kavanagh (7 January 1824–28 October 1877), born in Thurles, County Tipperary, moved aged one to London, then Paris. Kavanagh lived with her almost blind mother from the age of twenty, writing

---

[196] *The Christmas Bookseller* (1887), p. 202 (https://books.google.com.gi/books?id=yBADAAAAYAAJ&printsec=frontcover#v=onepage&q&f=false), "Just published: *A Short History of Ireland*."

[197] James McGuire et al., eds. *Dictionary of Irish biography* (2009).

[198] Judith Johnston, *Anna Jameson: Victorian, Feminist, Woman of Letters* (Aldershot: Scholar Press, 1997).

essays and short stories for various periodicals from 1846–1878: *Chambers Edinburgh Journal, Household Words, All the Year Round, The Month, People's Journal, Popular Record, Temple Bar,* and *Argosy.* Her children's book, *Three Paths* in 1847, was followed in 1848 by *Madeleine, a Tale of Auvergne,* and a string of novels set in France. Kavanagh returned to France with her mother in the early 1860s, where she died. Her *Women in France during the Eighteenth Century* and *Women of Christianity* in 1850–1852 remain pertinent, like her *French Women of Letters* and *English Women of Letters* in 1862. Kavanagh also wrote fairy tales and a *Queen Mab* in 1863. She was much translated.[199]

Margaret King [or **Margaret King Moore** or **Lady Mount Cashell** or **Mrs Mason**] (1773-January 1835), born in Mitchelstown, County Cork, was educated in 1787–1788 by Mary Wollstonecraft, appearing in Wollstonecraft's 1788 writings. In 1791, King married Stephen Moore, 2nd Earl Mount Cashell. She attended the Thelwall—Horne Tooke treason trials of 1794 and took the United Irish test, writing pamphlets opposing the Act of Union. In 1801, the Cashells began a Grand Tour, meeting Napoleon, Thomas Paine, and Pope Pius VII. In 1805, King left Stephen for George William Tighe. She contributed to Godwin's 1813–1820 *Stories of Old Daniel* and wrote *Advice to Young Mothers on the Physical Education of Children* in 1823 as well as two novels, one unpublished. In Pisa in 1820, the Shelleys visited them almost daily; Leopardi was a later guest. Widowed in 1822, King married Tighe in 1826.[200]

Elish Lamont [or **La Mont(e)**] (1800 or 1816–28 July 1870), born in Belfast, trained in London as a miniaturist, returning then to Belfast and working as a professional artist by 1837. Lamont opened a girls' school in 1851, leaving it by 1856. In 1857, she moved to Dublin, then England in later life, where her circle included John Ruskin and Charles Dickens. Lamont exhibited at the Royal Hibernian Academy in 1842–1858 and the Royal Academy of Arts in 1856–1859. She published various works in 1843: *The Northern Whig; Impressions, Thoughts and Sketches During Two Years in Switzerland; The Gladiators;* and *The Mission of the Educator.* In 1846, Lamont cowrote the volume *Christmas Rhymes, or Three Nights' Revelry;* she also published a novel

---

199 *Dictionary of National Biography* [DNB].
200 Edward C. McAleer, *The Sensitive Plant: A Life of Lady Mount Cashell* (Chapel Hill, NC: University of North Carolina Press, 1958).

in 1855, *Love Versus Money*.²⁰¹

Mary Leadbeater, née **Shackleton** (December 1758–27 June 1826), born in Ballitore, County Kildare, kept a fifty-five-volume diary beginning at age eleven; she also corresponded with Edmund Burke, George Crabbe, and Maria Edgeworth. Extracts appeared as *The Leadbeater Papers* in 1862. In 1784, Leadbeater visited London, meeting Crabbe and Sir Joshua Reynolds. She married fellow Quaker William Leadbeater in 1791. In her diary, Leadbeater describes in detail the effects of the 1798 Rebellion in Ballitore: the town was occupied by yeomanry, who ransacked and looted the houses and tortured and flogged the inhabitants; then by rebels, with reprisals; then by soldiers, with new reprisals and killings. Leadbeater published *Extracts and Original Anecdotes for the Improvement of Youth* in 1794. In 1808, she published *Poems*; in 1811 came *Cottage Dialogues among the Irish Peasantry*, with sequels in 1813–1814 and 1822.²⁰²

Sarah Leech (1809–1830), born in Ballylennan, County Donegal, lost her father aged three. At age six, Leech attended school for three months, learning how to read; she learned to write aged twelve, and began to spin yarn. Leech began composing poems in English and Ulster Scots in 1822; they were discovered and sent to the *Londonderry Journal*. She and her mother moved to near Lettergull that year. Leech's only volume, *Poems on Various Subjects*, appeared in 1828, with her at her spinning wheel as frontispiece and a preface describing her poverty. Leech became lame and, worried that she was losing her sight, ceased to supervise children. In her English poems, but not her Ulster Scots ones, Leech voices support for the Protestant Brunswick Clubs and distrust for priests. She is the only known Irish weaver poetess.²⁰³

Alicia Le Fanu (1791–29 January 1867), born in Dublin, moved to Devon and later Bath with her family in the 1790s. She was the niece of the writer Alicia Sheridan Le Fanu. Le Fanu began publishing in 1809, with *The Flowers; or, The Sylphid Queen: A Fairy Tale in Verse*. *Rosara's Chain; or, The Choice of Life: a Poem* followed in 1812; then the novels *Strathallan* in 1816, *Helen Monteagle* in 1818, *Leolin Abbey* in 1819, *Don Juan De Las*

---

201 James McGuire et al., eds. *Dictionary of Irish Biography* (2009).
202 Barbara Hughes, *Between Literature and History* (2010).
203 James McGuire et al., eds. *Dictionary of Irish Biography* (2009).

Sierras in 1823, and *Henry the Fourth of France* in 1826. In 1824, Le Fanu published a story collection and a volume on her grandmother: *Tales of a Tourist* and *Memoirs of the Life and Writings of Mrs Frances Sheridan*. Her death date has been recently determined.[204]

Alicia Sheridan Le Fanu (1753–1817), daughter of Thomas and Frances Chamberlaine Sheridan, was the sister of Richard Brinsley Sheridan and aunt of Alicia Le Fanu. She published the comedy *The Sons of Erin; Or, Modern Sentiment* in 1812.[205]

Elizabeth Emmet Lenox-Conyngham [or **Mrs. George Lenox Conyngham**], née **Holmes** (1800–c. 1889), born in Dublin, was the niece of Robert Emmet and daughter of the writer Mary Anne Holmes. She married George Lenox Conyngham in 1827. In 1833, Lenox-Conyngham published *The Dream, and Other Poems*, including some poems from her mother and translations from the German of Friedrich von Matthisson. Three more volumes followed: *Hella and Other Poems* in 1836, *Horae poeticae: Lyrical and Other Poems* in 1859, and *Eiler and Helvig: a Danish Legend in Verse* in 1863. She also published a *List of Italian Authors on Military Science*.[206]

Jane Susannah Anna Liddiard, née **Wilkinson** (29 April 1773–October 1819), born in County Meath, married Rev. William Liddiard in 1798. He was vicar of Culmullen, County Meath from 1807–1810 and then of Knockmark from 1810–1831. Liddiard published *Poems* in 1809; the couple moved to Bath from 1811–1813, where Liddiard published *The Sgelaighe or A Tale of Old* in 1811, purportedly from an old Irish manuscript. She describes her return to Ireland in *Kenilworth and Farley Castle*, 1813. In 1816, Liddiard published a volume in verse about Waterloo, *Evening after the Battle*. The anonymous volume *Mount Leinster* in 1819, which blames the 1798 Rebellion on the Penal Laws, is often attributed to Liddiard, but could be her husband's work.[207]

Catherine "Kate" Charlotte Maberly, née **Pritty** (1805–7 February 1875), born in Corville, County Tipperary, married William Leader Maberly in 1830. Maberly wrote predominantly historical fiction. Her

---

204 Fitzer, Anna M. "Fashionable Connections: Alicia LeFanu and Writing from the Edge." *Romanticism* (2018), 24.2: pp. 179–190.
205 Alicia Sheridan Le Fanu, *The Sons of Erin; Or, Modern Sentiment: A Comedy in Five Acts* (1812), http://irish-literature.english.dal.ca/texts/sons_of_erin.htm
206 James McGuire et al., eds. *Dictionary of Irish Biography* (2009).
207 Ibid.; *Orlando: Women's Writing in the British Isles*.

novels include *Display; The Locket; or, the History of Mr. Singleton; Emily, or the Countess of Rosendale; The Lady and the Priest. An Historical Romance*, about Henry II of England; *Leonora; Leontine, or the Court of Louis the Fifteenth; The Grand Vizier's Daughter. An Historical Romance of the Fifteenth Century; Melanthe; Or the Days of the Medici*; and *The Love-Match*. Maberly also published three non-fiction volumes—*Fashion and Its Votaries, The Present State of Ireland and Its Remedy*, and *The Art of Conversation with Remarks on Fashion and Address*—and an opera: *A Day Near Turin: An Opera in Two Acts*.[208]

Alicia Catherine Mant (15 July 1788–26 February 1869), born in Southampton, produced several novels and at least one game before marrying Rev. James Russell Phillott in 1835. She died in Ballymoney, County Antrim. Her publications include *Ellen; or, The Young Godmother*, 1812; *Caroline Lismore; or, The Errors of Fashion*, 1815; *The Canary Bird*, 1817; *Montague Newburgh; or, The Mother and Son*, 1817; *Margaret Melville, and The Soldier's Daughter; or, Juvenile Memoirs*, 1818; *The Cottage in the Chalk Pit*, 1822; *The Young Naturalist*, 1824; and the posthumous *Christmas, a Happy Time*, 1932.[209]

Harriet Evans Martin (?–1846) married Captain Robert Hesketh circa 1788, then Richard Martin MP in 1794. Their daughter was the writer Harriet Letitia Martin. In 1802, Martin published her *Remarks* [...], a study of the performances of the actor John Philip Kemble in *Hamlet* and *King Lear*. She also published *Historic Tales* in 1788 and a second novel, *Helen of Glenross*, in 1802.[210]

Harriet Letitia Martin (1801–1891), born in London, was the daughter of Harriet Evans Martin and aunt of Mary Letitia Martin. Martin spent her childhood in London, Galway, and Dublin. After her father's dismissal from the House of Commons for illegal election in 1826, the family followed him into exile in France until his death in 1834. Martin is said to have traveled in Europe and North America. In 1835, she published *Canvassing* in London; *The Changeling, a Tale of the Year '47* followed in 1848. She died in Dublin, where she lived with her sister in

---

208 *Dictionary of National Biography* [DNB].
209 Jan Mark, *The Oxford Book of Children's Stories* (Oxford: Oxford University Press, 1993).
210 Rolf Loeber, Magda Loeber, and Anne M. Burnham, *A Guide to Irish Fiction 1650–1900* (Dublin: Four Courts Press, 2006).

later years.[211]

Mary Letitia Martin (28 August 1815–7 November 1850), born in Connemara, was the niece of Harriet Letitia Martin and granddaughter of Harriet Evans Martin. She was fluent in Irish, English, French, and several other languages. In 1845, Martin published her first novel, *St. Etienne, a Tale of the Vendean War*. She married a cousin in 1847, Colonel Arthur Gonne Bell, who took the name Martin by Royal Licence. Martin's father died that year, and she inherited a large and heavily encumbered Connemara estate. In the next two years, her remaining fortune was destroyed in the famine as she attempted to provide for her tenants. Martin emigrated to Belgium, where she contributed to various periodicals. In 1850, her autobiographical novel *Julia Howard* appeared, and the Martins sailed for America. Martin gave birth on board the ship and died ten days after arrival. Her husband published her novel *Deeds, not Words* in 1857.[212]

Mary McDermott (fl. 1832) was living in Killyleagh, County Down, when her first known volume of poems appeared in 1832: *My Early Dreams*. McDermott also composed music to accompany her verses. A second volume appeared in 1859: *Lays of Love*.[213]

Anna Millikin (19 January 1764-at least 1849) was born at Castlemartyr, County Cork, the family leaving the Society of Friends for the established church. Millikin published early Gothic novels: *Corfe Castle, or, Historic Tracts*, 1793; *Eva, an Old Irish Story*, 1795; *Plantagenet; or Secrets of the House of Anjou: A Tale of the Twelfth Century*, 1802. Subscribers include Lord Boyle and the Freke family. Millikin also published *An Epitome of Ancient History* for children in 1808, and founded and contributed to the *Casket or Hesperian Magazine* (Cork, 1797–1798) with her brother Richard. Millikin was still alive in 1849, when she applied successfully to the Royal Literary Fund.[214]

Sydney, Lady Morgan, née **Owenson** (25 December 1781?–14 April

---

211 Rolf Loeber et al., *A Guide to Irish Fiction* (2006).
212 Helen Maher, *Galway Authors: a Contribution towards a Biographical and Bibliographical Index, with an Essay on the History and Literature in Galway* (Galway: Galway County Libraries, 1976).
213 Ann Ulry Colman, *Dictionary of Nineteenth-Century Irish Women Poets* (Galway: Kenny's Bookshop, 1996).
214 Claire Connolly, *A Cultural History of the Irish Novel, 1790–1829* (Cambridge: Cambridge University Press, 2012); James McGuire et al., eds. *Dictionary of Irish Biography* (2009).

1859), born either in Dublin or on the Irish Sea, lost her mother in 1789 and was sent away to school. In 1798, she became a governess, publishing her first volume of *Poems* in 1801, then a novel, *St. Clair; or, First Love* in 1802; and words set to Irish tunes, Thomas Moore's method: *Twelve Original Hibernian Melodies*, 1805 and *The Lay of the Irish Harp; or, Metrical Fragments*, 1807. And the novels continued: *The Novice of St. Dominick* and *The Wild Irish Girl*, 1806; *Woman; or, Ida of Athens*, 1809; *The Missionary*, 1811. Morgan tried drama in 1807: *First Attempt; or, the Whim of the Moment*, the year she published *Patriotic Sketches of Ireland*. She married Sir Thomas Charles Morgan in 1812. 1814 saw the novel *O'Donnel*, with more national and Irish tales in 1818–1827; 1817 saw *France*, 1821 *Italy*, then memoirs in 1859. Shelley and Byron admired her.[215]

Eibhlín Dubh Ní Chonaill [or **Eileen O'Connell**] (c. 1743–c. 1800), born in Derrynane, County Kerry, was an aunt of Daniel O'Connell. First married at fifteen, her husband died after six months. In 1767, she eloped with Captain Art Ó Laoghaire of the Hungarian Hussars, marrying that year. Abraham Morris, Sherriff of Cork, managed to have Art outlawed via the Penal Laws in 1773; a price was put on his head, and he was shot dead that same year. O'Connell's lament, the *Caoineadh Airt Uí Laoghaire*, has been described as the greatest poem composed in the British Isles in the eighteenth century. It was preserved for decades orally before being written down. A Coroner's Inquest found Morris guilty of murder, but the local magistracy found him not guilty. Green, who fired the fatal shot, was later decorated for valor.[216]

Máire Bhuí Ní Laoghaire (1774–c. 1848), born near Ballingeary, County Cork, married Séamus de Búrca in 1792. By 1847 the couple were unable to pay their landlord's rent increases; two sons were arrested, and they were evicted. Ní Laoghaire died in 1848. She was illiterate in both English and Irish, her songs preserved orally, the best-known being *Cath Chéim an Fhia* [The Battle of Keimaneigh], about a fight between the yeomanry and the Whiteboys. Father Donagh O'Donoghue published a book of her Irish poetry in 1931.[217]

Mary O'Brien (fl. 1785–1790), whose life is known only through her

---

215 Jacqueline E. Belanger, *Critical Receptions: Sydney Owenson, Lady Morgan* (London: Academica Press, 2007).
216 Robert Welch, *Concise Oxford Companion to Irish Literature* (Oxford: Oxford University Press, 2000).
217 James McGuire et al., eds. *Dictionary of Irish Biography* (2009).

writings, was the wife of Patrick O'Brien. She favored an independent Irish parliament and supported Charles James Fox and Richard Brinsley Sheridan, hoping for a regency and the fall of Pitt. Her works include the poems *The Pious Incendiaries*, 1785, and *The Political Monitor; or Regent's Friend*, 1790; the comedy *The Fallen Patriot*, 1794; and *Charles Henley*, published before 1790.[218]

Ellen Fitzsimon, née **Ellen Bridget O'Connell** (1805–27 January 1883), born in Derrynane, County Kerry, was the third child of Daniel and Mary O'Connell. She spoke several languages and was a close political ally of her father. Her poems appeared in *Irish Monthly, The Nation, Duffy's Fireside Magazine*, and the *Dublin Review*. She married Christopher Fitzsimon MP in 1825, and the couple had thirteen children. Fitzsimon published a volume of poems in 1863: *Derrynane Abbey in 1832, and Other Poems*.[219]

Adelaide O'Keeffe (5 November 1776–4 September 1865), born in Dublin, was sent by her father to a French convent aged seven, returning in 1789 to serve as her father's amanuensis for almost forty-five years. O'Keeffe's first published work was the historical novel *Llewellin* in 1799, a form she returned to thereafter, from her *Zenobia, Queen of Palmyra*, 1814, to *The Broken Sword, or, A Soldier's Honour: A Tale of the Allied Armies of 1757* in 1854. O'Keeffe's third novel, *Dudley*, in 1819, reworks Mme de Genlis's *Adèle et Théodore*, while her best-known prose work retells the Pentateuch: *Patriarchal Times; or, The Land of Canaan* in 1811. With Ann and Jane Taylor, O'Keeffe also published *Original Poems for Infant Minds* in 1804–1805, and more verse followed: *Original Poems Calculated to Improve the Mind of Youth* in 1808; *The Old Grand-Papa, and Other Poems* in 1812; and several more volumes of children's verse.[220]

Regina Maria Roche, née **Dalton** (1764–1845), born in Waterford, moved to Dublin with her family as a child. Her first two Gothic novels appeared under her maiden name: *The Vicar of Lansdowne: or, Country Quarters*, 1789, and *The Maid of the Hamlet*, 1793. She married Ambrose Roche in 1794 and moved to England, publishing the much-reissued and

---

218 Gregory A. Schirmer, *Out of What Began: A History of Irish Poetry in English* (Ithaca, NY: Cornell University Press, 1998).
219 Ann Ulry Colman, *Dictionary of Nineteenth-Century Irish Women Poets* (1996).
220 Donelle Ruwe, *British Children›s Poetry of the Romantic Era: Verse, Riddle, and Rhyme* (New York: Palgrave MacMillan, 2014).

translated tales *The Children of the Abbey*, 1796, and *Clermont*, 1798, one of Jane Austen's seven "horrid" novels in *Northanger Abbey*. Roche had financial problems after 1800's *Nocturnal Visit*, not writing again until help came from the Royal Literary Fund. She then wrote eleven more novels, most set in rural Ireland, to less popular acclaim: *Alvandown Vicarage* and *The Discarded Son*, 1807; *The Houses of Osma and Almeria*, 1810; *The Monastery of St. Columb*, 1814; and so forth. Her husband died in 1829 and Roche returned to Waterford.[221]

Elizabeth "Eliza" Ryves (1750–29 April 1797) lost her inheritance at her father's death and traveled to London in 1775 to petition the government. Unsuccessful, she began writing to support herself: *Poems on Several Occasions*, by subscription, 1777; *Ode to the Rev. Mr. Mason*, 1780; *Dialogue in the Elysian Fields, between Caesar and Cato*, 1784; *An Epistle to the Right Honourable Lord John Cavendish, Late Chancellor of the Exchequer*, 1784. Ryves wrote a novel, *The Hermit of Snowden*, 1789; she learned French to translate Rousseau's *The Social Contract*, Raynal's *Letter to the National Assembly*, and other pieces. Her two plays were unstaged: *The Debt of Honour* and *The Prude*, 1777. Her *The Hastiniad*, 1785, is Whig in politics. For some time, she wrote the historical and political sections of *The Annual Register*. She died in poverty.[222]

Mary Anne Sadlier (31 December 1820–5 April 1903), born in Cootehill, County Cavan, emigrated to Sainte-Marthe, Quebec on her father's death in 1844, marrying James Sadlier in 1846. In Canada, Sadlier published eighteen books: five novels, one volume of short stories, a catechism, and nine translations from the French, besides several articles provided free of charge to the *Pilot* and *American Celt*, very likely out of Irish sentiment. Two novels are set in Ireland: *Alice Riordan*, 1851, and *New Lights*, 1853, which deals with the Irish Famine. In total, Sadlier wrote twenty-three novels, translated seventeen books from the French, and wrote short stories and plays. In the early 1860s, the couple moved to New York City, and their home became a hub for the Catholic community there. Thomas D'Arcy McGee was a close friend. In later years, Sadlier lost the copyright to all her earlier works.

---

221 Seamus Deane, Andrew Carpenter, Angela Bourke, and Jonathan Williams, *The Field Day Anthology of Irish Writing*, 5 vols (New York: New York University Press, 1991–2002).
222 *Dictionary of National Biography* [DNB].

She died in Canada.[223]

Catharine Selden (fl. 1797–1817) is unknown outside her seven Gothic novels for London's Minerva Press, for whom she was a bestseller. The first is an imitation of Diderot's *La Religieuse*, 1792. They are: *The English Nun: a Novel*, 1797; *The Count de Santerre*, 1797; *Lindor; or Early Engagements*, 1798; *Serena*, 1800; *The Sailors*, 1800; *German Letters*, published in Cork, 1804; *Villa Nova: or, The Ruined Castle*, 1805; and *Villasantelle, or The Curious Impertinent*, 1817.[224]

Ann Elizabeth "Betsy" Sheridan Le Fanu (1758–4 January 1837) was the sister of Richard Brinsley Sheridan and of Alicia Sheridan Le Fanu. In 1791, she married Captain Henry Le Fanu, their daughter being Alicia Le Fanu, also a writer. Sheridan's works include *The Triumph of Prudence Over Passion*, 1781, published by 'the authoress of *Emmeline*,' and *The India Voyage*, 1804. Her extant journal and letters have been published.[225]

Mary Tighe (9 October 1772–24 March 1810), born in Dublin, married her first cousin Henry Tighe MP at 21, moving to London soon after 1800, where she met Thomas Moore. Her first publication, *Psyche, or the Legend of Love*, in Spenserian stanzas, appeared in fifty copies in 1805; she almost died that year of tuberculosis. In 1811, a posthumous edition of *Psyche* with other poems established Tighe's reputation. John Keats admired her work, and he, Moore, and Felicia Hemans wrote tributes. Tighe also wrote an unpublished novel, *Selena*, held in the National Library of Ireland and now available online. *Mary: a Series of Reflections during 20 Years*, edited by Tighe's brother-in-law William Tighe, appeared posthumously in 1811.[226]

Melesina Trench, née **Chenevix** [formerly **St George**] (22 March 1768–27 May 1827), born in Dublin, was orphaned aged three and raised by her grandfather, the Anglican Bishop of Waterford. He died in 1779 and her other grandfather took her in. She married Colonel Richard St George in 1786; he died in 1790. From 1799–1800, Trench traveled in Europe, meeting Lord Nelson, Antoine de Rivarol, Lucien

---

[223] Ann Ulry Colman, *Dictionary of Nineteenth-Century Irish Women Poets* (1996).
[224] *The Women's Print History Project*.
[225] William R. Le Fanu, ed. *Betsy Sheridan's Journal: Letters from Sheridan's Sister, 1784–1786 and 1788–1790* (Oxford: Oxford University Press, 1986).
[226] Harriet Linkin, ed. *The Collected Poems and Journals of Mary Tighe* (Lexington, KY: The University Press of Kentucky, 2005).

Bonaparte, and John Quincy Adams, as her journal and memoirs record. In 1800, Trench published *Mary, Queen of Scots, an Historical Ballad*; then *Campaspe, an Historical Tale* in 1815, each with other poems, and *Laura's Dream* in 1816. She married Richard Trench in Paris in 1803; he was detained after the end of the Peace of Amiens, and Trench petitioned Napoleon in person. Their son Richard Chenevix Trench published her diaries and letters posthumously: *The Remains of the Late Mrs. Richard Trench*, 1861.[227]

Eliza Dorothea Cobbe, Lady Tuite (c. 1764–1850), born in Dublin, married Sir Henry Tuite, 8th Baronet Tuite in 1784. He died in 1805; Tuite evidently retired to Bath in later years. Her poetical works include *To a Friend* in 1782; the patriotic and reformist *Poems. By Lady Tuite* in 1796; and *Miscellaneous Poetry* in 1841. Tuite also published a children's book: *Edwina and Mary*, 1838. Her first book includes five poems written "as a sylph."[228]

Katherine [or **Catherine**] **Wilmot** (c. 1773–28 March 1824) was born in Drogheda, County Louth, the family settling in Glanmire. Wilmot was friendly with Margaret King, Lady Mount Cashell, and joined the Mount Cashells for their Grand Tour in 1801–1803; her letters record meeting Napoleon Bonaparte, Angelica Kauffman, Talleyrand, Pope Pius VII, and others. Wilmot returned to Ireland via Germany and Denmark after Anglo-French hostilities resumed, leaving for Russia in 1805–1807 to fetch her sister Martha, living near Moscow. Wilmot later moved to France for a drier climate, where she died. Her detailed letters and diaries were published posthumously: *An Irish Peer on the Continent, 1801–03*, 1920; *The Russian Journals of Martha and Catherine Wilmot*, 1934; *More letters from Martha Wilmot; Vienna 1819–29*, 1935; and *The Grand Tours of Katherine Wilmot, France 1801–1803, and Russia 1805–07*, 1992.[229]

---

227 *Dictionary of National Biography* [DNB].
228 Stephen C. Behrendt, ed. *Irish Women Poets of the Romantic Period* (Alexandria, VA: Alexander Street Press, 2007) (https://edesiderata.crl.edu/resources/irish-women-poets-romantic-period).
229 James McGuire et al., eds. *Dictionary of Irish Biography* (2009); *Dictionary of National Biography* [DNB].

11. Writers from the Italian Peninsula

"Italy," said Metternich, "is a geographical concept."[1] Austria was not alone in perpetuating Italy's division: it took a millennium and a half from the fall of Rome before Garibaldi and Cavour managed to reunite the peninsula and its speakers of Italian in 1848–1871. Throughout our period, Italy was occupied and divided. One can, however, trace the beginnings of a national tradition in the writers of the period, and I have in fact identified eleven Italian women writers between 1776–1848—a substantial number, on a par with Sweden or Denmark.

Italy (11 writers)

Eleonora Anna Maria Felice de Fonseca Pimentel

Sonetti di Altidora Esperetusa in morte dell'unico figlio (1779)

II

> Figlio, mio caro figlio, ahi! l'ora è questa,
> Ch'i' soleva amorosa a te girarmi;
> E dolcemente tu solei mirarmi
> A me chinando la vezzosa testa.
>
> Del tuo ristoro indi ansiosa, e presta
> I'ti cibava; e tu parevi alzarmi
> La tenerella mano, e i primi darmi

---

1 *Mémoires [...] laissés par le Prince de Metternich*, ed. Richard de Metternich, 4th edn, 8 vols (Paris: Plon, 1883–1886), VII 415: 6 August 1847.

> Pegni d'amor: memoria al cor funesta!
>
> Or chi lo stame della dolce vita
> Troncò, mio caro figlio, e la mia pace,
> Il mio ben, la mia gioia ha in te fornita?
>
> Oh di medica mano arte fallace!
> Tu fosti, mal accorta in dargli aita,
> Di uccider più, che di sanar capace.[2]

Sonnets of Altidora Esperetusa on the Death of Her Only Son
II

> *Son, my dear son, alas! the time is now*
> *When I used to turn to you lovingly;*
> *And sweetly you used to look at me*
> *Bowing your charming head to me.*
>
> *Then anxious and attentive to your refreshment*
> *I nursed you; and you seemed to lift up*
> *Your tender hand, and to give me*
> *The first tokens of love: memory fatal to the heart!*
>
> *Now who has truncated the spirit of sweet life,*
> *My dear son, and has placed my peace,*
> *My good, my joy in you?*
>
> *Oh of medical hand fallacious art!*
> *You were ill-advised in giving him help,*
> *Capable more of killing than of healing.*

Pimentel's complete poetry is a relatively slim volume: under three hundred pages, and that with a long introduction. But here at least it seems worth preserving. Formally, this is a Petrarchan sonnet in Dante's favored hendecasyllables; it was published in 1779, five years before Charlotte Smith's *Elegiac Sonnets* relaunched the sonnet in English, but the sonnet is after all a resolutely Italian form. As for the topic, it is, like Rückert's and Mahler's

---

2   In Eleonora de Fonseca Pimentel, *Una donna tra le muse. La produzione poetica*, ed. D. De Liso et al. (Naples: Loffredo, 1999), pp. 101–102.

Kindertotenlieder, about the death of a child, being the second of Pimentel's *Sonnets of Altidora Esperetusa on the Death of Her Only Son*, and like Mahler's music, it is quite moving. "Alas!" writes Pimentel, "the time is now / When I used to turn to you lovingly;" one thinks of Mahler's "Wenn das Mütterlein," where as the mother enters, the speaker lifts his head, but she looks only for their lost daughter. Pimentel recalls how her infant son looked up as she nursed him, in an echo of countless Italian Madonna and Child paintings; the child would lift his hand and give her tokens of love. So much for the quatrains. The tercets turn in their *volta* to the doctors, better able to kill than to heal; the tone shifts from desolation to anger, perhaps regrettably, as the poem turns outward from nursing mother and child toward the doctors who failed them both. But the quatrains are splendid, and their virile, slightly Roman language is not without recalling that of Leopardi's *Canti* some fifty years later. Let us thus recall that Pimentel's involvement in the months-long Neapolitan Republic led to her public hanging in 1799.

In short, this is a scene of desolation. Just as Floresta's advice to her daughter occupies a privileged feminine space, that of mother and child, so Pimentel situates her sonnet squarely in the domestic sphere. But in this space, extreme grief is possible; there is meaning to the loss of an only child, there is weight, and in her quatrains, Pimentel has found the key to unlock that weight, in her portrait of the nursing pair. Just as Christ in any painting of Madonna and Child is destined for death, so the nursing son we see in ghostly outline in these quatrains is gone forever. Let these few lines be a fitting memorial to that small child and to irredeemable loss.

Teresa Landucci Bandettini [or **Amarilli Etrusca**] (11 August 1763–6 April 1837), born in Lucca, was orphaned by the age of seven and established as a dancer under the name 'Amarilli Etrusca.' She married Pietro Landucci after 1789, moving from dance to verse improvisation. Several volumes of her improvised verses appeared, in 1799, 1801, 1807, and 1835; but Bandettini preferred to publish her non-improvisational verse, from *Rime varie* in 1786 to *Versi* in 1833, including *Poesie diverse*, 1788; *Saggio di Versi*, 1799; *Poesie varie*, 1805; and *Rime*, 1809. Bandettini also published individual poems, odes, songs, sonnets, rhymes, hymns, elegies, and letters, three tragedies in 1794, 1814, and 1827, and prose fragments, 1820.[3]

---

3   Katharina M. Wilson, ed. *An Encyclopedia of Continental Women Writers* (1991); Natalia Costa-Zalessow, *Scrittrici italiane dal XIII al XX secolo. Testi e critica* (Ravenna: Longo, 1982).

Cristina Trivulzio di Belgiojoso (28 June 1808–5 July 1871), born in Milan, lost her father early and her mother remarried. In 1824, she married Prince Emilio Barbiano di Belgiojoso. Belgiojoso knew Mazzinian revolutionaries through her stepfather and her art teacher, Ernesta Bisi; Austria took note, and she left for Paris. Here, her salon drew Cavour and other revolutionaries. Her circle included Balzac, Musset, Hugo, Heine, Liszt, Tocqueville, Thierry, and Mignet. Belgiojoso took part in Italy's 1848 revolutions and in 1849's Roman Republic, publishing on both and fleeing to Turkey where she lived until her return to Italy in 1856. Between 1850–1858, she published in French on Turkey, exile, and Asia Minor. In 1866, Belgiojoso published *Della condizione delle donne e del loro avvenire* [Of Women's Condition and of Their Future], followed by observations on Italy and on European politics, 1868–1869.[4]

Maria Luisa Cicci (14 September 1760–8 March 1794), born in Pisa, lost her mother aged two. From age eight to age fifteen, her father put her in monasteries; she then returned home to study poetry, philosophy, physics, history, English, and French. Cicci was admitted to the Pisan Academy of Arcadia and the Sienese Accademia degli Intronati in 1786, taking the names 'Emenia Tindarida' and 'La Incognita.' Cicci lived and hosted a salon at her brother's house, refusing all marriage proposals before her early death. Cicci burned most of her writings before she died; however, her brother and friends transcribed some poems from memory and published them posthumously.[5]

Eleonora Anna Maria Felice de Fonseca Pimentel, known as **Eleonora de Fonseca Pimentel** (13 January 1752–20 August 1799), born in Rome, read Latin and Greek and spoke Italian, Portuguese, French, and some English. She moved to Naples with her family as a child. Pimentel married Lieutenant Pasquale Tria de Solis in 1778. Her first son died eight months later, and her husband's violence resulted in two miscarriages. Her father petitioned the court for his daughter's return, which was granted in 1784. Pimentel won several royal poetry competitions over the years, drawing praise from Metastasio and Voltaire; she also translated. In 1799, Pimentel founded, edited, and

---

4 Mariachiara Fugazza, Karoline Rörig, eds. *La prima donna d'Italia. Cristina Trivulzio di Belgiojoso tra politica e giornalismo* (Milano: FrancoAngeli 2010).

5 Béatrice Didier et al., eds. *Dictionnaire universel des créatrices* (2013), https://www.dictionnaire-creatrices.com/

wrote for a republican journal, *Il Monitore Napoletano*. Her leading role in the 1799 Neapolitan Republic led to her public hanging that year, after being denied beheading. Her last words were Virgil's: "Forsan et haec olim meminisse juvabit."[6]

Cornelia Barbaro Gritti [or **Aurisbe Tarsense**] (1719–19 April 1808), born in Venice, in 1736 married Gianantonio Gritti, arrested in 1757 for "depraved conduct" and imprisoned for life in the Fortificazioni di Cattaro. Gritti returned to her father and did not remarry. She trained as a poet with her father and with Carlo Innocenzo Frugoni, hosting a leading salon as 'Aurisbe Tarsense;' Carlo Goldoni dedicated his *La pupilla* to her in 1756. Some of Gritti's poems appeared in Venetian collections of the time, others in Goldoni's *Il raggiratore o Scherzi poetici*, also 1756, while other poems were occasional verses.[7]

Laura Beatrice Mancini, née **Laura Beatrice Oliva** (17 January 1821– 17 July 1869), born in Naples, married the *Risorgimento* figure Pasquale Stanislao Mancini in 1840. Mancini hosted a liberal salon in Naples until the couple moved to Turin after the 1848 Revolution. She published several volumes of poetry: *Ines*, 1845; *Colombo al convento della Rabida*, 1846; *Poesie varie*, 1848; *L'Italia sulla tomba di Vincenzo Gioberti*, 1853; and *Patria ed amore*, 1874. Many poems focused on contemporary political events, especially after 1860.[8]

Angelica Palli (1798–1875), born in Livorno to Greek parents, spoke Albanian, Greek, French, and Italian. She married Giampaolo Bartolomei. Palli wrote tragedies, dramas, short stories, romantic novels and poems, and her salon attracted Ugo Foscolo, Lord Byron, Alessandro Manzoni, Alphonse de Lamartine, and Giuseppe Mazzini. She corresponded with Champollion and translated Shakespeare, Victor Hugo, and Greek poets into Italian; a theme of her work is the Greek struggle for independence. In 1851, she published a feminist essay addressed to young newlyweds, *Discorso di una donna alle giovani maritote del suo paese*.[9]

---

6   Elena Urgnani, *La Vicenda Letteraria e Politica di Eleonora de Fonseca Pimentel* (Naples: La Città del Sole, 1998). The Latin says: "Perhaps even this will be worth remembering one day."
7   Alberto Maria Ghisalberti et al., eds. *Dizionario biografico degli italiani*, 100 vols (Rome: Istituto dell'Enciclopedia Italiana, 1960–2020).
8   Ghisalberti et al., eds. *Dizionario biografico degli Italiani* (1960–2020).
9   Christine Fauré, *Political and Historical Encyclopedia of Women* (London: Routledge, 2004).

Giulietta Pezzi (1812 or 1816–31 December 1878) was born in Milan to the editor of the *Gazzetta di Milano*, then Milan's official newspaper. Her first novel appeared in that organ; as a child, she frequented Milan's literary salons, meeting Carlo Cattaneo, Giuseppe Verdi, Honoré de Balzac, Vincenzo Bellini, Gaetano Donizetti, and Vincenzo Monti. In 1848, she met Giuseppe Mazzini, a decisive meeting. Her works include *Foglia d'autunno*, 1841; the novels *Gli artisti*, 1842, and *Egberto*, 1843; the drama *Carlo Sand*, 1848, dedicated to Mazzini; and the novel *Il nido delle rondini*, 1880, dedicated to her daughter Noemi. Pezzi's letters and personal papers were destroyed in a fire during World War Two.[10]

Diodata Saluzzo Roero (31 July 1774–24 January 1840), born in Turin, was in 1795 one of the first women admitted to the Roman Accademia dell'Arcadia, and later the first to join the Turin Accademia delle Scienze. In 1796, she published her first volume of poetry, *Versi di Diodata Saluzzo*. She married Count Massimiliano Roero di Revello in 1799; he died three years later, and she returned to her family. She published elegies, cantatas, songs, and odes; her *Due tragedie inedite* appeared in 1817, and in 1830, a collection of her short stories, *Novelle di Diodata Saluzzo Roero*. Her work drew praise from Ludovico di Breme, Alessandro Manzoni, Vittorio Alfieri, Vincenzo Monti, and Ugo Foscolo. *Poesie postume di Diodata Saluzzo* appeared in 1843.[11]

Clotilde Tambroni (29 June 1758–2 June 1817), born in Bologna and fluent in French, English, Spanish, and Italian, was admitted to the Roman *Accademia dell'Arcadia* in 1792. She was awarded the Chair of Greek Language at the University of Bologna in 1793, despite having no degree. Tambroni lost her position in 1798 after refusing the oath of loyalty to the new Cisalpine Republic, traveling then to Spain with her father. In 1799, she was given back the Chair of Greek Language and Literature in Bologna, without an oath. Tambroni retired in 1808 before Napoleon abolished the chair. She published occasional verses between 1792–1796—elegies, Pindaric and Sapphic odes—and her letters were published after 1804.[12]

---

10   Raffaello Barbiera, *Il salotto della contessa Maffei e la società milanese 1834–1886* (Milan: Fratelli Treves, 1895).
11   Letizia Panizza and Sharon Wood, *A History of Women's Writing in Italy* (Cambridge, UK: Cambridge University Press, 2000).
12   Rosie Wyles and Edith Hall, eds. *Women Classical Scholars: Unsealing the Fountain from the Renaissance to Jacqueline de Romilly* (Oxford: Oxford University Press, 2016).

Angela Veronese (20 December 1778–8 October 1847), born in Montebelluna, moved as a child to Treviso, then Venice with her family. She published her first volume in 1807 under an Arcadian name she gave herself: *Rime pastorali di Aglaja Anassillide*. Other volumes followed: *Alcune poesie pastorali edite ed inedite*, 1819; *Versi di Aglaja Anassillide*, 1826. In 1836, Veronese published the longer *Eurosia*. She appears in the Venetian anthology *Poesie scelte d'italiani viventi*, 1844, and was republished in 1973.[13]

---

13 Antonia Arslan, Adriana Chemello, and Gilberto Pizzamiglio, *Le stanze ritrovate. Antologia di scrittrici venete dal Quattrocento al Novecento* (Mirano-Venice: Eidos 1991).

12. Writers from the Low Countries

Belgium and the Netherlands were briefly united under the Dutch Crown from 1815 to 1830, a cohabitation whose popularity in Belgium may be gauged by Belgium's 1830 revolution to end it. Prior to 1792, Belgium, or Flanders and Wallonia, was Habsburg territory; then part of the French Republic and Empire; then at last independent after 1830, though divided still between speakers of French and Dutch, and forever at risk of splintering in two. The old oligarchical Dutch Republic, after the failed Patriot Revolution of 1786–1787, became a monarchy at the departure of the French in 1814 and remains so today. Here, the two national traditions are grouped under the heading The Low Countries since our headings respond not only to dynastic realities but also to geographical pressures. I have identified five Belgian women writers for the period 1776–1848 and seven Dutch.

Belgium (5 writers)

Josine Natalie Louise Bovie [or **Marie Sweerts**] (1810–11 January 1870) published a novella, *La Perdrix* [The Partridge], under the pen name 'Marie Sweerts.' She also wrote poetry and short stories and contributed to the *Revue de belgique*. In 1855, Bovie toured Italy with her sister Virginie, with whom she lived outside Brussels. *Contes posthumes*, a 339-page collection of Bovie's stories published within a year of her death, included *La Perdrix* and other stories, with topics ranging from suicide to incest. It was reviewed in the *Athenæum*.[1]

---

1   Eliane Gubin, ed. *Dictionnaire des femmes belges: XIXe et XXe siècles* (Brussels: Éditions Racine, 2006).

Joanna Courtmans, née **Joanna-Desideria Berchmans** (6 September 1811–22 September 1890), born in Oudegem, went to boarding school in Wallonia aged nine, then to Ghent from 1835–1844. In 1836, she married Jan Baptiste Courtmans, a co-founder of the Gentse Maetschappij van Vlaemsche Letteroefening. He taught her Flemish again and put her in touch with the Flemish Movement. Courtmans's first Flemish poem appeared in the *Nederduitsch letterkundig jaarboekje* in 1839; her poems thereafter won several prizes, at least eight volumes appearing before 1856. Jan Baptiste died in 1856, and Courtmans briefly opened a school to support her family. She also switched to prose after *Helena van Leliëndal* in 1855, notably with *Het geschenk van de jager* [The Gift of the Hunter] in 1865, which won a Dutch prize, and *Bertha Baldwin* in 1871. Courtmans published over thirty volumes of prose fiction between 1855–1882.[2]

Maria Doolaeghe (25 October 1803–7 April 1884) was born and died in Diksmuide. Her life is little-known outside her works, which include both prose fiction and poetry: *Nederduitsche letteroefeningen*, 1834; *Madelieven*, 1840; *De avondlamp*, 1850; *Sinte Godelieve, Vlaemsche legende uit de XIde eeuw*, 1862; *Winterbloemen*, 1868; *Najaarsvruchten*, 1869; *Madelieven en avondlamp*, 1876; *Najaarsvruchten en winterbloemen*, 1877; *Nieuwste gedichten*, 1878; and *Jongste dichtbundel*, 1884.[3]

Angélique Pollart d'Herimetz [or **Angélique de Rouillé**] (25 June 1756–4 February 1840), born in Ath and raised in a convent in Brussels, married Louis de Rouillé in 1777. He died in 1814, but the couple had lived mostly apart. Mistress of the manor of Ormeignies, Rouillé left an extensive correspondence; she also kept a diary. Ardent royalist, Rouillé welcomed Waterloo and accepted the Dutch royal presence in Belgium, though grudgingly. She detested liberalism. Rouillé made a last visit to Brussels and Antwerp to try out the railway.[4]

Coralie Adèle van den Cruyce [in marriage **Coralie de Félix de la Motte**] (13 October 1796–27 June 1858), born in Paris, wrote the plays *Les Orphelins de la grande armée*, 1834, and *Les Violettes*, 1836. Her work

---

2   Hugo Notteboom, Rik Van de Rostyne, and Michiel De Bruyne, eds. *Over mevrouw Courtmans' leven en werk* (Mevrouw Courtmans Comité, 1990).

3   Eliane Gubin, ed. *Dictionnaire des femmes belges* (2006); G.J. van Bork and P.J. Verkruijsse, *De Nederlandse en Vlaamse auteurs van middeleeuwen tot heden met inbegrip van de Friese auteurs* (Weesp: De Haan, 1985).

4   Armand Louant, *Une épistolière en Hainaut. Angélique de Rouillé, châtelaine d'Ormeignies (1756–1840)* (Mons: Société des Bibliophiles Belges, 1970).

Bas-bleus defends women's right to express themselves as writers. Van den Cruyce married Eugene-Francois-Auguste Pompée de Félix de la Motte; the couple were leading members of Brussels aristocratic life.[5]

The Netherlands (7 writers)

Anna Louisa Geertruida Bosboom-Toussaint (September 16, 1812-April 14, 1886)

Het huis Lauernesse (1840)

Eerste deel

I: In De Landsvrouw Maria

Nooit heb ik recht begrepen, waarom men lange inleidingen schrijft, om tot een eenvoudig romantisch verhaal te komen. Ik zie niet in, waarom lezer en schrijver met elkander eene lange reeks van volzinnen moeten doorworstelen, eer de een hooren en de ander spreken mag. Ik begin altijd liefst het eerst met hetgeen ik te vertellen heb: wat noodig is te weten en aangenaam, moet het verhaal zelf kunnen leeren; anders ware het beter, dat lezer en schrijver beiden niet begonnen.

Velen hebben zeker veelmalen de zon zien opgaan; allen hebben het ten minste éénmaal gezien, hoe de lichtgevende dochter der hemelen met langzame waardigheid zich verheft uit het Oosten, en de nevelen van zich wegschuift, zooals eene Oostersche bruid den sluier terugslaat van voor haar aangezicht, bij het eerste samenzijn met den echtgenoot. Zij is ook de jonge bruid der aarde: zij is ook de trouwe echtgenoote van den vroolijken dag, die met haar geboren wordt, om met haar weg te sterven: zij is ook ... dan wat is zij niet, dat niet door hare tallooze beschrijvers van haar is gezegt geworden! Wij willen niets toevoegen tot dien overvloed: maar wij vragen alleen, of er onder hen, die het zagen, niet ook sommigen waren, die het voor iets meer hielden dan voor eene schitterende tooneel-decoratie der Natuur, waarbij hunne toejuiching werd afgevraagd; of zij er ook wel eens bij gedacht hebben, hoe dit schouwspel, dat zich sedert den eersten scheppingsmorgen, door duizende jaarkringen heen, wiskundig zeker herhaalt, de dagelijksche waarachtige bekrachtiging is van het Goddelijk magtwoord, gesproken bij de Schepping: "Daar zij licht!" "Waar het zoo licht is in de wereld der Natuur, mogen de menschen het niet donker maken voor elkander, en er is nog een beter licht dan dat van de zon: het licht van de Openbaring."

---

5   Eliane Gubin, ed. *Dictionnaire des femmes belges* (2006).

Dat nieuwe scheppingswoord, gesproken door den mond van een bezield en krachtig man, in den aanvang der 16de eeuw, klonk voort in alle Vorstenstaten van Europa, en zoude ook weêrgalm vinden in het Graafschap van Holland.⁶

The Lauernesse House [First Part]
I: In The Landsvrouw Maria.

I have never really understood why people write long introductions to lead up to a simple romantic story. I do not see why reader and writer have to struggle through a long series of sentences before one can hear and the other may speak. I always prefer to start first with what I have to tell: what is necessary to know and pleasant, the story itself must be able to teach; otherwise it would be better that both reader and writer did not start.

Many have certainly seen the sun rise many times; all have seen at least once how the luminous daughter of the heavens with slow dignity rises from the East and pushes the mists away from her, as an Eastern bride draws back the veil from her face at the first meeting with her husband. She is also the young bride of the earth; she is also the faithful spouse of the cheerful day, that is born with her, to die away with her; she is also ... then what isn't she, that has not been said of her by her countless describers! We do not want to add anything to that abundance; but we only ask, whether among those who saw it there were not some who regarded it as something more than a splendid stage-decoration of Nature, in which their applause was invited; whether they have ever thought about how this spectacle, which has been repeated mathematically with certainty since the first morning of creation, through thousands of annual circles, is a daily true reinforcement of the Divine power spoken at Creation: "Let there be light!" Where it is so light in the world of Nature, people must not make it dark for each other, and there is a better light than that of the sun: the light of Revelation. That new word of creation, spoken through the mouth of an inspired and powerful man at the beginning of the sixteenth century, resounded in all the Principalities of Europe, and would also be echoed in the County of Holland.⁷

There is a certain irony to the opening of this novel, whose first paragraph wonders rather brusquely why people "write long introductions" while its second takes time to do exactly that. We have argued above that long introductions appealed to the Romantic period, for a variety of reasons, as they had not to the period's predecessors, who tended to begin *in medias res*.

---

6 Anna Louisa Geertruida Bosboom-Toussaint, *Het huis Lauernesse* (Rotterdam: D. Bolle, 1906).
7 Translation reviewed by Harry van der Linden.

The opening first-person narrator is here given a good deal of leeway to interact with the reading public: they are tonally charged and opinionated. Such narrators are relatively common in the Romantic period—again, one thinks of Dickens's Pip in 1861's *Great Expectations*—and less common prior to that. Unreliable narrators certainly exist in the eighteenth century—Des Grieux in the abbé Prévost's 1731 *Manon Lescaut*, for instance, or the letter writers of Pierre Choderlos de Laclos's 1782 *Liaisons dangereuses*—but that narration serves a specific moralistic purpose. Perhaps the closest parallel is Laurence Sterne's 1759 *Tristram Shandy*, where Tristram chats from start to finish. Sterne pioneered such conversational interludes, where narration is freed from the demands of plot; the device became frequent in the Romantic period, not least to open a novel.

The second paragraph, with its high tone, seems at first designed primarily to impress, or perhaps to co-opt for this novelistic production some of the prestige the epic took for granted. The sun, "luminous daughter of the heavens," is thus "the young bride of the earth," amid a string of other epithets. Such epithets stretch back to Homer, as Toussaint indicates in her mention of "countless describers;" they depend for their weight on Greco-Roman mythology, which may seem odd, given that the novel is about the Protestant Reformation. But having established her epic *bona fides*, with some added local color—"as an Eastern bride draws back the veil"—Toussaint turns from nature's spectacle to the Bible's "Let there be light," and contrasts sunlight with the "better light" of revelation. Toussaint has covered some ground from her opening epic invocation to the paragraph's conclusion, which focuses on a powerful man whose word of creation "would also be echoed in the County of Holland." Martin Luther nailed his ninety-five theses to the church door at Wittenberg in 1517; this novel opens in Holland in 1521.

As the opening irony suggests, or the text's abrupt passage from epic invocation to Luther, there is a certain lack of patina to this extract, as if it had not had time to age. One feels that Toussaint might have let it sit in the drawer for nine years, as Horace recommended, before publication.[8] Perhaps these ambiguities add a certain frisson to the text; I do not feel they add to its beauty. The problem may perhaps be laid at the feet of Toussaint's desire for epic; she has, in this novel, undertaken a large canvas, the arrival of the Reformation in Holland, and her opening invocation

---

8   "nonumque prematur in annum." *Ars poetica*, l.389, in Horace, *Satires and Epistles* (Oxford: Oxford University Press, 2011), p. 116.

dovetails neatly into that sweeping commission. But just as epic paintings had a certain baggage from which the nineteenth century struggled to free itself—one thinks of the Musée d'Orsay and its academic painters—so epic in literature risked leaving long traces on novels that undertook to cover that terrain. Being simple is sometimes a very difficult thing.

Anna Louisa Geertruida Bosboom-Toussaint (16 September 1812–14 April 1886), born in Alkmaar, published her first romance in 1837: *Almagro*. This was followed by *De Graaf van Devonshire* in 1838; *De Engelschen te Rome* [The English at Rome] in 1840; and *Het Huis Lauernesse* in 1841, a Dutch tale translated into several European languages. From 1840–1850, Toussaint published and conducted research resulting in an 1845–1855 trilogy: *De Graaf van Leycester in Nederland, De Vrouwen uit het Leycestersche Tijdvak* [Women of Leicester's Epoch], and *Gideon Florensz*. In 1851, she married Johannes Bosboom and added his name to hers. Toussaint later abandoned historical romance for contemporary novels: *De Delftsche Wonderdokter*, 1871, and *Majoor Frans*, 1875. Both did less well, though the latter was translated into English. A twenty-five-volume edition of her works appeared in 1885–1888.[9]

Isabelle de Charrière, née **Isabella Agneta Elisabeth van Tuyll van Serooskerken** [or **Belle van Zuylen**] (20 October 1740–27 December 1805), born in the château of Zuylen, near Utrecht, died in the canton of Neuchâtel, which then belonged to Prussia. Belle van Zuylen spoke French, English, German, Italian, and Latin, and studied mathematics and physics. She first published aged twenty-two: *Le Noble*, a satirical sketch. In 1771, she married Charles-Emmanuel de Charrière de Penthaz, and from 1782, began writing letters, pamphlets, tales, and novels, including the *Lettres neuchâteloises*, 1784; *Lettres de Mistriss Henley publiées par son amie*, 1784; *Lettres écrites de Lausanne*, 1785; *Caliste*, 1787; and *Trois femmes*, 1796, along with plays, political tracts, and operas. Her extensive correspondence includes James Boswell and Benjamin Constant. She also composed music for piano, harpsichord, and string instruments.[10]

---

9 Lia Van Gemert, *Women's Writing from the Low Countries 1200–1875: A Bilingual Anthology* (Amsterdam: Amsterdam University Press, 2011).
10 C.P. Courtney, *Isabelle de Charrière (Belle de Zuylen). A Biography* (Oxford: Voltaire Foundation, 1993).

Agatha ("Aagje") Deken (1741–14 November 1804), born in Nieuwer-Amstel, lost her parents in 1745 and was placed in an Amsterdam orphanage, remaining there until 1767. She then served in several families before starting a tea and coffee business. In 1775, Deken published *Stichtelijke gedichten*, a poetry volume written with her friend Maria Bosch, who died in 1773. In 1776, Deken began corresponding with Betje Wolff, then well-known. After Betje's husband died, they lived together, publishing their joint *Brieven* [Letters] in 1777, then novels, including the *Historie van den heer Willem Leevend*, 1784, and *Sara Burgerhart*, 1787. When the Patriot faction was defeated, the two moved to Trévoux in Burgundy in 1788; *Wandelingen door Bourgogne* [Wanderings in Burgundy] appeared in 1789. The two returned to the Netherlands in 1797, living in The Hague. They died nine days apart.[11]

Maria Aletta Hulshoff [or **Mietje**] (30 July 1781–10 February 1846), born in Amsterdam, held her Mennonite father's Patriotic and anti-Orangist views. She was taken into custody after her first democratic pamphlet in 1804, but released when the authorities could not prove she was the author. Her second pamphlet, *Oproeping aan het Bataafse volk* [An Appeal to the Batavian People], 1806, she wrote under her own name, predicting that Louis Bonaparte would be made King of Holland. The authorities destroyed all but five copies. Hulshoff's family smuggled her to Germany, but she returned to stand trial, mounted her own defense, and was given two years in prison. Exiting, she published a new pamphlet attacking conscription. Charged again, she fled to Amsterdam, then London and New York City, 1811–1820, where she published the *Peace-Republicans' Manual* in 1817. She returned to the Netherlands in 1820.[12]

Marguérite Emilie Luzac (30 November 1748–28 November 1788), born in Leiden, married Wybo Fijnje in 1775. Wybo was a Patriot and publisher of *Hollandsche Historische Courant* in Delft; after the British and Prussians crushed the Patriot Revolution in 1787, the couple fled to Antwerp, Brussels, then Watten in French Flanders, where Luzac died in 1788. Her letters were published in 2003 as *Myne beslommerde Boedel*.[13]

---

11 P.J. Buijnsters, *Wolff & Deken. Een biografie* (Leiden: Nijhoff, 1984).
12 Geertje Wiersma, *Mietje Hulshoff of de aanslag op Napoleon* (Amsterdam: Bert Bakker, 2003).
13 Emilie Fijnje-Luzac, *Myne beslommerde Boedel: brieven in ballingschap 1787–1788*, ed. Jacques J.M. Baartmans (Nijmegen: Vantilt, 2003).

Maria Petronella Woesthoven (25 October 1760–26 January 1830), born in Dantumawoude, was a member of the academy Amsteldamse Dicht- en Letteroefenend Genootschap, 1786, and the Kunst Wordt door Arbeid Verkregen, joining the executive committee in 1793–1794. Her poem *Amsteldamse*, 1787, earned a gold medal, and two other poems earned silver medals: *Kunstliefde Spaart Geen Vlijt*, 1788, and *De invloed van een vast geloof aan de voorzienigheid*, 1789. Woesthoven married Samuel Elter in 1785; they divorced in 1803, Samuel alleging she had slept with other men. She was found guilty but awarded custody of their son.[14]

Elizabeth "Betje" Wolff-Bekker (24 July 1738–5 November 1804), born in Vlissingen, married Adriaan Wolff in 1759; he was thirty years her senior. In 1763, Wolff published her collection *Bespiegelingen over het genoegen* [Reflections on Pleasure]. After her husband's death in 1777, she lived with Aagje Deken, the two dying nine days apart. They published together and it is difficult to determine the part of each: *Brieven* [Letters] in 1777, then novels, including the *Historie van den heer Willem Leevend*, 1784, and *Sara Burgerhart*, 1787. The Patriots were defeated in 1787 and the two fled to Burgundy, publishing *Wandelingen door Bourgogne* [Wanderings in Burgundy] in 1789 and translating the Swiss abolitionist Benjamin Sigismond Frossard in 1790. They returned to the Netherlands in 1797.[15]

---

14 *Digitaal Vrouwenlexicon van Nederland* (https://resources.huygens.knaw.nl/vrouwenlexicon).
15 P.J. Buijnsters, *Wolff & Deken* (1984).

13. Writers from the Swiss Confederation

Swiss independence from Austria, and with it the Swiss national tradition, begins early, in 1291. The French Revolution brought restructuring and regime change, and the tiny republic of Geneva joined the confederation at Napoleon's fall in 1814; but the Swiss story is one of continuity, not fragmentation. I have identified four Swiss women writers for the period 1776–1848, writing in French and German.

Switzerland (4 writers)

Marianne Ehrmann, née **Marianne Brentano-Corti** [or **Marianne Ehrmann-Brentano** or **Madame Sternheim**] (25 November 1755–14 August 1795), born in Rapperswil, lost her mother in 1770, her father in 1775, finding work as a governess. Around 1777, Ehrmann married, divorcing in 1779. She became insane and was confined for months. Around 1782, she went to Vienna, touring Europe for some years as an actress. In 1784, she published the tract *Philosophie eines Weibes* [Philosophy of a Woman]. She married Theophil Friedrich Ehrmann in 1785; in 1786, she published a play, *Leichtsinn und gutes Herz* [Frivolity and a Good Heart]. In Stuttgart after 1788, Ehrmann co-edited her husband's journal *Der Beobachter* and published the epistolary novel *Amalie*. She also wrote for the *Frauen-Zeitung* after 1787, and from 1790–1792 published *Amaliens Erholungsstunden*, then *Die Einsiedlerinn aus den Alpen* from 1792–1795.[1]

---

1   Annette Zunzer, *Marianne Ehrmann: Die Einsiedlerinn aus den Alpen* (Bern: Paul Haupt Verlag, 2002).

Valérie de Gasparin, née **Catherine-Valérie Boissier** (13 September 1813–16 June 1894), born in Geneva, traveled for two years in France and Italy before her first publication: *Nouvelles*, 1833. More than thirty other publications followed: poetry, novels, memoirs, essays. After her mother's death in 1836, Gasparin embraced the Protestant Réveil, and religion remained very important to her. She married Count Agénor de Gasparin in 1837, moving to Paris where he represented Bastia, Corsica from 1842. In 1847–1848, the couple traveled via Greece to Egypt and Jerusalem, as Gasparin recorded. Gasparin published *Des corporations monastiques au sein du protestantisme* in 1855, condemning the institution of deaconesses. In 1859, she founded the first lay school for caregivers, the *École de La Source*. She continued publishing after her husband's death in 1871, including translations from the English.[2]

Isabelle de Montolieu (7 May 1751–29 December 1832) published her first novel, *Caroline de Lichtfield*, in 1790; it was reprinted until the mid-nineteenth century. She published over 100 volumes of translations, including the first (unauthorized) French versions of two Jane Austen novels, *Sense and Sensibility* and *Persuasion*. Montolieu also produced the still-standard *Le Robinson suisse* [The Swiss Family Robinson] from Johann David Wyss's German original.[3]

Suzanne Necker, née Curchod (2 June 1737–6 May 1794), daughter of a pastor in the Pays de Vaud, married Jacques Necker in 1764, future finance minister of Louis XVI. Their daughter was Germaine de Staël. As Jacques became a minister, Necker founded their salon, arguably the last great salon of the Old Regime, welcoming Marmontel, La Harpe, Buffon, Grimm, Raynal, Bernardin de Saint-Pierre; also, Diderot, d'Alembert, Geoffrin, and du Deffand. Necker barely published during her life, perhaps at her husband's urging, but at her death, he brought out her notes and reflections in five volumes. She is known primarily for her *Mémoire sur l'établissement des hospices*, 1786, and for her *Réflexions sur le divorce*, 1794, written during her daughter's somewhat high-profile affair with Narbonne.[4]

---

2 Denise Francillon, ed. *Valérie de Gasparin, une conservatrice révolutionnaire. Cinq regards sur une vie* (Le Mont-sur-Lausanne: Éditions Ouvertures, 1994).
3 Béatrice Didier et al., eds. *Dictionnaire universel des créatrices* (2013).
4 Sonja Boon. *The Life of Madame Necker: Sin, Redemption and the Parisian Salon* (London: Routledge, 2011).

Conclusion:
La Condition féminine

This book chronicles seven decades of women picking up a pen and writing, across Europe and the European diaspora, from 1776 to 1848. Its period is, for want of a better phrase, the Romantic age, an age bracketed by revolutions in Europe and in the Americas. Indeed, it is a period of multiple revolutions, in government, in the arts, in science and technology, in the culture of the book. And women necessarily played a key role in this story, from the loom to the guillotine.

Our aim has been to reclaim a comprehensive corpus of women writers in this period—without exception, across fifty-one nations—and then to determine whether any universal principles or priorities can be identified within it. The method seems appropriate. The answer may be, as Zhou Enlai once said of the French Revolution's place in history, that it is too early to tell; but the question seems worth asking.[1]

Looking back over our 650-author corpus, certain patterns or priorities do begin to emerge. Religion, for instance, from hymn writing to missionary work. Women preachers—female sermons—are naturally in short supply (though there is Lucretia Mott), and it bears repeating that nuns' texts, notably in Latin America, were routinely mediated by male hands. Social justice appears, from prison reform to charity work to abolition. Mediation of others' work: translation in particular, but also dictation, as an amanuensis to a man. Reflections on the private sphere, in letters, diaries, memoirs, cookbooks. Children's literature and the education of the young. Admonitions to other women. The broad outlines of these priorities reflect that age-old topos, women's work. That is not new to the period, though specific content—for instance,

---

1   Zhou Enlai famously said this to Henry Kissinger in 1972.

the abolitionist cause—may well be. These outlines also go some way to separating the female written corpus from the male for the years 1776–1848. Other distinctions have been posited; let us begin with these. And then, moving beyond traditional women's work, we come—aptly enough, for this is an age of revolution—to transgression and revolt. One thinks of Gothic literature, for instance, that international phenomenon, with its contested epistemologies and its lurid plots. One thinks of women who were hanged, like Eleonora de Pimentel, or guillotined, like Olympe de Gouges. Of those who eloped or divorced—those assertions of female autonomy. But beyond these, one thinks of the journalists, the editors, the explorers, the inventors, the scientists, the philosophers, the military strategists—all those trespassers on the public sphere—and with them, one perhaps sees something new in the female condition, something to distinguish this age from those that preceded it.

It seems obvious that the age's men and women were conditioned equally, though perhaps differently, by the society in which they lived. This is true of the people in our book's cover painting, for instance, where Branwell Brontë has first painted himself in, then painted himself out of the group of his three sisters—a painting where success and failure, as often in Romantic art, are not so very far apart. It is true of Victor Hugo and Juliette Drouet, where Romanticism for Victor meant keeping Drouet, his mistress, shut up in her Paris apartment for fifty years, while for her it meant abandoning the stage to wait a half-century for Victor's visits. During his long exile on Guernsey, she lodged in a cottage within eyesight of the Hugo family home; he did not attend her funeral. And one might argue that certain defining aspects of Romanticism, like openness to passion or empathy for the oppressed, spoke directly to many women in the sphere the age accorded them. Elisavet Moutzan-Martinengou thus makes a remarkable witness to the Greek war of independence, from the home that she, unlike her tutor, is unable to leave. It is curious, though telling, to see how the Romantic movement later came to be gendered as male, with women cast, like Drouet, in subordinate roles. To this day, busts of Romantic men dot European cities, while busts of women, mostly nude, stand for abstract nouns like liberty or for goddesses or muses; and Drouet's work to this day is filed under H for Hugo in the Bibliothèque nationale de France. But that viewpoint is clearly a fiction, in a world where men and women equally are actors and have free will. Much work has been done to replace this patriarchal fiction with the reality of the Romantic field; may this book bring its own small contribution to that undertaking. One might indeed argue that Romanticism was essentially female in its bones, and that it is time for that truth to be rediscovered. The case can at least be made, as we have long seen it made to the contrary.

It remains true that women in the Romantic age, as today, faced constraints that men did not. Not only was their scope of action limited— Germaine de Staël as a man might have been prime minister of the France she loved, as her father was before her—but the field of literary creation was similarly barricaded against them. Thus, while career philosophers and scientists appear in this book, they are thin on the ground. One thinks of Gulliver in Lilliput, bound by a thousand threads, as one surveys this volume's impressive body of work. What, one wonders, might women have done on a playing field that was level? We can but speculate. But the achievements listed here—for every text listed is an achievement—are not promising, or relative, or partial. They are absolute. One indeed considers the gender that shapes every word here written, as science requires of us; but every work here listed stands autonomous, complete, and worthy of consideration on its own terms, like the author behind it.

And so, we return to the question of empathy, that Romantic theme. If sympathy travels downward, *de haut en bas*, empathy sees all of us as equal: "Am I not a man and a brother?" said Wedgwood's famous abolitionist medallion. Romantic creators, in their revolutionary context, felt empathy for madmen and chimney sweeps alike, for Kit Smart's cat Jeoffry or John Clare's badger, for every category of the voiceless and the oppressed.[2] Empathy recurs throughout this extensive corpus, and empathy is proper in considering it. It is not the critic's task to investigate whether a chair might make a good table; it is instead their task to recognize the chair in its own terms, as a specific chair, and determine what unique value lies in that. Perhaps the meaning of this book's title, *Women Writers in the Romantic Age*, is to be found in that perennial insight.

---

2   Madmen: Johann Wolfgang von Goethe, *Torquato Tasso* (1790); also, William Blake, "The Chimney Sweeper," published in two parts in *Songs of Innocence* (1789) and *Songs of Experience* (1794); Christopher Smart, "For I will consider my Cat Jeoffry." in *Jubilate Agno* (1759–1763); John Clare, "The Badger" (1835–1837).

Finally, this is, fundamentally, a women's written corpus; indeed, it is a complete corpus of all women's writing thus far identified within a field spanning seven decades and stretching from Lima to St Petersburg. It is delimited in space and time by the frontiers of the Romantic phenomenon—roughly speaking, Europe and the European diaspora between 1776 and 1848—and it shares with that Romantic phenomenon a variety of defining traits. Beyond these boundaries, we leave the field of Romantic creation, and women's writing may come to have different characteristics. But that would be the subject of another book.

Selected Bibliography

General

Adams, Henry Gardiner, ed. *A Cyclopædia of Female Biography: Consisting of Sketches of All Women Who Have Been Distinguished by Great Talents, Strength of Character, Piety, Benevolence, or Moral Virtue of Any Kind* (London: Groombridge & Sons, 1857)

Allibone, Samuel Austin. *A Critical Dictionary of English Literature, and British and American Authors, Living and Deceased, from the Earliest Accounts to the Middle of the Nineteenth Century* [...], 3 vols (Philadelphia, PA: J.B. Lippincott & co, 1859–1871)

Australian Dictionary of Biography, 19 vols (Canberra: Australian National University, 1966–2021)

Beeton, Samuel Orchart. *Beeton's Modern European Celebrities: A Biography of Continental Men and Women of Note* (London: Ward, Locke and Tyler, 1874)

Blain, Virginia, Patricia Clements, and Isobel Grundy, eds. *The Feminist Companion to Literature in English* (New Haven, CT: Yale University Press, 1990)

Bridenthal, Renate, Susan Mosher Stuard, and Merry E. Wiesner-Hanks, eds. *Becoming Visible: Women in European History*, 3rd edition (Boston, MA: Houghton Mifflin Company, 1998)

Buck, Claire, ed. *Bloomsbury Guide to Women's Literature* (London: Bloomsbury Publishing, 1992)

Burwick, Frederick, ed. *Encyclopedia of Romantic Literature* (Oxford: Blackwell, 2012)

Chisholm, Hugh, ed. *Encyclopædia Britannica*, 11th edition, 29 vols (Cambridge: Cambridge University Press, 1910–1911)

Claeys, Gregory, ed. *Encyclopedia of Nineteenth-Century Thought* (London: Routledge, 2005)

Clery, Emma. *The Rise of Supernatural Fiction, 1762–1800* (Cambridge: Cambridge University Press, 1995)

Cohen, Aaron I. *International Encyclopedia of Women Composers*, 2nd edition, 2 vols (New York: Books & Music, 1987)

Commire, Anne, and Deborah Klezmer, eds. *Women in World History: A Biographical Encyclopedia*, 17 vols (Waterford, CT: Yorkin Publications, 1999–2002)

Commire, Anne, and Deborah Klezmer, eds. *Dictionary of Women Worldwide: 25,000 Women Through the Ages*, 3 vols (Farmington Hills, MI: Thomson Gale, 2007)

Cook, Elizabeth. *Epistolary Bodies: Gender and Genre in the Eighteenth-Century Republic of Letters* (Stanford, CA: Stanford University Press, 1996)

Cypess, Rebecca. *Women and Musical Salons in the Enlightenment* (Chicago, IL: University of Chicago Press, 2022)

DeLamotte, Eugenia C. *Perils of the Night: A Feminist Study of Nineteenth-Century Gothic* (Oxford: Oxford University Press, 1990)

DeLamotte, Eugenia C., Natania Meeker, and Jean F. O'Barr, eds. *Women Imagine Change: A Global Anthology of Women's Resistance from 600 B.C.E. to Present* (London: Routledge, 1997)

Didier, Béatrice, Antoinette Fouque, and Mireille Calle-Gruber, eds. *Dictionnaire universel des créatrices*, 3 vols (Paris: Éditions des femmes, 2013)

Drake, Kimberly, ed. *The Slave Narrative* (Ipswich, MA: Salem Press, 2014)

Esterhammer, Angela, ed. *Romantic Poetry* (Amsterdam and Philadelphia: John Benjamins Publishing, 2002)

Fauré, Christine, ed., tr. Richard Dubois. *Political and Historical Encyclopedia of Women* (London: Routledge, 2002)

Gardner, Catherine Villanueva. *The A to Z of Feminist Philosophy* (Lanham, MD: Scarecrow Press, 2009)

Gillispie, Charles Coulston, ed. *Dictionary of Scientific Biography*, 18 vols (New York: Charles Scribner's Sons, 1970–1990)

Gilman, D. C., H. T. Peck, and F. M. Colby, eds. *New International Encyclopedia*, 17 vols (New York: Dodd, Mead, 1902–1904)

Green, Katherine Sobba. *The Courtship Novel, 1740–1820: A Feminized Genre* (Lexington, KY: University Press of Kentucky, 1991)

Hale, Sarah Josepha. *Woman's Record, or Sketches of All Distinguished Women from the Creation to A.D. 1854: Arranged in Four Eras: with Selections from Female Writers of Every Age*, 2nd edition (New York: Harper & Bros, 1855)

Herbermann, Charles, ed. *The Catholic Encyclopedia [...]*, 16 vols (New York: Encyclopedia Press, 1913–1914)

Hughes, William, David Punter, and Andrew Smith. *The Encyclopedia of the Gothic*, 2 vols (Chichester: Wiley-Blackwell, 2013)

Jeffares, Neil. *Dictionary of Pastellists Before 1800* (London: Unicorn Press, 2006)

Kass-Simon, Gabriele, Patricia Farnes, and Deborah Nash. *Women of Science: Righting the Record* (Bloomington, IN: Indiana University Press, 1993)

Kord, Susanne. *Women Peasant Poets in Eighteenth-Century England, Scotland, and Germany: Milkmaids on Parnassus* (London: Camden House, 2003)

Kramarae, Cheris, and Dale Spender. *Routledge International Encyclopedia of Women: Global Women's Issues and Knowledge*, 4 vols (London: Routledge, 2000)

Kramer, Jack. *Women of Flowers: A Tribute to Victorian Women Illustrators* (New York: Stewart, Tabori & Chang, 1996)

Lanser, Susan Sniader. *Fictions of Authority. Women Writers and Narrative Voice* (Ithaca, NY: Cornell University Press, 1992)

Larsen, Kristine. *The Women Who Popularized Geology in the 19th Century* (New York: Springer, 2017)

Lehner, Ulrich L., ed. *Women, Enlightenment and Catholicism: A Transnational Biographical History* (London: Routledge, 2018)

Letzter, Jacqueline, and Robert Adelson. *Women Writing Opera: Creativity and Controversy in the Age of the French Revolution* (Berkeley, CA: University of California Press, 2001)

Murray, Christopher John, ed . *Encyclopedia of the Romantic Era, 1760–1850*, 2 vols (London: Fitzroy Dearborn, 2004)

Pendergast, Sara, and Tom Pendergast, eds. *Reference Guide to World Literature*, 3rd edition, 2 vols (Detroit, MI: St. James Press, 2003)

Peterson, Linda H., ed. *The Cambridge Companion to Victorian Women's Writing* (Cambridge: Cambridge University Press, 2015)

Ogilvie, Marilyn, and Joy Dorothy Harvey, eds. *The Biographical Dictionary of Women in Science […]*, 2 vols (London: Routledge, 2000)

Olsen, Kirstin. *Chronology of Women's History* (Westport, CT: Greenwood Press, 1994)

Peterson, Linda H., ed. *The Cambridge Companion to Victorian Women's Writing* (Cambridge: Cambridge University Press, 2015)

Pitman, Emma Raymond. *Lady Hymn Writers* (London: T. Nelson and sons, 1892)

Reid, Martine, ed. *Femmes et littérature, une histoire culturelle*, 2 vols (Paris: Gallimard, 2020)

Robinson, Jane. *Wayward Women: A Guide to Women Travellers* (Oxford: Oxford University Press, 1990)

Sadie, Julie Anne, and Rhian Samuel, eds. *The Norton/Grove Dictionary of Women Composers* (New York: W.W. Norton & Co., 1994)

Sadie, Stanley, and John Tyrrell, eds. *The New Grove Dictionary of Music and Musicians*, 2nd edition, 29 vols (London: Macmillan Publishers, 2001)

Sage, Lorna, Germaine Greer, and Elaine Showalter, eds. *The Cambridge Guide to Women's Writing in English* (Cambridge: Cambridge University Press, 1999)

Singer, Isidore, ed. *The Jewish Encyclopedia* [...], 12 vols (New York: Funk & Wagnalls, 1901–1906)

Smith, Bonnie, ed. *The Oxford Encyclopedia of Women in World History*, 4 vols (Oxford: Oxford University Press, 2008)

Smith, Hilda L., and Berenice A. Carroll, eds. *Women's Political and Social Thought: An Anthology* (Bloomington, IN: Indiana University Press, 2000),

societyforthestudyofwomenphilosophers.org

Sol, Antoinette Marie. *Textual Promiscuities: Eighteenth-Century Critical Rewriting* (Bucknell, PA: Bucknell University Press, 2002)

Stein, Gordon. *Encyclopedia of Hoaxes* (Detroit, MI: Gale Research, 1993)

Summers, Montague. *A Gothic Bibliography* (London: The Fortune Press, 1941)

Todd, Janet M., ed. *A Dictionary of British and American Women Writers, 1660–1800* (Totowa, NJ: Rowman & Allanheld, 1985)

Uglow, Jennifer S; Frances Hinton, and Maggy Hendry, eds. *The Northeastern Dictionary of Women's Biography* (Boston, MA: Northeastern University Press, 1999)

Vincent, Patrick H. *The Romantic Poetess: European Culture, Politics, and Gender, 1820–1840* (Durham, NH: University of New Hampshire Press, 2004)

Warhol-Down, Robyn R., et al, eds. *WOMEN'S WORLDS: The McGraw-Hill Anthology of Women's Writing in English Across the Globe* (New York: McGraw-Hill, 2007)

Wettlaufer, Alexandra K. *Portraits of the Artist as a Young Woman: Painting and the Novel in France and Britain 1800–1860* (Columbus, OH: Ohio State University Press, 2011)

Wiles, Rosie, and Edith Hall, eds. *Women Classical Scholars: Unsealing the Fountain from the Renaissance to Jacqueline de Romilly* (Oxford: Oxford University Press, 2016)

Wilson, Katharina M., ed. *An Encyclopedia of Continental Women Writers*, 2 vols (New York and London: Garland Publishing, 1991)

Wilson, Katharina M., Paul Schlueter, and June Schlueter, eds. *Women Writers of Great Britain and Europe: An Encyclopedia* (London: Garland, 1997)

Wood, James, ed . *The Nuttall Encyclopædia* [...] (London: Frederick Warne, 1900)

Writers from British North America

Canada

Brown, George Williams. *Dictionary of Canadian Biography*, 15 vols (Toronto: University of Toronto/Université Laval, 1966–2005)

Buss, Helen M., and Marlene Kadar, eds. *Working in Women's Archives: Researching Women's Private Literature and Archival Documents* (Waterloo, Ontario: Wilfrid Laurier University Press, 2001)

Benson, Eugene, and William Toye, eds. *Oxford Companion to Canadian Literature*, 2nd edition (Oxford: Oxford University Press, 1997)

Canada's Early Women Writers https://cwrc.ca/project/canadas-early-women-writers

Canadian Women Artists History Initiative https://www.concordia.ca/finearts/art-history/research/cwahi.html

Gerson, Carole. *Canadian Women in Print, 1750–1918* (Waterloo, Ontario: Wilfrid Laurier University Press, 2010)

McMullen, Lorraine, and Sandra Campbell, eds. *Pioneering Women: Short Stories by Canadian Women: Beginnings to 1880* (Ottawa: University of Ottawa Press, 1993)

Morgan, Henry James, ed. *Types of Canadian Women and of Women who are or have been Connected with Canada* (Toronto: William Briggs, 1903)

New, William, ed. *Encyclopedia of Literature in Canada* (Toronto: University of Toronto Press, 2002)

Rose, George Maclean. *A Cyclopædia of Canadian Biography: Being Chiefly Men of the Time [...]*, 2 vols (Toronto: Rose Publishing Company, 1886)

The United States

American National Biography https://www.anb.org/

Appleby, Joyce, Eileen Cheng, and Joanne Goodwin. *Encyclopedia of Women in American History*, 3 vols (Armonk, NY: Sharpe Reference, 2002)

Atwater, Edward C. *Women Medical Doctors in the United States before the Civil War: A Biographical Dictionary* (Rochester, NY: University of Rochester Press, 2016)

Balkun, Mary McAleer, and Susan C. Imbarrato, eds. *Women's Narratives of the Early Americas and the Formation of Empire* (London: Palgrave Macmillan, 2016)

Barker-Benfield, G. J., and Catherine Clinton, eds. *Portraits of American Women: From Settlement to the Present* (New York: St Martin's Press, 1991)

Baym, Nina. *Woman's Fiction: A Guide to Novels by and about Women in America, 1820–70* (Champaign, IL: University of Illinois Press, 1993)

Baym, Nina, and Robert S. Levine, eds. *The Norton Anthology of American Literature*, 8th edition, 5 vols (New York: W.W Norton & Co., Inc., 2012)

Benbow-Pfalzgraf, Taryn, ed. *American Women Writers* [...], 2nd edition (Detroit: St. James Press, 2000)

Berkin, Carol. *First Generations: Women in Colonial America* (New York: Hill and Wang, 1996)

Berkin, Carol. *Revolutionary Mothers: Women in the Struggle for America's Independence* (New York: Knopf, 2005)

Bradshaw, Sidney Ernest. *On Southern Poetry Prior to 1860* [...] (Richmond, VA: B.F. Johnson publishing Company, 1900)

Brekus, Catherine A., ed. *The Religious History of American Women: Reimagining the Past* (Chapel Hill, NC: University of North Carolina Press, 2007)

Burt, Daniel S. *The Chronology of American Literature* (Boston, MA: Houghton Mifflin Company, 2004)

Cleveland, Charles Dexter. *A Compendium of American Literature, Chronologically Arranged, with Biographical Sketches of the Authors* [...] (Philadelphia, PA: Biddle, 1858)

Coggeshall, William Turner. *The Poets and Poetry of the West: With Biographical and Critical Notices* (Columbus, OH: Follett, Foster & Co., 1860)

Cullen-DuPont, Kathryn. *Encyclopedia of Women's History in America*, 2nd edition (New York: Facts on File, 2000)

Culley, Margo, ed. *A Day at a Time: The Diary Literature of American Women from 1764 to the Present* (New York: Feminist Press at CUNY, 1985)

Davidson, Cathy N. *Revolution and the Word: The Rise of the Novel in America* (Oxford: Oxford University Press, 1986)

Davidson, Cathy N., Linda Wagner-Martin, et al., eds. *The Oxford Companion to Women's Writing in the United States* (Oxford: Oxford University Press, 1995)

Derby, George, and James Terry White, eds. *The National Cyclopædia of American Biography: Being the History of the United States as Illustrated in the Lives of the Founders, Builders, and Defenders of the Republic* [...], 63 vols (New York: J. T. White, 1891–1984)

Diamant, Lincoln, ed. *Revolutionary Women in the War for American Independence: a One-Volume Revised Edition of Elizabeth Ellet's 1848 Landmark Series* (Westport, CT: Praeger Publishers, 1998)

Drake, Francis Samuel. *Dictionary of American Biography, Including Men of the Time* [...] (Boston, MA: James R. Osgood & Co., 1872)

Ehrlich, Eugene, and Gorton Carruth. *The Oxford Illustrated Literary Guide to the United States* (Oxford: Oxford University Press, 1982)

Eisenmann, Linda, ed. *Historical Dictionary of Women's Education in the United States* (Westport, CT: Greenwood Press, 1998)

Engle, Paul. *Women in the American Revolution* (Chicago, IL: Follett, 1976)

Evans, Elizabeth. *Weathering the Storm; Women of the American Revolution* (New York: Charles Scribner's Sons, 1975)

Fox-Genovese, Elizabeth, and Eugene D. Genovese. *The Mind of the Master Class: History and Faith in the Southern Slaveholders' Worldview* (Cambridge, UK: Cambridge University Press, 2005)

Gardner, Jared. *Master Plots: Race and the Founding of an American Literature, 1787–1845* (Baltimore, MD: Johns Hopkins University Press, 1998)

Gates, Jr., Henry Louis. *The Signifying Monkey: A Theory of African-American Literary Criticism.* New York: Oxford University Press, 1989)

Gates, Jr., Henry Louis, Valerie A. Smith, et al, eds. *The Norton Anthology of African American Literature*, 3rd edition, 2 vols (New York: W. W. Norton & Co., 2014)

Greeley, Horace. *Eminent Women of the Age; Being Narratives of the Lives and Deeds of the Most Prominent Women of the Present Generation* (Hartford, CT: S.M. Betts & Co., 1868)

Griswold, Rufus Wilmot. *The Female Poets of America* (Philadelphia, PA: Carey and Hart, 1849)

Grunwald, Lisa, and Stephen J. Adler, eds. *Women's Letters: America from the Revolutionary War to the Present* (New York: Dial Press, 2005)

Hackel, Heidi Brayman, and Catherine E. Kelly. *Reading Women: Literacy, Authorship, and Culture in the Atlantic World, 1500–1800* (Philadelphia, PA: University of Pennsylvania Press, 2009)

Haddad, John Rogers. *The Romance of China: Excursions to China in U.S. Culture, 1776–1876* (New York: Columbia University Press, 2008)

Hanson, E.R. *Our Woman Workers: Biographical Sketches of Women Eminent in the Universalist Church for Literary, Philanthropic and Christian Work* (Chicago, IL: Star and Covenant Office, 1884)

Harris, Sharon M. *Women's Early American Historical Narratives* (London: Penguin Classics, 2003)

Harris, Sharon M. *Executing Race: Early American Women's Narratives of Race, Society, and the Law* (Columbus, OH: The Ohio State University Press, 2005)

Hart, John Seely. *The Female Prose Writers of America. With Portraits, Biographical Notices, and Specimens of Their Writings* (Philadelphia, PA: E.H. Butler & Co., 1852)

Hodges, Graham Russell. *Encyclopedia of African American History, 1619–1895: From the Colonial Period to the Age of Frederick Douglass*, 3 vols (Oxford: Oxford University Press, 2006)

Hudock, Amy E., and Katharine Rodier. *American Women Prose Writers, 1820–1870* (Detroit, MI: Gale Research, 2001)

James, Edward T., Janet Wilson James, and Paul Samuel Boyer, eds. *Notable American Women, 1607–1950: A Biographical Dictionary*, 3 vols (Cambridge, MA: Harvard University Press, 1971)

Kerber, Linda K. *Women of the Republic: Intellect and Ideology in Revolutionary America* (Chapel Hill, NC: University of North Carolina Press, 1980)

Knight, Denise D., ed. *Writers of the American Renaissance: An A-to-Z Guide* (Westport, CT: Greenwood Press, 2003)

Kort, Carol. *A to Z of American Women Writers* (New York: Facts on File, 2000)

Kunitz, Stanley J., and Howard Haycraft, eds. *American Authors, 1600–1900: A Biographical Dictionary of American Literature* (New York: The H. W. Wilson Company, 1938)

Lauter, Paul, ed. *The Heath Anthology of American Literature*, 5th edition, 5 vols (New York: Houghton Mifflin Company, 2005)

Levernier, James A., and Douglas R. Wilmes, eds. *American Writers before 1800: a Biographical and Critical Dictionary* (Westport, CT: Greenwood Press, 1983)

Lindley, Susan Hill, and Eleanor J. Stebner. *The Westminster Handbook to Women in American Religious History* (Louisville, KY: Westminster John Knox Press, 2008)

Linkon, Sherry Lee. *In Her Own Voice: Nineteenth-century American Women Essayists* (New York: Taylor & Francis, 1997)

Logan, Mrs. John A. *The Part Taken by Women in American History* (Wilmington, DE: Perry-Nalle Publishing Company, 1912)

López Rodríguez, Miriam, and María Dolores Narbona Carrión, eds. *Women's Contribution to Nineteenth-Century American Theatre* (Valencia: Universitat de València, 2004)

Mainiero, Lina, et al., eds. *American Women Writers: a Critical Reference Guide from Colonial Times to the Present*, 5 vols (New York: Frederick Ungar, 1979–1994)

Malone, Dumas, ed. *Dictionary of American Biography*, 22 vols (New York: Charles Scribner's Sons, 1928–1958)

May, Caroline. *The American Female Poets: With Biographical and Critical Notices* (Philadelphia, PA: Lindsay & Blakiston, 1848)

McKenney, Janice E. *Women of the Constitution: Wives of the Signers* (Lanham, MD: Scarecrow Press, 2012)

Miller, Marla R. *The Needle's Eye: Women And Work in the Age of Revolution* (Amherst, MA: University of Massachusetts Press, 2006)

Mulford, Carla, Amy E. Winans, and Angela Vietto, eds. *American Women Prose Writers to 1820* (Detroit, MI: Gale Research, 1999)

Okker, Patricia. *Our Sister Editors: Sarah J. Hale and the Tradition of Nineteenth-Century American Women Editors* (Athens, GA: University of Georgia Press, 1995)

Onderdonk, James Lawrence. *History of American Verse (1610–1897)* (Chicago, IL: A.C. McClurg, 1901)

Page, Yolanda Williams, ed . *Encyclopedia of African American Women Writers*, 2 vols (Westport, CT: Greenwood Press, 2007)

Patterson, Daniel, Roger Thompson, and J. Scott Bryson, eds. *Early American Nature Writers: A Biographical Encyclopedia* (Westport, CT: Greenwood Press, 2008)

Peterson, Carla L. *Doers of the Word: African American Women Speakers and Writers in the North (1830–1880)* (New York: Oxford University Press, 1995)

Premo, Terri L. *Winter Friends: Women Growing Old in the New Republic, 1785–1835* (Urbana, IL: University of Illinois Press, 1990)

Price. Kenneth M., and Susan Belasco Smith. *Periodical Literature in Nineteenth-Century America* (Charlottesville, VA: University of Virginia Press, 1995)

Ranta, Judith A. *Women and Children of the Mills: An Annotated Guide to Nineteenth-Century American Textile Factory Literature* (Westport, CT: Greenwood Publishing Group, 1999)

Rawlings, Peter, ed. *Americans on Fiction, 1776–1900,* 3 vols (London: Pickering & Chatto, 2002)

Read, Thomas Buchanan. *The Female Poets of America: With Portraits, Biographical Notices, and Specimens of Their Writings* (Philadelphia, PA: E.H. Butler & Co., 1849)

Reed, Elizabeth Wagner. *American Women in Science Before the Civil War* (Minneapolis, MN: University of Minnesota, 1992)

Rines, George Edwin, ed. *The Encyclopedia Americana* [...], 16 vols (New York: Scientific American Compiling Dept., 1903–1905)

Robert, Dana Lee. *American Women in Mission: a Social History of Their Thought and Practice* (Macon, GA: Mercer University Press, 1997)

Scanlon, Jennifer, and Shaaron Cosner. *American Women Historians, 1700s-1990s: A Biographical Dictionary* (Westport, CT: Greenwood Publishing Group, 1996)

Shields, David S., ed. *American Poetry: The Seventeenth and Eighteenth Centuries* (New York: Library of America, 2007)

Shockley, Ann Allen. *Afro-American Women Writers 1746–1933: An Anthology and Critical Guide* (Boston, MA: G.K. Hall, 1988)

Shook, John R., ed. *The Dictionary of Early American Philosophers*, 2 vols (New York: Continuum, 2012)

Smith, Jessie Carney, and Linda T. Wynn . *Freedom Facts and Firsts: 400 Years of the African American Civil Rights Experience* (Canton, MI: Visible Ink Press, 2009)

Stabile, Susan M. *Memory's Daughters: The Material Culture of Remembrance in Eighteenth-Century America* (Ithaca, NY: Cornell University Press, 2004)

James Henry Stark. *The Loyalists of Massachusetts and the Other Side of the American Revolution* (Boston: W.B. Clarke Co., 1909)

Watts, Emily Stipes. *The Poetry of American Women from 1632 to 1945* (Austin, TX: University of Texas Press, 1977)

Weaks, Mary Louise, and Carolyn Perry, eds. *Southern Women's Writing: Colonial to Contemporary* (Gainesville, FL: University Press of Florida, 1995)

White, Barbara A. *American Women's Fiction, 1790–1870: A Reference Guide* (New York: Garland Pub., 1990)

White, James Terry. *The National Cyclopædia of American Biography*, 63 vols (New York: James T. White & Co., 1891–1984)

Who Was Who in America: Historical Volume, 1607–1896 (Chicago, IL: Marquis Who's Who, 1967)

Willard, Frances Elizabeth, and Mary Ashton Livermore. *A Woman of the Century: Fourteen Hundred-seventy Biographical Sketches Accompanied by Portraits of Leading American Women in All Walks of Life* (Buffalo, NY: Moulton, 1893)

Wilson, James Grant, and John Fiske, *Appletons' Cyclopaedia of American Biography*, 6 vols (New York: D. Appleton & Co, 1887–1889)

Yee, Shirley J. *Black Women Abolitionists: A Study in Activism, 1828–1860* (Knoxville, TN: University of Tennessee Press, 1992)

Yellin, Jean Fagan, and John C. Van Horne. *The Abolitionist Sisterhood: Women's Political Culture in Antebellum America* (Ithaca, NY: Cornell University Press, 1994)

Writers from France

Adler, Laure. *A l'aube du féminisme: les premières journalistes (1830–1850)* (Paris: Payot, 1979)

Bard, Christine, and Sylvie Chaperon, eds. *Dictionnaire des féministes: France, XVIIIe-XXIe siècle* (Paris: Presses universitaires de France, 2017)

Briquet, Fortunée Bernier. *Dictionnaire historique, littéraire et bibliographique des Françaises, et des étrangères naturalisées en France [...]* [1804] (Strasbourg: Presses universitaires de Strasbourg, 2016)

Carton, Henri. *Histoire des femmes écrivains de la France* (Paris: Dupret, 1886)

Cuisin, J.-P.-R. *Dictionnaire des gens de lettres vivants* (Paris: chez les marchands de nouveautés, 1826)

Decreus, Juliette. *Sainte-Beuve et la critique des auteurs féminins* (Paris: Boivin, 1949)

Diaz, Brigitte, and Jurgen Siess, eds. *L'épistolaire au féminin, correspondances de femmes, colloque de Cerisy-la-Salle [...]* (Caen: Presses universitaires de Caen, 2006)

Duhet, Paule-Marie. *Les femmes et la Révolution 1789–1794* (Paris: Julliard, 1971)

Finch, Alison. *Women's Writing in Nineteenth-Century France* (Cambridge, UK: Cambridge University Press, 2000)

Fraisse, Geneviève. *Muse de la raison: la démocratie exclusive et la différence des sexes* (Aix-en-Provence: Alinéa, 1989)

Gabrielli, Domenico. *Dictionnaire historique du Père-Lachaise: xviiie et xixe siècles* (Paris: Amateur, 2002)

Gautier, Théophile. *Portraits contemporains: littérateurs, peintres, sculpteurs, artistes dramatiques*, 2nd edition (Paris: Charpentier, 1874)

Guentner, Wendelin. *Women Art Critics in Nineteenth-Century France: Vanishing Acts* (Newark, DE: University of Delaware Press, 2013)

Hesse, Carla. *The Other Enlightenment: how French Women Became Modern* (Princeton, NJ: Princeton University Press, 2001)

Hoefer, Ferdinand, ed. *Nouvelle Biographie générale*, 46 vols (Paris: Firmin Didot, 1853–1866)

Jensen, Katharine Ann. *Writing Love: Letters, Women, and the Novel in France, 1605–1776* (Carbondale, IL: Southern Illinois University Press, 1995)

Larousse, Pierre, ed. *Grand dictionnaire universel du xixe siècle*, 17 vols (Paris: Administration du grand dictionnaire universel, 1866–1890)

Marand-Fouquet, Catherine. *La Femme au temps de la Révolution* (Paris: Stock, 1989)

Margadant, Jo Burr, ed. *The New Biography: Performing Femininity in Nineteenth-Century France* (Berkeley, CA: University of California Press, 2000)

Makward, Christiane P., Madeleine Cottenet-Hage, et al., eds. *Dictionnaire littéraire des femmes de langue française: de Marie de France à Marie NDiaye* (Paris: Karthala, 1996)

Melzer, Sara E., and Leslie W. Rabine. *Rebel Daughters: Women and the French Revolution* (Oxford: Oxford University Press, 1992)

Michaud, Joseph François, and Louis Gabriel Michaud, eds. *Biographie universelle, ancienne et moderne* [...], 85 vols (Paris: Michaud frères, 1811–1862)

Olivier-Martin, Yves. *Histoire du roman populaire en France: de 1840 à 1980* (Paris: Albin Michel, 1980)

Quérard, Joseph-Marie. *La France littéraire, ou Dictionnaire bibliographique des savants, historiens et gens de lettres de la France, ainsi que des littérateurs étrangers qui ont écrit en français* [...], 12 vols (Paris: Firmin Didot, 1827–1864)

Quérard, Joseph-Marie. *La littérature française contemporaine: XIXe siècle*, 6 vols (Paris: Daguin Frères, 1842–1857)

Reid, Martine. *Des femmes en littérature* (Paris: Belin, 2010)

Robert, Daniel. *Textes et documents relatifs à l'histoire des Eglises réformées en France (Période 1800–1830)* (Geneva: Librairie Droz, 1962)

Rosa, Annette. *Citoyennes: les femmes et la Révolution française* (Paris: Messidor, 1988)

Sainte-Beuve, Charles Augustin. *Causeries du lundi, Portraits de femmes et Portraits littéraires* (Paris: Garnier, 1881)

Schiffer, Liesel. *Femmes remarquables au xixe siècle* (Paris: Vuibert, 2008)

Sicard, Germain. ed. *Justice et politique: la Terreur dans la Révolution française* (Toulouse: Presses de l'Université Toulouse 1 Capitole, 1997)

Smart, Annie K. *Citoyennes: Women and the Ideal of Citizenship in Eighteenth-Century France* (Newark, DE: University of Delaware, 2011)

Société internationale pour l'étude des femmes de l'Ancien Régime https://siefar.org/

Soprani, Anne. *La Révolution et les femmes, 1789–1796* (Paris: MA Éditions, 1988)

Unwin, Timothy, ed. *The Cambridge Companion to the French Novel: From 1800 to the Present* (Cambridge: Cambridge University Press, 1997)

Vapereau, Louis Gustave, ed. *Dictionnaire universel des contemporains* (Paris: Hachette, 1858)

Writers from German Lands

Allgemeine Deutsche Biographie [ADB], 56 vols (Leipzig: Duncker & Humblot, 1875–1912)

Blackwell, Jeannine, and Susanne Zantop, eds. *Bitter Healing. German Women Writers 1700–1830* (Lincoln, NE: University of Nebraska Press, 1990)

Brinker-Gabler, Gisela, Karola Ludwig, and Angela Wöffen, eds. *Lexikon deutschsprachiger Schriftstellerinnen 1800–1945* (Munich: DTV, 1986)

Brümmer, Franz, ed. *Lexikon der deutschen Dichter und Prosaisten vom Beginn des 19. Jahrhunderts bis zur Gegenwart*, 8 vols (Leipzig: Reclam, 1913)

Chambers, Helen. *Humor and Irony in Nineteenth-Century German Women's Writing* (Rochester, NY: Camden House, 2007)

Dawson, Ruth P. *The Contested Quill: Literature by Women in Germany 1770–1800* (Newark, DE: University of Delaware, 2002)

Diethe, Carol. *Towards Emancipation: German Women Writers of the Nineteenth Century* (New York: Berghahn Books, 1998)

Elon, Amos. *The Pity of It All: A History of Jews in Germany 1743–1933* (New York: Henry Holt, 2002)

Frederiksen, Elke, and Elizabeth Ametsbichler, eds. *Women Writers in German Speaking Countries: a Bio-Bibliographical Critical Sourcebook* (Westport, CT: Greenwood Press, 1998)

Friedrichs, Elisabeth. *Die deutschsprachigen Schriftstellerinnen des 18. und 19. Jahrhunderts. Ein Lexikon* (Stuttgart: Metzler, 1981)

Garland, Mary, and Henry Garland. *The Oxford Companion to German Literature*, 3rd edition (Oxford: Oxford University Press, 1997)

Groß, Heinrich. *Deutsche Dichterinnen und Schriftstellerinnen in Wort und Bild*, 3 vols (Berlin: Fr. Thiel, 1885)

Hardin, James, and Christoph E. Schweitzer, eds. *German Writers in the Age of Goethe: Sturm und Drang to Classicism* (Detroit, MI: Gale Research, 1990)

Hertz, Deborah. *Jewish High Society in Old Regime Berlin* (New Haven and London: Yale University Press, 1988)

Joeres, Ruth-Ellen B., and Mary Jo Maynes, eds. *German Women in the Eighteenth and Nineteenth Centuries, A Social and Literary History* (Bloomington, IN: Indiana University Press, 1986)

Klemme, Heiner F., and Manfred Kuehn, eds. *The Bloomsbury Dictionary of Eighteenth-Century German Philosophers* (London: Bloomsbury, 2016)

Kontje, Todd Curtis, *Women, the Novel, and the German Nation, 1771–1871: Domestic Fiction in the Fatherland* (Cambridge: Cambridge University Press, 1998)

Konzett, Matthias, ed. *Encyclopedia of German Literature*, 2 vols (Chicago, IL: Fitzroy Dearborn, 2000)

Mikus, Birgit. *The Political Woman in Print: German Women's Writing 1845–1919* (Bern: Peter Lang AG, 2014)

Neue Deutsche Biographie [NDB], 28 vols (Berlin: Duncker & Humblot, 1953–2024)

Porterfield, Allen Wilson. *An Outline of German Romanticism: 1766–1866* (New York: Ginn, 1914)

Susman, Margarete. *Frauen der Romantik* (Jena: Diederichs, 1929)

Touaillon, Christine. *Der deutsche Frauenroman des 18. Jahrhunderts* (Vienna and Leipzig: Braumüller, 1919)

Writers from Habsburg Territories

Austria

Daviau, Donald G., ed. *Major Figures of Nineteenth-Century Austrian Literature* (Riverside, CA: Ariadne Press, 1998)

Österreichisches Biographisches Lexikon 1815–1950 [ÖBL], 16 vols (Vienna: Austrian Academy of Sciences, 1957–2022)

Schmid-Bortenschlager, Sigrid, and *Hanna Schnedl-Bubeniček. Österreichische Schriftstellerinnen 1880–1938: eine Bio-Bibliographie* (Stuttgart: H.-D. Heinz, 1982)

Wurzbach, Constant v., ed . *Biographisches Lexikon des Kaiserthums Oesterreich* [...], 61 vols (Vienna: L. C. Zamarski, 1877–1961)

Croatia

de Haan, Francisca, Krassimira Daskalova, and Anna Loutfi, eds. *A Biographical Dictionary of Women's Movements and Feminisms: Central, Eastern and South Eastern Europe, 19th and 20th Centuries* (Budapest: Central European University Press, 2006)

Knjiženstvo—Theory and History of Women›s Writing in Serbian until 1915 http://knjizenstvo.etf.bg.ac.rs/en

Czechia

Iggers, Wilma Abeles. *Women of Prague: Ethnic Diversity and Social Change from the Eighteenth Century to the Present* (Providence, RI: Berghahn Books, 1995)

Writers from Latin America and the Caribbean

Argentina

MacIntyre, Iona. *Women and Print Culture in Post-Independence Buenos Aires* (Rochester, NY: Tamesis, 2010)

Marting, Diane E., ed . *Spanish American Women Writers: A Bio-Bibliographical Source Book* (Westport, CT: Greenwood Press, 1990)

Meachem, Susanne. *Women's Actions, Women's Words: Female Political and Cultural Responses to the Argentine State* [Doctoral Dissertation] (Birmingham, AL: University of Birmingham, 2010)

Méndez Rodenas, Adriana. *Transatlantic Travels in Nineteenth-Century Latin America: European Women Pilgrims* (Lewisburg, PA: Bucknell University Press, 2014)

Menton, Seymour. *Latin America's New Historical Novel* (Austin, TX: University of Texas Press, 1993)

Bolivia

Foster, David William, ed. *Handbook of Latin American Literature*, 2nd edition (New York: Garland, 1992)

Imbert, Enrique Anderson. *Spanish American Literature: A History* (Detroit, MI: Wayne State University Press, 1963)

Ferro, Hellén. *Historia de la poesía hispanoamericana* (New York: Las Américas, 1964)

Brazil

Bernd, Zila. *Littérature brésilienne et identité nationale: Dispositifs d'exclusion de l'Autre* (Paris: L'Harmattan, 1995)

Budasz, Rogério. *Opera in the Tropics: Music and Theater in Early Modern Brazil* (Oxford: Oxford University Press, 2019)

Schumaher, Schuma, and Erico Vital Brazil. *Dicionário mulheres do Brasil: de 1500 até a atualidade* (Rio de Janeiro: Jorge Zahar, 2000)

Silva, Jacicarla Souza da. *Vozes femininas da poesia latino-americana: Cecília e as poetisas uruguaias* (São Paulo: Editora UNESP, 2009)

Chile

Cano Roldán, Imelda (Sor). *La mujer en el Reyno de Chile* (Santiago: Gabriela Mistral, 1981)

Casazza, Roberto, et al, eds. *Artes, ciencias y letras en América colonial*, 2 vols (Buenos Aires: Teseo, 2009)

Pereira, Ronan Alves, César Ceriani Cernadas, and María Julia Carozzi. *Ciencias Sociales y Religión en América Latina: Perspectivas en Debate* (Buenos Aires: Editorial Biblos, 2007)

Goić, Cedomil, *Letras del Reino de Chile* (Madrid, Iberoamericana Editorial, 2006)

Guardia, Sara Beatriz, ed. *Mujeres que escriben en América Latina* (Lima: Centro de Estudios La Mujer en la Historia de América Latina, CEMHAL, 2007)

Hintze, Gloria María. *Escritura femenina: diversidad y género en América Latina* (Mendoza: Universidad Nacional de Cuyo, Facultad de Filsofía y Letras, 2004)

Lavrín, Asunción, and Rosalva Loreto López, eds. *Diálogos espirituales: manuscritos femeninos hispanoamericanos siglos XVI-XIX* (Mexico City: Instituto de Ciencias Sociales y Humanidades de la Benemérita Universidad Autónoma de Puebla, 2006)

Memoria Chilena https://www.memoriachilena.gob.cl/602/w3-channel.html

Montecino Aguirre, Sonia. *Mujeres chilenas: fragmentos de una historia* (Santiago: Editorial Catalonia, 2008)

Colombia

Cortés, José Domingo, ed. *Poetisas Americanas: Ramillete Poético del Bello Sexo Hispano-Americano* (Paris: Bouret, 1896)

Cuba

Foster, David William, and Daniel Altamiranda, eds. *From Romanticism to Modernismo in Latin America* (New York: Garland, 1997)

Meléndez, Concha. *La novela indianista en Hispanoámerica (1832–1889)* (Madrid: Hernando, 1934)

Sommer, Doris. *Foundational Fictions, the National Romances of Latin America* (Berkeley, CA: University of California Press, 1991)

Mexico

Díaz, Mónica. *Indigenous Writings from the Convent: Negotiating Ethnic Autonomy in Colonial Mexico* (Tucson, AZ: University of Arizona Press, 2010)

Writers from Ottoman Europe

Greece

Denissi, Sophia. "The Greek Enlightenment and the Changing Cultural Status of Women." *ΣΥΓΚΡΙΣΗ/Comparison* 12 (2001), pp. 42–47

Serbia

Hawkesworth, Celia. *Voices in the Shadows: Women and Verbal Art in Serbia and Bosnia* (Budapest: Central European University Press, 2000)

Hawkesworth, Celia. *A History of Central European Women's Writing* (Berlin: Springer, 2001)

Milisavac. Živan, ed. *Jugoslovenski književni leksikon* [Yugoslav Literary Lexicon] (Novi Sad: Matica srpska, 1971)

Writers from Romanov Territories

Poland

Bibliografia Literatury Polskiej—Nowy Korbut [A Bibliography of Polish Literature], 18 vols (Warsaw: Państwowy Instytut Wydawniczy, 1963–)

Polski Słownik Biograficzny [A Dictionary of Polish Biography], 55 vols (Kraków: Polish Academy of Learning, Polish Academy of Sciences, 1935–)

Russia

Barker, Adele Marie, and Jehanne M. Gheith, eds. *A History of Women's Writing in Russia* (Cambridge: Cambridge University Press, 2002)

Cornwell, Neil, and Nicole Christian. *Reference Guide to Russian Literature* (Chicago, IL: Fitzroy Dearborn, 1998)

Энциклопедический словарь Брокгауза и Ефрона [Brockhaus and Efron Encyclopedic Dictionary], 86 volumes (St. Petersburg and Leipzig: Brockhaus and Efron, 1890–1907)

Engel, Barbara A. *Mothers and Daughters: Women of the Intelligentsia in Nineteenth-Century Russia* (Cambridge: Cambridge University Press, 1983)

Gheith, Jehanne M. *Finding the Middle Ground: Krestovskii, Tur, and the Power of Ambivalence in Nineteenth-Century Russian Women's Prose* (Evanston, IL: Northwestern University Press, 2004)

Great Soviet Encyclopedia, The. 3rd edition, 31 vols (New York: Macmillan, 1973–1983)

Greene, Diana. *Reinventing Romantic Poetry: Russian Women Poets of the Mid-Nineteenth Century* (Madison, WI: University of Wisconsin Press, 2004)

Kahn, Andrew, Mark Naumovich Lipovetsky, Irina Reyfman, and Stephanie Sandler. *A History of Russian Literature* (Oxford: Oxford University Press, 2018)

Kelly, Catriona, ed. *An Anthology of Russian Women's Writing, 1777–1992* (Oxford: Oxford University Press, 1994)

Ledkovsky, Marina, Charlotte Rosenthal, and Mary Fleming Zirin. *Dictionary of Russian Women Writers* (Westport, CT: Greenwood Press, 1994)

Levitt, Marcus C., ed. *Early Modern Russian Writers, Late Seventeenth and Eighteenth Centuries* (Detroit, MI: Gale Research, 1995)

Polovtsov, A.A, Русский биографический словарь [Russian Biographical Dictionary], 25 vols (St Petersburg: Imperial Russian Historical Society, 1896–1918)

Terras, Victor. *A History of Russian Literature* (New Haven, CT: Yale University Press, 1991)

Ukraine

Kubijovyč, Volodymyr, and Arkadii Zhukovsky, eds. *Encyclopedia of Ukraine*, 5 vols (Toronto: University of Toronto Press, 1984–1993)

Manning, Clarence A. *Ukrainian Literature: Studies of the Leading Authors* (Plainview, NY: Books for Libraries Press, 1944/1971)

Skrypnik, Mary, ed. and tr. *Written in the Book of Life: Works by 19th-20th Century Ukrainian Writers* (Moscow: Progress Publishers, 1982)

Writers from Scandinavia

Denmark

Andersen, Anton. *Danske Forfatterinder i det nittende Hundredaar* [...] (Copenhagen: E. Langhoffs Forlag, 1896)

Bricka, Carl Frederik. *Dansk biografisk Leksikon*, 27 vols (Copenhagen: J.H. Schulz, 1933–1944)

Howitt, William, and Mary Howitt. *The Literature and Romance of Northern Europe: Constituting a Complete History of the Literature of Sweden, Denmark, Norway and Iceland* [...], 2 vols (London: Colburn & Co., 1852)

Jensen, Elisabeth Møller. *Nordisk kvindelitteraturhistorie* [The History of Nordic Women's Literature], 5 vols (Copenhagen: Rosinante, 1993–1998)

Larsen, Jytte, Grethe Ilsøe, and Hanne Rimmen Nielsen, eds. *Dansk Kvindebiografisk Leksikon*, 4 vols (Copenhagen: Rosinante, 2000)

Nørballe, Inge. *Guldalderdigtere. Portrætter og poesi* [Golden Age Poets. Portraits and Poetry] (Copenhagen: Høst, 1999)

The History of Nordic Women's Literature https://www.kau.se/en/node/37172

Wiene, Inger. *En historie om kvindelige håndværkere i 200 år* (Copenhagen: SFAH, 1991)

Finland

Lappalainen, Päivi, and Lea Rojola, eds. *Women's Voices: Female Authors and Feminist Criticism in the Finnish Literary Tradition* (Helsinki: Finnish Literature Society, 2007)

Klinge, Matti. *Suomen kansallisbiografia* [National Biography of Finland], 11 vols (Helsinki: Suomalaisen Kirjallisuuden Seura, 2003–2008)

Knif, Henrik, et al. *Biografiskt lexikon för Finland*, 4 vols (Stockholm: Atlantis, 2008–2011)

Suomen kansallisbiografia [The National Biography of Finland], https://openlibrary.org/books/OL16394345M/Suomen_kansallisbiografia

Svenska Litteratursällskapet i Finland https://www.sls.fi/sv/

Zilliacus-Tikkanen, Henrika. *När könet började skriva—Kvinnor i finländsk press 1771–1900* [When Gender Started to Write - Women in Finnish Media 1771–1900] (Helsingfors: Suomen Tiedeseura, 2005)

Norway

Beyer, Edvard, ed. *Norges Litteraturhistorie*, 6 vols (Oslo: Cappelen, 1974–1975)

Helle, Knut, ed. *Norsk biografisk leksikon*, 10 vols (Oslo: Kunnskapsforlaget, 1999–2005)

Høgh, M., and F. Mørck, eds. *Norske kvinder. En oversigt over deres stilling og livsvilkaar i hundredaared 1814–1914*, 2 vols (Kristiania: Berg & Høgh, 1914)

Store norske leksikon https://snl.no/

Sweden

Berg, P.G., and Wilhelmina Stålberg, eds. *Anteckningar om Svenska Qvinnor* (Stockholm: P.G. Berg, 1864)

Berger, Margareta. *Pennskaft: kvinnliga journalister i svensk dagspress 1690–1975* (Stockholm: Norstedt, 1977)

Boëthius, Bertil. *Svenskt biografiskt lexikon* [Dictionary of Swedish Biography], 34 vols (Stockholm: Bonnier, 1918–)

Bohman, Nils, et al., eds. *Svenska män och kvinnor: biografisk uppslagsbok*, 8 vols (Stockholm: Albert Bonniers Förlag, 1942–1955)

Christensson, Jakob. *Signums svenska kulturhistoria* [Swedish culture history by Signum], 8 vols (Stockholm: Signum, 2004–2009)

Forsås-Scott, Helena. *Swedish Women's Writing: 1850–1995* (Atlantic Highlands, NJ: Athlone Press, 1997)

Hofberg, Herman, Frithiof Heurlin, Viktor Millqvist, and Olof Rubenson, eds. *Svenskt Biografiskt Handlexikon* [...] [Swedish Biographical Dictionary], 2nd edition, 2 vols (Stockholm: Bonnier, 1906)

Leijonhufvud, Sigrid, and Sigrid Brithelli. *Kvinnan inom svenska litteraturen intill år 1893. En bibliografi* [...] (Stockholm: Norstedt, 1893)

Öhrberg, Ann. *Vittra fruntimmer. Författarroll och retorik hos frihetstidens kvinnliga författare* (Stockholm: Gidlunds Förlag, 2001)

Österberg, Carin, Inga Lewenhaupt, and Anna Greta Wahlberg. *Svenska kvinnor: föregångare, nyskapare* (Lund: Signum, 1990)

Svenskt kvinnobiografiskt lexikon (SKBL) [Biographical Dictionary of Swedish Women] https://skbl.se/en

Writers from Spain and Portugal

Portugal

Bermúdez, Silvia, and Roberta Johnson. *A New History of Iberian Feminisms* (Toronto: University of Toronto Press, 2018)

Boxer, C.R. *Women in Iberian Expansion Overseas: Some Facts, Fancies and Personalities* (Oxford: Oxford University Press, 1975)

Esteves Pereira, João. *Portugal - Diccionário Histórico, Chorográphico, Heráldico, Biográphico, Bibliográphico, Numismático e Artístico*, 7 vols (Lisbon: João Romano Torres, 1904–1915)

Portuguese Women Writers—womenwriters (16th-19th centuries) http://www.womenwriters.nl/index.php/Portuguese_Women_Writers

Spain

Capel, Rosa, ed . *Mujeres para la Historia. Figuras destacadas del primer feminismo* (Madrid: Abada Editores, 2004)

Etienvre, Françoise, *Regards sur les Espagnoles créatrices (XVIIIe-XXe siècle)* (Paris: Presses Sorbonne Nouvelle, 2006)

Flores, Angel, and Kate Flores. *Hispanic Feminist Poems from the Middle Ages to the Present: A Bilingual Anthology* (New York: Feminist Press, 1986)

Ibiza i Osca, Vicent. *Les dones al món de l'art. Pintores i escultores valencianes (1500–1950)* (Valencia: Institució Alfons el Magnànim, Centre Valencià d'Estudis i d'Investigació, 2017)

Palmer, Simón, and María del Carmen. *Escritoras españolas del siglo XIX: manual bio-bibliográfico* (Madrid: Castalia, 1991)

Pérez, Janet, and Maureen Ihrie. *The Feminist Encyclopedia of Spanish Literature*, 2 vols (Westport, CT: Greenwood Press, 2002)

Writers from the British Isles

Great Britain

Aaron, Jane. *Nineteenth-Century Women's Writing in Wales: Nation, Gender and Identity* (Cardiff: University of Wales Press, 2010)

Backscheider, Paula R., ed. *Restoration and Eighteenth-Century Dramatists* (Detroit, MI: Gale Research, 1989)

Backscheider, Paula R. *Eighteenth-Century Women Poets and Their Poetry: Inventing Agency, Inventing Genre* (Baltimore, MD: Johns Hopkins University Press, 2008)

Battestin, Martin C., ed. *British Novelists, 1660–1800* (Detroit, MI: Gale Research, 1985)

Behrendt, Stephen C. *British Women Poets and the Romantic Writing Community* (Baltimore, MD: Johns Hopkins University Press, 2009)

Belchem, John, ed. *A New History of the Isle of Man* (5 vols), *Vol. V: The Modern Period, 1830–1999* (Liverpool: Liverpool University Press, 2000)

Brake, Laurel, and Marysa Demoor. *Dictionary of Nineteenth-Century Journalism in Great Britain and Ireland* (Ghent: Academia Press, 2009)

Burroughs, Catherine, ed. *Women in British Romantic Theatre: Drama, Performance, and Society, 1790–1840* (Cambridge: Cambridge University Press, 2000)

Clemit, Pamela. *The Cambridge Companion to British Literature of the French Revolution in the 1790s* (Cambridge, UK: Cambridge University Press, 2011)

Cook, Daniel, ed. *Scottish Poetry, 1730–1830* (Oxford: Oxford University Press, 2023)

Copeland, Edward. *Women Writing about Money: Women's Fiction in England, 1790–1820* (Cambridge, UK: Cambridge University Press, 1995)

Craciun, Adriana. *Fatal Women of Romanticism* (Cambridge: Cambridge University Press, 2003)

Darton, F.J. Harvey, and Brian Alderson. *Children's Books in England: Five Centuries of Social Life*, 3rd edition (New York: Cambridge University Press, 1982)

Desmond, Ray. *Dictionary of British and Irish Botanists and Horticulturalists Including Plant Collectors, Flower Painters and Garden Designers* (London: Taylor & Francis, 1977)

Donkin, Ellen. *Getting Into the Act: Women Playwrights in London 1776–1829* (London: Routledge, 1995)

Eger, Elizabeth. *Bluestockings Displayed: Portraiture, Performance and Patronage, 1730–1830* (Cambridge, UK: Cambridge University Press, 2013)

Ewan, Elizabeth L., Sue Innes, Siân Reynolds, Rose Pipes. *The Biographical Dictionary of Scottish Women* (Edinburgh: Edinburgh University Press, 2007)

Finberg, Melinda C., ed. *Eighteenth-Century Women Dramatists* (Oxford: Oxford University Press, 2001)

Fullard, Joyce, ed. *British Women Poets, 1660–1800: An Anthology* (Troy, NY: Whitston Publishing Company, 1990)

Garside, Peter, and Karen O'Brien, eds. *The Oxford History of the Novel in English*, Volume 2, *English and British Fiction 1750–1820* (Oxford: Oxford University Press, 2018)

Gifford, Douglas, and Dorothy McMillan, eds. *A History of Scottish Women's Writing* (Edinburgh, Edinburgh University Press, 1997)

Graham, Henry Grey, *The Social Life of Scotland in the Eighteenth Century* (London: A. & C. Black, 1899)

Gray, Sara. *Dictionary of British Women Artists* (Havertown, PA: Casemate Publishers, 2009)

Grenby, Matthew. *The Anti-Jacobin Novel: British Conservatism and the French Revolution* (Cambridge, UK: Cambridge University Press, 2001)

Hartley, Cathy. *A Historical Dictionary of British Women*, 2nd edition (London: Routledge, 2003)

Howard, Rachel. *Domesticating the Novel: Moral-Domestic Fiction, 1820–1834* (Ph.D. thesis, Cardiff University, 2007)

Ingamells, John. *A Dictionary of British and Irish Travellers in Italy 1701–1800* (New Haven, CT: Yale University Press, 1997)

Johns, Alessa. *Women's Utopias of the Eighteenth Century* (Champaign, IL: University of Illinois Press, 2003)

Johns, Alessa, *Bluestocking Feminism and British-German Cultural Transfer, 1750–1837* (Ann Arbor, MI: University of Michigan Press, 2014)

Labbe, Jacqueline M., ed. *The History of British Women's Writing, 1750–1830: Volume Five* (London: Palgrave Macmillan, 2010)

Levine, Philippa. *The Amateur and the Professional: Antiquarians, Historians and Archaeologists in Victorian England, 1838–1886* (Cambridge, UK: Cambridge University Press, 1986)

Link, Frederick M., ed. *English Drama, 1660–1800: A Guide to Information Sources* (Detroit, MI: Gale Research, 1976)

Lonsdale, Roger, ed. *Eighteenth Century Women Poets* (Oxford: Oxford University Press, 1989)

Looser, Devoney. *British Women Writers and the Writing of History, 1670–1820* (Baltimore, MD: Johns Hopkins University Press, 2000)

Mark, Jan. *The Oxford Book of Children's Stories* (Oxford: Oxford University Press, 1993)

Maxwell, Richard, and Katie Trumpener, eds. *The Cambridge Companion to Fiction in the Romantic Period* (Cambridge, UK: Cambridge University Press, 2008)

Mitchell, Sally, ed. *Victorian Britain: an Encyclopedia* (1988. London: Routledge, 2011)

Moine, Fabienne. *Women Poets in the Victorian Era. Cultural Practices and Nature Poetry* (Burlington, VT: Ashgate, 2015)

Mudge, Bradford K., ed. *British Romantic Novelists, 1789–1832* (Detroit: Gale Research, 1992)

Olson, Paul A. *The Kingdom of Science: Literary Utopianism and British Education, 1612–1870* (Lincoln, NE: University of Nebraska Press, 2002)

Orlando: Women's Writing in the British Isles from the Beginnings to the Present (Cambridge: Cambridge University Press) https://orlando.cambridge.org/

Oxford Dictionary of National Biography [DNB] (Oxford: Oxford University Press) https://www.oxforddnb.com/

Ruwe, Donelle. *British Children's Poetry of the Romantic Era: Verse, Riddle, and Rhyme* (London: Palgrave Macmillan, 2014)

Saglia, Diego. *Poetic Castles in Spain: British Romanticism and Figurations of Iberia* (Amsterdam: Rodopi, 2000)

Shteir, Ann B. *Cultivating Women, Cultivating Science: Flora's Daughters and Botany in England, 1760–1860* (Baltimore, MD: Johns Hopkins University Press, 1996)

Sutherland, John. *The Longman Companion to Victorian Fiction* (Harlow: Pearson Longman, 2009)

The Women's Print History Project https://womensprinthistoryproject.com/

Watson, George, ed. *The New Cambridge Bibliography of English Literature*, 5 vols (Cambridge: Cambridge University Press, 1969–1977)

Wordsworth, Jonathan. *The Bright Work Grows: Women Writers of the Romantic Age* (Poole: Woodstock Books, 1997)

Ireland

Adelaide, Debra. *Australian Women Writers: A Bibliographic Guide* (London: Pandora, 1988)

Behrendt, Stephen C., ed. *Irish Women Poets of the Romantic Period* (Alexandria, VA: Alexander Street Press, 2007) https://edesiderata.crl.edu/resources/irish-women-poets-romantic-period

Behrendt, Stephen C., ed. *Romantic-Era Irish Women Poets in English* (Cork: Cork University Press, 2021)

Bourke, Angela, ed. *The Field Day Anthology of Irish Writing: Irish Women's Writing and Traditions*, 2 vols (New York: New York University Press, 2002)

Boylan, Henry. *A Dictionary of Irish Biography*, 3rd Edition (Dublin: Gill and MacMillan, 1998)

Colman, Anne Ulry. *Dictionary of Nineteenth-Century Irish Women Poets* (Galway: Kenny's Bookshop, 1996)

Connolly, Claire. *A Cultural History of the Irish Novel, 1790–1829* (Cambridge: Cambridge University Press, 2012)

Coughlan, Patricia, and Tina O'Toole, eds. *Irish Literature: Feminist Perspectives* (Dublin: Carysfort Press, 2008)

Darcy, Ailbhe, and David Wheatley, eds. *A History of Irish Women's Poetry* (Cambridge: Cambridge University Press, 2021)

Deane, Seamus, Andrew Carpenter, Angela Bourke, and Jonathan Williams. *The Field Day Anthology of Irish Writing*, 5 vols (New York: New York University Press, 1991–2002)

Foster, John Wilson. *The Cambridge Companion to the Irish Novel* (Cambridge: Cambridge University Press, 2006)

Froggatt, Richard. *The Dictionary of Ulster Biography* (Ulster History Circle) https://www.newulsterbiography.co.uk/

Hamilton, C. J.. *Notable Irishwomen* (Dublin: Sealy, Bryers & Walker, 1904)

Harte, Liam, ed. *A History of Irish Autobiography* (Cambridge: Cambridge University Press, 2018)

Jackson, Alvin, ed. *The Oxford Handbook of Modern Irish History* (Oxford: Oxford University Press, 2014)

Killeen, Jarlath. *The Emergence of Irish Gothic Fiction: History, Origins, Theories* (Edinburgh: Edinburgh University Press, 2014)

Loeber, Rolf, Magda Stouthamer-Loeber and Anne M. Burnham, *A Guide to Irish Fiction 1650–1900* (Dublin: Four Courts Press, 2006)

Looser, Devoney. *The Cambridge Companion to Women's Writing in the Romantic Period* (Cambridge: Cambridge University Press, 2015)

McCarthy, Justin, Maurice Francis Egan, Douglas Hyde, Charles Welsh, Lady Gregory, and James Jeffrey Roche, eds. *Irish Literature*, 10 vols (Philadelphia, PA: J.D. Morris & Co., 1904)

McGuire, J.I., and James Quinn, eds. *Dictionary of Irish Biography: from the Earliest Times to the Year 2002*, 9 vols (Cambridge: Cambridge University Press, 2009)

Murphy, James H., ed. *The Oxford History of the Irish Book*, 5 vols. *IV: The Irish Book in English, 1800–1891* (Oxford: Oxford University Press, 2011)

O'Shaughnessy, David, ed. *Ireland, Enlightenment and the English Stage, 1740–1820* (Cambridge: Cambridge University Press, 2019)

Prendergast, Amy . *Literary Salons Across Britain and Ireland in the Long Eighteenth Century* (London: Palgrave Macmillan, 2015)

Schirmer, G.A *Out of What Began: A History of Irish Poetry in English* (Ithaca, NY: Cornell University Press, 1998)

Sihra, M. *Women in Irish Drama: A Century of Authorship and Representation* (London: Palgrave Macmillan, 2007)

Sweeney, Fionnghuala, Fionnuala Dillane, and Maria Stuart. *Ireland, Slavery, Anti-Slavery, and Empire* (London: Routledge, 2020)

Todd, Janet. *Rebel Daughters: Ireland in Conflict 1798* (London: Viking, 2003)

Webb, Alfred. *A Compendium of Irish Biography* [...] (Dublin: M. H. Gill & Son, 1878)

Welch, Robert. *Concise Oxford Companion to Irish Literature* (Oxford: Oxford University Press, 2000)

Writers from the Italian Peninsula

Arslan, Antonia, Adriana Chemello, and Gilberto Pizzamiglio. *Le stanze ritrovate. Antologia di scrittrici venete dal Quattrocento al Novecento* (Mirano-Venice: Eidos 1991)

Buti, Maria Bandini. *Enciclopedia Biografica e Bibliografica Italiana*, 6: *Poetesse e scrittrici*, 2 vols (Rome: Istituto Editoriale Italiano, 1941–1942)

Costa-Zalessow, Natalia. *Scrittrici italiane dal XIII al XX secolo. Testi e critica* (Ravenna: Longo, 1982)

Di Fazio, Rossana, and Margherita Marcheselli . *Enciclopedia delle donne* https://www.enciclopediadelledonne.it/edd.nsf/home?readform

Fortune, Jane, and Linda Falcone. *Invisible Women*: *Forgotten Artists of Florence* (Florence: The Florentine Press, 2010)

Ghisalberti, Alberto Maria, et al., eds. *Dizionario biografico degli italiani*, 100 vols (Rome: Istituto dell'Enciclopedia Italiana, 1960–2020)

Marrone, Gaetana, Paolo Puppa, and Luca Somigli. *Encyclopedia of Italian Literary Studies*, 2 vols (London: Routledge, 2007)

Panizza, Letizia, and Sharon Wood, eds, *A History of Women's Writing in Italy* (Cambridge: Cambridge University Press, 2000)

Russell, Rinaldina, ed. *Italian Women Writers: A Bio-Bibliographical Sourcebook* (Westport, CT: Greenwood Press, 1994)

Wyles, Rosie, and Edith Hall, eds. *Women Classical Scholars: Unsealing the Fountain from the Renaissance to Jacqueline de Romilly* (Oxford: Oxford University Press, 2016)

Writers from the Low Countries

Belgium

Gubin, Éliane, Catherine Jacques, Valérie Piette, and Jean Puissant, eds, *Dictionnaire des femmes belges: xixe et xxe siècles* (Brussels: Racine, 2006)

van Bork, G.J., and P.J. Verkruijsse, *De Nederlandse en Vlaamse auteurs van middeleeuwen tot heden met inbegrip van de Friese auteurs* (Weesp: De Haan, 1985)

van Rokeghem, Suzanne, Jeanne Vercheval-Vervoort, and Jacqueline Aubenas, *Des femmes dans l'histoire en Belgique, depuis 1830* (Brussels: Luc Pire, 2006)

The Netherlands

Digitaal Vrouwenlexicon van Nederland https://resources.huygens.knaw.nl/vrouwenlexicon

van Gemert, Lia, et al, eds. *Women's Writing from the Low Countries 1200–1875: A Bilingual Anthology* (Amsterdam: Amsterdam University Press, 2010)

Writers from the Swiss Confederation

Switzerland

Dupree, Mary Helen. *The Mask and the Quill. Actress-Writers in Germany from Enlightenment to Romanticism* (Bucknell, PA: Bucknell University Press, 2011)

Fleig, Anne. *Handlungs-Spiel-Räume: Dramen von Autorinnen im Theater des ausgehenden 18. Jahrhunderts* (Würzburg: Königshausen & Neumann, 1999)

Index

Index of Listed Writers

Acland, Lady Christian Henrietta Caroline [or Lady Harriet Acland] 203
Adams, Abigail 18–19
Adams, Hannah 19
Adams, Lois Bryan 27
Agoult, Marie Catherine Sophie de Flavigny, Comtesse d' [or Daniel Stern] 85–86, 91, 98
Ahlgren, Catharina 187
Akhmatova, Elizaveta Niklaevna [or Leila] 160
Alexander, Cecil Frances 264–265
Ali, Mrs Meer Hassan 229
Allart de Méritens, Hortense Thérèse Sigismonde Sophie Alexandrine [or Prudence de Saman L'Esbatx], known as Hortense Allart 86
Almeida Portugal, Leonor de, 4th Marquise of Alorna, 8th Countess of Assumar [or Alcipe] 194
Amory, Katharine Greene 19
Ancelot, Virginie 86
Andersen, Clara Elisabeth [or Paul Winter] 169
Annenkova, Varvara Nikolaevna 160
Arbouville, Sophie d' 86
Arenal Ponte, Concepción 197
Arnaud, Angélique [or Marie Angélique Bassin] 87
Arnim, Bettina von 104, 107, 109
Arriagada García, María del Carmen Thomasa del Rosario 132
Arsić, Eustahija 146
Audubon, Lucy Bakewell 27

Austen, Jane 204, 212, 220–221, 223, 226–229, 281, 302
Austin, Sarah 229–230
Avdeyeva, Yekaterina Alekseyevna 160
Ayzac, Félicie Marie Émilie d' 87

Babois, Marguerite Victoire 87
Bacon, Delia Salter 27
Baden, Charlotte 169–170
Bailey, Abigail Abbot 19
Bailey, Margaret Jewett Smith 28
Bailey, Margaret L. 28
Baillie, Joanna 204, 209, 215, 230, 235
Baker, Harriette Newell Woods 28
Balfour, Clara Lucas 230
Ball, Catherine [or 'Baroness de Calabrella'] 234–235
Ball, Martha Violet 29
Bandettini, Teresa Landucci [or Amarilli Etrusca] 287
Bannerman, Anne 230–231
Barbauld, Anna Laetitia 203–204, 208–209, 223, 230, 254
Bardonneau, Elizabeth "Eliza" Ann Ashurst 231
Barnard, Frances Catherine [or Mrs. Alfred Barnard] 231
Barnes, Charlotte Mary Sanford 29
Barnes, Lucy 20
Barrell, Maria 204
Bartolini, Louisa Grace 231–232
Bateman, Sidney Frances 29
Battie, Henrietta 265
Bawr, Sophie, Baronne de 87–88

Bayard Cutting, Elise Justine 29
Beauclerc, Amelia 232
Beaufort, Louisa Catherine 265
Beauharnais, Fanny de 88
Beavan, Emily Elizabeth Shaw 13
Beckwith, Julia Catherine 13–14
Belgiojoso, Cristina Trivulzio di 288
Belloc, Louise Swanton 88
Berger, Christina Charlotta Ulrika 187–188
Berkeley, Elizabeth, Princess [or unofficially Margravine of Brandenburg-Ansbach], previously Elizabeth Craven, Baroness Craven 208
Bertin, Louise-Angélique 88
Beverley, Elizabeth [or Mrs. R. Beverley] 232
Biehl, Charlotta Dorothea 170
Biggs, Rachel Charlotte 232
Billings, Mary C. [after first marriage, Granniss; after second marriage, Webster; after third marriage, Billings] 30
Bilozerska-Kulish, Oleksandra Mikhailovna [or Hanna Barvinok] 167
Birch-Pfeiffer, Charlotte 105
Bleecker, Ann Eliza 20–21
Blessington, Marguerite Gardiner, Countess of 265–266
Bludova, Countess Antonina Dmitrievna 161
Böhl de Faber y Ruiz de Larrea, Cecilia Francisca Josefa [or Fernán Caballero] 198
Boigne, Adélaïde Charlotte Louise Éléonore, Comtesse de, known as Adélaïde de Boigne 89
Bolander, Sophie Christina Mathilda 188, 192
Bolton, Sarah Tittle 30
Bosboom-Toussaint, Anna Louisa Geertruida 4, 295, 298
Bošković, Anica 117–119

Botta, Anne Charlotte Lynch 30, 44
Bovie, Josine Natalie Louise [or Marie Sweerts] 293
Brandão, Beatriz Francisca de Assis 127, 131, 133
Bremer, Fredrika 69, 188, 190
Briest, Caroline Philippine von [or Caroline de la Motte Fouqué] 109
Brontë, Anne 221, 229, 233
Brontë, Charlotte 105, 221, 229, 233
Brontë, Emily Jane 221, 229, 233
Brooke, Charlotte 266
Brooks, Maria Gowen [or Gowan] 30–31
Browne, Frances 266
Browne, Maria da Felicidade do Couto, known as Maria Browne 193
Brown, Phoebe Hinsdale 31
Brun, Friederike 170
Brunton, Mary 234
Bryant, Charity 31
Buchholm, Magdalene Sophie 183
Budmani, Lukrecija Bogašinović 118–119
Bunbury, Selina 267
Bunina, Anna Petrovna 161
Burdon, Hannah Dorothy [or later Madame Wolfensberger or Lord B*******] 234
Burke, Anne 267
Burney, Frances [or Fanny Burney or Madame d'Arblay] 204, 221, 270–271
Burrell, Sophia, Lady 205

Cabrera y Heredia, Dolores 198
Callan, Margaret [or Thornton MacMahon] 267
Campbell, Dorothea Primrose 235–236
Campbell, Harriette 235
Campbell, Juliet Hamersley Lewis [or Judith Canute] 31
Candeille, Amélie-Julie [or Émilie] 89

Canfield, Francesca Anna [or Salonina] 32
Card, Mary Birkett 268
Carlyle, Jane Baillie 235
Carmichael, Rebekah [or Rebecca], later, Hay 205
Carney, Julia Abigail Fletcher [or Julia, Minnie May, Frank Fisher, Sadie Sensible, Minister's Wife, Rev. Peter Benson's Daughter] 32
Carroll, Anna Ella [or Hancock] 32
Carstens, Fredrika Wilhelmina [or R] 175, 177–178
Carter, Elizabeth [or Eliza] 205, 215, 219
Cartwright, Mrs H. 206
Cary, Alice 33, 37
Cary, Phoebe 33
Cary, Virginia Randolph 33–34
Case, Luella Juliette Bartlett 34
Cate, Eliza Jane 34
Catlow, Agnes 236
Caulkins, Frances Manwaring 35
Chabaud-Latour, Suzanne Rosette [or Rosine] de 89
Chalmers, Margaret 236
Chamberlain, Betsey Guppy 35
Chandler, Elizabeth Margaret 35–36
Charrière, Isabelle de [or Belle van Zuylen] 298
Chastenay, Louise-Marie-Victoire "Victorine" de 89–90
Cheesborough, Essie Blythe [or Motte Hall, Elma South, Ide Delmar, and E. B. C.] 36
Cheney, Harriet Vaughan 14, 22, 36
Chesebro', Caroline 37
Chetwode, Anna Maria [or Miss Chetwode] 268
Chézy, Helmina von 105, 108
Child, Lydia Maria 37
Choiseul-Gouffier, Sophie de 150
Chubbuck, Emily, later Emily Judson [or Fanny Forester] 37–38
Cicci, Maria Luisa 288

Clark, Emily Frederick 206
Clarke, Olivia, Lady 268
Cobb, Eunice Hale 38
Cobbold, Elizabeth [or Carolina Petty Pasty] 206
Cockburn, Alison [or Alison Rutherford or Alicia Cockburn] 207
Colet, Louise 90
Collett, Jacobine Camilla 183
Colquhoun, Janet [or Lady Colquhoun of Luss] 207
Condict, Jemima 20
Cottin, Marie Sophie Risteau 48, 91, 211
Cottnam, Deborah How 14
Courtmans, Joanna 294
Coxe, Margaret 38
Craik, Helen 207–208
Cristall, Ann Batten 208
Crocker, Hannah Mather 38–39
Croker, Margaret Sarah 208
Crowen, Susan (Akin) [or Mrs T.J. Crowen] 39
Cuenca de Moreno, María Guadalupe 129
Cushing, Eliza Lanesford 14, 22, 36
Cutter, Eunice Powers 39
Czartoryska, Elżbieta "Izabela" Dorota 153–154
Czartoryska, Princess Maria [formerly Duchess Maria of Württemberg] 154

Dashkova, Princess Yekaterina Romanovna 163, 268
da Silva e Orta, Margarida Teresa 127, 193–194
Davidson, Lucretia Maria 40
Davidson, Margaret Miller 40
Davies, Catherine 48, 236
Davis, Mary Elizabeth Moragne [or A Lady of South Carolina; M. E. Moragne] 40
Deffand, Marie de Vichy-Chamrond,

Marquise du 91, 96, 302
Deken, Agatha ("Aagje") 299–300
Deroin, Jeanne 91
Desbordes-Valmore, Marceline Félicité Josèphe 40, 87, 92, 94
Deverell, Mary 209
Dickinson, Rebecca 20
Dinnies, Anna Peyre [or Moina] 40–41
d'Istria, Dora [pen name of Duchess Helena Koltsova-Massalskaya] 146
Dodd, Mary Ann H., later Shutts 41
Doherty, Ann 237
Doolaeghe, Maria 294
Douglass, Sarah Mapps 41
Downing, Mary 269
Drinker, Elizabeth Sandwith 20
Droste zu Hülshoff, Anna Elisabeth "Annette" Franziska Adolphine Wilhelmine Louise Maria, Baroness von, known as Annette von Droste-Hülshoff 101–106
Dudevant, Amantine Lucile Aurore Dupin de Francueil, Baronne [or George Sand] 98
Dumont, Julia Louisa 41
Dunker, Conradine Birgitte 183
Duras, Claire Louisa Rose Bonne, Duchesse de, known as Claire de Duras 3, 92, 150

Eames, Elizabeth Jessup [or Stella and Mrs. E. J. Eames] 42
Écherolles, Alexandrine des 93
Edgeworth, Frances Anne "Fanny" 265, 269
Edgeworth, Maria 88, 222, 237, 249, 258, 269, 275
Edmond, Amanda Maria Corey [or A.M.E.] 42
Ehrmann, Marianne [or Marianne Ehrmann-Brentano or Madame Sternheim] 301
Eldridge, Elleanor 43

Ellet, Elizabeth Fries 43, 66, 80
Elliot, Jane Evans 43
Elwood, Anne 238
Embury, Emma Catherine [or Ianthe] 44
Engelhard, Magdalene Philippine 106
Épinay, Louise Florence Pétronille Tardieu d'Esclavelles d', known as Louise d'Épinay 93
Evans, Mary Ann [or George Eliot] 188, 229, 238, 244, 257

Falkman, Ulrica Charlotta 189
Fanshawe, Catherine Maria 209
Farnham, Eliza 44
Farrar, Eliza Ware 44–45
Faugères, Margaretta 21
Fay, Eliza 238
Fenimore Cooper, Susan Augusta 45
Fenn, Ellenor [or Mrs. Teachwell, or Mrs. Lovechild] 209
Fenno, Jenny 21
Fenwick, Isabella 239
Fergusson, Elizabeth Graeme [or Betsy Graeme] 21
Ferrier, Susan Edmonstone 239
Ficquelmont, Dorothea "Dolly" de 161–162
Field, Elizabeth "Eliza" [or Elizabeth Jones or Elizabeth Jones Carey, or Kecheahgahmequa] 239
Fischer, Caroline Auguste 106
Fisher, Sarah Logan 22
Fiszerowa, Wirydianna, later Wirydianna Kwilecka 154
Fitton, Sarah Mary [or Margaret] 269
Fitzsimon, Ellen 280
Floresta Brasileira Augusta, Nísia [pseudonym of Dionísia Gonçalves Pinto] 127, 132
Flygare-Carlén, Emilie 184–185, 189–190
Follen, Eliza Lee Cabot 45
Fonseca Pimentel, Eleonora Anna Maria Felice de, known as Eleonora

de Fonseca Pimentel 285, 288
Forkel-Liebeskind, Sophie Dorothea Margarete "Meta" 106
Forman, Charlotte [or Probus] 210
Foster, Hannah Webster 22, 36
Fouqueau de Pussy, Jeanne-Justine 93
Fry, Caroline, later Mrs Caroline Wilson 239–240
Fry, Elizabeth 240
Fuller, Anne 270
Fuller, Sarah Margaret 42, 46, 52, 60, 66, 80

Gales, Winifred Marshall 22
Galloway, Grace Growden 22–23
Gálvez, María Rosa de 198–199
Gambold, Anna Rosina Kliest 46
Gardiner, Jane Arden 210
Gasparin, Valérie de 302
Gauvin, Julienne Joséphine [or Juliette Drouet] 92, 304
Gayle, Sarah Ann Haynsworth 46
Gay, Sophie 86, 93–94
Geille de Saint-Léger, Anne-Hyacinthe [or Anne-Hyacinthe de Colleville] 94
Genlis, Stéphanie Félicité, Marquise de Sillery, Comtesse de, known as Félicité de Genlis 94, 108, 243, 280
Gilman, Caroline Howard [or Mrs. Clarissa Packard] 46–47
Girardin, Delphine Gay de [or Vicomte de Launay] 86, 94
Glover, Jean [or Jennifer Glover] 210
Goddard, Abba [or A. A. G., A. A. Goddard, and A. G. A.] 47
Godefroy, Eliza Anderson [or Beatrice Ironside] 47–48
Godwin, Catherine Grace 240
Gomersall, Ann 211
Gómez de Avellaneda, Gertrudis 125–126, 128, 133, 136
Gorriti, Juana Manuela 128, 137–139, 177
Gould, Hannah Flagg 48

Gouze, Marie Olympe [or Olympe de Gouges] 89, 95, 304
Grant, Beatrice 240–241
Granville, Harriet Leveson-Gower, Countess 248–249
Gratz, Rebecca 48
Gravallius, Wilhelmina Carolina 189
Gray, Catherine Rebecca [or Grey], Lady Manners, later, Lady Huntingtower 270
Gray, Jane Lewers 48–49
Greenland, Emma Jane [after marriage, Hooker] 211
Green, Mary Anne Everett 241
Green, Sarah 270
Griffith, Elizabeth 271
Griffith, Mary 49
Griffitts, Hannah 23
Grimké, Sarah Moore 49–50
Grimké Weld, Angelina Emily 50
Grimstone, Mary Leman [or Oscar] 241–242
Gritti, Cornelia Barbaro [or Aurisbe Tarsense] 289
Grosvenor, Harriet Ward Sanborn 50
Grouchy, Marie Louise Sophie de [or de Condorcet] 90
Gullbransson, Abela Maria 189
Günderrode, Karoline Friederike Louise Maximiliane von [or Tian] 104, 106–107
Gunning, Elizabeth 211–212, 218
Gunning, Susannah 211–212
Gyllembourg-Ehrensvärd, Baroness Thomasine Christine 170–171

Hack, Maria 242
Hahn-Hahn, Ida, Countess von 107
Hakewill, Maria C. 242
Hale, Mary Whitwell [or Y.L.E.] 50
Hale, Sarah Josepha Buell 51
Hall, Agnes C. [or Rosalia St Clair] 242–243
Hall, Anna Maria [or Mrs S.C. Hall] 271

Hall, Louisa Jane 51
Hall, Sarah Ewing 51
Hamilton, Elizabeth 212
Hamilton, Lady Mary [or Lady Mary Walker] 212–213
Hamilton, Marianne-Caroline 271–272
Hanck, Marie Kirstine Henriette 171
Hanway, Mary Ann 213
Harbison, Mary Jane 'Mercy' 23
Harding, Anne Raikes 243
Hardy, Elizabeth 229, 272
Harley, Martha [later Hugill] 213
Hays, Mary 208, 213–214
Hegermann-Lindencrone, Mette Louise Christiane Frederikke 171
Heiberg, Johanne Luise 171–172
Hemans, Felicia Dorothea 243, 246, 282
Hendriks, Rose Ellen, later Rose Ellen Temple 244
Hennell, Mary 244
Hensel, Luise 107
Herbert, Dorothea 272
Herbert, Jane Emily 272–273
Herbert, Sarah 14
Hervey, Elizabeth 214
Herz, Henriette Julie 107–108
Hesketh, Harriett [or Harriett Cowper] 214
Hewitt, Mary Elizabeth, later Mary Elizabeth Stebbins [or Ione and Jane] 52
Hillard, Harriett Low 52
Hjärne, Gustafva Sofia 178–179
Hoare, Sarah 244
Hoffmanowa, Klementyna 151–155
Holcroft, Fanny Margaretta 214–215
Holford, Margaret [known as "the elder"] 215
Holmes, Mary Anne 273, 276
Hooper, Ellen Sturgis 52
Hooper, Lucy 52–53
Hore, María Gertrudis 199

Howland, Esther Allen 53
Huber, Therese 106, 108, 112
Hughes, Mary [or Hughs] 244–245
Hunter, Anne 215, 230
Hussey, Anna Maria 245
Hyneman, Rebekah 53

Inchbald, Elizabeth 215, 254
Inglis, Frances "Fanny" Erskine, later Marquesa of Calderón de la Barca 245
Inglis, Margaret Maxwell 245
Ishimova, Aleksandra 162

Jackson, Rebecca Cox 54
James, Maria 54
Jameson, Anna Brownell 273
Jarnević [or Jarnjević], Dragojla 119
Jebb, Ann 208, 216
Jerauld, Charlotte A. [or Charlotte] 54
Jewsbury, Maria Jane, later Maria Jane Fletcher 246
Johnson Erwin Dudley, Margaret 55
Johnson, Susannah Willard 23
Johnstone, Christian Isobel 246
Johnston, Elizabeth Lichtenstein 55
Jones, Eliza Grew 55–56
Jones, Hannah Maria 246–247
Joyes y Blake, Inés 199

Karacs, Teréz 122–124, 165
Karsch, Anna Louisa 108
Kavanagh, Julia 273–274
Keir, Susanna 216
Kemble, Frances Anne 247
Kennedy, Grace 247
Kent, Elizabeth "Bessy" 247–248
Ker, Anne 216
Khvoshchinskaya, Nadezhda Dmitryevna [or V. Krestovsky] 162
Kielland, Susanne Sophie Catharina Gustava, known as Gustava Kielland 180, 182, 184
Kilner, Mary Ann 217, 220

King, Margaret [or Margaret King Moore or Lady Mount Cashell or Mrs Mason] 274, 283
Kinkel, Johanna 108–109
Kinzie, Juliette Augusta Magill 56
Kirkland, Caroline Mathilda Stansbury 56
Kniazhnina, Yekaterina Aleksandrovna 162
Knight, Anne 248
Knorring, Sophie Margareta von 190
Knös, Thekla Levinia Andrietta 190
Koren, Christiane 184
Krüdener, Beate Barbara Juliane Freifrau von [or Julie de Krüdener] 4, 150

Lacroix, Anne-Marie 95
Lamont, Elish [or La Mont(e)] 274
Landon, Letitia Elizabeth [or 'L.E.L.'] 248
Lard (Laird), Rebecca Hammond 23–24
La Roche, Marie Sophie von 104, 109
La Tour-du-Pin Gouvernet, Henriette Lucy Dillon, Marquise de 95
Leadbeater, Mary 275
Leech, Sarah 275
Lee, Eliza (Buckminster) 56
Lee, Hannah Farnham Sawyer 57
Lee, Jarena 57
Lee, Mary Elizabeth [or M.E.L. and A Friend] 57–58
Le Fanu, Alicia 275–276
Le Fanu, Alicia Sheridan 276
Lencastre, Catarina Micaela de Sousa César e, known as Catarina de Lencastre 194
Lennox, Charlotte 217
Lenox-Conyngham, Elizabeth Emmet [or Mrs. George Lenox Conyngham] 276
Leslie, Eliza 58
Lespinasse, Julie Jeanne Éléonore de 91, 95–96

Le Vert, Octavia Walton 58
Lewald, Fanny 109–110
Lewis, Estelle Anna [or Stella] 58–59
Lickbarrow, Isabella 249
Liddiard, Jane Susannah Anna 276
Lindqvist, Fredrika Lovisa 178
Ljungstedt, Aurora Lovisa [or Claude Gérard] 190
Logan, Deborah Norris 59
Lomax, Judith 59
Loud, Marguerite St. Leon 60
Lovisa de la Myle, Agatha 178
Lowell, Maria White 60
Lozano y Velázquez de Vilchez, Enriqueta 199
Łubieńska, Tekla Teresa 155
Ludvigsen, Anna Christiane Lauterup 172
Luzac, Marguérite Emilie 299
Lyon, Agnes 217

Maberly, Catherine "Kate" Charlotte 276–277
Mancini, Laura Beatrice 289
Manning, Anne 249
Mann, Mary Tyler Peabody 60
Mant, Alicia Catherine 277
Marcet, Jane 249–250
Marishall, Jean [or Jane Marshall] 218
Marović, Ana Marija 147
Martin, Emma 250
Martin, Harriet Evans 277–278
Martin, Harriet Letitia 277–278
Martin, Mary Letitia 277–278
Martin, Sarah 250–251
Massanés i Dalmau, Maria Josepa [or Josepa Massanés or Josefa Massanés] 200
Mather, Elizabeth Louisa 61
Maurice, Mary Atkinson 251
May, Caroline [or Caromaia] 61
Mayo, Sarah Carter Edgarton 61
McCord, Louisa Susannah Cheves 61–62

McDermott, Mary 278
McDougall, Frances Harriet Whipple Green 62
McIntosh, Maria Jane [or Aunt Kitty] 62
Medina, Louisa [or Louisa Honore de Medina, Louisa Medina Hamblin, or Louisine] 63
Mereau, Sophie Friederike 110
Meteyard, Eliza [or Silverpen] 251
Miller, Lydia Mackenzie Falconer [or Mrs. Harriet Myrtle] 252
Miller, Maria Morris 15
Millikin, Anna 278
Minifie, Margaret 211, 218
Mjödh, Barbara Catharina 178–179
Moïse, Penina 63
Monk, Maria 15
Montefiore, Judith, Lady 252
Montolieu, Isabelle de 229, 302
Moodie, Susanna 15
Moore, Jane Elizabeth 7, 218
Moore, Milcah Martha 23–24
More, Hannah 54, 209, 219, 222, 225, 254
Morgan, Sydney, Lady 262–264, 268, 279
Morrell, Abby Jane 63–64
Morton, Sarah Wentworth Apthorp 24
Mott, Lucretia 64, 74, 303
Moutzan-Martinengou, Elisavet 4, 143–145, 166, 304
Mowatt Ritchie, Anna Cora, later Mowatt, later, Ritchie [or Isabel, Henry C. Browning, and Helen Berkley] 64
Mujía, María Josefa 126, 129
Mundt, Clara [or Luise Mühlbach] 110
Murray, Judith Sargent Stevens 24

Nakwaska, Anna 155
Naubert, Benedikte 110
Necker, Suzanne 99, 302
Nelson, Esther 253
Němcová, Božena 120–122, 138, 153, 165
Newell, Harriet 64–65
Nicholson, Asenath Hatch 65
Nichols, Rebecca S. [or Ellen and Kate Cleaveland] 65
Ní Chonaill, Eibhlín Dubh [or Eileen O'Connell] 279
Nielsen, Birgitte Dorothea Henriette [or Theodora] 172
Ní Laoghaire, Máire Bhuí 279
Noel, Ellen Kyle [or Mrs. J.V. Noel] 15
Nyberg, Julia Kristina [or Euphrosyne] 190–191

Obrenović, Princess Anka, later Anka Konstantinović 147
O'Brien, Mary 280
O'Keeffe, Adelaide 280
Opie, Amelia 219–220
Osgood, Frances Sargent 43–44, 66, 79
Otté, Elise Charlotte 172
Otto-Peters, Louise [or Otto Stern] 111

Palli, Angelica 289
Palmer, Alicia Tindal 253
Panet, Louise-Amélie [or Berczy] 16
Parkes, Fanny [or Parks] 253
Parsons, Eliza 219–220
Parsons, Gertrude 253–254
Paul, Susan 66
Peabody, Elizabeth Palmer 66–67
Peacock, Lucy 220
Peirson, Lydia Jane Wheeler [or Pierson] 67
Peña i Nicolau, Victòria [or Victoria Peña de Amer] 200
Peña y Lillo Barbosa, Josefa de los Dolores [or Sister Josefa de los Dolores or Sister Dolores Peña y Lillo] 132–133
Penrose, Elizabeth [or Mrs Markham] 250

Pezzi, Giulietta 290
Pfeiffer, Ida Laura 115–116, 257
Phelps, Adaliza Cutter 67
Phelps, Elizabeth Porter 24–25
Phelps, Elizabeth Wooster Stuart [or H. Trusta] 67
Pichler, Caroline [or Karoline] 116
Pickard, Hannah Maynard [or A Lady] 16
Plessen, Louise Scheel von 173
Ploennies, Luise von 111
Plummer, Rachel Parker 68
Plumptre, Anne 216, 220
Pollart d'Herimetz, Angélique [or Angélique de Rouillé] 294
Porter, Agnes 220–221
Porter, Jane 254
Prince, Mary 254
Prior, Margaret, later Allen; then, Prior 68
Pulszky, Theresa 116
Purbeck, Elizabeth, and Jane Purbeck 221
Purvis, Sarah Louisa Forten [or Ada, Magawisca] 68–69
Pusich, Antónia Gertrudes 195
Putnam, Mary Traill Spence Lowell 69

Radcliffe, Ann 221, 224, 267
Ramsay, Martha Laurens 25
Randolph, Mary 69–70
Raoul, Marie-Françoise [or Fanny Raoul] 96
Read, Martha Meredith 70
Recke, Elisabeth Charlotte Constanzia "Elisa" von der 111
Reenstierna, Märta Helena [married name von Schnell] 191
Rémusat, Claire Élisabeth Jeanne de Vergennes, Comtesse de, known as Claire de Rémusat 96–97
Reventlow, Julie 173
Reventlow, Sophie Frederikke Louise Charlotte 173
Riccoboni, Marie-Jeanne 97

Ridgway, Marianne, later Mrs. Thomas Postans or Marianne Young 262
Ritter von Scherer, Sophie 116
Robert, Antoinette Henriette Clémence 97
Roberts, Eliza 221–222
Robinson, Mary 222, 270
Robinson, Therese Albertine Luise von Jakob [or Ernst Berthold, ein Frauenzimmer, Talvj] 70
Roche, Regina Maria 280–281
Roland de la Platière, Marie Jeanne 'Manon' 97
Romer, Isabella Frances 255
Rósa Guðmundsdóttir [or Vatnsenda-Rósa] 180
Roscoe, Margaret 255
Rosende, Petrona 128, 139–140
Rostopchina, Yevdokiya Petrovna 156, 159–160, 162–163, 264
Rowson, Susanna 25
Runeberg, Fredrika Charlotta 179
Rush, Rebecca 70
Ryves, Elizabeth "Eliza" 281

Sadlier, Mary Anne 281–282
Sáez Pérez de Vernet, María 129
Salm, Constance Marie Pipelet or Constance, Princesse de 96
Saluzzo Roero, Diodata 290
Sánchez de Gómez, María Josefa Acevedo [or Josefa Acevedo or Josefa Acevedo de Gómez] 133
Sandbach, Margaret 255
Sanders, Elizabeth Elkins 70–71
Sanguszko, Barbara Urszula 155–156
Sansay, Leonora 71
Saunders, Esther "Hetty" 71
Schlegel, Dorothea Friederike von 105, 112
Schlegel-Schelling, Caroline 112
Schoolcraft, Jane Johnston [or Bamewawagezhikaquay] 71–72
Schopenhauer, Johanna 112–113
Schwartz, Marie Sophie [or Fru

M.S.S.] 191
Scott, Alicia Ann, Lady John 258
Scott, Harriet Anne Scott, Lady 255
Scott, Jane Marie 222
Scott, Julia H. 72
Scott, Mary [after marriage, Mary Taylor] 222–223
Sedgwick, Catharine Maria 40, 69, 72
Selden, Catharine 282
Senancour, Virginie de 98
Seward, Anna 223
Shelley, Mary Wollstonecraft 225, 256
Sheridan Le Fanu, Ann Elizabeth "Betsy" 282
Shirreff, Emily Anne Eliza 256
Sigourney, Lydia Huntley 72–73
Silfverstolpe, Magdalena Sofia "Malla" 191–192
Silva-Bazán y Sarmiento, Mariana de [or Mariana de Silva-Meneses or Sarmiento de Sotomayor] 200
Simcoe, Dame Elizabeth Posthuma 16
Sinclair, Catherine 256–257
Sinnett, Jane 257
Sleath, Eleanor 223
Smirnova, Alexandra Osipovna 163
Smith, Anna Young 25
Smith, Charlotte 224, 286
Smith, Elizabeth 241
Smith, Elizabeth Oakes [or E] 73
Smith, Margaret Bayard 73–74
Somerville, Elizabeth 257
Somerville, Mary [formerly Greig] 249–250, 257–258
Souza-Botelho, Adélaïde-Emilie [or Émilie-Adélaïde] Filleul, Marquise de 98
Spence, Elizabeth Isabella 258
Staël-Holstein, Anne-Louise-Germaine Necker, Baronne de, known as Germaine de Staël 99
Stanhope, Louisa Sidney 258–259
Stanton, Elizabeth Cady 33, 74
Stein, Charlotte Albertine Ernestine von 113
Stephens, Ann Sophia [or Jonathan Slick] 74
Stockton, Annis Boudinot 25–26
Stoddard, Lavinia 74–75
Stokkenbech, Maria Engelbrecht [also E.M. Stokkenbeck] 6, 173–174
Stowe, Harriet Elisabeth Beecher 14, 75, 88, 230
Strussenfelt, Constantina Carolina Amalia "Amelie" von 188, 192
Strussenfelt, Ulrika "Ulla" Sophia von 192
Stuart, Lady Louisa 224
Sullivan, Arabella Jane 259
Swanwick, Anna 259
Swedenmarck, Catharina Charlotta 179
Swift, Mary Amelia 75

Taggart, Cynthia 75
Takách, Judit Dukai [or Malvina] 124
Tambroni, Clotilde 290
Taylor, Ann [or Ann Martin] 259–260, 280
Taylor, Jane Agnew 76, 280
Temple, Laura Sophia 260
Tenney, Tabitha Gilman 76
Thayer, Caroline Matilda Warren 76
Thompson, Jane Tonge 260
Thomson, Katherine [or Mrs. A.T. Thomson or Grace Wharton] 260
Thoresen, Anna Magdalene 174
Tighe, Mary 218, 271, 282
Tomlinson, Sarah Windsor 260–261
Tonge, Grizelda Elizabeth Cottnam [or Portia] 16
Townsend, Eliza 76
Townsend, Mary 77
Trench, Melesina [formerly St George] 282–283
Tristán y Moscoso, Flore Célestine Thérèse Henriette [or Flora Tristan] 99
Tuite, Eliza Dorothea Cobbe, Lady 283

Tuthill, Louisa Caroline [various pen names] 77

van den Cruyce, Coralie Adèle [in marriage Coralie de Félix de la Motte] 294–295
Van Lennep, Mary Elizabeth 77–78
Varnhagen, Rahel Antonie Friederike 113–114
Veintimilla de Galindo, Dolores 136
Veronese, Angela 291
Vidal, Mary Theresa 261
Vigée Le Brun, Marie Louise Élisabeth 99–100

Wacklin, Sara Elizabeth 179
Ward, Julia Rush Cutler 78
Ware, Katharine Augusta 78
Warren, Mercy Otis 26
Waterman, Catharine Harbison, later Esling 78
Welby, Amelia Ball Coppuck [or Amelia or 'Minstrel-girl'] 79
Wells, Anna Maria 79
Wells, Helena, later Whitford 26
Welsh, Jane Kilby [or Welch] 79
Whatman, Susanna 224
Wheatley Peters, Phillis 26
Whitman, Sarah Helen Power 80
Wildermuth, Ottilie 113–114

Wilkinson, Eliza Yonge 27
Williams, Catharine R. 80
Williams, Helen Maria 220, 223–225
Williams-Wynn, Charlotte 261
Wilmot, Katherine [or Catherine] 283
Wirt, Elizabeth Washington Gamble 80–81
Woesthoven, Maria Petronella 300
Wolff-Bekker, Elizabeth "Betje" 300
Wollstonecraft, Mary 24, 70, 130, 132, 206, 208, 210, 212, 214, 219, 225, 256, 274
Wolzogen, Caroline von 114
Wood, Sarah "Sally" Sayward Barrell Keating 81
Wordsworth, Dorothy Mae Ann 261–262
Worm, Pauline Frederikke 174
Worthington, Jane Taylor 81

Xovellanos y Xove Ramírez, Xosefa de 201

Yearsley, Ann [or Lactilla] 225
Young, Mary Julia 226

Zhukova, Maria Semyonovna 164
Zitz-Halein, Kathinka 114
Żmichowska, Narcyza [Gabryella] 156

Index of Names

Adams, John 18–19, 26
Adams, John Quincy 283
Aeschylus 259
Agassiz, Louis 116
Alembert, Jean Le Rond d' 91, 93, 96, 302
Alexander I, Emperor of Russia 150, 162
Alfieri, Vittorio 214, 243, 290
Alighieri, Dante 286

Almqvist, Carl Jonas Love 192
Andersen, Hans Christian 171, 182, 266
Angoulême, Marie Thérèse Charlotte, Duchess of 255
Anthony, Susan B. 33, 74
Aragon, Louis 92
Arnim, Achim von 104–105
Asbjørnsen, Peter Christen 166
Atterbom, Per Daniel Amadeus 191–

192
Atwood, Margaret 15
Audubon, John James 27
Augustus III of Poland 151, 153

Babbage, Charles 258
Bach, Johann Christian 211
Bacon, Francis 27
Baggesen, Jens Immanuel 106
Balzac, Honoré de 85, 92, 94, 98, 221, 288, 290
Barnum, P.T. 33
Baudelaire, Charles 90, 92
Beauharnais, Joséphine de 88
Beaumarchais, Pierre-Augustin Caron de 90
Beccaria, Cesare 90
Beckford, William 214
Beethoven, Ludwig van 105, 116
Bellini, Vincenzo 290
Belloc, Hilaire 88
Bentham, Jeremy 229
Bentley, Richard 239
Berlioz, Hector 88
Bernadotte, Jean-Baptiste 169
Bernardin de Saint-Pierre, Jacques-Henri 85, 94, 302
Beronja, Vladislav 11, 118–119
Berry, Marie-Caroline of Bourbon-Two Sicilies, Duchesse de 95
Bertin, Louis François 88
Bird, Robert Montgomery 63
Bismarck, Otto von 101
Björk 180
Blackwood, William 239
Blanc, Louis 98
Boieldieu, François-Adrien 87
Bolívar, Simón 125, 129
Bonaparte, Caroline 236
Bonaparte, Jérôme-Napoléon 47
Bonaparte, Louis 299
Bonaparte, Lucien 283
Bonaparte, Napoléon 94–95, 99, 283
Bonstetten, Charles Victor de 170

Bordeaux, Henri d'Artois, Duc de 97
Boswell, James 223, 298
Brentano, Clemens 104, 107, 110
Brissot de Warville, Jacques-Pierre 97
Broglie, Victor, Duc de 89
Browning, Elizabeth Barrett 56, 269
Browning, Robert 259–260
Brown, John 39
Brumoy, Pierre 217
Bryant, William Cullen 31, 56
Buffon, Georges-Louis Leclerc, Comte de 94, 99, 302
Bulwer-Lytton, Edward 63, 190
Bürger, Gottfried August 106
Burke, Edmund 219, 225, 275
Burns, Robert 205, 207, 210, 245
Burr, Aaron 71
Byron, George Gordon, Lord 88, 99–100, 114, 145, 209, 256, 266, 270, 279, 289

Cadell, Robert 239
Cagliostro, Count Alessandro di [Giuseppe Balsamo] 111
Calderón de la Barca, Pedro 214
Calhoun, John C. 58
Campbell, Elizabeth, Duchess of Argyll 75
Carducci, Giosuè 232
Carlyle, Thomas 235–236, 261
Caroline, Princess of Wales 216
Catherine II the Great, Empress of Russia 154
Cattaneo, Carlo 290
Cavour, Camillo Benso, Count of 285, 288
Chamisso, Adalbert von 105
Champollion, Jean-François 289
Charlotte, Princess of Wales 232
Charlotte, Princess Royal, Queen of Württemberg 209
Chartres, Louise Marie Adélaïde de Bourbon, Duchesse de 87, 94
Chateaubriand, François-René, Vicomte de 84, 86, 92–93, 150, 194

Chatterton, Thomas 40
Choderlos de Laclos, Pierre 297
Chopin, Frédéric 85, 98, 155
Clare, John 305
Clay, Henry 54, 58
Clinton, DeWitt 78
Coleridge, Samuel Taylor 170, 204, 246
Collins, Wilkie 105, 160
Comte, Auguste 251
Condillac, Étienne Bonnot de 96
Condorcet, Marie Jean Antoine Nicolas de Caritat, Marquis de 89–90, 96, 98
Constant, Benjamin 93
Cornwallis, Charles Cornwallis, 1st Marquess 26
Cottle, Joseph 208
Cousin, Victor 229
Cowper, William 214
Crabbe, George 229, 275
Crabb Robinson, Henry 259
Creuzer, Georg Friedrich 107
Cruikshank, Isaac 218
Csire, Márta 11, 123
Custine, Marquise de 93
Czartoryski, Prince Adam 153–155

Darwin, Charles 45, 245, 251
Darwin, Erasmus 216, 223
Delacroix, Eugène 86, 98, 145
Delany, Mary 215
De Quincey, Thomas 249
Derzhavin, Gavrila 161
Deschamps, Émile 94
Devonshire, Georgiana Cavendish, Duchess of 222
di Breme, Ludovico 290
Dickens, Charles 56, 88, 160, 182, 229, 260, 266, 269, 274, 297
Dickinson, Emily 8, 60
Diderot, Denis 93, 96, 163, 282, 302
Disraeli, Benjamin, 1st Earl of Beaconsfield 266
Donizetti, Gaetano 290

Dorat, Claude Joseph 88
Dorval, Marie 92, 98
Dostoyevsky, Fyodor 221
Douglass, Frederick 74
Douglas, William 258
Duarte Caetano, Luiza 11, 130
Ducis, Jean-François 87
Ducray-Duminil, François-Guillaume 220
Dumas, Alexandre, père 94, 96, 127, 196, 247

Éluard, Paul 122
Emerson, Ralph Waldo 27, 46, 52, 58, 188, 238
Emmet, Robert 273, 276
Enlai, Zhou 303

Fanon, Frantz 7
Faraday, Michael 250
Fénelon, François de Salignac de La Mothe 227
Fenimore Cooper, James 45
Fichte, Johann Gottlieb 110, 177
Fielding, Henry 177, 217, 221
Fillmore, Millard 32
Flaubert, Gustave 90, 98, 197
Fontenelle, Bernard Le Bouyer de 91, 211
Forster, Georg 108, 112
Foscolo, Ugo 213, 289–290
Fouquier-Tinville, Antoine Quentin 91
Fox, Charles James 203, 280
Francis II, Holy Roman Emperor 101, 115
Franklin, Benjamin 153, 163
Frederick II the Great of Prussia 108, 154
Frederick VII of Denmark 174
Frederick William II of Prussia 108
Frederick William IV of Prussia 240
Freud, Sigmund 186
Friedrich, Caspar David 186
Frossard, Benjamin Sigismond 300

Galiani, Ferdinando 93
Galvani, Luigi 177
Garibaldi, Giuseppe 97, 285
Garrick, David 217, 219, 222, 271
Garrison, William Lloyd 50, 66
Gaskell, Elizabeth Cleghorn 88
Gauguin, Paul 99
Gautier, Théophile 94
Gellert, Christian Furchegott 178
Gentz, Friedrich von 108, 113
Geoffrin, Marie Thérèse 302
George III, King of Great Britain and Ireland 21
George IV, King of the United Kingdom of Great Britain and Ireland 243
Gérard, François Pascal Simon 94
Gibbon, Edward 99
Gifford, John 253
Gilray, James 218
Girodet-Trioson, Anne-Louis 94
Gladstone, William Ewart 259, 262
Gleim, Johann Wilhelm Ludwig 108, 111
Gluck, Christoph Willibald 89
Godoy, Manuel 198
Godwin, William 214, 219, 225, 256
Goethe, Johann Wolfgang von 64, 70, 85, 105, 110–114, 138, 170, 229, 231, 259
Gogol, Nikolai 161, 163
Goldoni, Carlo 289
Goldsmith, Oliver 88, 90
Gonzaga, Tomás António 132
Greeley, Horace 33, 42, 44, 46, 73
Grégoire, abbé Henri Jean-Baptiste 19
Grétry, André Ernest Modeste 87
Grillparzer, Franz 116
Grimm, Friedrich Melchior, Baron von 93, 99, 302
Grimm, Jacob 106, 121, 165, 182
Grimm, Wilhelm 106, 121, 165, 170, 182
Griswold, Rufus 33, 42, 61, 78–80

Guizot, François 86, 89, 230
Gundulić, Ivan 119
Gustav III of Sweden 169, 171, 178–179

Hallam, Henry 249
Hamann, Johann Georg 111
Hamilton, Emma, Lady 100
Hancock, John 18, 26
Händel, Georg Friedrich 159
Hastings, Warren 238
Hawthorne, Nathaniel 27, 52, 66, 188
Heine, Heinrich 85, 114, 288
Heinse, Johann Jakob Wilhelm 109
Helvétius, Claude Adrien 89, 91, 97
Henry, Patrick 26
Hensel, Fanny Mendelssohn 109
Herder, Johann Gottfried 170
Hertz, Henrik 169, 171
Heyne, Christian Gottlob 108
Hogg, James 207
Holbach, Paul-Henri Thiry, Baron d' 93, 97–98
Homer 197, 297
Horace 33, 87, 297
Horne Tooke, John 274
Houdetot, Sophie d' 86
Hugo, Victor 84, 86–88, 90, 92–94, 105, 114, 124, 221, 288–289, 304
Humboldt, Alexander von 108, 113, 116, 172, 225
Humboldt, Wilhelm von 108, 113
Hume, David 97, 207
Hunt, Leigh 236, 247–248
Hutchinson, Thomas 38

Ibsen, Henrik 174
Irving, Washington 40, 48, 58, 116, 188
Isabey, Jean-Baptiste 94
Isbell, Margarita Madanova 11, 159

Jacobi, Friedrich Heinrich 109
Janin, Jules 94
Jean Paul [Johann Paul Friedrich Richter] 56, 108, 113
Jefferson, Thomas 1, 18, 21, 26, 34, 53,

59, 69, 73, 90, 227
Jeffrey, Francis 260
Johnson, Samuel 199, 205, 208–209, 217, 219, 223, 265
Jones, John Paul 207

Kant, Immanuel 111, 177
Karadžić, Vuk 146
Karamzin, Nikolay 163
Kauffman, Angelica 283
Kean, Edmund 254
Keats, John 60, 228, 248, 282
Kemble, John Philip 215, 247, 277
Kierkegaard, Søren 172
Klopstock, Friedrich Gottlieb 111, 170
Kościuszko, Tadeusz 154
Kossuth, Lajos 116
Kotzebue, August Friedrich Ferdinand von 220
Krasicki, Ignacy 156
Krylov, Ivan 162
Kulish, Panteleimon 167

Lacretelle, Jean Charles Dominique de 86
La Croze, Maturinus Veyssière 220
Lafayette, Marie-Joseph Paul Yves Roch Gilbert du Motier, Marquis de 31, 78, 231
Lafontaine, August Heinrich 243, 270
La Harpe, Jean-François de 94, 302
Lamartine, Alphonse Marie Louis Prat de 59, 86–88, 93–94, 289
Lamb, Charles 248
Lamennais, Félicité Robert de 98
Lameth, Marie-Anne, Comtesse de 89
La Motte Fouqué, Friedrich de 109, 113
Laplace, Pierre-Simon, Marquis de 258
Latouche, Hyacinthe-Joseph Alexandre Thabaud [or Henri] de 94
La Vallière, Louise, Duchesse de 217
Lavater, Johann Kaspar 32, 109, 172

Lavoisier, Antoine-Laurent de 98
Lawrence, Thomas 249
Ledru-Rollin, Alexandre Auguste 98
Lee, Sophia 221
Leopardi, Giacomo Taldegardo Francesco di Sales Saverio Pietro, Count 274, 287
Lermontov, Mikhail 116, 160–161, 163
Leroux, Pierre 98
Lessing, Gotthold Ephraim 104, 214
Lincoln, Abraham 32–33, 49, 55
Linnaeus, Carl 177
Liszt, Franz 288
Longfellow, Henry Wadsworth 72
Louis Philippe, King of the French 94, 124
Louis XVI, King of France and Navarre 99, 302
L'Ouverture, Toussaint 251
Lowell, James Russell 60, 69
Lundy, Benjamin 36
Luther, Martin 297
Luynes, Marie Brulart de La Borde, Duchesse de 91

Mackenzie, Henry 207
Mackintosh, James 260
MacPherson, James 121
Madison, Dolley 73
Mahler, Gustav 286–287
Malthus, Thomas 251
Manzoni, Alessandro 289–290
Marivaux, Pierre Carlet de 91, 93, 97
Marmontel, Jean-François 93–94, 98, 302
Marshall, John 209, 217
Mars, Mademoiselle 92
Marx, Karl 1, 124
Matthisson, Friedrich von 170, 276
Mazzini, Giuseppe 46, 231, 289–290
Melville, Herman 71
Mendelssohn, Felix 112
Mendelssohn, Moses 107, 112–113
Mérimée, Prosper 86, 89, 98

Merry, Robert 214
Metastasio, Pietro 132, 155, 288
Metternich, Klemens von 285
Michael III of Serbia, Prince 147
Mickiewicz, Adam 153, 155, 158–160, 163
Mignet, François Auguste Marie 288
Mill, John Stuart 229, 243, 259
Mirabeau, Honoré Gabriel Riqueti, Count of 108
Moe, Jørgen 166
Monboddo, James Burnett, Lord 207
Monet, Claude 85
Montagu, Elizabeth 206, 215, 219
Montagu, Lady Mary Wortley 224
Montesquieu, Charles de 103
Monti, Vincenzo 290
Moore, Thomas 218, 265, 279, 282
Moratin, Leandro Fernández de 214
Morris, Gouverneur 34, 98
Mozart, Wolfgang Amadeus 116, 219
Müller, Johannes von 108, 170
Müller, Wilhelm 107
Murat, Prince Achille 236–237
Musset, Alfred de 86, 90, 94, 98, 288

Napoleon III, Emperor of the French 58
Narbonne-Lara, Louis Marie Jacques Amalric, Comte de 99, 302
Necker, Jacques 99, 302
Nelson, Horatio, Lord 283
Newbery, Elizabeth 209
Newbery, John 218
Newman, John Henry 240
Newton, John 18, 89
Nicholas I, Emperor of Russia 160
Nicolai, Christoph Friedrich 111
Niebuhr, Barthold Georg 108
Nightingale, Florence 240
Nodier, Charles 94, 213
Novalis [Georg Philipp Friedrich von Hardenberg] 112

Obradović, Dositej 146
O'Connell, Daniel 279
Oehlenschläger, Adam 171–172
Ossian 70, 197, 205
Owen, Robert 238, 242, 250

Paine, Thomas 219, 225, 274
Paley, William 177
Paul, Emperor of Russia 150
Paulin, Roger 11, 103
Pellico, Silvio 43
Percy, Bishop Thomas 121, 166
Perrault, Charles 121
Pétion de Villeneuve, Jérôme 97
Petrarch, Francis 59, 231
Pierce, President Franklin 64
Pitt, William 280
Pius IX, Pope 58
Pius VII, Pope 274, 283
Pixérécourt, René Charles Guilbert de 211
Poe, Edgar Allan 27, 30–31, 33, 40, 42–43, 56, 58–60, 64, 66, 79–80, 221
Poniatowski, Józef 154
Poniatowski, Stanisław August 156
Potter, Bishop Alonzo 54
Pradier, James 90, 92
Prévost, abbé Antoine François 297
Priestley, Joseph 216
Proudhon, Pierre-Joseph 91
Pushkin, Alexander 159, 161–163, 227

Quatrefages de Bréau, Jean Louis Armand de 172
Quintana, Manuel José 198

Rachel, Mademoiselle 86
Racine, Jean 135, 139, 155
Ranke, Franz Leopold von 230
Raynal, abbé Guillaume Thomas François 93, 99, 281, 302
Récamier, Juliette 86, 89, 93–94, 96, 150
Reed, Elizabeth Wagner 77, 79
Reeve, Clara 206
Reynolds, Joshua 249, 275

Ricardo, David 237
Richardson, Samuel 218
Rivarol, Antoine de 283
Robertson, William 207
Robespierre, Maximilien François Marie Isidore de 71, 97, 124
Rossini, Gioachino Antonio 129
Rousseau, Jean-Jacques 84, 93–94, 153, 177, 222, 281
Rückert, Friedrich 108, 286
Runeberg, Johan Ludvig 179
Ruskin, John 274

Sainte-Beuve, Charles Augustin 86, 92
Saint-Lambert, Jean François de 93
Saint-Simon, Claude-Henri de 86–87
Salmhoferová, Naděžda 11, 121
San Martín, José de 125
Sappho 59, 194
Savigny, Friedrich Carl von 107
Schelling, Friedrich Wilhelm Joseph 112–113, 177
Schiller, Friedrich 108, 110–111, 113–114, 170, 247
Schlegel, August Wilhelm 99, 106, 112–113, 139, 170
Schlegel, Friedrich 108, 112–113, 116
Schleiermacher, Friedrich 108, 113
Schoolcraft, Henry Rowe 71
Schopenhauer, Arthur 112
Schubert, Franz 105, 107, 116
Schumann, Clara 106
Schumann, Robert 106
Scott, Walter 48, 70, 138, 207, 209, 217, 219, 221–224, 230–231, 234–237, 239, 246, 254, 263
Senancour, Étienne-Jean-Baptiste-Pierre-Ignace Pivert de 84
Shakespeare, William 27, 112, 171, 177, 197, 247, 271, 273, 289
Shelley, Percy Bysshe 243, 256, 274, 279
Sheridan, Richard Brinsley 219, 222, 271, 276, 280, 282
Sherman, William Tecumseh 43

Shishkov, Alexander 161
Shpylova-Saeed, Nataliya 11
Siddons, Sarah 215, 247
Smart, Christopher 305
Smith, Adam 90, 97
Smith, Sydney 230
Soulié, Frédéric 93
Soumet, Alexandre 93–94
Southey, Robert 31, 40, 208, 225, 237, 246, 249
Spencer, Herbert 238
Spenser, Edmund 220
Spinoza, Baruch 238
Stendhal [Henri Beyle] 86, 88, 96
Sterne, Laurence 21, 84, 297
Strauss, David Friedrich 238
Suard, Jean-Baptiste-Antoine 93, 98
Sue, Eugène 93, 97, 190, 269
Sully, Maximilien de Béthune Sully, Duke de 217

Talleyrand-Périgord, Charles-Maurice de 94–95, 97–98, 225, 283
Tallien, Thérésa 96
Talma, François-Joseph 89, 92–93
Tegnér, Esaias 192
Tennyson, Alfred, Lord 259
Thackeray, William Makepeace 204, 260
Thiers, Marie Joseph Louis Adolphe 89
Thoreau, Henry David 45, 52
Thrale, Hester 205
Thucydides 152
Tieck, Ludwig 112–113
Tocqueville, Alexis Charles Henri Clérel, Comte de 288
Trollope, Anthony 160
Turgenev, Ivan 161
Turgot, Anne Robert Jacques 90, 96

van der Linden, Harry 11, 296
Verdi, Giuseppe 290
Verlaine, Paul 92
Vernet, Horace 94

Verri, Alessandro 32
Victoria, Queen of the United Kingdom of Great Britain and Ireland 15, 58, 240
Vigny, Alfred Victor, Comte de 85–86, 90, 93–94
Virgil 289
Voltaire [François-Marie Arouet] 84, 91, 93–94, 146, 153–155, 163, 177, 288
Vukić, Joakim 146
Vyazemsky, Prince Pyotr 161–163

Wagner, Richard 86
Wales, George Augustus Frederick, Prince of 204, 222
Walpole, Horace 91, 186, 208, 218–219
Washington, George 18, 20, 22, 25, 69, 207
Weber, Carl Maria von 104–105
Webster, Daniel 54, 58

Wedgwood, Josiah 221, 252, 305
Wergeland, Henrik 183
Werner, Zacharias 103, 155
West, Benjamin 100
Wheatley, John 17–18
Whitman, Walt 27
Whittier, John Greenleaf 33
Wieland, Christoph Martin 109, 112, 146, 187
Wilkes, John 210
Willis, Nathaniel Parker 37
Wilson, Katharina M. 5
Woolf, Virginia 8
Wordsworth, William 17, 204, 209, 239–240, 246, 249, 261
Wyss, Johann David 302

Xenophon 205

Zhukovsky, Vasily 161–163
Zola, Émile 160

Index of Topics

abolitionism 18, 21, 28–29, 37, 45, 47, 49–50, 60, 66, 69, 74, 89, 95, 135–136, 205, 214, 216, 219, 224–225, 247, 251, 254, 268, 300, 304–305
abuse 28, 254
Africa 7, 17, 26, 73, 116
African Americans 29, 41, 43, 66–67
amanuensis 6, 8, 45, 215, 247, 266, 280, 303
America 1–5, 7, 9, 13–14, 17–19, 24, 26–27, 29, 38, 46–47, 49, 55, 59–61, 63–64, 66–67, 70, 72–73, 76–78, 80, 92, 115–116, 123, 125, 132, 135–136, 139, 143–144, 188, 203, 211, 244, 247, 250–251, 264, 277–278, 303
annuity 219, 245
anonymity 3, 7–8, 14, 22, 27, 31, 36–37, 47, 51–52, 56, 62, 73, 76–77, 81, 86, 91–93, 95, 106, 110, 112–114, 133, 153, 171, 174, 178, 183, 190, 198, 204–205, 207–209, 211, 214–217, 220–221, 224, 229, 231–232, 237, 241, 243, 245–246, 248–249, 251–252, 255, 270, 272, 276
Argentina 126–129, 139
atheism 44, 250–251
Australia 7, 13, 261, 267
Austria 115, 193, 199, 227, 237, 285, 288, 301
autobiography 2, 19, 24, 31, 54, 57, 75, 98, 109–110, 116, 124, 133, 144, 146, 172, 174, 189, 216, 222, 251, 278

biography 3, 40, 64, 66, 73, 79, 113–114, 128, 133, 195, 198, 204, 214, 219, 226, 232, 239, 252–253, 255, 267, 273
Bluestocking 205, 215, 217, 230
botany 15, 62, 177, 223, 236, 244, 248,

270
Brazil 127–128, 130–132, 139, 193–194

Calvinism 20, 38, 71
Catholicism 107, 112, 245, 253
charity 45, 77, 80, 178, 188, 257, 265, 268, 271, 303
childbirth 6, 55, 68, 96, 110, 146, 161, 192, 231–232, 240
children 6, 14–16, 18–19, 23, 25, 28, 39, 42, 51, 53, 55, 58, 63, 69, 72, 76–80, 89, 93, 113–114, 154–156, 162, 167, 171, 173, 178, 180, 182, 184, 190–191, 194–196, 199, 204, 206, 209, 212, 217–221, 224, 231, 237, 239–240, 242–244, 248, 250, 252, 256–257, 259, 261, 266, 270, 272–275, 278, 280, 283
Chile 126–128, 132–133
China 7, 52, 115
Classicism 108, 165, 197, 199
Colombia 125–126, 133
colonialism 2, 7, 14, 18, 21, 23, 26, 128, 133, 135, 139, 224
Confederacy 53, 62, 101, 109, 155, 301
convent 2, 15, 60, 87, 92–93, 97–99, 107, 129, 133, 141, 194, 199, 280, 294
cookbooks 39, 53, 58, 65, 252, 303
correspondence 16, 25–26, 37, 45, 59, 81, 88, 91, 97, 104–107, 112–113, 132, 156, 170, 173, 178, 189, 205, 213–214, 220, 223, 236–237, 245–246, 249, 263, 275, 289, 294, 298
court 72, 74, 97, 99–100, 102, 109, 147, 161, 163, 173–174, 200, 250, 260, 288
Cuba 31, 60, 71, 125–128, 133–136, 188

debt 6–7, 24, 26, 164, 204, 210, 216, 222–224, 235, 238, 272
Declaration of Independence 1, 8, 25, 59, 125, 227
diary 2, 16, 19–20, 22–23, 25, 38, 40, 43, 46, 52, 59, 77, 129, 133, 152–153, 162, 173, 183–184, 191, 209–210, 220, 234, 239–240, 260, 275, 283, 294, 303

Dissenter 213, 223
dressmaking 6, 54, 251

education 26, 31, 75, 116, 132, 139, 153, 155, 161–162, 173, 178, 187–188, 198–199, 207, 212, 225, 229, 238, 251, 256–257, 268, 303
England 13, 15, 22, 25, 27–29, 44, 49, 55, 58–59, 61, 66, 77, 89, 91, 100, 109, 129, 166, 172, 194, 196–197, 203–204, 210, 212, 217, 220, 229, 235–238, 241, 247, 249–254, 256–257, 259–262, 264, 266, 268, 271–272, 274, 277, 279, 281
epic 31, 84, 191, 194, 224, 297–298
estate 22, 49, 99, 155, 173, 178, 191, 208, 237, 241, 255, 278
Europe 1, 3–7, 11, 22, 26, 30–31, 45, 47, 60, 63–65, 72, 78, 99–100, 109, 111, 115, 118, 121, 124, 132, 138, 143–144, 150, 163, 170, 186, 267, 273, 277, 283, 296, 301, 303, 306
exile 92, 95, 99, 139, 155–156, 159–160, 170, 173, 200, 237, 277, 288, 304

famine 65, 237, 241, 278, 281
fashion 134, 222
feminism 46, 54, 69, 131–132, 139, 145, 199, 222, 251, 256, 289
France 5, 11, 25, 44, 48–49, 57, 64, 83, 85, 89, 92, 94, 98, 100, 109, 123, 152, 163–164, 203, 210, 212, 220, 224–225, 229, 232, 237, 241, 247, 250, 256, 266, 269, 274, 276–277, 279, 283, 302, 304–305
friendship 66, 80, 105, 113, 199, 236, 239

Germany 5–6, 22, 67, 70, 96, 101–103, 105, 113, 115, 170, 173–174, 179, 190, 203, 221, 229–230, 257, 261, 283, 299
Girondins 97, 225
Gothic 6, 81, 138, 186, 213, 216, 219, 231–232, 258, 267, 270, 278, 280, 282, 304
governess 6, 27, 60, 63, 86, 89, 95, 114,

156, 179, 188–189, 192, 210, 215, 221, 231, 233, 235–236, 243, 245, 260, 267–269, 273, 279, 301
Greece 115, 143–146, 150, 240, 243, 302

Haiti 71, 125, 140
health, illness 39, 58, 60–61, 68, 75, 161, 163, 190, 196, 203, 207, 235, 237, 246, 253, 261, 286
history 5, 16, 26, 46, 56, 69–70, 72, 77, 86, 99, 101, 114, 121, 139, 150, 152, 166, 230, 241, 250, 254, 260, 263–264, 288, 303
household 45, 53–54, 69, 94, 156, 166, 224, 239, 246–247, 249, 264
hymn 7, 18, 26, 31, 33–34, 38, 45, 49–50, 63, 78, 81, 89, 182, 264–265, 287, 303

independence 2, 13, 106, 121, 125, 131, 135, 139, 143, 145, 149, 153, 176, 219, 265, 289, 301, 304
India 7, 65, 115, 207, 229, 238, 246, 253, 262, 282
insanity 43, 252, 301
Ireland 3, 14, 30, 48, 65, 203, 210, 218, 220, 240, 262, 264, 267–270, 272–273, 276–277, 279, 281–283
Italy 46, 95, 101, 109, 113, 115, 119, 147, 170, 234, 242–243, 249, 256, 258, 261, 266, 273, 279, 285, 288, 293, 302

Judaism 53, 109, 113

liberalism 44, 96, 193, 289, 294

manuscript 2, 14, 21, 25, 31, 35–36, 45–46, 55, 59, 80–81, 118–119, 132–133, 141, 156, 173, 184, 214, 217, 221–222, 229, 232, 234, 238, 246, 265, 276
memoir 2, 4, 15, 19, 23, 38, 55–56, 69, 72, 86, 89–90, 93, 95, 97, 111, 114, 124, 132, 152, 154–155, 161, 163–164, 170, 174, 183–184, 192, 205, 208–210, 217, 219–220, 224–225, 231, 234, 241, 244, 247, 250, 253, 257, 260–261, 269, 272, 279, 283, 302–303
men 3, 6, 8, 55, 110, 123, 128, 134, 139, 153, 181, 196, 300, 304–305
Methodism 14, 28, 57, 68, 239
Mexico 2, 125–126, 140–141, 245
mill 6, 34–35
Minerva Press 208, 213–214, 218, 226, 232, 235, 270, 282
miscarriage 167, 239, 288
Moravians 31, 46, 48, 73, 150, 254
music 25, 85, 87–88, 90, 105–109, 138, 154, 164, 180, 188, 199, 214–215, 230, 269, 278, 287, 298

Native Americans 7, 23, 35–37, 67, 71–72
nature 122, 176–177, 185–186, 191, 296–297

opera 25, 87–89, 93, 111, 127, 146, 159, 199, 272, 277, 298

painting 15–16, 86–87, 89–91, 94, 103, 112, 132, 147, 186, 200, 211, 232, 234, 240, 287, 298, 304
pamphlet 20–21, 32, 37, 70–71, 152, 216, 232, 244, 273–274, 298–299
periodicals, journals, magazines 14–16, 28–34, 36–38, 41, 45–49, 51–52, 57, 60–62, 65–67, 69, 72–78, 87, 91, 93–94, 96, 98, 108–111, 114, 124, 128, 139, 147, 153–154, 156, 160, 162–163, 187, 189, 191–193, 195, 198–199, 204, 217, 231, 235, 239, 241–243, 245–246, 252, 254–256, 262, 265–266, 268, 273–274, 278, 282–283, 289, 301
Peru 3, 9, 99, 125–126, 128, 137–139, 224
piano 60, 77, 105, 129, 147, 195, 298
poetry 8, 14–15, 24, 28, 30, 32–34, 37, 42, 44, 54, 59–61, 63, 67–68, 75–77, 79–80, 88, 91–92, 94, 96, 108, 110–111, 119, 132–133, 136, 146, 156, 162–163, 171–172, 174, 178, 183–184, 186, 188, 191, 194, 198–201, 205, 207, 209, 219, 222–223, 225–226, 230, 238–240, 248–249, 260, 266, 269, 273, 279, 286, 288–290,

293–294, 299, 302
Poland 112, 115, 149, 151–154, 156, 159, 163, 174, 227, 264
Portugal 125, 127, 193–194
posthumous 16, 20, 25, 30, 36, 40, 44, 46, 49, 51, 65, 67–68, 86, 89, 91, 106, 133, 163, 171, 177, 183, 189, 198, 200, 206, 221, 229, 234–235, 240–241, 244, 250, 266, 273, 277, 282–283, 288
poverty, penury 6, 75, 91, 97, 123, 162, 210, 217, 222, 224–225, 236, 265, 275, 281
pregnancy 85, 99, 136, 203, 223, 233, 256
prison 6–7, 14, 22, 24, 26, 44, 53, 68, 91, 97, 99, 112, 145, 156, 158–160, 166, 192, 194, 197–198, 204, 210, 222, 224, 250–251, 272, 289, 299, 303
Protestantism 56, 89, 103, 108, 124, 223, 254, 275, 297, 302
Prussia 101, 108, 112–113, 154, 227, 229, 240, 261, 298

Quakerism (Society of Friends) 7, 20, 22–24, 35, 49–50, 59–60, 64, 68–69, 71, 77, 219, 223, 240, 242, 248, 268, 275, 278

realism 183
republic 46, 83, 119, 133, 287–290, 293, 301
revolution 1, 21, 26, 44, 69, 83, 85, 99, 107, 109, 116, 124, 267, 288, 293, 303–304
Romanticism 1, 5, 7–8, 12, 153, 166, 228, 304–305
Royal Literary Fund 7, 206, 211, 216, 220, 226, 235, 246–247, 267, 278, 281
Russia 3, 9, 70, 146, 149, 154, 156, 161–163, 169, 176, 227, 268, 283

sales 37, 264
school 6, 8, 14, 16, 25–26, 29, 31–32, 35, 38, 41–42, 45–46, 48–50, 54, 56–57, 61, 64, 68, 72–73, 76–77, 80, 106, 124, 127, 132, 139, 155, 162, 165,

171, 174, 179, 183, 191–192, 207, 209–211, 219, 222, 224–225, 233, 235, 240, 243, 245, 248, 250–252, 267–268, 274–275, 279, 294, 302
Scotland 4, 6, 65, 172, 235, 240–241, 257, 273
sentiment 119, 149, 227, 281
ship 14, 26, 65, 185, 196–197, 240, 278
sibling, brother, sister 8, 14–15, 20, 24, 26, 29, 31, 33–34, 36, 40, 43, 47, 49–50, 56–57, 60–62, 68–69, 71, 75, 77, 79, 96, 104, 106, 112–114, 119, 121, 129, 154, 156, 160, 165–166, 171, 179, 182–183, 188, 192, 201, 207, 209–212, 214, 217–218, 220–221, 233, 236–237, 240, 244–245, 247–249, 251–252, 254, 256, 261–262, 265–269, 272–273, 276, 278, 282–283, 288, 293, 304–305
slavery 7–8, 15, 17–19, 23–27, 29, 32, 36–37, 39, 41, 43, 45, 47, 49–51, 55, 57, 62, 64, 66, 68, 71–75, 77, 103, 135, 144–145, 159, 199, 204, 212, 224, 231, 254, 256, 268
socialism 87, 97–98
song 87, 93, 105, 107, 119, 172, 180, 182, 184, 189–191, 210, 215, 217, 230, 246, 258, 279, 287, 290
Spain 125, 135–136, 174, 193, 195, 198–199, 290
suffrage 44, 49, 61–62, 74, 156, 256
suicide 24, 57, 98, 104, 107, 109, 136, 198, 234, 293
Switzerland 92, 146, 155, 198, 234–235, 254, 261, 274, 301

teaching 16, 35, 37, 41, 46, 49, 61, 204, 251, 257
temperance 7, 38, 60, 66, 68, 230
tenant/landlord 237, 278–279
theater 63, 88, 94, 136, 171, 174, 194–195, 205, 210, 215, 217, 222, 230, 247, 265, 268, 271
Tory 22, 218, 224, 270
translation 3, 9, 11, 29, 43, 48, 53, 57, 66, 88, 90, 106, 112, 130, 147, 160,

163, 186–187, 190, 211, 220, 222, 226, 234, 237–239, 243, 247, 251, 257, 271, 276, 281, 302–303
travel 35, 85, 102, 108, 132, 134, 146, 164, 170, 174, 196, 219–220, 234–235, 239, 252, 255, 257–258, 262, 267, 305
tuberculosis, consumption 14, 32–33, 40, 42, 52–53, 66, 72, 190, 233, 253, 270, 282

Unitarianism 19–20, 22, 36, 47, 51, 76, 251
United States. *See* America
Uruguay 125, 129, 139–140

war 14, 19–20, 23, 25–26, 32–33, 36, 39, 46–48, 50, 53, 55–56, 59, 70–71, 77, 79, 85, 99, 135, 145, 154, 193, 198, 203–204, 304, 311, 315
Whig 207, 237, 251, 271, 274, 281
widow 14, 30, 52, 75, 87, 91, 107, 109, 120, 131, 146, 156, 173, 183, 191, 197, 200, 211, 214–216, 267, 274
women's rights 1, 19, 38, 60, 62, 73, 110, 119, 124, 139, 183, 248, 256

About the Team

Alessandra Tosi was the managing editor for this book and proof-read the manuscript. Adèle Kreager compiled the index.

Jeevanjot Kaur Nagpal designed the cover. The cover was produced in InDesign using the Fontin font.

Jeremy Bowman typeset the book in InDesign and produced the paperback and hardback editions and created the EPUB. The main text font is Tex Gyre Pagella and the heading font is Californian FB.

Cameron Craig produced the PDF edition.

The conversion to the HTML edition was performed with epublius, an open-source software which is freely available on our GitHub page at https://github.com/OpenBookPublishers

This book was peer-reviewed by two referees. Experts in their field, our readers give their time freely to help ensure the academic rigour of our books. We are grateful for their generous and invaluable contributions.

This book need not end here...

Share

All our books — including the one you have just read — are free to access online so that students, researchers and members of the public who can't afford a printed edition will have access to the same ideas. This title will be accessed online by hundreds of readers each month across the globe: why not share the link so that someone you know is one of them?

This book and additional content is available at
https://doi.org/10.11647/OBP.0458

Donate

Open Book Publishers is an award-winning, scholar-led, not-for-profit press making knowledge freely available one book at a time. We don't charge authors to publish with us: instead, our work is supported by our library members and by donations from people who believe that research shouldn't be locked behind paywalls.

Join the effort to free knowledge by supporting us at
https://www.openbookpublishers.com/support-us

We invite you to connect with us on our socials!

BLUESKY	MASTODON	LINKEDIN
@openbookpublish.bsky.social	@OpenBookPublish@hcommons.social	open-book-publishers

Read more at the Open Book Publishers Blog
https://blogs.openbookpublishers.com

You may also be interested in:

Destins de femmes
French Women Writers, 1750-1850
John Claiborne Isbell
https://doi.org/10.11647/OBP.0346

An Outline of Romanticism in the West
John Claiborne Isbell
https://doi.org/10.11647/OBP.0302

Romanticism and Time
Literary Temporalities
Sophie Laniel-Musitelli and Céline Sabiron (eds)
https://doi.org/10.11647/OBP.0232

Prismatic Jane Eyre

Close-Reading a World Novel Across Languages

Matthew Reynolds (ed.)

https://doi.org/10.11647/OBP.0319

Breaking Conventions

Five Couples in Search of Marriage-Career Balance at the Turn of the Nineteenth Century

Patricia Auspos

https://doi.org/10.11647/OBP.0318

Women in Nineteenth-Century Russia

Lives and Culture

Wendy Rosslyn and Alessandra Tosi (eds)

https://doi.org/10.11647/OBP.0018

www.ingramcontent.com/pod-product-compliance
Lightning Source LLC
Chambersburg PA
CBHW051535230426
43669CB00015B/2607